VENICE

THE RISE TO EMPIRE

*

JOHN JULIUS NORWICH

ALLEN LANE

ALLEN LANE

Penguin Books Ltd

17 Grosvenor Gardens, London SW1W 0BD

First published in 1977

Copyright © John Julius Norwich, 1977

ISBN 0 7139 0742 8

Set in Monotype Garamond

Printed in Great Britain by
Ebenezer Baylis & Son Ltd
The Trinity Press, Worcester and London

For Jason
and in memory of the grandfather he never knew
who loved Venice
and should have written this book

Contents

7

CONTENTS

List of Illustrations

The author and publishers are grateful to the following for permission to use photographs: Osvaldo Böhm, Venice, for nos. 1, 3, 6, 7, 8, 9, 10, 11, 13, 15, 16, 17, 20, 22, 23, 25, 26: Courtauld Institute of Art for nos. 4, 5, 24, 27, 29, 30: Bodleian Library, Oxford, for nos. 14, 28; Mansell Collection for nos. 18, 19, 21; the Italian Tourist Office for no. 2 and the Trustees of the British Museum for no. 12.

LIST OF MAPS

Acknowledgements

During the shamefully long time that I have been working on this book, I have received help and encouragement from many friends, both English and Venetian. Some debts, however, must be individually acknowledged, and my particular thanks must go to Mollie Philipps, for her unflagging – and invaluable – work on the bibliography and illustrations; to Joe Links, himself the author of one of the most delightful books on Venice ever written, for the loan of books and for his eagle-eyed scrutiny of the proofs; to Peter Lathrop Lauritzen for the bottomless erudition with which he cleared up several knotty problems on the spot; to Jean Curtis and Euphan Scott for their patient typing and retyping of an almost indecipherable manuscript; to Barbara Reynolds for allowing me to use her translation of the Ariosto epigraph to Chapter 2; to Douglas and Sarah Matthews for the index; and to my wife Anne for the countless hours she has spent designing yet another lovely jacket.

Almost every word in the pages which follow was written in the Reading Room of the London Library, my debt to which – as to every member of its superb staff – can only be recorded, never measured.

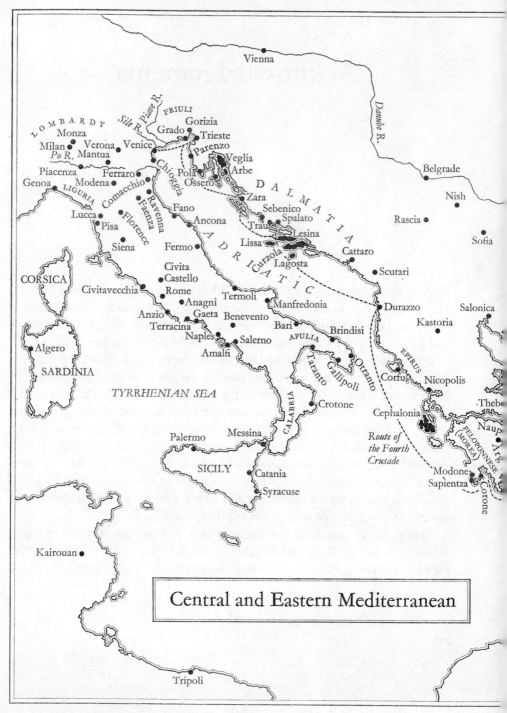

Central and Eastern Mediterranean

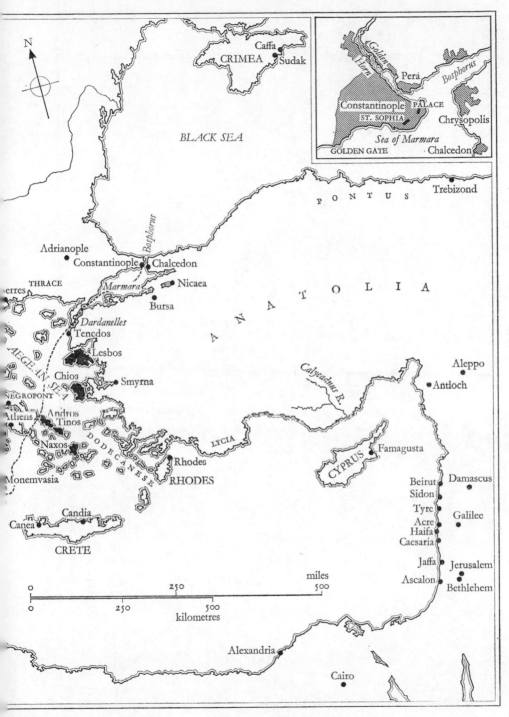

N

BLACK SEA

CRIMEA
Caffa
Sudak

Bosphorus

PONTUS

Trebizond

Adrianople

Constantinople Chalcedon
THRACE
erres *Marmara* Nicaea

Bursa

A N A T O L I A

Dardanelles
Tenedos

Lesbos

D
AEGEAN SEA
Chios Smyrna

NEGROPONT

Athens Andros
Tinos

Naxos
DODECANESE
LYCIA

Monemvasia

Rhodes
RHODES

Calycadnus R.

Aleppo

Antioch

CYPRUS
Famagusta

Beirut Damascus
Sidon
Tyre Galilee
Acre
Haifa
Caesaria

Jaffa Jerusalem
Ascalon
Bethlehem

Candia
Canea
CRETE

miles
0   250   500
0   250   500
kilometres

Alexandria

Cairo

Pera *Bosphorus*

Golden Horn

Constantinople PALACE
ST. SOPHIA
Chrysopolis

Sea of Marmara
GOLDEN GATE Chalcedon

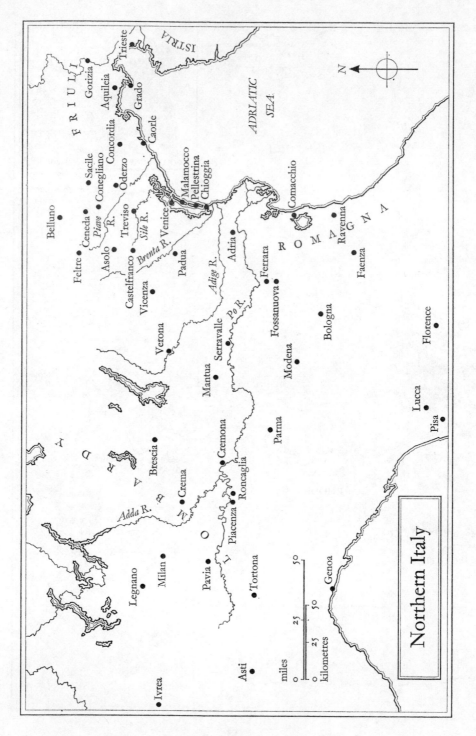

Northern Italy

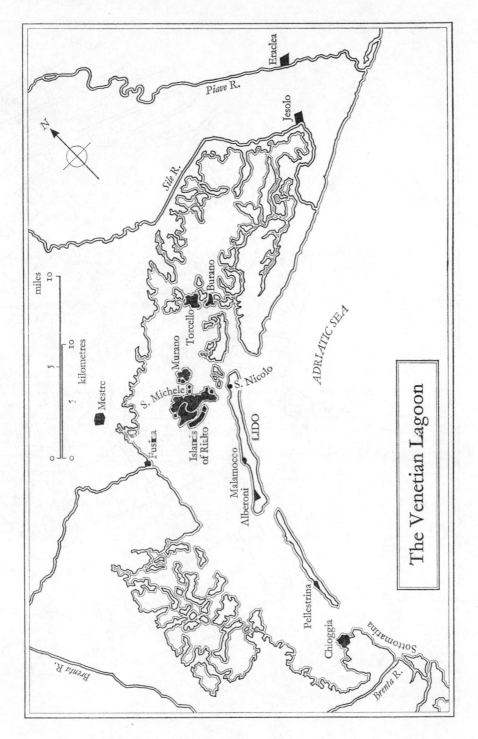

The Venetian Lagoon

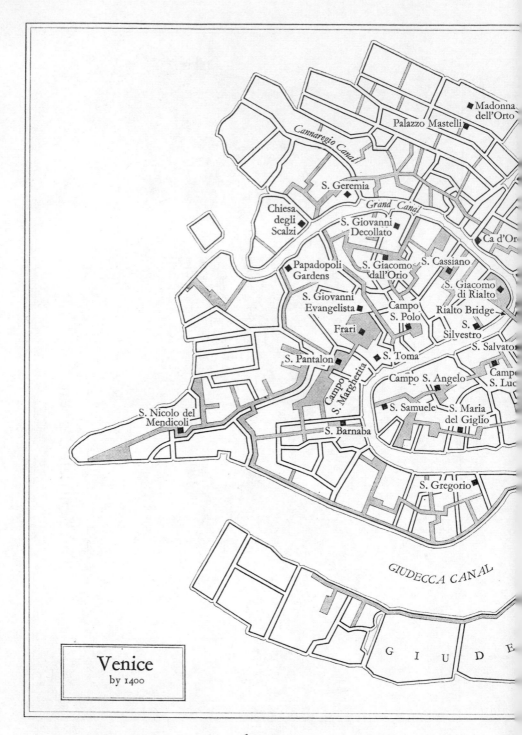

Venice
by 1400

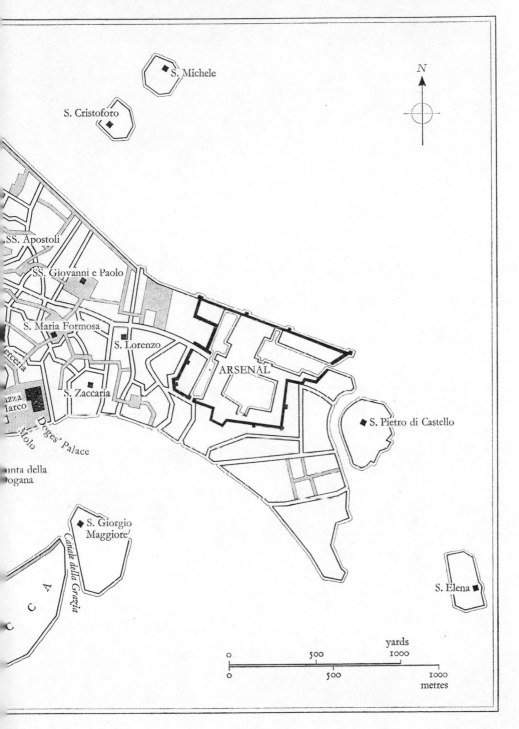

S. Michele

S. Cristoforo

N

SS. Apostoli

SS. Giovanni e Paolo

S. Maria Formosa

S. Lorenzo

ARSENAL

Merceria

S. Zaccaria

S. Pietro di Castello

Piazza S. Marco

Doges' Palace

Molo

Punta della Dogana

S. Giorgio Maggiore

Canale della Grazia

S. Elena

GIUDECCA

| yards |
| 0   500   1000 |
| 0   500   1000 |
| metres |

Introduction

First experiences should be short and intense. When my parents took me to Venice in the summer of 1946, we stayed only a few hours; but I can still feel – not remember, *feel* – the impact it made on my sixteen-year-old brain. With his usual blend of firmness and commonsense, my father limited to two the buildings we actually entered: the Basilica of St Mark and Harry's Bar. For the rest of the time, wandering on foot or drifting gently in a gondola, I subconsciously absorbed the first essential Venetian lesson – a lesson, incidentally, that poor Ruskin, beavering away at his crockets and cusps round the Doges' Palace, never learnt: that in Venice, more than anywhere else, the whole is greater than the sum of the parts. However majestic the churches, however magnificent the *palazzi*, however dazzling the pictures, the ultimate masterpiece remains Venice itself. Interiors, even the great golden mystery of St Mark's, are but details. The relation of Piazza and Piazzetta, the sublime setting of S. Giorgio Maggiore at precisely the right angle to the Molo, the play of light at a canal's curve, the slap of water against the hull of a gondola, the all-pervading smell of the sea – for let there be no mistake about it, except when the wind is blowing across from Mestre and Marghera, Venice is the sweetest-smelling city in Europe – these are the first things to be experienced and understood. There will be time for Titian and Tintoretto later. Even Carpaccio must wait his turn.

As we wandered and drifted, my father talked about Venetian history, and I learned that Venice was not just the most beautiful city that I had ever seen; she had also been an independent republic for over 1,000 years

– longer than the period separating us from the Norman Conquest – during much of which she had been mistress of the Mediterranean, the principal crossroads between East and West, the richest and most prosperous commercial centre of the civilized world. Her unique system of government, he admitted, was stern, occasionally even harsh; but he believed that it had a better record of fairness and justice than any other in Europe, and that it had been much maligned by historians. For that very reason, one of these days, he intended to write a history of Venice himself and set the record straight.

We departed, that first day, just as dusk was falling and the lights were coming on along the Grand Canal; I have never left any city with such bitter regret. But the next year we were back again, for longer; I began to explore on my own, and discovered what I now know to be one of the major pleasures of life: that of walking through Venice at night. By eleven the streets are virtually deserted by all but the cats; the lighting, limited to the occasional ordinary electric bulb, is perfect; the silence is broken only by one's own footsteps and the occasional ripple of unseen water. On those walks, now nearly thirty years ago, I fell in love with the city. I have walked it, and loved it, ever since.

My father died on New Year's Day, 1954. Although he left a considerable collection of books on Venice and a few pages of notes, his long-projected history remained unwritten. The need for it, however, seems to me to be greater now even than it was in his day. More and more people visit this most magical of cities every year; more and more publicity is rightly given to its desperate struggle for survival; and yet, despite a plethora of admirable guide-books, descriptive essays, surveys of art and architecture and historical studies of individual periods, I know of only one (and that all too short) consecutive general history of the Republic written in English in the twentieth century. In the nineteenth, admittedly, there were several; but all of these, to my possibly jaundiced eye, tend to veer between the inaccurate and the unreadable – or, indeed, as often as not, to combine the two.

This book, then, is an attempt to fill the first half of the gap – to tell the story of Venice from her misty beginnings to the year 1400, when she stood on the threshold of her golden age. A sequel will describe her apogee and her decline, ending on that sad day for Europe when Napoleon, the self-styled 'Attila of the Venetian People', dealt the 1,000-year-old Republic its death-blow and Doge Ludovico Manin slowly removed his ducal cap, murmuring that he would not be needing it again. Ideally, I should have preferred to span the whole period with a single book; but I very soon became aware that some 1,400 years of history simply could not be adequately dealt with in one volume of manageable size. Any attempt to do so would have meant either so sketchy a coverage as to leave the story disconnected and important points obscure, or a factual recital so dry and unadorned as to have been a penance to writer and readers – if any – alike. Venetian history is particularly susceptible to this latter danger, if only because of the instinctive horror, amounting at times almost to a phobia, shown by the Republic to the faintest suggestion of the cult of personality. Sooner or later, anyone tackling the subject finds himself looking wistfully across to the *terra firma* and that superb, swaggering pageant of Medici and Malatesta, Visconti and della Scala, Sforza and Borgia and Gonzaga. The echoing names of Venice, by contrast, evoke *palazzi* more often than people, and it is hard to find much human interest in the decrees and deliberations of the faceless Council of Ten.

Yet there are compensations. The sheer individuality of the place, for one thing. For Venice, alone of all the still great cities of Italy, was born and brought up Greek. It is no accident that she possesses the greatest Byzantine church in the world that is still used for Christian worship, and a Patriarch to preside in it. Long after she shed her dependence on Constantinople she continued to turn her back on Italy and to look resolutely eastward; the nightmare tangle of medieval Italian politics, of Guelf and Ghibelline, Emperor and Pope, feudal baron and civic commune – none of this was for her. And by the time she did at last condescend to carve out a mainland empire, her character was fixed in its own unique and quirkish mould.

Secondly, there is the unchanging quality of the city itself. Protected by the waters of her lagoon throughout her independent history from all foreign invaders except the last – and, in the present century, from the more insidious menace of the motor car – Venice still maintains essentially the same appearance that she presented to the world not only in the days of Canaletto but even in those of Carpaccio and Gentile Bellini. This apparent triumph over time would be an extraordinary phenomenon in any city; when the city happens to be the most beautiful in the world, the phenomenon becomes a miracle. It is also a particular blessing for the historian since it enables him to conjure up, in his own imagination at any rate, a vision of his subject at earlier periods far clearer and livelier than would have been possible anywhere else in Europe.

But this is not a work of imagination, and I have tried to keep mine firmly in check. Nor, on the other hand, is it a work of profound scholarship; the sheer time span has forced me to keep the narrative moving ahead at all costs, and there has been little opportunity for detailed analysis. The one luxury I have allowed myself has been the occasional reference to buildings and monuments still standing in Venice today which have a direct bearing on the events described. For the rest, my only aim has been to tell the story as concisely and coherently as possible; my only regret that the task of doing so has fallen to me rather than to my father, who would have done it so much more brilliantly, a quarter of a century ago.

Il n'est pas rare de voir de grandes émigrations de peuples inonder un pays, en changer la face et ouvrir pour l'histoire une ère nouvelle; mais qu'une poignée de fugitifs, jetée sur un banc de sable de quelques cents toises de largeur, y fonde un état sans territoire; qu'une nombreuse population vienne couvrir cette plage mouvante, où il ne se trouve ni végétation, ni eau potable, ni matériaux, ni même de l'espace pour bâtir; que de l'industrie nécessaire pour subsister, et pour affermir le sol sous leurs pas, ils arrivent jusqu'à présenter aux nations modernes le premier exemple d'un gouvernement régulier, jusqu'à faire sortir d'un marais des flottes sans cesse renaissantes, pour aller renverser un grand empire, et recueillir les richesses de l'Orient; qu'on voit ces fugitifs tenir la balance politique de l'Italie, dominer sur les mers, réduire toutes les nations à la condition de tributaires, enfin rendre impuissants tous les efforts de l'Europe liguée contre eux: c'est là sans doute un développement de l'intelligence humaine qui mérite d'être observé.

Daru, *Histoire de la République de Venise*

Part One

The Barbarian Invasions
to the
Fourth Crusade

Question: *Quid est mare?*
Answer: *Refugium in periculis.*

Alcuin's Catechism

Beginnings

[to 727]

A few in fear
Flying away from him, whose boast it was
That the grass grew not where his horse had trod,
Gave birth to Venice. Like the water-fowl,
They built their nests above the ocean waves;
And where the sands were shifting, as the wind
Blew from the north or south – where they that came
Had to make sure the ground they stood upon,
Rose, like an exhalation from the deep,
A vast metropolis, with glistening spires,
With theatres, basilicas adorned;
A scene of light and glory, a dominion,
That has endured the longest among men.

Samuel Rogers

The origins of Venice encircle her still. No great city has managed to preserve, in its immediate surroundings, so much of the atmosphere and environment which gave it birth. The traveller approaching Venice, whether by sea as she should be approached, or by land across the causeway, or even by air, gazes out on the same flat, desolate expanse of water and reed and marsh that the first Venetians chose for their own; and is struck, more forcibly every time, not just by the improbability but by the sheer foolhardiness of their enterprise. It is a curious world, this world of the Venetian lagoon; over 500 square miles of brackish water, much of it shallow enough for a man to wade through waist-deep, but criss-crossed with deeper channels along which the river Brenta and its fellows make their tortuous way to the open sea; studded with shoals formed by the silt which they and other, grander streams like the Po and the Adige have brought down from the Alps; scored with endless lines of posts and piles driven into its sandy bed to mark invisible but important features – lobster pots and fishing-grounds, wrecks and cables, moorings, shallows, and recommended routes to be followed by the *vaporetti* that ply to and fro between the city and the outlying islands. In any season, under any light, it appears strangely devoid of colour; the water is not deep enough to take on either the rich, velvety blue of the central Mediterranean or that astringent green that characterizes much of the Adriatic. And yet, especially on autumn evenings when the days are drawing in and the surface glistens like oil under a low, misty sun, it can be beautiful – so beautiful that one is surprised that the great Venetian painters, seduced as always by the splendour of their city, took so little interest in their less immediate surroundings. How differently the Dutch would have reacted! But then the Venetian school was essentially joyous; the lagoon, for all its beauty, can be quite unutterably sad. Who in their senses, one wonders, would leave the fertile plains of Lombardy to build a settlement – let alone a city – among these marshy, malarial wastes, on little islets of sand and couchgrass, the playthings of current and tide?

This is a question to which there can be only one answer, since there is only one motive strong enough to induce so apparently irrational a step – fear. The first builders of Venice were frightened men. Where they originally came from is immaterial; Illyria probably, though there is a tradition as old as Homer himself that they were of Anatolian stock, and had fled westward after the fall of Troy. However that may be, by about A.D. 400, when the history of Venice begins, they were living prosperous, cultivated lives in a chain of splendid cities of the Roman Empire like Padua and Altino, Concordia and Aquileia, strung out along the northern and north-western shores of the Adriatic, looking to the lagoon for their supplies of salt and fresh fish but for very little else.

So, doubtless, they would have continued, given half a chance. But then, in the early years of the fifth century, the barbarians swept down. The Goths came first under their leader Alaric, falling on Aquileia in 402, pillaging and burning their way through the rich provinces of Istria and Venetia, sending a tremor of shock and foreboding down the whole length of Italy. The populations of the towns and villages fled before them, seeking a refuge at once unenviable and inaccessible, where their enemies would have neither the incentive nor the ability to follow them. Thus it was that the wisest came to the islands of the lagoon. There, they believed, these savages from landlocked central Europe, lacking both ships and knowledge of the sea, would – with any luck – ignore them, turning their attention instead to the richer and far more tempting prizes on the main-land. They were right. As further surges of invaders followed during the next few years, rolling in an intermittent avalanche down the peninsula, so more and more fugitives found their way through the channels and shoals to safety. In 410 Alaric sacked Rome; and eleven years later the

28

city of Venice was formally brought into being – at the stroke of noon on Friday 25 March 421.

So, at least, runs the old and venerable Venetian tradition. Unfortunately the document on which it is based, connecting the foundation with a visit by three consuls sent out from Padua to establish a trading-post on the islands of the Rialto, is a good deal more plausible than it is authentic. Such a mission may well have landed on the islands; it may even, as the document goes on to assert, have celebrated the event by raising up a church dedicated to St James.[1] But certainly the Paduans made little or no attempt to follow up this early attempt at colonial expansion, while the date given with such formidable exactitude seems rather too early for any independent initiative on the part of the islanders themselves. In the first half of the century at least, few of them yet saw themselves as permanent residents. When each wave of barbarians had passed, the majority would return to their homes – or what was left of them – and try to resume their old mainland lives. It was only later that their descendants came to understand that this was not to be.

For the Goths were merely the beginning. In 452 they were followed by a new scourge, fiercer and far more cruel – Attila the Hun, advancing remorselessly over North Italy, leaving a trail of devastation and destruction behind him. He too attacked Aquileia, which defended itself heroically for three months until its besiegers, unaccustomed to such resistance, were minded to give up the attempt and pass on to some easier victim. But one day Attila, on a tour of the walls, looked up and noticed a flight of young storks heading away from the city with their young. 'He seized,' – the quotation from Gibbon is irresistible – 'with the ready penetration of a statesman, this trifling incident which chance had offered to superstition', and pointed it out to his soldiers as a sure sign that Aquileia was doomed. Thus encouraged, they renewed their efforts; and a day or two later the ninth greatest metropolis in the Roman Empire was little more than an empty shell.

In the years that followed, more and more towns and villages and homesteads suffered a similar fate; and the flow of refugees increased. Many continued to return to the mainland when the danger had passed but there were many others who, finding their new lives more congenial than they had expected, made up their minds to stay. Thus, as conditions

1. It is this legend that lies at the root of the claim of the church of S. Giacomo di Rialto to be the oldest in Venice. The present building, however, goes back no further than the end of the eleventh century (see p. 106, n. 1).

on the mainland deteriorated, the island communities grew and began to prosper; and in 466 their respective representatives met together at Grado to work out a rudimentary system of self-government, through tribunes elected annually by each of them. It was a loose association at this stage, and one that was not even confined to the little archipelago which we now know as Venice; Grado itself lies on its own lagoon due south of Aquileia, some sixty miles away. But that distant assembly marks, more accurately than anything else, the beginning of the slow constitutional process from which the Most Serene Republic was ultimately to evolve.

Self-government, to be sure, is not the same as independence; yet the geographical isolation of these early Venetians did enable them to hold themselves politically aloof from the successive upheavals by which Italy was now being shaken. Even the fall of the Roman Empire of the West and the dethronement of its last Emperor, the callow young Romulus Augustulus, by the barbarian Odoacer caused few ripples out in the lagoons. And when Odoacer was in his turn overthrown by Theodoric the Ostrogoth, even Theodoric may have been a little unsure how far he could presume on Venetian obedience. A letter, addressed in the year 523 to 'the maritime tribunes' from his capital at Ravenna by his praetorian prefect Cassiodorus, certainly seems somewhat fulsome for what must have been after all a fairly routine piece of government business. 'The Istrian harvests of wine and oil', writes Cassiodorus,

have this year been particularly abundant, and orders have been given for their safe transport to Ravenna. Pray show your devotion, therefore, by bringing them hither with all speed. For you possess many vessels in the region . . . and you will be, in a sense, sailing through your native country. Besides your other blessings, there is open to you a way which is ever free of danger; for when the winds rage and the sea is closed against you, you may sail up the pleasantest of rivers. Your ships need fear no angry gusts, since they may continually hug the shore. Often, with their hulls invisible, they seem to be moving across the fields. Sometimes you pull them with ropes, at others men help them along with their feet . . .

For you live like sea birds, with your homes dispersed, like the Cyclades, across the surface of the water. The solidity of the earth on which they rest is secured only by osier and wattle; yet you do not hesitate to oppose so frail a bulwark to the wildness of the sea. Your people have one great wealth – the fish which suffices for them all. Among you there is no difference between rich and poor; your food is the same, your houses are all alike. Envy, which rules the rest of the world, is unknown to you. All your energies are spent on your salt-fields; in them indeed lies your prosperity, and your power to purchase those things which you have not. For though there may be men who have little need of gold, yet none live who desire not salt.

Be diligent, therefore, to repair your boats – which, like horses, you keep tied up at the doors of your dwellings – and make haste to depart . . .[1]

Even when allowances are made for Cassiodorus's naturally florid style, the impression he leaves is unmistakable: though these strange water-people could be extremely useful to the central government, they must be handled with care. Yet the real value of his letter lies in the picture that it gives – the earliest that has come down to us – of life in the lagoons.[2] It shows, too, that the twin pillars on which the future greatness of Venice was to be based – commerce and sea power – were even then firmly in position. Already those early settlers had trade in their blood. The salt that they gathered from their shallow pans was not only a valuable commodity in itself; it could also be used to preserve the fish and game that they netted with almost equal ease from the waters and marshes around them. By the middle of the sixth century the flat-bottomed Venetian trading barge was a common sight along the rivers of north and central Italy.

A rudimentary navy, too, was taking shape. In Theodoric's day, so far as we can tell, it was called upon mainly for the occasional transportation of essential supplies to Ravenna; but the peace that Theodoric had brought to the peninsula did not long survive his death. Though his original invasion had been carried out under Byzantine auspices, his subsequent rule had been absolute; he had brooked no interference, from Constantinople or anywhere else. Under him, Italy was no longer in any real sense part of the Eastern Empire. To make matters worse, he and his subjects after him had continued zealously to uphold their Arian beliefs. Arianism – according to which Christ was not truly divine, but merely a creation of God the Father and therefore inferior to Him – had long since been condemned as heresy; unfortunately, however, it had been preached by the first Christian missionaries whith whom most of the barbarians had come in contact, and it was still openly professed by nearly all the tribes of Europe. Theodoric himself was a tolerant man, who protected all shades of religious belief and had decreed particularly severe penalties for anti-semitism; but the faith of his people made them fair

1. *Variarum*, Book XII, Letter 24.

2. For a more recent, but inevitably less authentic, attempt to recreate the atmosphere of sixth-century Venice, it is interesting to compare d'Annunzio's violently chauvinistic play *La Nave*, set in Venice in A.D. 552.

game for Byzantine ambitions. Thus it was, in 535, that the Emperor Justinian launched his great campaign for the reconquest of his Italian heritage, entrusting the task to his most gifted general, Belisarius.

Once again the people of the lagoons remained, so far as they were able to remain, on the sidelines; but once again their ships were in urgent demand, this time for less peaceful purposes. In 539 Belisarius and his army reached the walls of Ravenna. The Venetians were requested to hold their harbours ready for any Greek ships that might arrive with reinforcements, sending all their own available smaller vessels to assist in the blockade of the capital.

Ravenna fell; Italy became imperial once again; and though many years were to pass before peace returned to the whole peninsula, the old Roman provinces of Venetia and Istria, territorially unchanged, readily submitted to their new Greek masters. To their inhabitants this was no hardship. Day-to-day administration continued as before in the hands of their own elected tribunes; their relations with the imperial authorities were distant but cordial. In 551 we find them helping Belisarius's successor, the septuagenarian eunuch Narses, by bringing a contingent of Lombard mercenaries by sea to Ravenna after they had been cut off by floods. In return, Narses is said to have built two churches on the islands of Rialto. One, which bore the names of Sts Geminianus and Menna – a curious twinning of a bishop of Modena and an obscure Phrygian martyr – probably stood in what is now the middle of St Mark's Square; the other, occupying the site of the present chapel of St Isidore in the basilica itself, was dedicated to Venice's first tutelary saint, St Theodore of Amasea, who can still be seen with his dragon-crocodile on the western column of the Piazzetta.

Twice in twelve years the Venetians had come to the aid of Constantinople, with a fleet that was now beyond doubt the most powerful in the Adriatic. They may well therefore have been treated with some special consideration by the imperial Exarch at Ravenna and his provincial governor, the *magister militum*; and something of the kind is certainly suggested by the *Altino Chronicle*, a gloriously ungrammatical hotch-potch of fact and legend put together in the twelfth century which remains, for better or worse, one of our principal sources for these early years. It tells a slightly garbled story of how, after the death of Justinian in 565 had brought about Narses' disgrace and dismissal, his successor Longinus paid an official visit to the lagoon. The Venetians' address to him on this occasion is worth quoting:

The Lord, who is our help and protection, has preserved us that we may live in these watery marshes, in our huts of wood and wattle. For this new Venice which we have raised in the lagoons has become a mighty habitation for us, so that we fear no invasion or seizure by any of the Kings or Princes of this world, nor even by the Emperor himself . . . unless they come by sea, and therein lies our strength.

Despite the implied defiance of these words, Longinus seems to have been given an enthusiastic enough reception, 'with bells and flutes and cytherns and other instruments of music, loud enough to drown the very thunder of heaven'. Later, Venetian ambassadors accompanied him to Constantinople and returned with the first formal agreement to be concluded between Venice and Byzantium according to which, in return for their loyalty and service when required, the settlements were assured of military protection and trading privileges throughout the Empire.

The *Altino Chronicle* claims that Longinus deliberately refrained from demanding any formal oath of submission, and for the next thousand years patriotic local opinion was staunchly to maintain that Venice was never entirely subject to Byzantium. The words quoted above – transcribed, let it be remembered, after an interval of some six centuries – are another reflection of this attitude; it is only in the past hundred years or so that Byzantine scholars have looked hard and mercilessly at the contemporary evidence and have established beyond question that the early Venetians, whether or not they enjoyed special privileges, remained subjects of the Empire in the fullest sense of the term, just as surely as their less fortunate neighbours on the mainland. Independence did not miraculously descend on them at their city's birth; like their democratic institutions, it was to grow, slowly and organically, over the years – which may be why it lasted so long.

Eunuchs, as everybody knows, are dangerous people to cross; and the dismissal of Narses, if tradition is to be believed, had far greater consequences for Venice – and indeed for all Italy – than the clarification of her political status. The old man had served his Emperor well. At an age when he might have expected a comfortable retirement he had been fighting one desperate campaign after another, up and down the whole length of the peninsula. Even after his final defeat of the Ostrogoths among the foothills of Vesuvius in 553, his task was not done. He had at once embarked on a programme of reorganization and reconstruction – on which he was still engaged, twelve years later at the age of eighty-seven, when the blow fell. As a crowning insult after his dismissal, the Empress

Sophia sent him a golden distaff and invited him, since he was no true man, to go and spin in the apartments of her women. 'I will spin her such a skein,' Narses is said to have muttered, 'that she shall not find the end of it in her lifetime'; at once he sent off messengers, laden with all the fruits of the Mediterranean, to the Lombard King Alboin in what is now Hungary, inviting him to lead his people down to the land which brought forth such abundance.

Alboin accepted, and in 568 the Lombards invaded Italy in the last, and the most lasting, of the barbarian invasions. Once again the long trains of refugees made their way from the mainland cities to the settlements in the lagoons; but now there was a difference. No longer did they come as individual frightened men and women, intending to remain in their self-inflicted exile only until better times returned. They had lost their faith in those better times. They had had enough of the bloodshed and the rapine and the wanton destruction that grew worse with every new visitation of this human plague. Now they arrived *en masse*, whole communities together, led by their bishops bearing the sacred relics which, enshrined in the churches that they were to build in their new homes, would provide a symbolic continuity with their former lives – the one tangible link between the past and present.

The early histories are rich in the stories and legends connected with these new migrations as, during the next seventy years, Lombard power spread over Italy. The *Altino Chronicle* records, for example, how Bishop Paul of that city heard a voice from heaven commanding him to climb to the top of a nearby tower and look at the stars; and how those stars showed him – presumably by the paths made by their reflections on the water – the island to which he must lead his flock. They settled in Torcello, naming it after the 'little tower' the bishop had climbed. Similarly, with episcopal if not always divine guidance, the people of Aquileia – now laid waste for the third time in 150 years – found their way to Grado, those of Concordia to Caorle, those of Padua to Malamocco. Finally in 639, in the reign of the Emperor Heraclius, the Lombards captured Oderzo – whose inhabitants, together with the Greek provincial administration, fled to the already existing settlement of Cittanova at the mouth of the Piave. Oderzo had been the last imperial foothold in mainland Venetia. Henceforth, apart from an isolated corner of the Istrian peninsula, the once-great province was reduced to the settlements on the lagoon. Its provincial capital was Cittanova, now renamed Heraclea in honour of the Emperor; but Torcello seems to have been considered as of at least equal importance and it was there, in that same year of 639,

34

that a basilica was erected in honour of the Virgin, with Heraclius himself as its patron. The document recording its foundation still exists, and even identifies the Byzantine officials concerned – Isaac, Exarch of Ravenna, and Maurice, his *magister militum*; so indeed does the church itself, now known as the cathedral of S. Maria Assunta.[1]

But for the later history of the Republic the most important of these flights from Lombard domination was also one of the first – that from Aquileia to Grado. The see of Aquileia had traditionally been founded by St Mark himself, in consequence of which its metropolitan Archbishop – later to bear the title of Patriarch – was supreme in the lagoons, occupying a place in the Italian hierarchy second only to that of the Pope of Rome. At the time of which we are speaking, however, this honour was more theoretical than real, since the Archbishop Paulinus had led his followers not only away from heresy (the Lombards being Arian to a man) but also, almost simultaneously, into schism. The historical and theological reasons for his break with Rome – the Schism of the Three Chapters, as it is generally called – need not detain us here. What is significant for our purposes is the fact that, ecclesiastically speaking, Venice was born schismatic; and though the Metropolitan of Grado was to return to the Roman fold in 608 the schism continued, in the person of a rival Archbishop at old Aquileia, for nearly another century – during which each persisted in his denunciation of the other as an impostor and reciprocal anathemas thundered backwards and forwards between the two. At last the dispute was settled, but the old unity was gone. Aquileia and Grado continued independently of each other as separate sees, the first with authority over the old mainland territories of the province, the second covering Istria and the lagoons. Their mutual jealousies were to poison Venice's relations with the mainland, both political and religious, for generations to come; but it was the Patriarch of Grado who occupied the ancient episcopal throne in which St Mark had once sat, now re-erected in the great church built there by Paulinus and his followers soon after their arrival. That church still stands. It is dedicated, surprisingly, not to the Evangelist but to St Euphemia, the leader of an obscure group of local virgins martyred at Aquileia soon after his departure; but it begins the association of St Mark with Venice which was merely to be confirmed when his body was brought from Alexandria some 250 years later.

1. The cathedral was rebuilt in 864 and again in 1008; and it is this latter structure that we see today. The superb mosaics are slightly later, dating from the twelfth and thirteenth centuries. Owing to the ever-shifting contours of the Adriatic coast, Heraclea has now disappeared, virtually without trace. It probably stood not on the site of the present village that bears its name, but a few miles to the south-east, near Cortelazzo.

With this sudden new influx of permanent settlers Venice began to develop fast; but she was not yet, in any sense of the word, a city. Despite the two churches built by Narses, the islands of Rialto which comprise the Venice we know today were, in the sixth and seventh centuries, still largely uninhabited. At this stage the future Republic was nothing more than a loose association of island communities, dotted about over a wide area and with little effective unity except that which was imposed by its Byzantine overlords. Even its Latin name, and the one invariably used by its inhabitants, was a plural – *Venetiae*[1] – and it still had no real nucleus. Heraclea was the seat of the Byzantine governor, Grado that of the Patriarch; neither amounted to more than a large village. More prosperous than either was Torcello, whose superiority as a commercial centre was recognized but, with the passage of time, increasingly resented by her neighbours. As the individual settlements grew, such stresses and strains were probably inevitable; the Venetians of the seventh century seem to have preserved little enough of that prelapsarian innocence that had so struck Cassiodorus in the sixth. The old-established tribunes and the more recently arrived bishops tended always to contest one another's authority, while differences between one community and the next were more and more liable to lead to open fighting which the Byzantine authorities were powerless to control. The imperial presence at Heraclea prevented the Venetians themselves from producing a leader who might have given them the cohesion they needed; and there is no telling how long this unsatisfactory state of affairs might have continued but for the events of the year 726, when Byzantine Italy underwent the crisis that was ultimately to bring about its downfall.

This crisis had begun when the Byzantine Emperor Leo III ordered the destruction of all icons and holy images throughout his dominions. The effect of his decree was immediate and shattering. Everywhere men rose in wrath; the monasteries, in particular, were outraged. In the eastern provinces of the Empire, where the cult of icons had reached such proportions that they frequently served as godparents at baptisms, a puritan reaction had been inevitable and Leo had found some measure of support; but in the more moderate West, which had done nothing to deserve them, the new laws were rejected with indignation. The imperial province in

1. It would be pleasant, but by no means easy, to accept the traditional theory about the origin of the name. Sansovino – the scholar-son of the architect, whose *Venetia, città nobilissima et singolare, descritta in XIII libri*, published in 1581, remains one of the greatest works on the city ever penned – states it thus: 'It is held by some that this word VENETIA signifies *VENI ETIAM*, that is, Come again, and again, for however oft you come, you will always see new things, and new beauties.'

Italy, enthusiastically encouraged by Pope Gregory II, turned against its masters. Paul, Exarch of Ravenna, was assassinated, his provincial governors put to flight. Throughout the Exarchate the rebellious garrisons – all of whom had been recruited locally – chose their own commanders and asserted their independence. In the lagoon communities, their choice fell on a certain Ursus, or Orso, from Heraclea, who was placed at the head of the former provincial administration and given the title of *Dux*.

There was nothing especially remarkable about this last development; the same thing was happening almost simultaneously in many other insurgent towns. What distinguishes Venice from the rest is the fact that Orso's appointment inaugurated a tradition which was to continue, unbroken, for over a thousand years; and that his title, transformed by the rough Venetian dialect into *Doge*, was to pass down through 117 successors before the Republic's end.

One of the most infuriating aspects of early Venetian history is the regularity with which truth and legend pursue separate courses. This is a tendency of which the reader will already be only too well aware; and if he happens to have read any of the standard English works on the subject he will also know that the above account of the way the Doges began is by no means that which has been generally accepted in the past. If you believe that Venice was born in freedom you cannot at the same time accept the theory of a revolt against a foreign oppressor. According, therefore, to the authorized version, a general assembly of all the people of the lagoons had been summoned to Heraclea in 697 by the Patriarch of Grado. Pointing out that their internal conflicts were putting the whole future of the state in jeopardy, he had proposed that the Venetians should elect a single ruler in place of the twelve tribunes. Their choice had fallen on a certain Paoluccio Anafesto who, as their first Doge, shortly afterwards concluded a treaty of friendship with the Lombard King Liutprand.

As a story, this sounds perfectly probable. It certainly commands the respect due to age, since it goes back at least as far as the beginning of the eleventh century, to John the Deacon, putative author of the earliest history of Venice that we possess. And in every list of Doges, there, sure enough, is Paoluccio's name at the head; we even have an imaginary portrait of him to start off the long series around the walls of the *Sala del Maggior Consiglio* of their palace. Unfortunately, he never existed; not at least as a Doge, nor even as a Venetian. Nor was there ever any treaty with Liutprand. All we learn from the original sources is that a certain *dux* Paulicius, with Marcellus, his *magister militum*, was responsible for fixing the Venetian boundary-line near Heraclea and that this line was later accepted by the Lombards. Venetia being as we now know a Byzantine province at that time, the obvious and indeed the only legitimate conclusion to be drawn from this is that the mysterious Paulicius was none other than Paul, Exarch of Ravenna from 723 until his murder by the rebels in 727 – the very year, incidentally, to which John the Deacon ascribes the death of Paoluccio. As an imperial viceroy his authority would have been indispensable for any frontier delimitation, as would that of the provincial governor Marcellus – who, by a similar triumph of wishful thinking, has gone down in history as the city's second Doge. It is the historians of Venice, just as much as her architects, who have sunk their foundations into shifting sands.

· 2 ·

Emergence

[727–811]

Lor mostra appresso un giovene Pipino
Che con sua gente par che tutto copra
Dalle Fornaci al lito pelestino;
E faccia con gran spesa e con lung' opra
Il ponte a Malamocco; e che vicino
Giunga a Rialto, e vi combatta sopra.
Poi fuggir sembra, e che i suoi lasci sotto
L'acque, che 'l ponte il vento e 'l mar gli han rotto.

Pepin the Younger he moves on to show,
Who with his army seems to cover all
The region from the outlet of the Po
As far as Pellestrina's littoral;
Who builds a pontoon bridge at Malamocco;
Whose troops attack Rialto, but to fall
Into the depths of the lagoon and drown
When wind and water wash the structure down.

Ariotso, *Orlando Furioso*
Canto XXXIII (Tr. Barbara Reynolds)

Byzantine Italy's insurrection against her Greek masters did not last long.
Pope Gregory, who had provided the moral leadership, himself had no
wish to see the power of the Lombard heretics further strengthened; it
soon became clear that the provisions of the iconoclast decree neither
would nor could be seriously enforced in the West; and as tempers cooled
there seemed to emerge a general feeling that so long as the newly
established democratic institutions could still be maintained in the
individual cities, these would be well advised to continue as before in at
least nominal adherence to the Empire. Thus it comes as no surprise to
learn that within a few years of the uprising Doge Orso was granted the
imperial title of *Hypatos*, or Consul – a distinction of which he seems to
have been so proud that his descendants came to surname themselves
Ipato. Whatever developments might have occurred in the political sphere,
Venice's institutional and emotional links with Constantinople clearly

remained unbroken. And Orso was only the first of many Doges who were to puff themselves up with Byzantine honorifics; resonant appellations like *patricius*, *proedrus* or *spatharius* appear regularly and, one sometimes suspects, indiscriminately up to the tenth century and even later. Before long the Doge's dress was to be modelled on that of the Exarch, and even on that of the Emperor himself; the ducal ceremonial was deliberately to reflect the imperial usages; Sunday prayers in St Mark's were to echo the Greek liturgy current in St Sophia. Many a Byzantine maiden was to be shipped off to the West, into the arms of a Venetian bridegroom; many a Venetian was to send his son eastward to finish his education in Constantinople.

Politically, however, the Empire's grip on Venice had been loosened. To be sure, the Greeks did not relinquish it without a struggle; but it was by now clear that Byzantine power in North Italy was dying. When in 742, after a short interregnum, Orso's son Teodato – or Deusdedit, as he is sometimes rather pedantically called – was elected second Doge of Venice, simultaneously transferring his seat of government from imperial Heraclea to the more central and republican Malamocco,[1] he found himself for all practical purposes a sovereign ruler.

Ravenna finally fell in 751, and though the vacuum left in the lagoons was more apparent than real, the Lombards might have been expected to move into Venice to fill it. Fortunately, Liutprand's successor King Aistulf had more pressing problems on his mind. In that very same year, beyond the Alps, the young Pepin – son of Charles Martel – had deposed the Merovingian King Childeric and seized the Frankish throne. Almost at once, at the invitation of Pope Stephen III, he had crossed into Italy and twice, in quick succession, had smashed the Lombard armies. Henceforth, though the greater part of his conquests was bestowed on Stephen – leading to the foundation of the Papal State and the temporal power of the Pope – the Franks were to be the controlling force in North Italy. Yet once again Venice was spared. The region of the lagoons had not formed part of the territorial redistribution; the Franks were in no hurry to extend their power any further around the Adriatic; and it was not till sixty years after the fall of the Exarchate that the Venetians were at last obliged to defend their young Republic by force of arms.

This is not, however, to say that the second half of the eighth century

---

1. Old Malamocco did not occupy the same site as the present village, but further across the Lido on the eastern shore. It was swept away by the sea in 1105 (see p. 106).

promised to be very much more peaceful for them than the first half had been. Venice might have found a form of government that suited her; but she had not yet achieved either internal stability or cohesion. The various settlements were still at loggerheads and even within the individual communities, seething as they were with family feuds and factional strife, flash-point was never far away. Like his father, Doge Teodato came to a violent end – being deposed and blinded by his successor who, scarcely a year later, suffered a similar fate. The fourth Doge lasted a little longer; but after eight years, becoming resentful of the two tribunes who were now elected every year to prevent the abuse of the ducal power, he too was eliminated.

With the election of Maurizio Galbaio in 764, the situation began to improve. A well-born Heraclean, claiming descent from the Emperor Galba,[1] he represented a return to the old pro-Byzantine tradition. His enemies, both the stauncher republicans and those who believed the best hopes for Venetian prosperity to lie in close association with the rising Kingdom of the Franks, would probably have branded him a reactionary; and their suspicions would have been confirmed when, in 778, he associated his son Giovanni with him in the dogeship. For the embryonic Republic, this step was as dangerous as it was unprecedented. Teodato Ipato, it was true, had succeeded his father, but his succession had not been immediate and in any case had been sanctioned by the popular vote. The elevation of Giovanni Galbaio, on the other hand, meant that he would automatically assume full powers on Maurizio's death without his subjects' approval – without, indeed, their being even consulted. To the republicans at least, the fact that the old Doge had taken the trouble to seek and obtain the consent of the Emperor in Constantinople is unlikely to have been much consolation.

It was a bad augury for the future; and the wonder is not only that Maurizio managed to carry out his intention but that in 796 Giovanni was permitted in his turn to associate his own son with him, thereby pushing Venice one step further along the road to a hereditary monarchy. The most likely explanation lies in the fact that the average Venetian was tired of bloodshed, and longed for a system by which one ruler might quietly succeed another with the minimum disruption of everyday life – and, of course, of trade. There was nothing new in this; smoothness of succession has always been one of the most telling arguments in favour of the hereditary principle and, for many nations of the world, has amply

1. The Galbaio family later assumed the name of Querini, in which guise it was to play a leading part in later centuries.

justified it in practice. But it was not for the Venetians, as events were soon to show.

The first of the Galbaii, reactionary or not, did much to deserve their confidence. For twenty-three years he ruled them strongly and well. As their prosperity increased and their numbers grew they began to spread themselves, moving out to various islands in the lagoon which, for one reason or another, the earlier settlers had tended to ignore. The Rialtine group in particular, lying about half-way between the outer line of sand-banks and the mainland shore, had remained almost deserted since the days of Narses. Muddy rather than sandy, difficult of access owing to the surrounding shallows, low-lying and thus susceptible to floods when the *acqua alta*, or high water, came surging in from the Adriatic, these islands had never before seemed a particularly tempting site for intensive colonization. But they were central, and to those who were revolted by the endless bickering and squabbling of the older communities they offered a chance of peace and a fresh start. And so, during the eighth century, building there suddenly began in earnest. At first it seems to have been concentrated at the eastern end, on the little island of Olivolo on which the Trojans, fleeing westward after the destruction of their city, were reputed to have built a fortress and which was consequently later to be known as Castello. It was here in about 775 that Doge Maurizio founded a new bishopric, and transformed a small church bearing the names of St Bacchus and St Sergius into a cathedral dedicated to St Peter.[1]

That same year the old Doge died and his son, as had been expected, gathered all the reins of power into his own hands. Alas, Giovanni Galbaio possessed little of his father's flair: he proved quite unable to deal with the developing situation in the rest of Italy, where the Franks were rapidly consolidating their position and presenting an ever-growing threat to the Republic's independence. Pepin was dead, and had been succeeded by his son Charles – Charlemagne – who had spent much of the previous fifteen years in Italy. During that time he had conceived a cordial dislike of the Venetians whom he suspected, with good reason, of making huge profits out of the slave trade, and he had already on one occasion appealed to the Pope to take active measures against them. The Pope for his part had, since Pepin's defeat of the Lombards, found

---

1. Another legend attributed the choice of the site to St Peter himself, appearing miraculously to the Bishop of Heraclea and indicating 'the place where he had seen a herd of oxen and sheep feeding together'. S. Pietro di Castello has since been rebuilt several times, most recently in 1598, in a rather unsuccessful pastiche of Palladio. It continued to be the cathedral church of Venice throughout the lifetime of the Republic. Only in 1807 did it yield the title to St Mark's, which till then had technically been nothing but the chapel of the Doges' Palace (see pp. 53–4).

himself master of a considerable section of the Italian peninsula; to defend and preserve it, however, he was utterly dependent on the Kingdom of the Franks. His pro-Frankish policies were naturally supported by the large majority of the Latin clergy; and so it had come about that to the two traditional factions which had already long existed in Venice – those which, at the risk of over-simplification, could be described as the pro-Byzantine at Heraclea and the republican at Malamocco – there had now grown up a third, containing a strong clerical element, which stood for the Frankish alliance.

All through the closing years of the century this third party continued to gain in strength; and it received still further impetus when, on Christmas Day 800, Charlemagne was crowned by the Pope as Emperor of the West. Under the leadership of the Patriarch of Grado – who had for some time shown himself openly rebellious towards the central authority on Malamocco – it now began seriously to threaten the security of the state. Doge Giovanni, who had by now followed his father's example and associated his son, another Maurizio, with him on the ducal throne, was fully aware of the danger; and in an effort to curb the Patriarch's influence within the Church he had recently appointed a young Greek called Christopher to the new see of Olivolo. Unfortunately, Christopher could not take up his duties without prior consecration by the Patriarch; and this ceremony, less because of the bishop's age – which was just sixteen – than because of his prematurely pronounced anti-Frankish tendencies, His Beatitude obstinately refused to perform. The Doge's reply was to send his son with a squadron of ships to Grado. The Patriarch was seized and dragged up to the top of his palace tower from which, already badly wounded, he was hurled to the ground.

Political assassinations seldom achieve the purpose for which they are intended. Horror at the crime spread far beyond Grado, where for generations to come men were to claim that they could still see the bloodstains on the paving beneath the tower; and Maurizio was hardly home before news arrived that the murdered Patriarch's nephew, Fortunatus, had been elected in his stead. More bitterly opposed to the regime of the Galbaii than even his uncle had been, Fortunatus had immediately escaped to Frankish territory; meanwhile other, secular leaders of the opposition, fearing like him that recent events in Grado might prove a prelude to a reign of terror in Venice itself, removed themselves simultaneously to Treviso where, under the leadership of a former tribune named Obelerio degli Antenori, they settled down to plot the two Doges' overthrow. In 804 they succeeded. A popular rising deposed the Galbaii, who were lucky to get away with their lives; young Bishop Christopher followed them into exile; and Obelerio returned in triumph to Venice, where he was at once raised to the supreme power.

But if the Venetians thought that this last *coup* would bring an end to their problems, they were soon disillusioned. Obelerio lost no time in elevating his brother Beato to share his throne, and the new tandem soon proved almost indistinguishable from the old. Internal unrest grew worse than ever. The upheavals of the past two years had aroused still fiercer passions which in their turn had brought about new scores to settle, new insults to be avenged. The age-long feud between Heraclea and Mala-mocco blazed up again and continued until the former was attacked and reduced to ashes. Before many months had passed it looked as though the two hapless rulers would go the way of their predecessors. But now there reappeared on the scene the Patriarch Fortunatus, fresh from the court of Charlemagne, with an offer. If Obelerio would reinstate him, making open avowal of Frankish sovereignty over Venice and the lagoons, the Doge and his brother could rely on the protection of the Western Empire.

Although Obelerio and his brother had led the opposition to the pro-Byzantine Galbaii, their hostility had been more personal than political and they had never shown any particular sympathy for the Franks. Now, however, they had little choice. Thus, on Christmas Day 805 at Aachen, the rulers of Venice did homage to Charlemagne as Emperor of the West – Obelerio even going so far as to choose for himself from among the ladies of the court a Frankish bride, who returned with him to take her place as the first *dogaressa* known to history.

The news of Venice's treachery – for so, understandably, it was considered – was received with deep displeasure at Constantinople. The Byzantines, who had always justifiably considered themselves the rightful inheritors of the Roman Empire, had not yet completely recovered from the shock of Charlemagne's coronation. When, two years later, the reigning Empress Zoë had not immediately rejected his proposal of marriage, they had lost no time in deposing her and banishing her, somewhat inappropriately, to the island of Lesbos; and the new Emperor Nicephorus, though he soon came to accept the Western Empire as a fact of life, was by no means disposed to submit to this still more recent blow to his sovereignty without protest. In 809 a Byzantine squadron sailed up the Dalmatian coast and anchored in the lagoon.

It was received coldly. The admiral's attempts at negotiations were frustrated and envenomed at every turn until at last, losing patience, he was somehow persuaded to attack – not Venice itself, but a Frankish flotilla based at Comacchio, some forty miles to the south. It proved stronger than he had thought. A few days later he retired, beaten and humiliated, to his base at Cephalonia.

In Venice now the situation was as confused as ever it had been. The renewed hostility between the two rival Empires was reflected in a fresh upsurge of party strife. Obelerio and Beato, who had now raised yet a third brother, Valentino, to share their ducal dignity, played their last card. Invoking the agreement of 805, they sent messengers to Pepin at Ravenna, inviting him to occupy Venice and to garrison the entire province. And Pepin accepted. By the terms of the treaty he had little option; he might, nevertheless, have taken the trouble to find out for himself just what his reception was likely to be.

Pepin's expedition, hastily and inadequately prepared, set out from Ravenna early in 810. He found the Venetians ready for him, but not in the sense that he had been led to expect. The people of the lagoons, faced at last with a common danger, had forgotten their internal differences. The explanations and protests of their three Doges they simply ignored; the brothers were traitors, but there would be time to deal with them afterwards. Entrusting the defence of the Republic to one of the older settlers of Rialto, a certain Agnello Participazio,[1] they blocked the channels, removed all buoys and markers, and prepared to face the enemy with everything they had.

Although Pepin met with furious resistance from the moment his army entered Venetian territory, he had little difficulty in making himself master of Chioggia and Pellestrina, at the southern end of the lagoon. But at the Malamocco channel, dividing the island of Pellestrina from that of Malamocco (now better known as the Lido) he was brought to a halt. Of what happened next, there has come down to us a lively account by, of all people, the Byzantine Emperor Constantine VII Porphyrogenitus, in a treatise on imperial administration which he wrote for his son in the middle of the tenth century. Though not quite contemporary, it is probably as reliable as any other source we possess.

The Venetians, seeing King Pepin coming against them with his army and intending to ship his cavalry over to the island of Malamaucus . . . blocked up the passage with a barricade of projecting stakes. So the people of King Pepin, being rendered helpless – for they could not cross elsewhere – encamped on the mainland opposite for six months, fighting with them every day. And the

1. His name is also found in the alternative version of Particiaco. Later, in the tenth century, the family changed it altogether to Badoer, in which form it still exists.

Venetians went on ship-board, and took up a position behind the stakes they
had fixed, but Pepin stood with his people on the sea shore. And the Venetians
fought with arrows and other missiles, preventing them from crossing over to
the island. So King Pepin, at a loss, appealed to the Venetians saying 'Ye are
under my hand and my providence, since ye belong to my land and my dominions.' But the Venetians answered him, 'We will be the servants of the Roman
Emperor,[1] and never shall be thine.'

In other directions, Pepin's armies continued to advance. Grado fell,
and so, probably, did those old enemies Heraclea – what was left of it – and
Jesolo. But the Malamoccans, their women and children evacuated to
Rialto, showed no signs of weakening; the legend runs how one day,
hearing that Pepin was determined to starve them out, they showed him
the futility of his hopes by bombarding his army with bread. Meanwhile
spring had turned to summer, and the fever-ridden shores of the *lidi*
began to take their toll of the invaders. Rumours spread, too, that a huge
Byzantine fleet was already sailing to Venice's relief. Pepin knew that he
had failed, and gave the order to withdraw. The state of his own health
may have influenced his decision, for within a few weeks he was dead.

It has been fashionable, in recent years, to accuse the Venetians of
having exaggerated the importance of their victory; and indeed, gazing at
the two gigantic paintings by Vicentino which commemorate it in the
Sala dello Scrutinio of the Doges' Palace, one can hardly argue that the
theme has been underplayed. It is true that Pepin did not leave until the
Venetians, to get rid of him, had agreed to pay an annual tribute, and that
this tribute continued to be exacted for well over a century; it is equally
true that even though he failed in his most important object, he extended
his authority all around the lagoon and well beyond it. But the conquered
towns were not to remain in Frankish hands for long; and in any case the
significance of the year 810 far exceeds that of any individual political or
military event. More than once in the past, the lagoon settlers had asserted
their right to exist as an independent entity; in that year, for the first time,
they fought for it and proved it. And in doing so they also proved
something else – that whatever the rivalries and jealousies of those early
times, in a moment of real crisis they were capable of seeing themselves
not as men of Malamocco or Chioggia, of Jesolo or Pellestrina, but as
Venetians. Pepin had marched against a group of bickering communities;
he had been defeated by a united people.

And now, as if in search of some visible sign of their reconciliation, the

1. i.e. the Emperor at Constantinople, whose subjects continued to call themselves Ῥωμαῖοι
– Romans.

eyes of that people turned towards Rialto and its little cluster of islands that had never been embroiled in the squabbles of their neighbours – that had, on the contrary, served as a refuge for citizens of other, unhappier settlements who had fled from the advancing invader just as their ancestors had fled 300 and 400 years before. Malamocco, valiantly as it had defended itself as a community, had failed as a capital. Its last trio of Doges, the Antenori, had been a disaster. It had never acquired that degree of political neutrality that any federal capital must possess. Moreover, as Pepin had shown, it was vulnerable to attack. It had staved off the enemy once, but only after a hard struggle; next time it might not be so lucky. The outer seaboard of the lagoon, along the line of the *lidi* – those long, narrow sandbanks that protected it from the open Adriatic – was now revealed to be no safer than the mainland.

The islands of the Rialtine archipelago – Rialto itself with Dorsoduro, Spinalunga (the present Giudecca), Luprio (the area around S. Giacomo dell' Orio) and Olivolo (now known as Castello) – possessed neither of these disadvantages. More and more did they appear as a haven of moderation, toleration and good sense in a sea of bitterness and hatred. From their position in the centre of the lagoon, almost impossible of access to those who were unfamiliar with the shoals and shallows that surrounded them, they were superbly placed to defy an attacker. After the fall of Grado they possessed in S. Pietro di Castello the only national ecclesiastical centre remaining to the Republic. Their inhabitants, being at once champions of and refugees from practically all shades of political opinion, were collectively impartial. The hero of the hour, that Agnello Participazio who had turned back the forces of the Western Empire, was himself a Rialtine. To Rialto, then, the capital was moved. The three Doges were exiled. In a last-minute attempt to save their throne and their reputations, they had turned their coats and taken up arms against the invaders they had themselves invited; but it was a pathetic ploy, and it had deceived no one. In their place the Venetians elected the only possible candidate – Agnello himself, whose modest house on the Campiello della Cason (near S. Canciano) became the first Doges' Palace in the Venice that we know today.

Theoretically, the province of Venetia was still part of the Byzantine Empire. But it was by this time entirely autonomous, and the imperial government at Constantinople – which could not have done anything about it anyway – was quite content that it should remain so. The important thing now was to obtain recognition of its autonomy in the

West as well. Within a month or two of Pepin's retreat a Byzantine legate arrived in Venice on his way to the Frankish court at Aachen.

The Byzantines, once they had become accustomed to the idea, had found themselves resenting Charlemagne's existence rather less than might have been expected. Subconsciously, perhaps, they understood that for the new, emerging Europe one Emperor was no longer enough. Constantinople might be the theoretical repository of Roman law, civilization and imperial traditions; but in spirit Constantinople was now entirely Greek. Rome, shattered as she was by the barbarians and demoralized by centuries of near-anarchy, was still the focal point of Latin culture; it was Aachen, not Byzantium, that had re-established the *Pax Romana* in the West.

Had Charlemagne been thirty years younger, he might have been less ready to accept the Byzantine proposals; but he was old and tired, more concerned with the division of his Empire between his surviving heirs than with further territorial extensions. He always maintained that his imperial coronation had taken him by surprise. It had certainly embarrassed him, and he had been careful never to suggest any aggressive designs on the Empire of the East. Byzantine recognition of his own imperial title was all he sought; given that, he asked nothing better than friendly relations with his fellow-Emperor Nicephorus, for which the surrender of his tenuous claim to Venice seemed a small enough price to pay.

The treaty between the two Empires that was agreed in the spring of 811 (although, owing to the deaths of both Charlemagne and Nicephorus, it was not ratified till three years later) gave each what it required – at a price. The Franks obtained recognition of their imperial status while, for the Byzantines, Charlemagne's renunciation of all his claims over the province of Venetia meant not only the continuation of their own suzerainty but also the assurance that the leading maritime power in the Adriatic could not be mobilized against them. The gain on each side, however, involved a corresponding concession by the other; only for Venice herself were the benefits unmitigated. Henceforth she was to enjoy all the advantages, partly political but above all cultural and commercial, of being a Byzantine province, without any real diminution of her independence. For many years to come, the Doges might continue, legally speaking, to be officials of Byzantium, loaded with Byzantine honorifics and, on occasion, with Byzantine gold. But they were none the less Venetians, elected by Venetians, and the Eastern Empire was never again seriously to interfere with their affairs. It is always dangerous to press historical comparisons too far, particularly when dealing with institutions remote alike in time and spirit; but if we think of Venice, in her relations with Constantinople, as enjoying for the next two centuries something akin to what we should now call Commonwealth status, perhaps we should not be so very far wrong.

There were other advantages too. The *Pax Nicephori*, as it came to be called, separated Venice from the rest of Italy and so enabled her to escape, just in time, the political upheavals which were soon to change the face of the peninsula and indeed much of western Europe. Thanks to her links with Byzantium she remained virtually untouched by the feudal system, by communal government of the kind that later became the rule in Lombardy and Tuscany, and by the seemingly endless wars of Guelf against Ghibelline that were intermittently to continue, in one form or another, almost as long as the Republic itself. Thus, paradoxically, it was through her very submission to the Empire of the East that her independence was achieved and her future greatness assured.

The City Rises Up

[811–900]

'And so Barnabas took Mark, and sailed unto Cyprus.' If as the shores of
Asia lessened upon his sight, the spirit of prophecy had entered into the heart
of the weak disciple who had turned back when his hand was on the plough,
and who had been judged, by the chiefest of Christ's captains, unworthy
thenceforward to go forth with him to the work, how wonderful would he
have thought it, that by the lion symbol in future ages he was to be represented
among men! . . .

Ruskin, *The Stones of Venice*

With peace restored to the lagoon, Doge Agnello was free to turn his
attention to a new problem, every bit as challenging as that which he had
just surmounted. The islands of Rialto, flat, muddy and often waterlogged,
were neither large enough nor firm enough to accommodate the new
influx of settlers. If they were to be made into a capital worthy of the
growing Republic, they would have to be strengthened, drained and –
wherever primitive methods of land reclamation made it possible –
enlarged. They must be protected, too, from the sea, against which the
outer line of *lidi* provided a not always effective barrier. To undertake
these tasks the Doge appointed a commission of three men. Nicolò
Ardisonio was to fortify the *lidi*, buttressing them artificially where
necessary; Lorenzo Alimpato was entrusted with the digging of canals,
the shoring up of islands and the preparation of building sites; while
the buildings themselves were made the responsibility of Agnello's close
kinsman, Pietro Tradonico.

These buildings were still for the most part modest, two-storey
structures, lightly constructed to minimize subsidence and usually
thatched with straw. Already, like Venetian houses today, they tended to
have two front doors, one giving out on the land – probably with a little
patch of garden for vegetables – and the other opening directly on to the

water. Wood was still the most popular building material; it was light, easy to transport, abundant – thanks to the pine forests around the lagoon – and cheap. Bricks, so characteristic of later Venetian architecture, were still almost unknown; the mud of the lagoon was too soft and thin. For the more important buildings where wood seemed insufficiently durable or impressive, there remained only one answer – stone, and in particular the hard, white stone of the Istrian peninsula.

But stone presented its own problems, notably that of weight. The only means of establishing a firm enough foundation for it was to drive thousands of wooden piles into the ooze, so close that they touched one another and their sawn-off tops made a virtually unified, solid surface. It was a long and laborious process, but it worked; many houses in Venice today still stand on piles sunk almost 1,000 years ago, and the technique was to be continued well into the twentieth century.[1] In the ninth, however, it was still in its infancy; there were few stone buildings except the churches – and the great palace that Agnello began for himself and his successors near the old church of St Theodore.

Of this first Doges' Palace nothing now remains. Though it occupied the same site as the present one, its appearance must have been very different; heavily battlemented, with corner towers and drawbridges, it was more a fortress than anything else – and no wonder, in view of the Republic's recent history. Architecturally, it cannot have compared with the splendid edifice that was simultaneously rising just behind it to the east. This was the church and convent of S. Zaccaria, designed to receive the mortal remains of the father of John the Baptist, recently presented to Venice in a gesture of friendship and goodwill by the Byzantine Emperor, Leo V the Armenian. Leo may well have gone even further and paid for the whole building himself; he certainly sent architects and craftsmen from Constantinople. Alas, their work too has disappeared. S. Zaccaria, like most of the older churches of Venice, has been rebuilt and restored so often as to be unrecognizable for what it originally was. But its importance in the early history of the Republic was considerable, and there will be more to say of it as we go on.

This initial period of carefully planned construction laid down the lines on which the new capital was to develop and gave it the basic shape it still preserves. Inevitably, however, the Doge had other more immediate problems to contend with – for the gravest of which he was himself

1. Even so colossal a structure as Longhena's church of the Salute, built between 1630 and 1687 on the end of Dorsoduro (the firmest, as its name implies, of all the Rialtine islands), rests entirely on such piles – according to one record, 1,156,627 of them.

responsible. Though by far the most enlightened ruler that Venice had yet produced, he too fell into the temptation of trying to make his office hereditary; and since his elder son Giustiniano was away in Constantinople he raised the younger, Giovanni, to share the dogeship with him. Giustiniano returned in wrath and demanded that his brother be deposed – a step which drove Giovanni in his turn into a fury, and shortly afterwards into exile. But these family quarrels, undignified as they were, never seriously threatened the security of the state. The building work went on uninterrupted; and Agnello Participazio can be accounted, more than anyone else, the first architect of modern Venice. It was only sad for him that he did not live to witness what was, perhaps, the most important single event in the spiritual life of the Republic – that which did more than any other to strengthen its ecclesiastical independence and to focus its national pride and which, incidentally, gave the city its most glorious and enduring monument.

One day – so the story goes – when St Mark was travelling from Aquileia to Rome, his ship chanced to put in at the islands of Rialto. There an angel appeared to him and blessed him with the words '*Pax tibi, Marce, evangelista meus. Hic requiescet corpus tuum.*'[1] The historical evidence for this story is, to say the least, uncertain; the prophecy – since St Mark later became Bishop of Alexandria and remained there till he died – would have seemed improbable; but the legend certainly came in very handy when, in 828 or thereabouts, two Venetian merchants returned from Egypt with a corpse which they claimed to be that of the Evangelist, stolen from his Alexandrian tomb. As might be expected, the details of this enterprise vary from one account to the next; the consensus seems, however, to be that the Christian guardians of the shrine, concerned for the future of their church under Saracen rule, were somehow persuaded – or bribed – to cooperate. The shroud was slit up the back, the body removed and the remains of St Claudian, which lay conveniently near at hand, substituted for it. It was then put into a large basket and carried down to the harbour, where a Venetian ship was waiting.[2]

1. 'Peace be unto you, Mark, my evangelist. On this spot shall your body rest.' The first of these sentences must be familiar to all visitors to Venice, since it is inscribed upon the open book that the ubiquitous winged lion of the city holds in his paw. One of the few exceptions is the stone lion outside the Arsenal; the message being thought too conciliatory for so warlike an institution, his book is held defiantly closed.

2. One account asserts that there were no less than ten Venetian vessels in the port of Alexandria at the time. If so, it is a significant indication of the growth of the merchant fleet of the Republic.

By this time the odour of sanctity that issued from the body was becoming so strong that, in the words of one chronicler,[1] 'If all the spices of the world had been gathered together in Alexandria, they could not have so perfumed the city.' Suspicions were understandably aroused, and local officials arrived to search the ship; but the Venetians had covered their prize with quantities of pork, at the first sight of which the officials, pious Muslims to a man, cried *'Kanzir, kanzir!'* – 'Pig, pig!' – and fled in horror. The body was then wrapped in canvas and hoisted up to the yard-arm, where it remained till the vessel was out of harbour. Even now the dangers were not over, for the vessel headed straight for some uncharted reef and would surely have foundered had not St Mark himself roused the sleeping captain and induced him, just in time, to lower his sail. At last, however, it was brought safely to Venice, where its precious cargo was received with appropriate rejoicing.

Now this story – which is admirably depicted, down to the very cries of the customs men, high on the mosaic walls of the present Basilica[2] – is something more than just another of those legends in which early Venetian history is so rich. That a body thought to be that of St Mark was brought to Venice at this time is generally believed to be a historical fact; and it is equally beyond doubt that Giustiniano Participazio – now sole Doge since the death of his father in 827 – instantly commanded that a special chapel should be built for its reception, in the *brolo* or garden separating the church of St Theodore from his own palace. There is a strong possibility, even, that the whole expedition from Alexandria had been undertaken on the secret orders of the Doge. If the Republic were to command respect in the new Europe that was gradually taking shape around it, it needed some special prestige beyond that which wealth or sea power alone could confer; and in the Middle Ages, when politics and religion were still inextricably intertwined, the presence of an important sacred relic endowed a city with a mystique all its own. The body of St Zacharias might be better than nothing, but it was not really enough. That of an Evangelist, on the other hand, would endow Venice with Apostolic patronage and place her on a spiritual level second only to Rome itself, with a claim to ecclesiastical autonomy – further strengthened by the patriarchal status of her bishop – unparalleled in Latin Christendom.

Similarly, there was no reason why a spiritual advantage should not be turned to straightforward political ends; and here again the relic arrived at an opportune moment. Barely a year before, in 827, a synod at Mantua

1. Martino da Canale, Ch. XI.
2. Above the south transept, near the chapel of S. Clemente.

THE CITY RISES UP

headed by representatives of the Pope and the Western Emperor had
proposed the restoration of the old Patriarchate of Aquileia, giving it
authority over the see of Grado. Since Aquileia was part of the Western
Empire, such a decision might have constituted a serious threat to
Venetian independence. Now, with the body of St Mark slammed, as it
were, on to the scales in favour of Grado, the Mantuan decision could be
safely ignored. Grado remained the metropolitan see to which the
Church of Venice, revived and regenerated in the name of the Evangelist,
owed its ecclesiastical allegiance.

It might in these circumstances have been expected that Doge Giustiniano would consign the body to the new cathedral at Olivolo. His decision
to preserve it instead in an obvious dependency of his own palace
deliberately associated it from the outset with the civil rather than with
the religious authorities of the state.[1] From that moment on, old St
Theodore and his dragon were relegated to the top of a column in the
Piazzetta and, for all practical purposes, forgotten. St Mark became the
patron of Venice. His lion, its wings outstretched, its forepaw proudly
indicating the angelic utterance, was to be emblazoned on banners and
bastions, on poops and prows, whenever and wherever the Venetian
writ was to run; his name above all others was invoked by the faithful
at prayer and by the soldiers and sailors of the Republic as they went
into battle.

History records no more shameless example of body-snatching; nor
any – unless we include the events associated with the Resurrection – of
greater long-term significance. But once the Venetians had the Evangelist
safely among them, they adopted him as their own, more whole-heartedly
than any other tutelary saint in any other city. As their guardian, over the
centuries, they were to work him hard and to try him sorely; but as their
patron they were never to fail him in their love and veneration.

And he, for his part, was to serve them well.

The first church of St Mark – smaller and less magnificent than that which
now stands on the same site but still, by the standards of the day, a
building fit for an Evangelist to dwell in – received its formal consecration

1. It also conferred on the shrine of St Mark a primacy which has never been lost. 'I am
aware of no other city of Europe in which its cathedral was not the principal feature. But the
principal church in Venice was the chapel attached to the palace of her prince and called the
"Chiesa Ducale". The patriarchal church, inconsiderable in size and mean in decoration,
stands on the outermost islet of the Venetian group, and its name, as well as its site, are probably unknown to the greater number of travellers passing hastily through the city.' Ruskin,
The Stones of Venice, I, ix.

only four years later, in 832.[1] By that time Doge Giustiniano, three years in his grave, had been succeeded by his younger brother. He had always despised Giovanni, and from what we can gather from the scant sources available, he was probably right. Had the new Doge not already reigned briefly at his father's side he would never have been chosen; as it was, his fecklessness and general apathy soon became more than his subjects could stand. On 29 June 836, the feast of St Peter and St Paul, just as he was leaving S. Pietro di Castello after mass, he was seized by some of his own subjects and compelled to abdicate. Then, tonsured and forcibly ordained, he was sent to end his days in a monastery at Grado.

One of the main reasons for the Venetians' dissatisfaction with Giovanni Participazio had been his ineffectiveness in dealing with a new menace which was now looming ever larger on the horizon. For some years already, Adriatic trade had been harassed by Slav pirates, slipping out from their lairs in the hidden creeks and inlets of the Dalmatian coast around the mouths of the Narenta[2] and Cetina rivers and falling upon any well-laden merchantman that caught their fancy. Early successes had caused a rapid growth in their numbers, to the point where Venetian captains were becoming chary of putting to sea and Venetian commerce was being threatened with slow strangulation. Nor was Venice the only sufferer; the Western Empire too was beginning to feel the pinch as sea communications with Ravenna, Padua and the other cities of imperial Italy became progressively harder to keep open.

Firm action against these pirates was thus a matter of high priority for any new ruler; and Pietro Tradonico from Jesolo, now raised from his position on the building commission to be the eleventh Doge of Venice, was not a man to shirk his responsibilities. Within three years of his election we find him leading a naval expedition to Dalmatia; and in 840, his hand strengthened by the moderately successful outcome of these operations, he sent an ambassador to the Franks to conclude a treaty with Charlemagne's grandson, the Emperor Lothair. Much of this treaty was a simple confirmation of previous agreements, but it is remarkable for two reasons. First, the original manuscript of it still exists, the oldest Venetian diplomatic document to have been preserved. Secondly, it contains an explicit pledge by the Doge to bear responsibility for the defence of the Adriatic against the Slavs or any other enemy, together with the implicit

1. Though usually described as a basilica, this first church was not built on the basilican plan any more than its successors. Like them, it was almost certainly modelled on the Church of the Holy Apostles at Constantinople – now long since destroyed – and was cruciform, as was the custom for Apostolic churches.

2. Now better known by its Slavonic name of Neretva.

acknowledgement by Lothair of his own naval weakness and Venice's consequent rights over the central Mediterranean.

At about this time, too, another race was giving another Empire still graver cause for concern. In 827 a Byzantine governor of Sicily named Euthymius, in an effort to avoid the consequences of his recent elopement with a local nun, had proclaimed his independence and invited the Aglabi Saracens of North Africa to support him. It was just the opportunity they needed. Landing in strength along the south-west coast they soon got rid of Euthymius, and before their conquest was complete they were already using the island as a springboard from which to attack the Byzantine province of Apulia. There, the Greek garrisons in Bari, Brindisi and Otranto found themselves as helpless against this new enemy as the Franks had been against the Dalmatians. In the past thirty years the Emperors at Constantinople, reassured by their friendship with Venice and the growing Venetian power at sea, had allowed themselves to neglect their own bases in the Adriatic. Even on the Eastern shores, the once formidable strongholds of Durazzo and Cephalonia were no longer able to launch an offensive on any scale. Thus it was that in 840 or thereabouts – at roughly the same time as the Venetian plenipotentiaries were signing their treaty with Lothair – there arrived at Rialto no less a personage than the Patriarch of Constantinople himself, to confer upon the Doge the title of *spatharius* and seek his active help against the Saracen peril.

Tradonico responded at once. The Saracens, he saw, constituted a far more serious threat in the long term than any number of Slav corsairs; it was in the interests of Venice, just as much as of Constantinople, to prevent them from establishing themselves in the narrow waters. The Venetian navy was quickly made ready, and early in 841 sixty of its largest ships, each carrying some 200 men, sailed out of the lagoon to their appointed rendezvous with a Byzantine squadron. The combined fleet then moved on southward, until it came upon the Saracens off the little Calabrian port of Crotone.

Whether the Greek admiral fled at the first engagement – as the Venetians were later indignantly to aver – or whether the fault lay elsewhere, we shall never know; but the Christian defeat was total. The pride of the Venetian navy went to the bottom, the land force which had been disembarked near Taranto was wiped out. The Saracen fleet then advanced unhindered up the Adriatic, sacking Ancona and reaching the very edge of the lagoon before the shoals and currents swirling around the delta of the Po forced it to turn back.

Once again Venice had been saved by her geography; but this time she had no cause to congratulate herself on her good fortune. The sea that she had claimed as her preserve, and that the two great Empires of Europe had recognized as such only a year before, had been openly demonstrated to be nothing of the kind. The very next year was to see the Saracens pressing yet further up the coast, the Venetians powerless as ever to check them. Meanwhile the Narenta pirates, seeing that they had less to fear than they had imagined, grew bolder and still more predatory. It was to be many decades before these twin scourges were finally eliminated and the Adriatic approaches made safe again for Venetian and imperial shipping.

After so complete a débâcle, it was inevitable that Venice's relations with Byzantium should have suffered a sharp deterioration. The old links were still there, but they were becoming more tenuous all the time. With the Empire of the West, on the other hand, once the principle of independence – both political and ecclesiastical – had been properly established, friendship continued to blossom. In 856 Lothair's son and successor, the young Emperor Lewis II, went so far as to pay a state visit to Venice with his Empress. They were met and entertained by the Doge and his son Giovanni – whom, it is hardly necessary to add, he had associated with himself on the ducal throne – at Brondolo, a little to the south of Chioggia; thence they were conveyed with much pomp to Rialto, where they remained three days, in the course of which the Emperor stood godfather to Giovanni's little daughter.

On the domestic front, too, Doge Pietro had his problems. It was now nearly half a century since the Venetian capital had been established on the islands of Rialto; after all that had gone before, it was hardly likely that their comparative freedom from factional strife – one of the principal reasons for their selection – should last for ever. Despite her Adriatic enemies, Venice was now the leading emporium and clearing-house in the Christian Mediterranean. Trade was expanding in all directions; the advantage went to the first to seize it; and in the prevailing atmosphere of commercial ruthlessness and cut-throat competition, new jealousies and resentments were bound to arise. Many of the recent settlers had brought their old animosities with them. For most of his 28-year reign – the longest of any Doge to date – Pietro Tradonico kept the peace with remarkable success; it was only after the death of Giovanni – one of the few associate Doges to justify an institution that was nearly always disastrous – that he found that he could no longer hold the balance between the factions. Perhaps he resorted to repressive measures which his subjects found intolerable, perhaps he showed too much favour towards one group and thereby antagonized another; whatever the reason, a conspiracy took shape, and on 13 September 864 the conspirators struck. It was the eve of the Exaltation of the Cross, a day on which by tradition the Doge attended mass at S. Zaccaria; and as the old man – with well over fifty years' service to the state behind him, he cannot have been far short of eighty – was leaving the church after vespers, he was sprung upon by an armed band and left dead in the square. The ensuing struggle between his attendants and the attackers soon led to a riot; we read that the nuns of the convent attached to the church did not at first dare to venture out to rescue the body. Not until after nightfall could it be brought to safety and given a decent burial.

Meanwhile the servants of the murdered Doge – probably a bodyguard of Croatian slaves – had hurried back to the palace and barricaded themselves in. There, while the street fighting raged throughout the city, they kept up their resistance for several days until they heard that five of the leading conspirators had in their turn met their deaths at the hands of the mob. Only then did peace return sufficiently for a certain Orso, a nobleman whose principal qualification was that he had had no part in the plot, to be elected to the supreme power.

Tradition, unsupported by any firm historical evidence, maintains that this new Doge was of the family of Participazio. Three of his four predecessors had borne this name, and the fourth, Pietro Tradonico, had been closely related by marriage; if, therefore, tradition is to be trusted, we must see the new election as indicating a further drift towards the hereditary principle. But Orso, whether a Participazio or not, showed no disposition to allow the old order of things to continue. Immediately on his accession he launched a radical programme of reform; and his first target was his own authority.

From the beginnings of her independence, Venice had been theoretically a democracy. Not only was the dogeship itself an electoral office, but the Doge was attended by two tribunes whose explicit purpose was to prevent him from abusing it. Furthermore, there had always been provision for what was known as the *arengo*, when all the citizens met in general assembly to vote on major decisions affecting the security of the state. But democracies are unstable institutions; they need constant maintenance if they are to work. In Venice, over the years, the tribunes had declined in importance, the *arenghi* were never called, and public affairs had become the preserve of whatever little clique chanced to surround the Doge of the day. Orso now instituted a system of elected *giudici*, or judges – high state officials, part ministers, part magistrates, who formed the nucleus from which the future ducal *curia* was to grow and provided an effective check on the arbitrary misuse of the supreme power. Meanwhile changes in the structure of local government brought the outlying islands into closer dependence on the central administration.

Having reorganized the governmental machine, Orso next turned his attention to Church affairs. Here, by contrast, he adopted a policy of decentralization. Several of the old bishoprics in and around the lagoon had ceased to exist, or had returned to the cities from which they had been driven by the barbarian invasions; there remained only Grado, Altino and Olivolo, to which the new diocese of Equilo had recently been added, with the result that many outlying areas were falling increasingly under the influence of the Patriarch of Aquileia or other equally undesirable ecclesiastics in the territory of the Western Empire. To counteract this tendency Caorle, Malamocco, Cittanova – the old Heraclea – and Torcello, which heretofore served only as the occasional seat of the Bishop of Altino, were all given sees of their own. Neither the new bishops nor the old were in any way subordinated to the civil power of the Republic; but their very independence increased their loyalty. Within a few years we find all the newly appointed bishops supporting the Doge in one of his periodic disputes with the Patriarch of Grado, and three times in a single year refusing summonses from the Pope himself to attend a synod in Rome to settle the matter.

Another dispute, with the Patriarch of Aquileia this time, was even more satisfactorily handled. This rascally primate seems somehow to have acquired temporal control over a large part of the duchy of Friuli – from which, probably as a result of pique over the new bishoprics, he was conducting his own armed campaign against Venetian merchants. Orso's answer was an economic blockade. The mouths of all rivers passing through Aquileian territory were closed and all exports to and from the city banned. The Patriarch was brought to his knees; and it is worth noting that in the ensuing treaty, while Orso was prepared to accept that the Venetian merchants trading with Aquileia should continue to pay reasonable duties on their goods, he cheerfully stipulated that his own personal trading representatives in the area should be exempt from all taxation. There spoke the authentic voice of Venice. The state might come first, but enlightened self-interest was never very far behind.

Orso's constitutional reforms, far-reaching as they were, did not extend to the problem of nepotism. Like most of his predecessors he had associated his son with him during his lifetime, and on his death in 881 this son,

Giovanni, assumed the throne in smooth and undisputed succession. But Giovanni was himself no longer young and his health was uncertain; after a few years' ineffectual struggle he had to admit himself unequal to his office. His subjects agreed. Constitutionally, yet at the same time showing more determination to be heard than at any previous time in Venetian history, they demanded not his abdication – for they seem to have been genuinely fond of him – but the enthronement at his side of the 45-year-old Pietro Candiano.

Alas, only five months later, on 18 September 887, Pietro was killed while leading an expedition against the Dalmatian pirates, the first Doge to die in battle for the Republic. Reluctantly, old Giovanni took up the reins again until a successor could be found; and this time the people's choice fell on Pietro Tribuno, great-nephew of that ill-fated Doge Tradonico whose murder had caused such havoc in the city a quarter of of a century before.

Pietro Candiano's reign had been brief, bellicose and – at least so far as the Doge himself was concerned – disastrous; that of Pietro Tribuno was to be long and in the main peaceful, with its single emergency ending in Venice's most dazzling military triumph since her victory over Pepin. Tribuno began, auspiciously enough, by renewing the treaty agreements with the Western Empire, first in 888, the year of his accession, and then again in 891. Since Giovanni Participazio had negotiated a similar renewal with the Emperor Charles the Fat as recently as 883, it may be wondered whether so much diplomatic activity was strictly necessary; but at this crucial stage in her political development Venice was still steering a course of extreme delicacy between the two imperial whirlpools, a course on which she was in constant danger of being sucked into one or the other. It was vital for her to seize every opportunity she could of taking her bearings and adjusting her trim. Seldom, in so doing, did she fail to improve her position. Thus, a few years before, a clause had been written into the agreement by which any murderer of a Doge who sought refuge in the Empire should be fined 100 pounds of gold and banished – a mild enough penalty, one would have thought, under the circumstances. In 888 the terms went considerably further: henceforth any Venetian anywhere in imperial Italy would remain under the jurisdiction of the Doge and subject to the laws of Venice rather than to those of the Empire. This provision was directed not only against criminals – extradition, of a kind, had been allowed for since the days of Lothair. Its principal effect was to guarantee to Venetian merchants in Italy the protection of their own law, and thereby to encourage them to extend their operations further and further afield.

Thus, with trade expanding, the economy developing steadily, shipbuilding in full swing, a new iron-founding industry growing fast[1] and the city taking ever more splendid shape as the work of clearance, drainage, reclamation and construction gathered impetus, the last decade of the ninth century proved for the Venetians the happiest and most prosperous of all. Then, in 899, came crisis – with the appearance on the horizon of a new enemy. By this time men might have been forgiven for thinking that the age of the barbarians was past; but the Magyars proved them wrong. Emerging, like so many of their predecessors, from the steppes of Central Asia, they had crossed the Carpathians for the first time only three years before; their savagery and brutality were still unblunted. Several shocked chroniclers of the time go so far as to describe them as cannibals – which, on occasion, they may well have been. Already in 898 they had briefly raided the Veneto, but had withdrawn again before much harm had been done. In the following year, however, they returned in strength and, after an initial reverse, overran the whole Lombard plain. Then they turned towards Venice.

One by one, the cities around the lagoon fell to the Hungarian horde: Cittanova, Fine and Equilo first, then Altino, and the hinterland north and west to Treviso and Padua. Next, swinging south, the Magyars advanced along the *lidi* from Chioggia and Pellestrina up towards Malamocco. They reached Albiola without much difficulty, but there – almost exactly where Pepin had come to grief ninety years before – they found Tribuno and his army awaiting them. Coming as they did from the centre of the Asiatic land mass, they had no knowledge or understanding of the sea; the portable coracles which they used for crossing rivers were useless against the Venetian ships. Their defeat was quick and complete. Once again the lagoon had saved the city.

But was even the lagoon enough? Pietro Tribuno did not think so. Some future aggressor, more disciplined and experienced in seamanship, might succeed where the Magyars had failed. Once inside the line of *lidi* he would find the islands of Rialto still largely unprotected. And so the Doge gave orders for the building of a bastion from the castle on the eastern side of Olivolo down to what is now the Riva degli Schiavoni and thence all the way along to S. Maria Zobenigo, and for the manufacture of a great chain of iron which could be stretched across the Grand Canal

1. On his accession in 864 Orso Participazio had sent the Byzantine Emperor Basil I a peal of twelve bells cast in a Venetian foundry.

from the church of S. Gregorio on Dorsoduro to the opposite bank.[1]

The chronicler John the Deacon, writing about 100 years after the event, sees the construction of this bulwark as marking the moment when the Rialtine settlement first properly became what he calls a *civitas*. The term is untranslatable; a city, in our sense of the word – although a very small one – had existed there since the days of Doge Agnello and the transfer of the central government. But Pietro Tribuno's wall, and the emergency that brought it into being, gave the citizens a new feeling of cohesion and community that was to have its own importance in the years to come; and one can only hope that the few crumbling remnants of it that still survive at the southern end of the Rio dell' Arsenale will continue to be treated by the authorities of today with the respect that is their due.

1. The precise spot is now occupied by the seventeenth-century Palazzo Gaggia, two buildings to the east of the Palazzo Contarini-Fasan ('Desdemona's house'). It is interesting to note that the churches of S. Maria Zobenigo (del Giglio) and S. Gregorio already existed as landmarks in Venice at this time. They are both still there, though the present structures are of later date: the former – so-called after its founders, the family of Jubanico – now a seventeenth-century building, the latter a fifteenth. A neighbouring *calle* is still called the *Calle del Bastion*.

· 4 ·

The Adventurer and the Saint

[900–991]

É necessario ad un principe, volendoli mantenere, imparare a potere essere non buono, ed usarlo o non usarlo secondo la necessità.

A prince who wishes to maintain his position must learn how not to be good, and make use or not make use of that knowledge as necessary.

Machiavelli, Il Principe, Ch. XV

Exalted by her victory over the Hungarians, elevated by her new civic pride, strengthened and protected by her rapidly rising fortifications, Venice entered the tenth century in a mood of confidence. Her enemies were scattered, the two Empires grateful and admiring: trade had never been better. The future looked bright indeed. Pietro Tribuno continued to reign wisely and well till 912, when he died and was buried in S. Zaccaria; and his successor, another Orso Participazio, pursued similarly peaceable policies with similar success for a further twenty years before retiring – voluntarily – to the monastery of S. Felice in 932. For the next forty-four years Venice was to be dominated by one of the most remarkable families in all her early history – the Candiani.

The first Candiano Doge has already made his all-too-brief appearance in these pages, dying in action against the Dalmatian pirates in 887. He was now to be followed by his son, and then – after a brief and wholly unmemorable hiatus in 939 – by his grandson and great-grandson. All four, confusingly, were named Pietro; all seem to have been endowed with more energy than their fellow-men, more aggressiveness, more self-confidence. All were arrogant and headstrong; one was a national disaster; none were dull. The second of the line was hardly settled on his throne before he began a bitter economic blockading war against Istria; not long after, following a trifling diplomatic incident, he burnt Venice's neighbour and potential rival, Comacchio, to the ground. The third sailed twice against the Narenta pirates who had killed his grandfather and forced them to their knees. And so we come to the fourth; but the wild and almost incredible career of Pietro Candiano IV cannot be conveniently summed up in a few words; it deserves to be recounted in detail.

His father must have regretted for the rest of his life the decision, only four years after his own accession in 942, to associate young Pietro with him on the ducal throne. From the outset, the boy showed himself a rebel. Whether, as some suggest, he was a corrupt and vicious debauchee or whether, as seems more likely, the rift was fundamentally political is not altogether clear. What is certain is that relations between father and son and their respective factions rapidly deteriorated to the point where open warfare broke out in the streets of the city. Finally the young man was captured, narrowly escaping with his life; it was only thanks to his father's intercession with the judicial authorities that his sentence was commuted to one of perpetual banishment. Thus it was that he was able to enlist as a soldier of fortune under the banners of Guy, Marquis of Ivrea, who in 950 was crowned King of Italy. Away in exile, however, his resentment continued to grow; and a few years later we find him in command of a squadron of corsairs, blockading no less than seven of the Republic's galleys at the mouth of the Po.

Over the centuries, the Venetians had suffered more than most peoples from the effects of piracy. There was no crime that they detested more, none that they were readier to condemn. The old Doge bore his son's shame as long as he could, but a terrible epidemic of plague that struck the city in 959 finally broke his spirit and he died the same year. And then an extraordinary thing happened. The people met together and elected young Pietro in his stead.

If the reasons for the original banishment are hard to analyse, those for this sudden volte-face are harder still. The most probable theory points, quite simply, to another one of those unexpected swings of the political pendulum; Pietro was young, go-ahead and, from what we can deduce, possessed of a certain glamour. A born leader, he was also a Candiano. Finally, there was the practical consideration – and the Venetians were nothing if not practical – that, as past experience had proved, he could be a dangerous thorn in their flesh; it was better to have him on their side than against them. At any rate the decisive votes were cast, and 300 ships were sent down to Ravenna to bring the new Doge back to the lagoon in suitable state.

It was a dark day for Venice when they did so. Though Pietro Candiano no longer had a parent to oppose, he soon proved as resolute as ever in his opposition to all those principles that his father had represented – the old, austere, republican virtues on which the state had been founded and had grown to greatness, the high standards of moral behaviour expected of – if not always evinced by – its leaders, the mistrust of personal pomp and ostentation. Pietro had lived in the sophisticated courts of the mainland; they had given him a taste for luxury, as well as for an autocracy unfettered by the nicely calculated checks and balances with which the Doges of Venice were increasingly hamstrung. He was, however, entirely without the subtlety to see how these controls could be circumvented; and though happy to work constitutionally in matters where he could expect a measure of popular support, in those arising from his insatiable appetite for self-aggrandizement he tried to ride roughshod over the opposition. In Venice, such a man could never last for long.

His energies were not at first entirely misdirected. Within a year or so of his accession he imposed new and severe restrictions on the slave trade, with harsh penalties – physical, financial and even spiritual – for offenders. The traffic was still not altogether forbidden; special provision was made for it to continue where it was necessary 'for the purposes of government'. But the new laws were stringent enough to arouse the potentially dangerous indignation of the Venetian slave traders themselves; and it was probably this consideration that prompted the Doge to draft them not in his name alone but also in those of the Patriarch, bishops and nobles of the city. Whatever the reason for this collective responsibility, it seems to have been taken as a precedent; from this time forward, references to similar councils became increasingly frequent in Venetian legislation.

Pietro's future conduct, however, was a good deal less circumspect. During his exile he had allowed his eye to fall on Waldrada, sister of the Marquis of Tuscany who was at that time one of the richest and most powerful of the Italian princes. He now divorced his Venetian wife, packing her off to end her days in the convent of S. Zaccaria, and brought Waldrada to Venice as his bride – together with an immense dowry of lands in Friuli, the March of Treviso, Adria and the Ferrarese. There was, be it noted, no question of these lands becoming Venetian territory; they were to be the personal property of Pietro. Thus the Venetians suddenly saw, in place of the Doge they thought they had elected, a powerful feudal baron with huge estates on *terra firma* held in vassalage of the Western Emperor – so much for Venice's hard-won independence – living in state like some perfumed princeling of Byzantium, and insulated from his subjects by a bodyguard of foreign mercenaries raised on his mainland dominions.

All this was bad enough; but popular dissatisfaction increased still further when the Doge, who soon after his accession had made his son

c

Vitale Bishop of Torcello – having had the rival candidate blinded and imprisoned – in 969 procured for him the Patriarchate of Grado. In the past century the Patriarchate had grown steadily in wealth and influence, with the result that the new incumbent found himself second only to his father not just in the hierarchy of the state but also as a landowner, master of nearly all the coast and its hinterland between his see and the Venetian lagoon. Through this he would travel in princely pomp with an extensive retinue, while the local inhabitants came out to do him homage and the monasteries along the way vied with each other in the lavishness of their hospitality.

With the civil and ecclesiastical authority now firmly gathered into his hands, Pietro Candiano was – or seemed to be – all-powerful. Unfortunately, like so many of his otherwise talented family, he never knew when to stop; and when, in the summer of 976, he called on his Venetian subjects to help defend his personal interests in the Ferrarese, the people rose against him. Their first attack on his palace was unsuccessful; the building proved to be too well fortified and the attackers were forced to retire. But now, more determined than ever, they set fire to the neighbouring houses. The timber went up like matchwood in the summer heat, and the flames soon spread to the palace itself.

For the events that followed we have the authority of John the Deacon, an authority and perhaps even an eye-witness. Desperate and choking, the Doge with his young wife and infant child tried to escape through the atrium of St Mark's, only to find their passage blocked by a group of nobles. Vainly Pietro pleaded with them, promising satisfaction for all their demands if his and his family's lives could be spared. 'But, affirming him to be a man most wicked [sceleratissimus] and deserving of death, they cried out with fearsome voices that he should have no means of escape. And they instantly surrounding him, and setting about him cruelly with the points of their swords, his immortal soul left its bodily prison to seek the haunts of the blessed' – a destination which, from what we know of Pietro Candiano IV, it is unlikely to have found.

Somehow the Dogaressa Waldrada managed to escape with her life; but her baby, run through with a spear, shared the fate of its father. The two bodies were then thrown on to a boat and carted off to the common slaughter-house, where they were rescued only by the intervention of a certain Giovanni Gradenigo, 'a most saintly man', who arranged an obscure but seemlier burial. The convent of S. Zaccaria had now become the traditional resting-place for deceased Doges, but there could be no question of using it on this occasion. Pietro and his child were borne secretly away across the lagoon to the remote abbey of Sant' Ilario, beyond Fusina, while the Venetians, their tempers cooled at last, settled down to rebuild their ravaged city.

Some 300 buildings had been destroyed or badly damaged by the fire, among them St Mark's itself, the Doges' Palace, and the newly completed S. Maria Zobenigo. Of the old church of St Theodore, which dated back to the time when even the churches were built of wood, scarcely a stick remained standing. Venice had got rid of her Doge, but she had paid dearly for her mistake.

Pietro Candiano had been a child of his century – a century which, following the break-up of Charlemagne's Empire in 888, had witnessed the steady political disintegration of Italy. In the north, Lombardy had remained prey to the Magyars for more than fifty years after they had been turned back from the Venetian lagoon. In the south, the Byzantine Empire had shown itself more and more unable to control either the Lombard princelings – who thought of nothing but their own glorification – or the maritime city-republics of Naples, Amalfi and Gaeta, whose loyalties lay in the direction whence the most favourable trade wind happened at the time to be blowing. Between the two, the Papacy presented the most unedifying spectacle of all – under such creatures as John X, strangled in the Castel Sant' Angelo by his mistress's daughter so that she could install her own bastard son by a former Pope in his place; or John XII, who was consecrated at the age of seventeen and during whose reign, according to Gibbon, 'we learn with some surprise that the Lateran Palace was turned into a school for prostitution; and that his rapes of virgins and widows had deterred the female pilgrims from visiting the tomb of St Peter, lest, in the devout act, they should be violated by his successor.'

But if John XII marked the nadir of the papal pornocracy, he was also unwittingly responsible for Italy's deliverance. In 962, defenceless against the encroachments of Berengar II, King of Italy, on his northern borders, he appealed for help to Duke Otto of Saxony who, having recently driven the Hungarians from the Lombard plain, was now the dominant force in North Italy. Otto hurried to Rome, where John – no doubt remembering Pope Leo and Charlemagne – hastily crowned him Emperor. It was the Pope's undoing. His debaucheries were bad enough, but when two years later he also gave signs of insubordination towards the Emperor he had created, the latter promptly summoned a synod and had him deposed. Berengar soon surrendered; Otto was supreme; and the Empire of the West was reborn, to continue in one form or another virtually uninterrupted until the age of Napoleon.

In South Italy the new order had little immediate effect. It would take another 100 years and a Norman conquest to re-establish order there. In the North, however, it brought about a general revulsion against the debauchery and licence of recent years – encouraged, perhaps, by the reflection that the end of the first Christian millennium was fast approaching and with it, as many believed, that of the world itself. This revulsion may well have played its part in the decision taken by the people of Venice to get rid of the fourth Candiano, and is still more likely to have affected them when, on 12 August 976 in the cathedral church of S. Pietro di Castello, they elected his successor.

With Pietro Orseolo I we encounter the only Doge in Venetian history – possibly the only republican head of state anywhere – to have been subsequently canonized. Whether he deserved his halo is open to question; to leave wife, child and heavy political responsibilities at the age of fifty for the peace of a monastic cell would not nowadays be considered much of a qualification for sainthood. From his earliest youth, however, Pietro Orseolo seems to have been a genuine ascetic; and during the two short years of his reign he ruled Venice with a wise and above all a generous hand. He found the Republic in grave financial straits. Candiano's extravagances had emptied the coffers; the Dogaressa Waldrada, who had taken refuge at the German imperial court, was claiming the return of her formidable dowry; meanwhile there was the whole centre of Venice to be rebuilt. So great had been the devastation that Orseolo had been obliged to transfer the seat of government to his own private house, some distance along the Riva beyond the charred remains of the Doges' Palace; and it was from there that he set to work to put the city on its feet again. For the first time, a tithe was imposed upon all Venetians; Waldrada – who, considering everything, was lucky to be alive at all – was paid off in full; while the Doge devoted a great part of his personal fortune – enough, we are told, to yield an annual 8,000 ducats for eighty years – to the rebuilding of the Palace and of the Basilica of St Mark, and to the erection of a new hospital across the Piazzetta, more or less on the site now occupied by the Marciana Library and the eastern end of the Procuratie Nuove.[1]

1. It was as part of his reconstruction of St Mark's that Pietro Orseolo ordered from Constantinople an altar-screen of what Yeats was to describe, 1,000 years later, as 'hammered gold and gold enamelling'. Enlarged and remodelled over the centuries, it is now known as the *Pala d'Oro*.

All too soon, however, there appeared on the scene the faintly sinister figure of a certain Guarinus, otherwise known as Warren, abbot of the monastery of St Michael of Cuxa, a Benedictine foundation near Prades in the French Pyrenees.[1] We cannot be sure how far this man was to blame for the Doge's subsequent action. He may have been deliberately sent as an agent from the Ottonian court where Waldrada, unappeased, had stepped up her diplomatic offensive against Venice with the enthusiastic assistance of her stepson Vitale Candiano, Patriarch of Grado; he may have been just another of those well-meaning but misguided medieval ecclesiastics whose ideal world consisted of one enormous monastery and who spent their lives persuading one public figure after another to retreat into the cloister. Or he may have been neither: Peter Damian, that most uncharitable of saints, attributes the events that followed to the guilty conscience of the Doge himself, whom he accuses of complicity in his predecessor's overthrow and in the destruction of the Palace.[2] On Warren's first visit to Venice in 977, his blandishments, if such there were, had no immediate effect; a year later, however, on the pretext of a pilgrimage to Jerusalem, the abbot was back again – and this time he succeeded. It had been a bad year. Opposition was mounting both inside and outside the city; the tithe was increasingly resented; and although Pietro Orseolo was still spending as much as ever on his own account, he had doubtless come to understand that generosity and popularity are two very different things. He may too have begun to suspect a lack within himself of that last ounce of moral fibre necessary to withstand the pressures by which he was surrounded. On 1 September 978, he took the easy way out and fled. Under the cover of darkness, and accompanied only by his son-in-law Giovanni Morosini and a certain Gradenigo – the same, in all probability, who had retrieved the Candiano corpses two years before – he slipped across the lagoon to Sant' Ilario, where horses were waiting. Having shaved off his beard before his departure he passed unrecognized, and a few weeks later the former Doge was safe in the abbey of his friend. There he lived another nine years, and there his body was preserved until 1732, the year after his canonization, when at the command of Louis XV it was returned to Venice.

1. The monastery was dissolved and destroyed during the French Revolution, and though it has since been resurrected by the Cistercians it retains little of its former glory. There is a reconstruction, containing many of the original capitals, in the Cloisters of the Metropolitan Museum of Art, New York.

2. *Vita Sancti Romualdi*, Ch. V.

The reign of Orseolo's successor, the weak and probably invalid Vitale Candiano,[1] was little more than an interregnum. After only fourteen months in office he too retired to a monastery, leaving the throne to yet another member of his family. Tribuno Memmo, or Menio, was distinguished for his knowledge of horticulture, but for very little else. He was the son-in-law of the murdered Pietro, a fact which did not deter him from proclaiming, on his accession in 979, a general amnesty to all those who fled after the assassination. But if he hoped by this means to restore peace to the lagoon, he was unsuccessful. Venice remained torn by factional strife, with the two principal parties now polarizing themselves each around a leading family and looking respectively to the Eastern and Western Empires for support. On the one side were the Morosini, champions of the old link with Byzantium; on the other the Coloprini, who put their trust in the Empire of the West and its energetic young Emperor, Otto II.

Otto had succeeded his father in 973, at the age of eighteen. For the next seven years he had been busy consolidating his position north of the Alps; then, in December 980, angered and alarmed by the incursions of the Sicilian Muslims in Apulia and Calabria, he headed south into Italy with the object of freeing the peninsula once and for all from Saracen occupation. The fact that the beleaguered provinces were technically part of the Byzantine Empire did not worry him overmuch; his wife Theophano was sister of the two jointly reigning Emperors of Byzantium, Basil II and Constantine VIII, who were far too taken up with problems nearer home to give these distant and to them relatively unimportant possessions the attention they deserved. To begin with, the campaign went well enough; but in the summer of 982, as he was advancing south-westward into Calabria, Otto was surprised by a Saracen force near Stilo. His army was cut to pieces. He himself escaped only by swimming to a passing ship, concealing his identity and later, as the vessel approached Rossano, jumping overboard again and striking out for the shore.

But his determination remained firm; the following June found him at Verona preparing a fresh campaign and, incidentally, renewing the usual treaty of trade and protection with Venice. He did so, probably, in all good faith; but shortly afterwards there arrived at his court a party of Venetians led by Stefano Coloprini, who had killed one of the Morosini faction in the square of S. Pietro di Castello and had been obliged to flee

---

1. Not to be confused with his namesake, the Patriarch of Grado. His relationship with the other, more famous members of his family is uncertain.

for his life. He had now come to Otto with a proposal. Venice, for all her growing power, still remained dependent on the mainland for her lines of communication and supply. If these were to be cut, she would be brought rapidly to her knees and obliged to accept Coloprini as Doge, who would in return subject the city to imperial suzerainty. The entire Venetian fleet would then be available to Otto for his next campaign against the Saracens.

The prospect of adding this brightest of jewels to his crown was more than the ambitious young Emperor could resist. The treaty he had just renewed was forgotten; instead, he declared an immediate blockade of the Republic. His vassal the Duke of Carinthia was ordered to ensure that the Marches of Verona, Istria and Friuli were closed to Venetian commerce, while the Coloprini and their followers were posted at strategic points along roads and rivers. As autumn turned to winter Venice, still devastated by the conflagration of seven years before, demoralized by civil strife and ruled by an indecisive and vacillating Doge, now found herself faced with the twin threats of famine and an imperial take-over. In one respect the crisis was even greater than in the days when she had met the challenge of Pepin, or later of the Magyars. Then at least she had had the surrounding waters to protect her, with their treacherous shoals and currents that none but her own sailors knew. This time the attackers were themselves Venetians, for whom the lagoon had no secrets. And how many agents and supporters had they left within the city? Panic-stricken, the populace fell upon the houses of those of the Coloprini who had remained behind and razed them to the ground, seizing the women and children as hostages. Then, powerless to do more, they awaited the onslaught.

It never came. Stefano Coloprini suddenly died, and was followed to the grave in December of the same year – 983 – by the Emperor Otto himself, stricken down at the age of twenty-eight by an overdose of medicine (four drachms of aloes) following a fever. His mother Adelaide, who became co-regent in the place of her three-year-old grandson, would probably have liked to carry on the blockade; but the influence of Otto's Byzantine widow Theophano, with whom she shared the regency, was too strong. The best she was able to achieve was an amnesty under which the Coloprini and their fellow rebels were permitted to return to Venice. They would have been better advised to stay away. Their old enemies, the Morosini, had not forgotten their murdered kinsman. They were sworn to vengeance and their memories were long. In 991 they attacked three of the Coloprini just as the latter were boarding

71

a boat outside the newly rebuilt Doges' Palace, ran them through with their swords and hurled them into the water.

It was perhaps not altogether fair to blame Tribuno Memmo for this new outrage. He was certainly related to the Morosini by marriage; and in 982 when Giovanni Morosini, back in Venice after settling his fugitive father-in-law at St Michael of Cuxa and now himself a monk, was looking for land on which to found a Benedictine monastery, the Doge had offered him the little island opposite the palace, known then as the Island of the Cypresses and now as that of S. Giorgio Maggiore. In so far as he took sides at all, therefore, Memmo's sympathies were clear. But he was a gentle, peace-loving man and the last thing he would have wished to see was his city, after nearly a decade of comparative tranquillity, torn asunder yet again by internecine warfare. Blamed, however, he was, attacked and reviled until there was no course open to him but that which had been taken by his two immediate predecessors. He too withdrew to a monastery – S. Zaccaria this time, just behind his former palace – there to end his days in the obscurity he should never have left.[1]

1. Surprisingly enough, this most forgettable of Doges is the earliest to boast a permanent memorial in Venice – even though he had to wait nearly 500 years for it, until Palladio rebuilt the church of S. Giorgio Maggiore in the late sixteenth century. It takes the form of a portrait bust set above a symbolic sarcophagus in a niche on the left-hand side of the façade, in recognition of the fact that it was Memmo to whom, with Giovanni Morosini, the original foundation owed its existence.

The Determined Dynasty

[991–1032]

La puissance dépend de l'empire de l'onde;
Le trident de Neptune est le sceptre du monde.

Lemierre

The tenth century had opened in Venice on a note of triumph, with the repulse of the Magyar invaders. It had not, however, fulfilled its early promise. Of the past fifty years, all but two – those covering the brief reign of Pietro Orseolo I – had seen the fate of the Republic entrusted to members, by blood or marriage, of the family of Candiano, whose policies had brought it to the brink of disaster. By their arrogance and ambition – or, as with the last reigning member of their clan Tribuno Memmo, by sheer ineptitude and the inability to give a strong lead in moments of crisis – they had alienated the Empire of the West, largely ignored that of the East, and encouraged dissension at home. As the final decade of the century began, Venice was sick to the heart. A casual visitor might have been impressed by the outward signs of prosperity – the ships in the harbour, the merchandise on the Rialto, the sables and the silks and the spices; but the Republic was no longer feared and respected by her neighbours as once she had been and, as her reputation had waned, so too had her morale. Her own particular form of national pride – that consciousness of being a race apart, springing from a different element, pursuing an individual destiny – which had given courage and cohesion to her founding fathers and impelled their successors to the threshold of greatness seemed to be draining away. Desperately now, Venice needed a strong hand to guide her, to weld her again into a nation, to restore her self-confidence and her self-respect.

And she found it. Old Pietro Orseolo, when he had fled from family and responsibilities thirteen years before, had left behind him a young son, also called Pietro; and it was this son, still only thirty years old, that the Venetians acclaimed in 991 as their new ruler. They could not have made a better choice. Statesman, warrior and diplomatist of genius, Pietro

Orseolo II towers above the other Doges of his day like a giant among pygmies; and from the outset his subjects seem to have recognized his greatness. With his accession, the feuding that had so long poisoned civilized life stopped as suddenly as if it had never happened. It was as though the Venetians had grown up once again into an adult, responsible and gifted people, and now stood ready to follow him on the road to glory.

But for Venice glory meant trade; and the first task of Pietro Orseolo as Doge was to restore friendly and mutually advantageous trading relations with the two Empires. Within a year he had negotiated with Basil II in Constantinople commercial terms more favourable than any that Venice had previously enjoyed. An imperial chrysobul dated March 992 undertook to admit *bona fide* Venetian goods – though not those from other sources carried on Venetian ships – at tariffs far lower than those imposed on foreign merchandise in general. Almost as important, Venetian merchants in Constantinople were henceforth to be directly subject to the Grand Logothete, a high palace official roughly comparable to the Minister of Finance. This spared them the delays and frustrations for which Byzantine bureaucracy was famous and virtually assured them the ear, in emergencies, of the Emperor himself. In return, the Venetian fleet was to be kept ready to transport imperial troops at short notice wherever they might be needed.

With the young Emperor of the West the Doge achieved similar success – perhaps even more, owing to the mutual admiration and affection that rapidly grew up between them. Otto III was an extraordinary child. Born in 980, Emperor at the age of three, he grew up combining the traditional ambitions of his line with a romantic mysticism inherited from his Greek mother, and forever dreaming of a great Byzantinesque theocracy that would embrace Germans, Italians and Slavs alike, with God at its head, and himself and the Pope – in that order – as His twin viceroys. The pursuit of this dream made him still more preoccupied with affairs in Italy than his father had been before him; a young man's hero-worship for the ablest ruler west of Constantinople did the rest. In 996, when Otto crossed the Alps for the first time in his life on the way to his imperial coronation in Rome, he was able to make an impressive demonstration of his friendship. First he compelled two refractory bishops to restore to Venice certain territories that they had wrongfully appropriated for themselves; next he granted the Doge the right to establish Venetian warehouses and trading-stations along the banks of the Piave and the Sile, simultaneously guaranteeing safe conduct and tax exemptions for all Venetians on imperial territory. Most significant of all, he sent personally for Orseolo's third son to join him at Verona, and there stood sponsor to him at his confirmation, bestowing on him his own name, Otto.

Thus, by the end of his fifth year in office, Pietro Orseolo II had assured the commercial prospects of the Republic with the two greatest powers in Christendom. Now more than ever the broad rivers of northern Italy were thronged with Venetian barges, their gunwales sunk almost to the water-line beneath their cargoes of iron and wood, corn and wine, salt and – in spite of everything – slaves; battling their way upstream to the great clearing-houses of Verona, Piacenza or Pavia, whence they would be transported by land across the Apennines to Naples, Amalfi and their neighbours or over the Alps to Germany and northern Europe. Other, heavier vessels would meanwhile beat south-east down the Adriatic, round the Peloponnese, northward again to Constantinople and even, occasionally, the Black Sea. Yet others concentrated on a newer market, still more rapidly expanding: the world of Islam. Heretofore, though there had always been some measure of trade with the Arabs – it was, after all, Venetian merchants who had stolen the body of St Mark from Alexandria – commercial dealings had always been inhibited by such factors as the Saracens' predilection for piracy, Venetian memories of their great attack on the lagoon that had so nearly succeeded 150 years before, and the revulsion still felt by much of western Christendom at the suggestion of any degree of friendly relations with the infidel. Here was yet another attitude that Pietro Orseolo was determined to dispel. Off went his ambassadors to every corner of the Mediterranean where the green banner of the Prophet flew – to Spain and Barbary, Sicily and the Levant; to the courts of Aleppo, Cairo and Damascus, to Cordova, Kairouan and Palermo. Emir after Emir received them with courtesy and accepted their proposals. Agreement after agreement was brought back with pride and satisfaction to the Doge. His imperial neighbours to East and West, ever anxious at the growing Muslim menace in South Italy, might be horrified at his actions and accuse him of treachery to the Faith. But for Pietro, true Venetian that he was, commerce was always preferable to bloodshed – and a good deal more profitable as well.

To the unfettered expansion of Venetian trade, one obstacle only now remained – the Slav pirates of the Dalmatian coast. The last major expedition against them – that led by Pietro Candiano I in 887 – had ended in catastrophe, with the death of the Doge in battle; and though some sixty years later his grandson had managed in part to retrieve the honour of his family and the Republic, the menace was now as great as ever it had been – so great, in fact that throughout the second half of the tenth century Venice had acquired the habit of paying an annual tribute of protection money to ensure the free passage of her ships through the narrow Adriatic waters. But Pietro Orseolo was not a man to submit to blackmail. On his accession he forbade all further payments and, when the next was due, sent six Venetian galleys across to Dalmatia to guard against possible reprisals. Inevitably, a battle followed. The island of Lissa,[1] one of the principal pirate strongholds, fell to the Venetians, who returned joyfully to the lagoon, their vessels crammed to capacity with prisoners of both sexes.

Venice had won the first round, but the pirates were not beaten. Their main concentrations, around the mouths of the Narenta and the Cetina, had not even been affected; and they now turned the full force of their anger against the defenceless inhabitants of the coastal cities. Racially and linguistically, these people had nothing in common with their assailants. The pirates were Croats, a Slav people who had pushed westward from the Carpathians in the sixth and seventh centuries as part of the general Slavonic expansion across the Balkan peninsula, and in the tenth had founded a kingdom of their own. This Croatian Kingdom, however, had never comprised the whole coast of Dalmatia, where the populations of Pola, Zara, Traù and Spalato,[2] and of many other smaller communities along the coast, were the descendants of a Latin-speaking race whose forbears had been citizens of the Roman Empire and who looked upon their Croatian neighbours as barbarian upstarts. These populations, except that of Zara, were all technically subject to Constantinople; their subjection, however, was more theoretical than real. As one historian puts it, 'the name of the Emperor was officially honoured and respected, but he was not obeyed, for he gave no orders'.[3] Knowing only too well, therefore, that help could never be expected from that direction, they appealed to Venice.

If Orseolo needed any further excuse to complete the work he had started, here was the perfect one ready to hand. On 9 May, A.D. 1000 – it

1. Now Vis. Dalmatian place-names present something of a problem, since the classical Latin or Italian versions commonly used by most historians of the period often bear little or no resemblance to their modern Slavonic counterparts. In this book the contemporary Italian names are used throughout, but all modern Slavonic equivalents will be given in footnotes and, in brackets, in the index.

2. Now Pula, Zadar, Trogir and Split.

3. R. Cessi, *Cambridge Medieval History*, Vol. IV, Part I, p. 269.

was Ascension Day – the Doge heard Mass in the cathedral of S. Pietro di Castello, and received from the Bishop of Olivolo a consecrated standard.[1] Thence he proceeded in state to the harbour where the great Venetian fleet lay waiting for him, boarded his flagship and gave the signal to weigh anchor. After a night at Jesolo, the fleet came the next morning to Grado, where the Patriarch – still that same old Vitale Candiano who, after over thirty years in office, seems to have given up political intrigue and settled down as a loyal servant of the Republic – ceremonially greeted them and invested the Doge with relics of St Hermagoras.[2] Finally on 11 May, now spiritually as well as materially equipped for the tasks that lay ahead, the expedition set sail across the Adriatic.

John the Deacon's account of the journey down the Dalmatian coast reads more like the record of a triumphal progress than that of a military campaign. Bishops, barons and city priors welcomed the Venetians at every port of call; civic receptions were held in the Doge's honour; holy relics were brought out for his inspection and adoration. Oaths of fidelity were freely sworn; on occasion young men even rallied, uninvited, to the Venetian colours. At Traù the brother of the Croatian King made voluntary submission, even leaving a hostage in the person of his young son, who was later to receive the Doge's daughter in marriage. It was only when the fleet reached Spalato that Orseolo made direct contact with the enemy, whose leaders came up from the Narenta delta to discuss terms. They were in no position to drive a hard bargain; in return for the Venetian withdrawal they willingly agreed to forgo their annual tribute and to cease their molestation of the Republic's galleys travelling on their lawful occasions.

Unfortunately, however, the Narentines could not speak for all the offshore islands. Curzola[3] proved rather less cooperative and had to be subdued by force, while the men of Lagosta,[4] putting their trust in the almost legendary impregnability of their island fortress, prepared a still more formidable resistance. But the besiegers were equal to the challenge. Advancing under a hail of rocks and stones from the upper ramparts, they soon succeeded in breaching the base of one of the towers – fortunately for them, the one on which Lagosta depended for its water supply.

1. Gfrörer believes that this banner bore, possibly for the first time, the now familiar Venetian emblem of the winged lion with the open book in its paws.

2. The friend and disciple of St Mark, who appointed him first Bishop of Aquileia. He was later beheaded under Nero.

3. Korčula.

4. Lastovo.

And so, writes John the Deacon – who, as Orseolo's friend and most trusted servant, was very probably present:

the enemy, now dejected in spirit, laid down their arms and on bended knees begged nothing more than that they should be delivered from the dreaded peril of death. Therefore the Doge, who was a merciful man, resolved to spare them all, insisting only that their town should be destroyed . . . The Archbishop of Ragusa met him with his clergy, swore allegiance to the Doge and made him many signs of homage[1] . . . Thence, passing once again by the cities through which he had come, he returned in great triumph to Venice.

His subjects greeted him with jubilation, and no wonder. How long the pirates of the Narenta would keep their oath was an open question; but they had at least seen that the Republic was not in a mood to be trifled with, and the fate of Lagosta would not quickly be forgotten. Besides, Venice had now gained a hold over the eastern coast of the Adriatic such as she had never before enjoyed. It was still not technically Venetian territory; the cities and towns of Dalmatia, while swearing their oaths of fidelity and agreeing to pay an annual tribute,[2] had been careful to recall the overall suzerainty of Byzantium, which the Doge in his turn had willingly recognized. But the way was now clear for the opening of warehouses and trading-posts in the principal sea-ports, and for the consequent expansion of trade in the interior of the Balkan peninsula.

Strategically, too, Venice had gained much; henceforth she would have an alternative source of food in an emergency. Although the Rialtine islands were still only partially built over, the patches of productive land remaining on them had long been inadequate to satisfy a rapidly growing population. For her food supplies, Venice was obliged to look to the mainland; hence her consternation during Otto II's landward blockade seventeen years before. In the foreseeable future any such blockade might be a mild inconvenience; it would certainly be no worse. A few ships dispatched across the Adriatic would be back a few days later with all the corn and provisions the city might need. Finally, the pine forests of Curzola and other islands guaranteed a virtually inexhaustible stock of timber for the Venetian shipyards.

And so there was added to the Doge's other honorifics the mellifluous

1. This last assertion, it is only fair to state, has been hotly denied by certain historians of Ragusa – now Dubrovnik.

2. From Arbe (Rab), ten pounds of raw silk; from Ossero (Osor) on the island of Cherso (Cres), forty marten skins; from Veglia (Krk), fifteen marten skins and twenty fox skins; from Pola (Pula), 2,000 pounds of oil for the basilica of St Mark. Spalato (Split) undertook to equip two galleys and one barque whenever the Venetians sent a fleet to sea.

title of *Dux Dalmatiae*; and in further commemoration of the expedition it was decreed that on every succeeding Ascension Day – the anniversary of the fleet's departure – the Doge, with the Bishop of Olivolo and the nobles and citizens of Venice, should sail out again by the Lido port into the open sea for a service of supplication and thanksgiving. In those early days the service was short and the prayer simple, though it asked a lot: 'Grant, O Lord, that for us and for all who sail thereon, the sea may ever be calm and quiet.' The Doge and his suite were then sprinkled with holy water while the choir chanted the text from the fifty-first Psalm 'Purge me with hyssop, and I shall be clean'[1] and what was left of the water was poured into the sea. Later, as the tradition grew more venerable, so the ceremony grew more elaborate, and included the casting of a propitiatory golden ring into the waves; thus it was slowly to become identified with a symbolic marriage to the sea – the *Sposalizio del Mar* – a character that it was to retain till the end of the Republic itself.[2]

For Otto III, the new millennium had had less auspicious beginnings. In furtherance of his wild politico-mystical ambitions, the young Emperor had settled in Rome, where he had built himself a magnificent new palace on the Aventine. Here he lived in a curious combination of splendour and asceticism, surrounded by a court rigid with Byzantine ceremonial, eating in majestic solitude off gold plate, then occasionally shedding his purple dalmatic for a pilgrim's cloak and trudging barefoot to some distant shrine. But he had retained all his old admiration for Venice – seeing her, perhaps, as the one place in Italy where Western practicality and Byzantine mysticism were fused into one – and he hoped, as ever, to make her the instrument of his Italian policies.

He was disappointed. When an imperial embassy arrived on the Rialto soon after the Doge's return from Dalmatia with a proposal for joint operations in North Italy, it met with a firm but polite refusal. Orseolo understood, better than any Doge before him, how much Venice's fortunes depended on the sea. Territorial acquisitions on the mainland had no part in her greatness. He may, on the other hand, have been rather more interested in another suggestion which was put to John the Deacon by the Emperor at about the same time: that Otto should pay a

1. The text is not quite as surprising as it may appear at first sight. In the Latin Vulgate, the first word is more accurately translated by *aspergere* – 'sprinkle' – as it is in the New English Bible. Hyssop branches were used as an aspergent rather than an aperient.
2. See also p. 140.

secret visit to the Doge in Venice 'to hear his wise counsel and for the sake of the love he bore him'.

Unless the Emperor feared an attempt at assassination, his insistence on secrecy is hard to understand. Historians have argued that it was made necessary by the confidential nature of the subjects that he wanted to discuss; but a publicly announced visit would not have prevented privately held discussions and, in any case, both Emperor and Doge were to reveal the fact, if not the details, of the visit within a day or two of Otto's departure. It was admittedly unusual, in those pre-Crusading days, for an Emperor to leave the boundaries of his Empire; there were, however, no particular risks involved. Whatever the reasons, Otto was adamant, and the preparations – which involved John, as the Doge's secret emissary, passing the best part of a year shuttling between the two rulers – were made far longer and more laborious than they would otherwise have been. They were doubtless complicated still further when, in February 1001, the people of Rome rose up in rebellion against the Emperor and drove him from their city.

Otto does not appear to have been unduly discouraged. He celebrated Easter at Ravenna, where John the Deacon was with him to discuss last-minute arrangements. He then gave out that he proposed to spend a few days taking a health cure on the island of Pomposa[1] at the mouth of the Po. Accommodation at the abbey was actually prepared for him, but within a few hours of his arrival he slipped unseen down to the shore where John had a boat waiting and, attended only by a few of his closest associates, sailed off to Venice. After a day and a night in heavy seas he landed during a violent storm on the island of S. Servolo,[2] where Doge Pietro was waiting to greet him. John the Deacon has left us an eye-witness account of what followed. The night, he tells us, was so black that the two could scarcely see each other's faces. It was the Doge – who may not have been in the best of tempers – who began the conversation. 'If you wish to see the monastery of S. Zaccaria,' he remarked to the muffled shape beside him, 'you had better go there at once, so that you may be safely received before dawn within the walls of my palace.' By now Otto and his friends must have been in a state of some exhaustion; but Pietro was merciless. The secrecy had been the Emperor's idea; it was Otto who had involved him in all this inconvenience, subterfuge and

1. The abbey church still stands, together with many of the monastic buildings.
2. S. Servolo is now known to every Venetian as the home of one of the two main lunatic asylums of the city – a function it has fulfilled since 1725, when the Council of Ten set it aside for 'maniacs of noble family in comfortable circumstances'.

embarrassment; it was he, finally, who had dragged him out to this godforsaken island on this cold, stormy night. Very well: he must take the consequences.

There is no indication, in John's chronicle or anywhere else, that Otto was particularly eager to see S. Zaccaria or, even if he were, why his visit there should be so urgent. But he did as he was told. Orseolo did not accompany him. Instead he hurried back to the palace, ostensibly to prepare for the Emperor's reception; in fact, we may devoutly hope, to bed.

This furtive atmosphere was preserved throughout the Emperor's stay. The members of the imperial suite were publicly received by the Doge the next morning, as he emerged from the half-completed basilica of St Mark after Mass. They formally presented their letters of credence as representatives of their master – who, they claimed, had remained for reasons of health in Pomposa – whereupon Pietro Orseolo welcomed them in the name of the Republic, gave orders for their proper accommodation, and then himself slipped away to the remote eastern tower of the palace, where he had secretly installed Otto with a couple of attendants. Even now, John tells us, he took his meals publicly with the others, since 'he could not spend all day with the Emperor for fear of arousing the suspicions of any of his subjects'. If nothing else, it was a good excuse – and it allowed Otto, conspicuously disguised as a poor man, to visit the other churches and monuments in which he professed such an interest.

Some consultations were doubtless held, though no record of them has come down to us. Presents were exchanged, including an ivory throne and footstool for the Emperor; in return, Otto released the Venetians from the obligation to provide him every year with a *pallium* or state robe – a form of tribute which, together with an annual payment of fifty pounds of silver, had been in force since the days of his grandfather, Otto the Great – and, to cement their friendship still further, stood godfather for the second time to one of Pietro's children – on this occasion a new-born baby daughter, whom he personally held at the font. Then, probably not more than two days after his arrival, he slipped out of Venice as quietly as he had come, attended only by John the Deacon and his two personal servants, leaving the rest of his party to take their official departure on the following day.

Once back in Ravenna, however, he immediately announced where he had been; and, obviously by prior arrangement, the Doge made a similar and roughly simultaneous public statement in Venice – which, if John's account is to be believed, was enthusiastically acclaimed by the people.

Again it is not easy to see why; the Venetians dearly loved a show, and the secrecy surrounding the imperial visit had robbed them of a splendid one. But Orseolo's declaration would not have failed to emphasize the effect on the Republic's prestige – to say nothing of his own – of a free decision by the Emperor of the West to leave his dominions for the first time in his life in order to see Venice for himself, to worship at her shrines, admire her beauty and to drink at her fountain of experience and political wisdom. We can only assume that their gratification outweighed their disappointment.

Certainly Venice derived greater benefit from the visit than did Otto. Determined to re-establish himself in Rome, the young Emperor now returned there and prepared to besiege the city. Reinforcements were summoned from Germany; but just as they reached him, and while the Byzantine bride he had so long desired was still on her way from Constantinople, he was struck down by a sudden fever – probably smallpox – and died at the castle of Paterno, near Città Castellana, on 24 January 1002. He was just twenty-two years old. Surprisingly – though in the circumstances fortunately – he had expressed a wish to be buried not in Rome with his father,[1] but in Charlemagne's old capital of Aachen. Thither his body was taken, through hostile Roman territory, by a group of his faithful followers; and there it lies to this day, in the choir of the cathedral.

The death of Otto III did not deflect Pietro Orseolo II from his policy of close friendship with the Empire of the West. When, a month later, the Lombards rose in revolt under Ardoin, Marquess of Ivrea, and crowned him King in defiance of imperial claims, Pietro unhesitatingly backed the legitimate Emperor, Otto's second cousin, Henry II 'the Holy' of Bavaria. He was rewarded before the year's end with a new charter in which he was addressed as 'Doge of Venice and Dalmatia' and all previous privileges were confirmed; and he was also fortunate enough to have other children to whom he could invite an Emperor to stand godfather. The usual arrangements were made, and when Henry paid his first visit to Italy in 1004 the youngest of those sons was there at Verona to meet him. A service of confirmation followed, at which the Emperor acted as sponsor and gave the boy his name. The future of Venetian-imperial relations seemed to be set fair.

It might have been expected that the Doge would have chosen his eldest son rather than his youngest for so signal an honour; but Giovanni

1. The tomb of Otto II can still be seen in the crypt of St Peter's. He is the only Western Emperor to have been buried in Rome.

Orseolo was being kept for Byzantium. Pietro had never allowed his *rapprochement* with Otto or Henry to affect his friendship with Basil II. His Dalmatian adventure, if not actually cleared in advance with Constantinople, had certainly found favour with the Emperor of the East, whose rights he had been scrupulously careful to uphold and who was only too happy that Venice should take on the responsibility of policing a region that he was unable to cope with himself. Since then the Doge had acquired even more merit in Byzantine eyes by leading another expedition, smaller but still more valiant, to the relief of the city of Bari. As capital of the so-called Capitanata – the Byzantine province of South Italy which claimed suzerainty over all the land south of a line drawn from Terracina in the west to Termoli on the Adriatic coast – Bari was the largest and most important Greek community in the peninsula. In April 1002, however, it had been attacked by the Saracens and all that summer it lay under siege. Then on 6 September, a Venetian fleet under Orseolo's personal command had forced the blockade, brought provisions to the starving city and, after a three-day battle outside the harbour, had put the aggressors to flight.

The fact that Venice's intervention had been unsolicited – though she had had obvious reasons of her own for wishing to check the expansion of Saracen power in Italy – had further increased the gratitude of the Byzantines; and Orseolo must have seen that now was the moment to consolidate his advantage. Having first associated the nineteen-year-old Giovanni with him on the ducal throne, he sent him off with his younger brother Otto on a state visit to Constantinople, where it was arranged for him to marry the Princess Maria Argyra, niece of the two joint Emperors.[1] The ceremony took place in the imperial chapel, with the Patriarch officiating and the co-Emperors both present to crown the bridal pair in the Eastern fashion – simultaneously bestowing upon them the relics of St Barbara. Magnificent celebrations followed, after which the couple withdrew to a palace which had been put at their disposal. The young Dogaressa was in an advanced state of pregnancy by the time they returned to Venice.

Pietro Orseolo II was now at the climax of his career. By his statesmanship he had raised the Republic to new heights of prosperity and prestige. By his valour he had averted, for many years to come, the two

---

1. Throughout his reign, Basil II, the Bulgar-Slayer, – one of the greatest Emperors in Byzantine history – technically shared the throne with his brother, Constantine VIII. Constantine was, however, a pleasure-loving nonentity who remained in the background, playing virtually no part in political affairs. For the purposes of this history he can be ignored.

principal threats to its security – the Slavs to the east and the Saracens to
the south. He had established a Venetian presence – and a modified form
of dominion – over the Dalmatian coast. Meanwhile, on a personal level,
he had bound his family by bonds of marriage or compaternity to both
the Byzantine and the Western Empires and, for the first time in sixty
years, has associated a son with him as Doge. But, as his power and reputation grew, so too did the trappings of majesty with which he tended to
surround himself. It was not surprising that many Venetians began to
wonder whether success was not going to his head and whether he was not
secretly planning, as more than one of his predecessors had planned before
him, to establish a hereditary monarchy throughout the lagoon.

Then, suddenly, his world collapsed. In the autumn of 1005 a blazing
comet appeared in the southern sky, remaining there for three months.
Everyone knew it to be a portent; and sure enough early the following
year Venice was struck by famine – a famine that the new Dalmatian
sources of supply, which had suffered as much as those on the Italian
mainland, could do nothing to alleviate. In its wake came plague, carrying
off – among many hundreds of more humble citizens – young Giovanni,
his Greek wife and their baby son. St Peter Damian, with ill-concealed
satisfaction, attributes the Dogaressa's death to divine retribution for
her sybaritic oriental ways:

Such was the luxury of her habits that she scorned even to wash herself in
common water, obliging her servants instead to collect the dew that fell from
the heavens for her to bathe in. Nor did she deign to touch her food with her
fingers, but would command her eunuchs to cut it up into small pieces, which
she would impale on a certain golden instrument with two prongs and thus
carry to her mouth. Her rooms, too, were so heavy with incense and various
perfumes that it is nauseating for me to speak of them, nor would my readers
readily believe it. But this woman's vanity was hateful to Almighty God; and
so, unmistakably, did He take his revenge. For He raised over her the sword
of His divine justice, so that her whole body did putrefy and all her limbs began
to wither, filling her bedchamber with an unbearable odour such that no one
– not a handmaiden, nor even a slave – could withstand this dreadful attack on
the nostrils; except for one serving-girl who, with the help of aromatic concoc-
tions, conscientiously remained to do her bidding. And even she could only
approach her mistress hurriedly, and then immediately withdraw. So, after a
slow decline and agonizing torments, to the joyful relief of her friends she
breathed her last.[1]

1. Since Peter Damian does not refer to Maria Argyra by name, nor to the deaths – at the
same time and by the same causes – of her husband and son, some authorities have suggested
that he may have confused her with another Greek Dogaressa: Theodora, the wife of Doge

Giovanni and his wife died within sixteen days of each other, and were buried at S. Zaccaria in a single tomb. Pietro Orseolo was heart-broken. His dreams for the future vanished. Though not yet fifty, he seems to have lost the desire to live. Perhaps, like his father, he underwent a religious crisis. Unlike old Pietro, however, he did not retire to a monastery. Instead, he raised his third son, Otto, to the dogeship with him, made his will, leaving the bulk of his possessions to the Church and the poor, and then withdrew to a remote wing of the palace, separating himself even from his wife. Less than two years later, in 1008, he died.

Young Otto was still only sixteen. In the circumstances, it is odd that the Venetians should have made no objection when he joined his father on the throne; it is odder still that they should have allowed him to succeed to power without, so far as we know, a single voice being raised against him – the youngest Doge in Venetian history. But in the Middle Ages both men and women matured younger than they do now – for sixteen-year-olds to be given command of armies was by no means unheard of – and Otto Orseolo seems to have been old beyond his years. 'Catholic in faith, calm in purity, strong in justice, eminent in religion, decorous in his manner of life, well-endowed with wealth and possessions, and so filled with all forms of virtue that he was universally considered to be the most fitting successor of his father and grandfather' – thus Andrea Dandolo was to describe him, after a three-century interval which, if a poor guarantee of historical accuracy, at least argues a relatively unprejudiced standpoint.[1] Otto Orseolo had indeed inherited many of his father's characteristics, among them his taste for splendour and his love of power. The new Doge was familiar with the imperial courts of the West and the East, having received his religious confirmation at one and several high honours from the other; and the Magyar princess – daughter of the subsequently canonized King Stephen of Hungary – whom he married shortly after Pietro's death added still more lustre to his position. Like his father, he was quick to build up his image as a magnificent and majestic potentate – so far, at least, as the traditionally austere sensibilities of his subjects permitted.

Domenico Selvo (see p. 93). As Selvo became Doge only in 1071, however, and Peter Damian himself died in February 1072, this theory does not seem very probable. It may well be that Peter did not know about the plague – or if he did that he kept quiet about it, for the very good reason that it would have ruined his story.

1. John the Deacon's chronicle breaks off here, leaving us without any detailed or sustained contemporary record of events.

But for a young man of his ambitions, the outward trappings of power were insufficient. In 1017 the old Patriarch of Grado, Vitale Candiano, died at last, having occupied the patriarchate for as long as anyone could remember – well over half a century; and in his place Otto appointed his own elder brother, Orso. Orso had hitherto been Bishop of Torcello[1], a see which the Doge now passed on to yet another brother, Vitale. He should have known better. The new Patriarch cannot have been more than thirty, the new bishop ten years younger. Inevitably, the former jealousies concerning the Orseoli, the former fears that they were planning to set up some form of hereditary rule, sprang up again, more insistently than before. The dissatisfaction was not yet such as to provoke an uprising, and for a few more years all went smoothly enough; but it did mean that Otto could no longer rely on the goodwill and support of his people when, in 1019, the first serious cloud appeared on the horizon with the appointment of a noble Bavarian, Poppo of Treffen, to the Patriarchate of Aquileia.

History affords no more perfect example of that phenomenon so characteristic of the Middle Ages[2] – the worldly, ambitious warrior-priest. Hardly was he installed before he laid formal claim to the see of Grado as being historically part of his patriarchate, denouncing its legitimate incumbent, Orso, as a fraud and a usurper. His claim found little favour with the Pope, but a good deal more from the anti-Orseolo faction in Venice itself; in 1022–3 we find both the Doge and his brother fleeing the city and taking refuge in Istria. But now it was Poppo's turn to overreach himself. Without papal sanction, he marched into Grado and began systematically sacking the churches and monasteries, sending off their treasures to Aquileia. This was more than the people of Grado or the Venetians themselves could tolerate. There was an immediate reaction in favour of the Orseoli who returned in haste, drove out Poppo and his followers with surprisingly little fuss and resumed their former thrones, Orso in Grado, Otto in the Doges' Palace.

When, in 1024, a synod called in Rome by Pope John XIX dismissed Poppo's claims out of hand and reaffirmed the rights of Grado as an equal and independent see, it must have looked as though the Orseoli had surmounted their difficulties and were once again firmly entrenched in the seats of Venetian power. So they might well have been

1. It was during Orso's tenure of the see of Torcello that the present cathedral was built. It still stands today essentially as he left it. (See p. 35n.)

2. At least where western Europe is concerned; in the Orthodox world the tradition has continued up to the present day.

if the Doge had only shown a modicum of sensitivity to popular opinion. But Otto's ambitions were, as always, too strong for him, and two years later a further scandal over Church appointments brought matters finally to a head. His enemies acted quickly and decisively, and this time he had no opportunity to flee. He was seized, shorn of his beard, and dispatched to end his days in Constantinople.

Otto's successor, Pietro Barbolano – but, with that perverseness which characterizes so much of early Venetian nomenclature, more usually known as Centranico – could, at the time of his accession, boast one distinction only: that of having filched, some thirty years before, the relics of St Sabas from Constantinople and deposited them in the church of S. Antonino.[1] For four years he struggled to reunite the city, but his efforts were in vain. The old Orseolo policy of linking their family to the hereditary ruling dynasties of Europe began to pay off. In Constantinople, the Emperor had given an honourable refuge to Otto (his niece's brother-in-law) and had angrily withdrawn the trading privileges granted to old Pietro at the end of the previous century. The new Western Emperor followed suit, while King Stephen of Hungary, determined to avenge his exiled daughter and son-in-law, attacked Dalmatia and annexed a number of the coastal cities.[2] Venice herself remained torn by factions, among which the supporters of the Orseoli, who had remained strong in the city, became even stronger as the new government's problems multiplied and nostalgia for the old days grew. The crisis came in 1032, when Centranico in his turn was compelled to abdicate and Vitale Orseolo, the Bishop of Torcello, hurried off to Constantinople with an invitation to his brother to resume the throne. Meanwhile the third brother Orso, Patriarch of Grado, who like Vitale had managed to ride out the storm, temporarily took the power into his own hands.

All seemed set for a restoration; but Bishop Vitale reached Constantinople to find his brother already gravely ill, and Otto died before he could return to Venice. The Patriarch, who in the intervening months had continued to guide both the religious and the secular destinies of his

1. They were returned 973 years later – in 1965 – by Pope Paul VI at the request of the Orthodox Patriarch, who described movingly how the monks of St Sabas's foundation 'still gathered every evening at the empty tomb' (*The Times*, 18 March 1965).

2. This campaign was probably instigated by his nephew, Otto's son Peter, who was now living in Hungary – where indeed he was eventually to succeed Stephen on the throne. With the casuistry of the age, Peter would have had no difficulty in arguing that his grandfather had conquered Dalmatia for the benefit of the Orseoli, and not for the ungrateful Venetians who had banished them.

city, resigned as soon as the news reached him. An attempt to seize the throne by some obscure offshoot of the family, one Domenico Orseolo, was effortlessly scotched. A modern historian[1] has dismissed him as a *miserabile parodia*; he lasted for a day and a night, then fled to Ravenna.

The days of the Orseoli were passed. They would not return.

1. R. Cessi, *Storia della Repubblica di Venezia.*

· 6 ·

The Norman Menace

[1032–1095]

These men were brave, and skilled in naval warfare. They were sent forth at the imperial behest, by densely-peopled Venice, a land rich in wealth and in men, where the furthermost gulf of the Adriatic lies under the northern stars. The walls of this nation are surrounded by the sea, and its people cannot visit each others' houses unless they travel by boat. For they dwell ever among the waters, and no nation is more valiant than they in fighting at sea, or in steering their craft over the surface of the waves.

William of Apulia, a contemporary Norman Chronicler

The ignominious attempt by Domenico Orseolo to seize power in Venice proved catastrophic not only for himself but for his family. The Venetians, even those who had supported the restoration of Doge Otto, were shocked by his blatant presumption that the supreme authority in their city had become a perquisite of the Orseolo clan and showed their disgust in the clearest way possible – by conferring the dogeship on Domenico Flabanico, a wealthy silk-merchant who had led the insurrection six years before. Flabanico's known anti-dynastic views, plus the pattern of subsequent Venetian history, have together been responsible for a widely held theory that the new Doge introduced what almost amounted to a revised constitution for the state, according to which the practice of appointing co-regents – and thus in effect successors – was forbidden, and a period of tyranny gave place to one of democratic liberty. One authority[1] has even gone so far as to assert that a special law was passed, ostracizing the entire Orseolo family and debarring it in perpetuity from public office – this despite the fact that the two prelates Orso and Vitale are known to have continued in their respective sees until they died. In fact, such reform as there was resulted from a change not so much of laws but of attitudes. The necessary legislation providing

1. An anonymous annotator of the Ambrosian MS. of Andrea Dandolo's Chronicle – a version which, it is only fair to point out, was described by an eighteenth-century director of the Ambrosian Library in Milan as a *confusa indigestaque farrago*.

for the proper election of Doges and giving adequate powers to the popular assembly already existed. All that was required was the will to implement it. It was this will that Domenico Flabanico possessed and, in a way, personified. And he carried the people with him. During the seven and a half centuries that were to elapse before the Republic came to an end the names of certain leading families recur again and again in the list of Doges; considering that for most of that time Venice was an openly avowed oligarchy, it would be surprising if they did not. But on only two occasions in the whole period do we find the same name appearing twice consecutively; on both of these, the succession is from brother to brother rather than from father to son; and on neither is there any doubt as to the propriety of the election. After the fall of the Orseoli the practice of co-dogeship was never revived, or even indeed attempted.

The eleven-year reign of Domenico Flabanico, then, emerges as something of a milestone in Venetian history. At the same time it seems to have been unusually devoid of incident. The Republic was at peace again, factions were forgotten, and the citizens were able to concentrate on the two things they did best – making money, and enlarging and beautifying their city. This happy state of affairs was, however, rudely interrupted on the Doge's death. During the brief interregnum that followed, the unspeakable Poppo of Aquileia saw another opportunity to subjugate Grado and with the help of his usual army of thugs descended for the second time upon the luckless city, carrying off the few treasures that had somehow eluded him twenty years before. Fortunately Poppo himself died almost immediately afterwards, and his followers hastily fled at the approach of a Venetian fleet under the new Doge, Domenico Contarini; but although his action was formally condemned – and the rights and immunities of Grado confirmed – by the Pope in 1044, the rivalry between the two sees remained a vexed question for many years to come. It would probably have caused still more trouble than it did had not the Patriarchs of Grado, after the death of old Orso in 1045, sensibly decided to establish their principal residence in Venice. Thenceforth their connections with Grado were to grow ever more tenuous; and when in the fifteenth century the Pope officially recognized the transfer, he had little to change but their title.[1]

Apart from the relief of Grado, Doge Contarini's only foreign exploit

1. The first patriarchal palace in Venice stood on the Grand Canal, between the church of S. Silvestro and the Rialto bridge. It can be clearly seen in Carpaccio's *Cure of a Demoniac*, one of the series of paintings depicting the miracles of the Holy Cross, now in the Accademia.

was an expedition in 1062 to Dalmatia.[1] Here, particularly since the intervention of Stephen of Hungary forty years before, the situation was becoming ever more chaotic under the conflicting pressures of Hungarians, Croats and Byzantines. The Venetian recapture of Zara can hardly be said to have put an end to the confusion; but it doubtless reassured the local Latin populations who were feeling increasingly hemmed in, as well as providing a salutary reminder that the Doge did not bear the subsidiary title of Duke of Dalmatia for nothing. On the domestic front, throughout his twenty-eight years of office, Contarini was able to maintain the quiet prosperity inaugurated by his predecessor and to devote much of his time to works of piety – which, in true Venetian style, almost invariably resulted in the glorification of the city at least as much as that of the Almighty Himself. Deciding that old Pietro Orseolo's reconstruction of the fire-ravaged Basilica was no longer worthy of its surroundings, he called for new, more ambitious designs; meanwhile, out on the Lido, there arose a magnificent Benedictine monastery, founded and largely endowed by the Doge and dedicated to St Nicholas of Myra, patron of all who sailed the sea.

The present church of S. Nicolò di Lido is a rather pallid seventeenth-century affair; two splendid Veneto-Byzantine capitals flanking the monastery entrance are almost the only traces of the original structure. It certainly possesses none of the magical beauty of Venice's other (and far older) church with the same dedication, S. Nicolò dei Mendicoli.[2] Over the doorway into the church, however, is a memorial tablet to Contarini recording three military triumphs – the Dalmatian expedition, the recovery of Grado and, finally, the defeat of the Normans in Apulia.[3] The first two come as no surprise; the third is baffling. The Normans were never defeated in Apulia, where their record in the eleventh century is one of a steady succession of victories. Their only encounters with the Venetians were at sea, in the southern Adriatic, first off Durazzo in what is now Albania and later in the Corfu channel; and these took place between ten and fifteen years after Contarini's death. For the sake of his memory it is just as well that they did; for the last and ultimately decisive battle was a disaster for Venice and led to the downfall of his successor, previously one of the most popular Doges in her history.

1. Andrea Dandolo puts it in 1044, but his chronology at this point becomes a little muddled.

2. Recently restored by the British Venice in Peril Fund.

3. The inscription reads: *Domenico Contareno/qui rebellam Dalmatiam compressa foedera domuit/Gradum pulsu Aquileiense recepit/Normannos in Apulia vicit.*

To what, precisely, Domenico Selvo owed his popularity we cannot tell; but we can be sure that it was real enough because there has come down to us, by some lucky chance, a first-hand account of his election written by a parish priest of the church of S. Michele Archangelo, a certain Domenico Tino. It is the earliest eye-witness description of such a ceremony that survives, and it gives us an invaluable glimpse, after the quasi-tyrannies of former years, of the popular will once again in full operation.[1]

The date was 1071, the place – since St Mark's was full of Contarini's workmen – the new monastery church of S. Nicolò on the Lido. Previous Doges, when the basilica had not been available, had been chosen in S. Pietro di Castello; but S. Nicolò was a good deal larger, and its greater capacity was presumably considered to outweigh the difficulties of access. The authorities may indeed have hoped that the choice of so comparatively distant a venue might diminish the numbers of those attending; if so, they were disappointed, since Tino tells us that 'an innumerable multitude of people, virtually all Venice' was present, having sailed across the lagoon *in armatis navibus* – a phrase which suggests that part of the Republic's war fleet was requisitioned for the occasion.

Proceedings began with a High Mass at which, 'to the accompaniment of psalms and litanies', divine inspiration was sought for the choice of a Doge 'who would be both worthy of his nation and acceptable to its people. And now a great shout rose up to the very heavens, and, as with a single voice, all those present cried out, again and again and ever more loudly, the words *Domenicum Silvium volumus et laudamus*.' There could have been no clearer expression of the people's wish; the election was over. A party of the more distinguished citizens then lifted the Doge-elect and bore him, shoulder-high above the cheering crowd, to the quayside; meanwhile the choirs sang the *Kyrie* and *Te Deum*, the bells pealed out from the *campanili* and the oarsmen of the innumerable escorting craft, beating the flat of their blades upon the water, added their own thunderous applause. So it continued all the way back to the city. Selvo, barefoot now and clad only in a simple shift, was led in state to the Basilica where, amid the masons' ladders and scaffolding, he prostrated himself on the newly laid marble pavement, gave thanks, and received his staff of office at the High Altar. At this point – though Tino does not specifically tell us so – he presumably donned the ducal robes for the first time and made a formal procession to the palace, there

1. The complete Latin text can be found in Galicciolli, *Delle memorie Venete antiche,* Vol. VI, pp. 124–6.

to receive oaths of fidelity from his subjects and to distribute traditional gifts in return.

The reign of Venice's twenty-ninth Doge had begun; but Tino ends his account with a curious detail. 'Without delay,' he writes, 'the Doge gave orders for the restoration and improvement of the doors, seats and tables which had been damaged after the death of Doge Contarini.' Why, one asks, should this have been necessary? There is no evidence of any public disorder after Contarini's death. He was popular with his people; indeed, had he not been, it is hardly likely that Selvo, who had been one of his chief lieutenants, would have been elected with such speed and jubilation. We can only assume that the Venetians had at some moment in the past been ill-advised enough to adopt that barbarous tradition of papal Rome whereby, on the death of the Supreme Pontiff, the Lateran Palace was regularly ransacked by the mob. If so, they certainly abandoned the practice before very long; during future centuries the Doges' Palace was to be attacked on more than one occasion at moments of crisis, but there is no other record of its being broken into as a matter of course. Perhaps, in the eleventh century, the legal position with regard to the ownership of the palace contents on the death of a Doge had not been clearly defined. It soon would be; the days were shortly to come when anyone found guilty of seizure or damage to the property of the Republic would almost certainly spend the rest of a rather short life regretting it.

The first decade of Domenico Selvo's reign was tranquil enough. Soon after his accession he married the Byzantine Princess Theodora Ducas, sister of the reigning Emperor Michael VII, and before long he had restored relations with the Western Empire to a level unknown since the days of the Orseoli, though he narrowly escaped excommunication for himself and an interdict on the entire Republic when the great struggle between the Emperor Henry IV and Pope Gregory VII – better known as Hildebrand – was at its height. For Venice herself, at home and abroad, there was peace; and not till 1081, when the newly crowned Byzantine Emperor Alexius I Comnenus appealed for help against the Norman menace, was that peace disturbed.

The career of the Normans in South Italy and Sicily is one of the great epics of European history. At the time when Alexius made his appeal there were still old men in Apulia who could remember the years when that stream of foot-loose young adventurers had begun to trickle down across the Alps to carve out their fortunes with their swords. Within little more than a generation they had mopped up virtually the entire peninsula south of the Garigliano river; in 1053 they had crushed a numerically far superior army, led by the Pope in person, whom they had subsequently held captive for nine months. Six years later Robert de Hauteville, called Guiscard ('the Crafty'), had been invested by Pope Nicholas II with the Duchies of Apulia, Calabria and Sicily. This last investiture was somewhat premature. The Normans had not yet set foot in Sicily, which was still in Saracen hands. It was to be another thirteen years before Palermo was to surrender to Robert's army, and twenty more before his countrymen were in undisputed possession of the whole island. But even before the fall of the capital, Robert Guiscard's eyes had become fixed on something far beyond his dukedom. He had already begun to meditate the most ambitious undertaking even of his own extraordinary career: a concerted attack on the Byzantine Empire, with Constantinople itself as his final objective. Internal problems with his South Italian dominions prevented him from putting his cherished plan into operation for several years; but by late spring 1081 his invasion fleet was ready to sail. His first target was Durazzo, whence the 800-year-old Via Egnatia ran east across the Balkan peninsula to the imperial capital.

The moment he heard of Robert's landing on imperial territory, the Byzantine Emperor Alexius Comnenus had sent the Doge an urgent appeal for assistance. It was probably unnecessary; the threat to Venice implied by Norman control of the straits of Otranto was every bit as serious as that to the Empire. Certainly Domenico Selvo never hesitated. Giving orders for the immediate preparation of the war fleet, he himself assumed command and soon afterwards was sailing to the attack. Even then, he arrived only just in time. Though themselves delayed by violent storms in which they lost several of their ships, the Normans were already at anchor in the roadstead off Durazzo when the Venetian war galleys bore down upon them.

Robert Guiscard's men fought tenaciously, but their inexperience of sea warfare betrayed them. The Venetians adopted the old Byzantine trick of hoisting manned dinghies to the yard-arms, from which the soldiers could shoot down on the enemy below; it seems too that they had learnt the secret of Greek fire, since a Norman chronicler, Geoffrey Malaterra, writes of how 'they blew that fire, which is called Greek and is not extinguished by water, through submerged pipes, and thus cunningly burned one of our ships under the very waves of the sea.' Against such tactics the Normans were powerless; and it was a reduced and battered fleet that finally beat its way back into harbour.

The Norman army, however, which had disembarked before the battle, was still virtually unimpaired; and after an eight-month siege – during which, at one moment, it inflicted a crushing defeat on a Byzantine force commanded by the Emperor himself – it compelled the city of Durazzo to surrender. Alexius had already sent rich presents to Venice in gratitude for her help; he might have been rather less generous had he known that the fall of the city was due to the treachery of a resident Venetian merchant who arranged for the gates to be opened in return for the hand in marriage of one of Robert Guiscard's daughters.

Thus the first defeat inflicted by Venice on the Norman expeditionary force, crippling as it must have appeared at the time, was soon revealed as only a temporary setback. After the fall of Durazzo the local populations, many of whom felt no particular loyalty to the Byzantines in any case, offered little further resistance to Robert Guiscard's advancing army. Within a few weeks all Illyria had submitted, and soon afterwards the important Macedonian city of Kastoria, half-way across the Balkan peninsula, had followed suit. If Robert had been allowed to keep up his momentum there is little doubt that the next summer would have found him at the gates of Constantinople; and from there it would have been but a short step to his ultimate goal, the throne of the Emperors. It was his misfortune that at this most critical of moments an urgent appeal from the Pope demanded his immediate return.

The story of the capture of Rome by the Emperor Henry IV in the spring of 1084, of Pope Gregory VII's refuge in the Castel Sant' Angelo and of his eventual deliverance by Robert Guiscard, has no place in this book. It is enough here to record that throughout this *annus mirabilis* of Robert's career – when the former penniless brigand had both the Eastern and Western Emperors on the run before him and the greatest of all the medieval Popes in his power – he appears to have been dreaming only of getting back to the Balkans at the earliest possible moment. He had, we are told, sworn on the soul of his father to remain unbathed and unshaven until he could rejoin the army he had left with his son Bohemund at Kastoria; and the occasional reports that reached him in Italy, telling of new counter-offensives by the Byzantines on land and by the Venetians at sea, resulting in massive desertions by his own forces, can only have added to his impatience.

He was back in the autumn, to find the situation even worse than he had expected. A Venetian fleet had recaptured both Durazzo and Corfu; Norman-held territory was once more confined to an offshore island or two and a short strip of coast. But Robert, though now sixty-eight, showed no sign of dismay. Instead, he at once started to plan a new offensive against Corfu. Unfortunately bad weather delayed his ships until November, and when at last they were able to sail the defenders were ready for them. Outside the harbour of Cassiope, in the extreme north-east corner of the island, they were met by a combined Greek and Venetian fleet which inflicted on them a defeat every bit as damaging as that they had suffered off Durazzo the previous year. Still the Guiscard would not admit himself beaten. Three days later he led his navy out yet again – with still more disastrous results. Convinced of their victory, the Venetians sent their fastest pinnaces scudding back up the Adriatic to bring the news to the Rialto.

Throughout his long career, people had tended to underestimate Robert Guiscard; invariably – if they lived at all – they lived to regret it. For the Venetians, it was an understandable mistake; after the two preceding encounters, few of the Norman ships were in a condition to hoist sail, let alone to venture on yet a third battle. But Robert, seeing the pinnaces disappearing over the horizon, recognized his chance. Summoning every vessel he possessed that was still afloat, he flung the broken remnants of his fleet against the unsuspecting enemy galleys in a last desperate on-slaught. He had calculated it perfectly. The Venetians were caught utterly unawares, and scarcely had time even to take up a defensive formation before the Normans engaged. To make matters worse their larger ships, having already been emptied of ballast and provisions, rode so high in the water that when in the heat of the battle their entire com-plement of soldiers and crew all rushed to the same side of the deck, many of them capsized. (So, at least, reports Anna Comnena, the Emperor's daughter, in the remarkable history that she wrote of her father's reign;[1] but it is hard indeed to reconcile with what we know of Venetian seaman-ship.) Anna assesses the Venetian dead at 13,000, in addition to which she mentions a large number of prisoners – on whose subsequent muti-lations at the hands of their captors she dwells with the morbid pleasure that is one of her least attractive characteristics. Finally she invents a fourth action in which she claims that the Venetians had their revenge; but this story must regretfully be dismissed as wishful thinking. There is no trace of it in the Venetian records, nor indeed anywhere else; and if in fact the series of engagements had ended in a triumph for the Republic it is hardly likely that Doge Domenico Selvo would have been deposed and disgraced.

1. *The Alexiad*, Book VI.

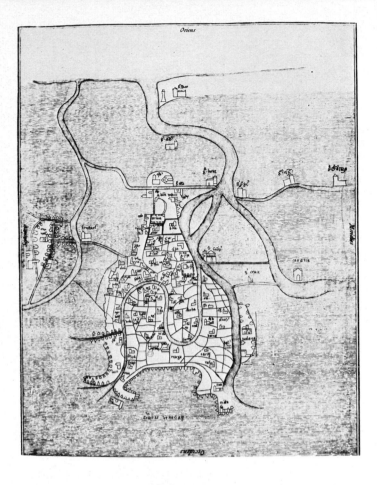

1. One of the earliest
surviving maps of Venice,
from a twelfth-century
manuscript in the Biblioteca
Marciana

2. The lion of St Mark, from
the column in the Piazzetta.
Its origins are uncertain –
perhaps Persian (fourth
century A.D.) or Chinese,
with wings added

3. The apse of the Cathedral of S. Maria Assunta, Torcello.
The mosaics of the Apostles date from *c.* 1100,
that of the Virgin about a century later

4. Torcello. An early eleventh-century Byzantine panel from the screen

5. A detail of the bronze doors of the Basilica of St Mark

6. SS. Maria e Donato, Murano. Late eleventh century

7. The cloister of S. Apollonia, twelfth–thirteenth century.
The only Romanesque cloister in Venice

8. Marble medallion of a
Byzantine Emperor (? tenth
century) in the Campiello
Angaran

9. An arch in the house of
Marco Polo, Corte Seconda
del Milion. Eleventh–twelfth
century

10. A Venetian ship of Marco Polo's time, from the inner right-hand lunette of the façade of St Mark's. The original was replaced in the seventeenth century; it is known only through this detail from Gentile Bellini's *Procession of the Cross in the Piazza S. Marco* in the Accademia

11 (*Right*). A Levantine merchant of the thirteenth century: sculpture in the Campo dei Mori

12. The first golden ducat, 1284, with the name of Doge Giovanni Dandolo, portrayed kneeling before St Mark

13. The Ca' da Mosto, twelfth–thirteenth century. The top two floors are later additions. In the sixteenth–eighteenth centuries it was the Albergo del Leon Bianco, Venice's most celebrated hotel.

14. Venice in c. 1400, from a manuscript of that date illustrating the departure of the elder Polos

15. The Basilica of St Mark, the Doges' Palace behind, and in the distance S. Giorgio Maggiore

16. The body of St Mark being carried into the Basilica.
This thirteenth-century mosaic in the extreme left-hand lunette of the
façade is the earliest-known representation of St Mark's
(the bronze horses are already in position)

17. The theft of the body of St Mark. A thirteenth-century mosaic in the Basilica

18. Doge, Patriarch, clergy and people pray
for the relics of the Evangelist to be rediscovered. South transept, St Mark's.

19. Their prayers are answered. Mosaics of later thirteenth century

20 (*Below left*). Thirteenth-century carving on a portal, St Mark's

21 (*Below right*). Baptistery, St Mark's. This mid-fourteenth-century mosaic
of Salome provides an invaluable illustration of contemporary Venetian fashion

22 (*Bottom*). The south wall, St Mark's. 'The front of St Mark's became rather
a shrine at which to dedicate the splendour of miscellaneous spoil, than the
organized expression of any fixed architectural law, or religious emotion.' (Ruskin) [?]

23 (*Top*). South front, the Doges' Palace. Fourteenth century

24 (*Above left*). Vettor Pisani – detail from his monument in SS. Giovanni e Paolo

25 (*Above right*). Doge Antonio Venier (1382-1400) by Jacobello dalle Masegne, Museo Correr

26. The tomb of Doge Andrea Dandolo. Baptistery, St Mark's.
'The best existing example of Venetian monumental sculpture.' (Ruskin)

27 (*Right*). The tomb of Doge Michele Morosini, SS. Giovanni e Paolo

28. The Fourth Crusade, from the original manuscript of Geoffrey de Villehardouin

29 (*Above left*). Doge Andrea Contarini (1368–82) from the Caresini Chronicle

30 (*Above right*). Doge Andrea Dandolo (1343–54) from the Caresini Chronicle

There is some doubt as to whether the Doge was in command of the fleet for the last catastrophe. If he was, his fate cannot have been entirely unmerited. But in other respects his policies had not been unsuccessful. The alacrity and enthusiasm with which he had responded to the Byzantine appeal for help had earned Venice the undying gratitude of the Emperor Alexius, who had not been slow in translating it into material form: annual subventions to all the churches in the city, including a special tribute to the treasury of St Mark's – 'the more acceptable', as Gibbon points out, 'as it was the produce of a tax on their rivals of Amalphi' – the grant of anchorages and warehouses along the Golden Horn and finally, in 1082, the extension of former trading privileges till they amounted to full exemption from all taxes and customs duties for Venetian merchants throughout the Empire. The importance of this last concession is almost impossible to exaggerate. Suddenly and at a single stroke, the Venetians found immense territories beckoning them – territories which, for all practical purposes, they could consider as their own. As the great French Byzantinist Charles Diehl put it, 'the Emperor flung open to them the gates of the Orient. On that day Venetian world trade began.'

But the fact remained that, in the short term, Venice had suffered not just a defeat but a humiliation. The cream of her fighting men was lost. Of her nine great galleys – the largest and most heavily armed of all the ships in her war fleet – two were in Norman hands and the other seven at the bottom of the sea, destroyed by an upstart nation with no experience of naval warfare whose own vessels at the time of the conflict had been scarcely able to stay afloat. Meanwhile the Normans were once again in control of the Adriatic approaches. The Venetians could not know that within a few months Robert Guiscard would die of typhoid on the island of Cephalonia, that his similarly stricken army would disintegrate and that the Norman threat would vanish, at least for the time being, as suddenly as it had arisen. For the moment a scapegoat was needed; and that scapegoat could be none other than the Doge himself.

It was all over quite quickly. Selvo seems to have made little or no attempt to defend himself. He was removed from power and packed off to a monastery, and by the end of the year his successor was already enthroned. Probably his spirit was broken, and he was glad enough to go; but it was a sad end to a reign that had begun with such bright promise just thirteen years before.

The historian Andrea Dandolo accuses the new Doge, Vitale Falier, of having 'persuaded the people, by means of promises and bribes, to depose his predecessor'. Perhaps he did; but Dandolo was writing 250 years later and his chronicle is at this point so sketchy and inaccurate that it hardly seems possible to condemn Falier on this testimony alone. An English historian[1] simply notes that 'the ten years of his authority contain little that was eventful and nothing that was unprosperous' – which is probably as good a summing-up as any.

These years, however, did include one great moment in Venetian history – the consecration of the new Basilica of St Mark, which still stands today. Work on this, the third building to occupy the site since the arrival of the Evangelist's remains two and a half centuries before, had been initiated by Doge Contarini and pursued still more enthusiastically by Domenico Selvo – who had even gone so far as to decree, at the outset of his reign, that every Venetian merchantman returning from the East must bring back, as part of its cargo, marbles or fine carvings for the decoration of St Mark's. It was Selvo, too, who had imported artists from Ravenna to begin the mosaic work that is still one of the supreme glories of the Basilica,[2] and we can only hope that, for a day or two during the summer of 1094, he was allowed to leave his cloister for the ceremony of consecration. If so, it may also have been given to him to witness one of the few miracles that the Venetians – a down-to-earth people even then, not normally given to imaginative flights of fancy – like to claim for their own.

After the burning of the original basilica in the great fire of 976 the body of St Mark, so the legend goes, disappeared without trace. It was not thought to have been consumed in the flames; the difficulty was that its precise location had been known to three people only, all of whom had perished before they could pass on their secret. And so, when the new building was at last complete, a three-day fast was declared for the whole city while the Doge, the Patriarch and all the bishops and clergy of the lagoons prayed that the precious relics might be rediscovered. On the third day – it was 25 June – their prayers were answered. Half-way through High Mass there was suddenly heard, from the south transept, the sound of crumbling masonry. All eyes turned to find that part of one of the main supporting piers had fallen away, revealing a hole from which there protruded a human arm. It was immediately recognized as being that of the Evangelist, whose body was now, amid scenes of great jubilation, removed *in toto* from its hiding-place and reburied in the crypt. There it

1. F. C. Hodgson, *The Early History of Venice*.

2. Some at least of the eleventh-century mosaics still exist – notably the portraits of saints in niches flanking the central door leading in from the narthex.

was to remain until 1836, when it was shifted to its present position beneath the high altar.[1]

The consecration of this third and final basilica of St Mark, whether or not accompanied by so signal a mark of divine favour, had an importance which went far beyond the boundaries of the city or the lagoon. Nowhere in the Western world, not in Ravenna or Aachen or even in Rome itself, had so sumptuous a monument been raised to the Christian God – ocular proof not so much of the piety of the Venetians (who were appreciably neither more nor less religious than their neighbours), as of their wealth, of the extent of their commercial Empire, and of the national pride – of a kind still unknown elsewhere in Europe – that was leading them to devote more and more of their private fortunes to the glory and splendour of their city. The lesson cannot have been lost on the Emperor Henry IV when he visited Venice in the summer of 1095, any more than on his numberless fellow-princes who, from the following year and for a century to come, were to pass through the city on their way to and from the East. But before this stream could begin, and indeed within a few weeks of the Emperor's visit, Vitale Falier was dead of the plague. He was buried at Christmas in the Basilica, where his tomb still stands, just inside the outer central doorway on the right, the oldest extant funerary monument in Venice. It was left to his successor to steer the Republic through those critical years of challenge that set the seal on the century – the years of the First Crusade.

1. Two delightful late thirteenth-century mosaics, on the end wall of the south transept, illustrate the discovery. Near by, on the pier just to the left of the Altar of the Sacrament, (Plates 18 and 19) a panel marks the precise place where the miracle occurred.

· 7 ·

In the Wake of the Crusade

[1095–1130]

Quale ne l'arzanà de' Viniziani
  Bolle l'inverno la tenace pece
  A rimpalmar li legni lor non sani,
Che navicar non ponno; e 'n quelle vece
  Chi fa suo legno novo e chi ristoppa
  Le coste a quel che più viaggi fece;
Chi ribatte da proda e chi da poppa;
  Altri fa remi e altri volge sarte;
  Chi terzeruolo e artimon rintoppa;
Tal, non per foco, ma per divin' arte,
  Bollia là giuso una pegola spessa,
  Che 'nviscava la ripa d'ogni parte.

For as at Venice, in the Arsenal
  In winter-time, they boil the gummy pitch
  To caulk such ships as need an overhaul,
Now that they cannot sail – instead of which
  One builds him a new boat, one toils to plug
  Seams strained by many a voyage, others stitch
Canvas to patch a tattered jib or lug,
  Hammer at the prow, hammer at the stern, or twine
  Ropes, or shave oars, refit and make all snug –
So, not by fire, but by the art divine,
  A thick pitch boiled down there, spattering the brink
  With viscous glue . . .

Dante, *Inferno*, XXI, 7–18
(Tr. Dorothy L. Sayers)

It was on Tuesday 27 November 1095, while Doge Falier lay on his deathbed, that Pope Urban II called upon Western Christendom to march to the rescue of the East. The response was enthusiastic and widespread. By 1 December Count Raymond of Toulouse and many of his lords had declared themselves ready to take the Cross. From Normandy and Flanders, from Denmark, Spain and even Scotland, prince and peasant alike rallied to the call. In Italy too the general reaction was much the same; the people of Bologna actually received a letter from the Pope cautioning them against excess of zeal and reminding them not to leave without the consent of their priests – and, in the case of recently married men, of their wives as well. Further south Robert Guiscard's son Bohemund, now Prince of Taranto, recognized the opportunity he had long been awaiting and raised a small army of his own. Pisa and Genoa, both rapidly gaining in importance as maritime powers, also scented new possibilities for themselves in the East and began to prepare their fleets.

But Venice hung back. Her own Eastern markets were already assured – particularly Egypt, which had become a major clearing-house for spices from India and the southern seas, providing in return a ready market for European timber and metal. Her people were too hard-headed to set much store by emotional outbursts about the salvation of Christendom; war was bad for trade, and the goodwill of the Arabs and the Seljuk Turks – who in the past quarter-century had overrun the greater part of Anatolia – was essential if the caravan routes to Central Asia were to be kept open. The new Doge, Vitale Michiel, preferred to wait, to judge for himself the scale of the enterprise and its prospects of success, before irrevocably committing the Republic. Not till 1097, when the first wave of Crusaders was already marching through Anatolia, did he even begin any serious preparations; and it was only in the late summer of 1099, after the Frankish armies had battered their way into Jerusalem, slaughtering every Muslim in the city and burning all the Jews alive in the main synagogue, that a Venetian fleet of 200 sail filed out through the Lido port.

In command was the Doge's son, Giovanni Michiel, while the spiritual well-being of the expedition was entrusted to Enrico, Bishop of Castello and son of the former Doge Domenico Contarini.[1] Down the Adriatic they went, calling in at the Dalmatian towns to pick up additional men and equipment, around the Peloponnese and so to Rhodes for the winter. There, according to one report, they received urgent representations from the Emperor Alexius, urging them to take no further part in the Crusade and to return home. Alexius had been horrified by the size of the Crusading armies. When he had first appealed to the Pope he had expected individual knights or small companies of trained mercenaries who would submit themselves to his authority and obey his orders; these voracious and utterly undisciplined hordes, some of them religious fanatics, others simple adventurers out for what they could get, had gone through his

1. The name of the see had recently been changed from Olivolo to Castello. It is with Enrico that we encounter this new title for the first time.

dominions like locusts and had totally destroyed that tenuous equilibrium of Christian and infidel on which the survival of his Empire now depended. Nor were they even confining their attacks to the Saracens: that same winter a Pisan fleet had actually been blockading the imperial port of Latakia while Bohemund – who had lost no time in carving out a principality for himself at Antioch – had attacked it simultaneously from the landward side. Considering the long history of Venetian–Byzantine friendship and the favoured treatment enjoyed by the Venetians throughout the Empire, Alexius can hardly have expected them to be guilty of similar conduct; by now, however, he was thoroughly disillusioned with the whole Crusade. If this was what was meant by a Christian alliance, he preferred to carry on alone. Meanwhile he had fought back hard at Latakia and the piratical Pisans had withdrawn, with ill grace, to Rhodes.

Thus, for the first time in their history, the Venetians and the Pisans found themselves face to face. The latter, despite their recent reverse, were in truculent mood; the former, who had watched Pisa's rise to power with misgivings that increased with every passing year, had no intention of allowing these impudent upstarts a share in the rich spoils of the Levant. The battle that followed was long, and costly to both sides. In the end the Venetians made their point; with twenty Pisan ships taken, together with 4,000 prisoners – nearly all of whom were released shortly afterwards – they were able to extract an undertaking from their defeated rival to withdraw altogether from the eastern Mediterranean. Like all such undertakings made under temporary duress, however, it was soon forgotten; and that encounter off the Rhodian shore proved to be only the first round in Venice's struggle with her commercial rivals which was ultimately to be measured not in years but in centuries.[1]

There can be few clearer indications of the spirit in which Venice had embarked on the Crusade than the fact that, six months after her fleet had set out, it had still not struck a single blow for Christendom, nor indeed even reached the Holy Land. As always in her history, Venice put her own interests first; and even now, as winter turned to spring, those interests demanded a few more weeks' delay for the greater glory of the Republic. Shortly before his departure, Bishop Enrico had visited his father's church of S. Nicolò on the Lido and prayed that it might be given to him to bring back the body of its patron from Myra to Venice. Now the city of Myra, St Nicholas's own bishopric and the place of his burial, stands on the mainland of Lycia almost opposite Rhodes. It had

---

1. There is a painting of this battle, by Vicentino, in the northernmost oval on the ceiling of the Sala dello Scrutinio of the Doges' Palace.

been largely destroyed by the Seljuk Turks, but the great church still stood – as indeed it still does – over the saint's tomb. The Venetians landed, burst in and soon came upon three coffins of cypress wood. In the first two they found the remains of St Theodore and of St Nicholas's uncle; the third, that of the saint himself, was empty. They interrogated the churchwardens, even subjecting them to physical violence in their determination to discover the whereabouts of the body; the unfortunate officials could only stammer that it was no longer in their possession, having been removed some years before by certain merchants from Bari. But the Bishop remained incredulous. Falling to his knees, he prayed loudly for the sacred hiding-place to be revealed. And, sure enough, just as the party was about to leave in disgust, a sudden fragrance in a remote corner of the church led them to another tomb. In it – so the story goes – lay the uncorrupted body of St Nicholas, clutching the palm, still fresh and green, that he had brought back from Jerusalem. All three corpses were triumphantly embarked and the ships, their mission accomplished, set sail at last for Palestine.

After the capture of Jerusalem in July 1099 the Crusading leaders had chosen as their sovereign Godfrey, Duke of Lower Lorraine. Refusing to wear a crown in the city where Christ had worn a crown of thorns, Godfrey had adopted the title of Defender of the Holy Sepulchre, and it was in this capacity that he received, in the middle of June 1100, a report that a large Venetian fleet had put in at Jaffa. The fighting was by no means over; much of the country still lay under Saracen occupation and Godfrey's own naval resources were poor. He hastened down to the coast to welcome the new arrivals, but by the time he reached Jaffa he was far from well. As he had stopped off on his way to attend a banquet given in his honour by his vassal, the Saracen Emir of Caesarea, there were the inevitable rumours of poison. In fact the trouble is more likely to have been typhoid; but at all events Godfrey was barely able to receive the Venetian leaders before being forced to retire in a state of collapse to Jerusalem – leaving his cousin, Count Warner of Gray, to negotiate on his behalf.

The Venetians' terms were hardly redolent of selfless Crusading zeal. In recognition of their assistance they asked free trading rights throughout the Frankish state, a church and a market in every Christian town and, in addition, a third of every other town that they might help to capture in the future. Finally, in return for an annual tribute, they demanded the entire city of Tripoli. Even if all this was granted, they undertook to remain in the Holy Land on this first visit for only two months, until 15 August.

It was a hard, typically Venetian bargain; and the speed with which the Franks accepted it shows how desperate they were for naval support. It was agreed that the first objective should be Acre, and that Haifa should follow; unfortunately for Crusading plans, however, a strong north wind delayed the ships near Jaffa, and while they were still there the news reached them that Godfrey was dead. Here was a problem. The Frankish leaders were all anxious to be in Jerusalem during the disputes over the succession and the inheritances that were bound to ensue. On the other hand, there was now less than a month before the date fixed by the Venetians for their return; it was unthinkable not to make use of a fleet whose cooperation had been so dearly bought. Further discussions accordingly produced a compromise: the assault on Acre would be postponed; the immediate objective would be Haifa, nearer and less strongly fortified.

Although Haifa was defended by a small Egyptian garrison, the real force of its resistance came from the predominantly Jewish population who, remembering what had happened to their brethren in Jerusalem less than a year before, fought with a bitter determination to preserve their city. But the Venetian mangonels and siege machines were too much for them, and on 25 July – within a week of Godfrey's death – they were obliged to surrender. Their fears proved to have been fully justified. A few managed to escape; the majority, Jews and Muslims alike, were struck down where they stood.

The Venetians themselves are unlikely to have played a leading part in the massacre. They were not a bloodthirsty people – merchants, not murderers. The Franks on the other hand had been guilty of this sort of thing before, not only in Jerusalem but in Galilee as well. The fact remains that this was a military alliance, and since Michiel, Contarini and their followers were present it is impossible to absolve the Venetians altogether from responsibility. Whether they themselves were conscious of it we cannot say; no mention of any atrocity occurs in the sketchy Venetian records. Nor is there any indication that they received the rewards guaranteed to them a month before, though they may have agreed to defer these until the political crisis was over. Soon after the fall of Haifa they set sail for home bearing with them, apart from the trophies and merchandise from the Holy Land, the saintly relics they had brought from Myra. On their arrival, which was neatly timed for St Nicholas's Day, they received heroes' welcomes from Doge, clergy and people, and the reputed body of the saint was reverently interred in Domenico Contarini's church on the Lido.

Did the ceremony have a slightly hollow ring? It should have done, because the luckless churchwardens of Myra had told the truth. Thirteen years before the Venetians arrived there, a group of Apulian merchants had indeed removed St Nicholas's body and had carried it back in triumph to Bari, where work had immediately begun on the basilica bearing his name – now one of the most superb romanesque churches in all Italy. Since the crypt of this glorious building had been consecrated as early as 1089 by Pope Urban himself, and since in the intervening years the great church must have been seen by countless Venetian sailors as it rose higher and ever higher above the city, it seems scarcely conceivable that the Doge and his advisers were unaware of the Bariot claims. As far as we know, however, they made no attempt to discredit them. We can only conclude that the whole thing was one gigantic exercise in self-deception; and that the Venetians, normally so level-headed, were yet perfectly capable of persuading themselves that black was white when the honour and glory and profit – for the financial advantages from the pilgrim traffic were not to be despised – of the Republic demanded that they should. So far as they were concerned, the true corpse of St Nicholas lay in his tomb on the Lido. Several centuries were to pass before the claim was discreetly withdrawn.

The new Doge who ascended the throne when Vitale Michiel died in 1102 is a faintly mysterious figure.[1] Of his origins or previous career we know nothing except that he was another member of the Falier family; nor has anyone ever provided a satisfactory explanation of his Christian name, unique in Venetian and indeed Italian history – Ordelafo. It has been pointed out that Falier is only a Venetian variant of the more usual Faledro, in which form his full name would be virtually a palindrome; perhaps therefore, it can be ascribed merely to some fantastic whim on the part of his parents. In any case there can be no doubt that this was the name by which he was generally known; we find it in several contemporary and near-contemporary documents, and also, in its abbreviated form, identifying his portrait (in Byzantine imperial robes) on the *Pala d'Oro*, Pietro Orseolo's great gold altar-screen in St Mark's which in 1105 Ordelafo had had remodelled and enriched.

1. Vitale Michiel's tomb has not survived. Surprisingly enough, however, that of his wife has. She appears to have died shortly before her husband and her tomb is in the atrium of St Mark's, not far from that of Vitale Falier on the other side of the main door.

This work on the *Pala d'Oro* must have been still in progress when Venice suffered the first of those terrible inundations to which, all through her history, she has been subject. They are due to a combination of factors – high tides, heavy rainfall, swollen rivers, strong and persistent south-easterly winds and other geophysical conditions which only have recently been understood. Occurring separately, these factors are quite frequent and cause no particular concern. When they coincide, on the other hand, they can be almost apocalyptic in their horror, and in January 1106 they coincided catastrophically. We need not necessarily believe the contemporary accounts of accompanying phenomena – the unseasonable heat that prostrated man and beast alike, the ominous rumblings from beneath the lagoon, the fish jumping in terror from the water, the meteors flashing across the sky; Venetian floods can be dramatic enough without such trimmings. On this occasion they swept away an entire community. Of the old town of Malamocco, once the capital of all the lagoon settlements, the outer bastion of defence that had so heroically saved the islands of Rialto from Pepin 300 years before, not a building remained. The very land on which it stood crumbled away, and as late as the eighteenth century the ruins of houses and churches, strewn over the bed of the lagoon, could still be discerned at low water. The surviving inhabitants fled, with such of the town's treasures as they had managed to save – including their prize relic, the head of St Fortunatus – to Chioggia, whither the old bishopric was shortly afterwards transferred; only much later did they return to the Lido, to build a new Malamocco on its present, more protected site further along the island to the west.

Though they too had suffered severely, the people of the Rialto doubtless congratulated themselves on having escaped the worst of the deluge; but the terrible year of 1106 had still scarcely begun. Within a few days a fire broke out in the house of the Zen family in SS. Apostoli, destroying the greater part of six parishes before it could be brought under control; and this was followed on 6 April by another, still greater conflagration which, beginning near S. Lorenzo, wiped out no less than twenty-four of the city's churches. Some idea of the fury of the flames, and of the wind which fanned them, can be gained from the fact that at least one of these fires actually crossed the Grand Canal.[1] At that time, it must be remembered, many of the smaller churches and almost all the

1. It did, however, fortunately spare the beautiful little church of S. Giacomo di Rialto which had been built a few years before – probably on the site of an earlier church (see p. 29) – for those using the new market, opened in the adjoining *campo* in 1097. Church and market-place still look much as they did at that time.

private dwellings in Venice were still built of wood; indeed it was only thanks to their stone and marble construction that the Basilica of St Mark and the Doges' Palace escaped with relatively minor damage. Thenceforth, however, the use of wood for building in all but the poorest quarters was actively discouraged. The fallen churches were rebuilt with the little red bricks known as *altinelle* and the hard white stone from Istria – more expensive perhaps, but infinitely more durable, and to this day the basic materials of Venetian architecture.

The after-effects of these three disasters, following so quickly one upon another, must have kept the Venetians fully occupied for the next year or two; and it was not till 1109 that Doge Ordelafo decided that the time had come for another expedition to the Holy Land, which he would lead himself. Once again, Venetian motives were something short of selflessly idealistic. As the Crusaders gradually consolidated their new dominions in Outremer, so the Christian populations had begun to increase and the markets to expand. But the days were past when Venice could rely on her traditional near-monopoly of the Levant trade. Pisa in particular seemed to have forgotten the promise extracted from her at Rhodes barely ten years before, and was obviously determined to assert herself in the eastern Mediterranean; another rising maritime Republic, Genoa, was not far behind. If Venice were not to be elbowed out altogether, her presence in the area was essential – and it would have to be a presence in strength.

Accordingly a Venetian fleet of some 100 sail left the lagoon in the summer of 1110, arriving in Palestine the following October. Its timing was excellent. King Baldwin I, the former Count of Boulogne who had succeeded Godfrey on the throne of Jerusalem – and who, unlike his predecessor, had felt no qualms about adopting the royal title – was besieging Sidon. Despite the assistance of a strong Scandinavian contingent he was not doing well, and the sudden appearance of the Venetians must have seemed like a godsend. Sidon surrendered on 4 December. Surprisingly, Venice does not seem to have received any land or privileges there; instead, she was granted a section of the city of Acre – in whose capture six years earlier she had played no part at all – together with the use of her own weights and measures and the right to maintain a resident magistrate.

These concessions were accepted with a gratitude somewhat tempered by the knowledge that Genoa and Pisa, both of whom had contributed far more to the early success of the Crusade, had been similarly favoured.

There could be no doubt, however, that Venice had done well out of the expedition, the more so since it was probably one of the vessels taking part that called on the return journey at Constantinople, whence it brought back yet another of those important relics by which the Middle Ages set so much store – the badly bruised body of St Stephen the Proto-martyr. On its arrival in Venice Doge Ordelafo carried it on his own shoulders to the ducal barge and, after heated argument between several rival churches all well aware of its potential value in terms of pilgrim traffic, deposited it in the monastery church of S. Giorgio Maggiore. Thenceforth, for nearly seven centuries until the fall of the Republic, the Doges would lead a torchlight procession to attend vespers in the church on Christmas Night, St Stephen's Eve.[1]

And yet, despite the gains borne home from the East and the promise of more to come, Venice felt herself inadequately equipped for the future. In little over a decade she had put some 300 men-of-war to sea, which was no mean achievement in itself; but if she were fully to exploit the new trading possibilities in the Levant – and hold her own against Pisan and Genoese competition – she would need more, both fighting vessels and merchantmen. An ambitious new shipbuilding programme was called for, and it was now that Doge Ordelafo made his most enduring contribution to the Republic. Hitherto the shipwrights of Venice had been scattered about all over the lagoon, many if not all of them running small private businesses of their own. Under his aegis shipbuilding became a nationalized industry. For its centre he chose two marshy little islands known as the *Zemelle* – 'the twins' in Venetian dialect – at the far end of the Riva to the east of the city; and here, over the next half-century, there grew up that mighty complex of dockyards, foundries, magazines and workshops for carpenters, sailmakers, ropemakers and blacksmiths that Dante described in the *Inferno* and that gave a new word to the English language and many others besides – the Arsenal.[2]

Naturally it would be rather longer before the Arsenal attained that formidable pitch of efficiency in mass production which ultimately enabled it to employ over 16,000 workers – nearly all of them specialists – and, when operating at full capacity, to turn out fully-equipped warships at the rate of one every few hours. Yet within little more than a decade it had transformed the Republic's shipbuilding. Never again would Venice, faced with a sudden emergency, have to rely on whatever vessels in a

1. St Stephen's tomb can still be seen in the north transept, whither it was moved in 1581 from the choir.

2. The word itself comes from the Arabic *Dar Sina'a* – House of Construction.

reasonable state of seaworthiness happened to be on hand. From now on she could plan ahead, undertaking long-term shipbuilding programmes as the situation demanded and state finances allowed. More important still, she could standardize designs and build up stores of spare parts, making it possible to complete even major refits in a fraction of the time that had previously been required. In such conditions too the designs themselves, as well as the techniques, could be revolutionized. It may be no coincidence that the foundation of the Arsenal roughly coincides with the development of rib and plank construction, by which a ship was assembled on a previously erected skeletal framework rather than being built steadily upwards from keel to gunwales; it is certainly true that the beginning of the twelfth century marks the moment when Venice began to design certain vessels primarily for war, and others for trade.

This distinction, however, must not be exaggerated. One of the secrets of Venice's rise to power lay in the fact that she never saw the twin necessities of defence and commerce as altogether separate. Her war captains, then and later, were never averse to trading on the side – a predisposition which meant that many of her military expeditions actually paid for themselves – while her merchant vessels had always to be ready to defend themselves against pirates or, occasionally, competitors. In feudal Europe, where the fighting nobility remained haughtily aloof from trade, such a system would have been unthinkable, but in Venice there was no separate military caste; the nobles were merchants, the merchants noble, and the interests of both were identical. Similarly, the warships produced by the Arsenal were endowed with as much storage space for additional cargoes as could be devised, and the merchantmen given plenty of provision for defence.

Even the Arsenal, however, could not function without raw materials; and the source of the most vital of those materials, timber, was soon seriously threatened. By far the greater part of it came from across the Adriatic, where the thickly wooded islands off the Dalmatian coast furnished an almost inexhaustible supply. The problem was that this territory, as we have seen, had long been coveted by the otherwise landlocked Kingdom of Hungary. Some years previously the Hungarian King Coloman, having annexed the Kingdom of Croatia, had descended upon the coast and captured several of its principal cities – an act of naked aggression which Venice, at that time fully occupied in the East, had been obliged to suffer in silence. Now at last she was able to retaliate. With the help of both Emperors, Henry V – who had visited the city two months before – and Alexius Comnenus, the cities were recovered;

alas, as soon as the conquerors had left for home the Hungarians swept down again. Ordelafo turned about at once and resumed the fight; but not for long. A week or two later, in the summer of 1118, he was killed in battle beneath the walls of Zara.[1]

Doge Ordelafo Falier, in the sixteen years of his reign, had won the deep affection and respect of his people. He had been a born leader of men and, seeing him fall, his followers – who, like all Venetians, hated to fight on land – panicked and fled. The Hungarians pursued them, cutting them down as they ran, and it was only a small proportion of those who had set out so confidently, so short a time before, that returned with the grim news to Venice.

Ordelafo's successor, Domenico Michiel, though present at Zara, had been powerless to prevent the rout. He was no coward; indeed the Altino Chronicle describes him as *vir bellicosus*, and in the years to come he was to give plenty more evidence of his valour. As the grandson of Doge Vitale Michiel and the son of Giovanni, leader of the 1099 expedition to the East, he had been brought up as a patriot, in the firm Venetian tradition of public service. Yet his first act as Doge was to send an embassy to Coloman's son, King Stephen II, to sue for peace. Considering the weakness of his position, the terms he gained were remarkable. Stephen willingly agreed to a five-year truce, during which a large part of the coast, together with the cities and the all-important forests, was allowed to remain in Venetian hands.

This generosity on the part of the Hungarians may to some extent have been due to the news that was trickling in during the summer of 1118 from Palestine. On 2 April, King Baldwin had died. Four months later, on 15 August, the Emperor Alexius Comnenus had followed him to the grave. Meanwhile the Saracens were growing stronger. The future of Christianity in the East looked bleak. Even in the West, the spectacle it presented was hardly edifying. The old struggle between Empire and Papacy showed no sign of being resolved; and when Pope Paschal II had died the previous January, the Emperor Henry V had been so outraged at the choice of his successor Gelasius II that he had nominated an anti-Pope and installed him at the Lateran, driving Gelasius into exile. The example was scarcely edifying; still, this was clearly no time for Christian nations to squabble amongst themselves. The two most powerful states in the central Mediterranean must compose their differences, if only temporarily, for Christ and the common good.

1. See the painting by Aliense in the Sala dello Scrutinio of the Doges' Palace.

Such, at least, seem to have been the arguments of the Doge's ambassadors, and as such King Stephen accepted them. How sincerely they were really believed in Venice is another question. The Venetians had many qualities but, as they had already demonstrated, crusading fervour was not one of them. They were interested in the Crusade only in so far as it opened up new commercial possibilities; it mattered little, if at all, to them whether their trading partners were Christian or Muslim so long as goods were delivered at the right prices and bills paid on time. It was four years more before they were to launch another expedition to the East; and when they did so their motives were, to say the least, mixed.

Not that their help was anything but desperately needed; for by then the Frankish states of Outremer were facing the gravest crisis in their short history. In June 1119 one of their leading princes, Roger of Antioch, had perished with virtually his entire army in a battle appropriately known as the Field of Blood; henceforth, just at the time they needed it most, they were to suffer from an acute shortage of manpower. Their problems were further aggravated by a fleet from Fatimid Egypt, whose ceaseless patrolling of the coast had made regular sea communications almost impossible. King Baldwin II's immediate reaction to the news of the Field of Blood had therefore been to appeal to Venice for help. The new Pope, Calixtus II, had supported him; and before the end of the year a general assembly of all the citizens of Venice had decided – though by no means unanimously – to respond.

Their decision was also influenced by another consideration. For some years now their relations with the Byzantine Empire had been deteriorating. We have seen how, at the time of the First Crusade, they had disregarded the pleas of Alexius Comnenus that they should return home. Even before then, their commercial expansion in the ports of the Aegean and the Black Sea had far exceeded what the Emperor had intended when he had granted special privileges to Domenico Selvo in 1082; and the process had continued until the Empire's own trade was threatened with strangulation. Thus, when Alexius's son John II succeeded to the Byzantine throne in 1118 one of his first acts had been to withdraw these privileges. The Venetians, he gave them to understand, were welcome to continue their normal mercantile activity; from now on, however, they would enjoy only the same treatment as was accorded to their competitors.

The anger with which this news was received on the Rialto was not altogether unjustified. On the assumption that the 1082 treaty would endure, the Venetians had involved themselves in considerable capital outlay; Genoa and Pisa were already giving them cause for concern; and this new blow was more than they were prepared to accept without active protest. The Doge's flagship that sailed out of the lagoon on 8 August 1122 with seventy-one men-of-war and many other smaller vessels in its wake may well have flown the Cross of Christ at its masthead; but it was directed, at least in the first instance, against a Christian and not an infidel enemy.

The fleet's initial objective was no further distant than Corfu, the scene of Venice's humiliation at the hands of Robert Guiscard nearly forty years before. The island had long been an important Byzantine outpost, defended by a strong and determined garrison. The Venetians besieged it for six months to no avail. They would probably have remained still longer had they not been recalled to their crusading vow by a ship sent specially from Palestine with reports of a new disaster: King Baldwin had been taken prisoner. Their presence was required at once if the Latin East was to survive. Reluctantly Doge Michiel gave the order to weigh anchor; but even then he seems to have felt no real urgency. In the course of a leisurely journey eastward he stopped to attack Greek shipping wherever he found it, and – if the Byzantine historian John Cinnamus is to be believed – even turned north into the Aegean, raiding and plundering Lesbos and Chios as well as Rhodes and Cyprus before dropping anchor at the end of May 1123 in the port of Acre.

Now at last the Venetians made amends for their past desultoriness. The Egyptian fleet, they learned, had given up its attempt to blockade Jaffa and had moved south again; it was now lying off Ascalon, the only coastal stronghold, apart from Tyre, still in Muslim hands. That was all the Doge needed to know. He quickly dispatched a flotilla of small ships in pursuit, to lure the Egyptians into battle, while the bulk of his fleet followed just below the horizon. The plan worked beautifully. No sooner had the Egyptians engaged than they found themselves surrounded and overwhelmingly outnumbered. Scarcely a single vessel escaped destruction or capture, the Doge himself winning particular distinction by personally sailing against the flagship of the Fatimid Admiral and sinking it. His victory was more decisive than he knew. Particularly since the loss of Sicily to the Normans at the end of the previous century, Muslim shipwrights had suffered from a chronic shortage of good timber, for which they were obliged to rely on imports from Europe; and when, for strategic reasons, these supplies were cut off[1] – or largely so – they were no longer able to build new vessels or even to keep existing ones in

1. The first such embargo had been ordered by Pietro Candiano IV as early as 960.

good repair. The Venetian victory off Ascalon thus effectively marked the end of Saracen sea power in the eastern Mediterranean.

When Domenico Michiel returned in triumph to Acre – having captured, by way of a bonus, ten fully-laden merchantmen *en route* – there was some hard bargaining to be done. The Franks were determined to make full use of his fleet for the capture of Tyre or Ascalon or both; but the Doge, having proved its worth so conclusively, was in a strong position. Negotiations dragged on for months. They were still in progress at Christmas, when Michiel attended the Nativity celebrations at Bethlehem and was royally entertained in Jerusalem by the Patriarch and other representatives of the captive King. Finally, in the first weeks of 1124, agreement was reached and a treaty signed. Its terms were even more favourable to the Venetians than those agreed in 1100, which Count Godfrey's death had rendered void. In every town of the Kingdom they were granted a street with a church, baths and a bakery, together with exemption from all tolls and customs dues. Their right to the use of their own weights and measures was confirmed, not only for transactions between themselves but for all others as well. Finally, they were promised a third of the cities of Tyre and Ascalon if they helped in their capture.

Now that the Doge knew where he stood, he delayed no longer but sailed northward to Tyre, while the Frankish army marched up simultaneously along the coast. Then as now, Tyre occupied the end of a short and narrow peninsula; its only link with the mainland was an artificial isthmus – hardly more than a causeway – which Alexander the Great had constructed nearly fifteen centuries before. Along this there ran an aqueduct, a lifeline for a city whose own wells and cisterns were quite inadequate for its population. Few places, in short, were more vulnerable to siege. Michiel beached his ships – all except one, which maintained a constant patrol round the seaward approaches – cut the aqueduct and, on 15 February 1124, began the siege.

Despite a steady bombardment from mangonels and catapults, the Tyrians defended their city bravely. The cisterns were full after the winter rains and food stocks were high; there was also a good chance of relief by the Egyptians from the sea or by a land army promised by the Emir of Damascus. But neither came. The Egyptian navy had not yet recovered from its recent defeat, and the Emir dared not march without its support. With the advent of high summer the parched garrison was obliged to capitulate. According to the terms of its surrender, there was no looting; the Christian army marched in on 7 July, and the standard of the King of Jerusalem was hoisted over the main gate, flanked on the two side towers by those of Tripoli and Venice. Michiel accepted his promised third of the city, which was given a Venetian governor, Venetian laws and a magnificent church dedicated to St Mark.

The Venetian overseas empire had begun; it was to endure nearly seven centuries, until the final downfall of the Republic – longer than any other in European history. But the Doge himself remained at Tyre no longer than the few days necessary to see that the Franks were true to their bargain. It was now two years since he had left Venice. Although the expedition had been an unqualified success, it had lasted long enough. One more coastal city remained in infidel hands – Ascalon – and the rewards for assisting in its capture would be considerable. But Ascalon would have to wait – which, for another thirty-nine years, it did. Well pleased with what he had achieved, Michiel returned home with his fleet, stopping only to eject the Hungarians from Spalato and to make a few casual raids on such Byzantine islands as he chanced to pass on the way. With him, it need hardly be noted, went still more relics – the body of St Donatus, brought from Cephalonia and now interred in the exquisite Romanesque church dedicated to him on the island of Murano; that of St Isidore, looted from Chios in circumstances not, perhaps, quite so ideal as those depicted on the wall of his chapel in the north transept of St Mark's; and finally the granite slab on which Christ himself is said to have stood when he preached to the men of Tyre, and which now crowns the altar in the baptistery of the Basilica.

Thus Domenico Michiel was in his turn received with exultation by his subjects, and when in the following year he scored more notable victories against the Hungarians in Dalmatia and the Byzantines in Cephalonia – inducing John Comnenus to restore all the commercial privileges he had withdrawn on his accession – his reputation was assured for ever. In later centuries, indeed, it became almost legendary. Certainly he is the only Doge to be commemorated three times over, by three different painters, in the Sala dello Scrutinio of the Doges' Palace which, with the neighbouring Sala del Maggior Consiglio, can be considered Venice's Hall of Fame;[1] and of the three events there portrayed, only one – the victory over the Egyptian fleet off Ascalon, by Peranda, above the third window on the Piazzetta side – is as historically accurate as even a Renaissance painter might be expected to make it. Further along the same wall there is a picture by Aliense described in the standard guide-

1. The triumphal arch along the end wall contains six small pictures by Lazzarini to the greater glory of the Doge Francesco Morosini, but these all form part of a single design.

book[1] as 'the Doge giving orders for sails and steering gear of the Venetian fleet to be pulled ashore, in order to demonstrate to the allies that the Venetian galleys will not depart until Tyre has been taken'. No chronicler of the time mentions such a gesture; the beaching of ships was normal practice if they were to remain unused for any length of time, and there is no reason to suppose that Michiel had any other idea in mind when he ordered it. The third picture, a small ceiling oval by Bambini, shows the Doge refusing the Crown of Sicily – which he was never offered. His last five years were in fact devoid of any foreign adventures; wisely, he concentrated on affairs within the Republic, where he instituted among other things a rudimentary form of street lighting – making Venice the first city in Europe, with the possible exception of Constantinople, to be regularly and compulsorily lit at night. Already in his day the *ancone* – those little, typically Venetian shrines to the Virgin or parish patron saint at the corners of the canals and principal *calli* – were beginning to appear in profusion; it was Domenico Michiel who, in 1128, arranged that a lamp should be lit in each of them at nightfall, the responsibility for its maintenance devolving on the local parish priest, the cost on the Republic. Then, two years later, after an eleven-year reign, he resigned the dogeship and retired to the monastery of S. Giorgio Maggiore, where he died soon afterwards and where his tomb still stands.

1. Lorenzetti.

· 8 ·

Between Two Empires

[1130–1172]

Perchè una gente impera e l'altra langue,
Seguendo lo giudicio di costei,
Che è occulta come in erba l'angue.

Therefore some rise to empire, some debase
According to the judgment of her pleasure
Who lieth hidden like a snake in grass.

Dante, *Inferno*, VII, 82
(Tr. J. I. Minchin)

The accession of the thirty-year-old Pietro Polani to the ducal throne left vacant by his father-in-law Domenico Michiel occurred within only a few weeks of two other elevations, far more momentous: of Norman Sicily from the status of a County to that of a Kingdom, and of Count Roger II de Hauteville, Robert Guiscard's nephew, to be its King. In Venetian eyes – indeed, in the eyes of most of Europe – the means by which Roger had achieved this success were not above reproach. A disputed papal election some months before had left two rival candidates, each with an arguably good claim, struggling for the Pontificate; one of them, Innocent II, thanks to the passionate advocacy of St Bernard of Clairvaux, soon had the greater part of Western Christendom behind him; the other, Anacletus, had turned to Roger, who had demanded a royal crown as the price of his support. In the circumstances, it was hardly to be expected that the partisans of Innocent would recognize the new Kingdom – which, moreover, both the Eastern and the Western Empires still claimed for their own; and their reluctance was still further increased by the disturbing speed with which Sicily under the Hautevilles had risen to wealth, prosperity and power. From its position in the dead centre of the Mediterranean the island commanded the trade routes between North and South, East and West, constituting a crossroads and a market-place for three continents; its Byzantine and Islamic past, together with its thriving Greek and Arab populations still living harmoniously together, gave the Sicilian ports a cosmopolitan character that no others could match. In the past two years Roger had absorbed into his own dominions virtually the whole Italian peninsula south of Rome, formerly the property of his feckless and fortunately infertile cousins; and this latest *coup*, by which he was enabled to treat with the princes of Europe as an equal, augured ill for the future.

Nowhere was this alarm more deeply felt than in Venice. Already Sicilian sea power was beginning to rival that of the Republic; and while the bazaars of Palermo and Catania, Messina and Syracuse grew more and more crowded, so dealings on the Rialto had begun, gently but perceptibly, to slacken. To make matters worse, Venetian merchantmen were suffering ever more frequent attacks from Sicilian privateers; by 1135 they could estimate their losses at 40,000 talents. When therefore in that same year a diplomatic delegation from Constantinople called in Venice on its way to the court of the Western Emperor Lothair II in search of financial and naval help for a projected joint expedition against the so-called King of Sicily, Polani not only agreed with enthusiasm but attached to the Byzantine party representatives of his own to lend additional weight to their appeal.

The expedition was duly mounted, and invaded South Italy the following year; but it was military rather than naval and Venice was not in the event asked to participate. This, as it happened, was just as well: despite a few tactical successes, the venture had no lasting effect on Sicilian power or prestige. The old Emperor himself died in December 1137 on his return journey across the Alps; less than eight weeks later the anti-Pope Anacletus followed him to the grave; and in July 1139 Pope Innocent, riding south at the head of an army of his own, was ambushed by Roger and taken prisoner, being released only after he had reluctantly confirmed his captor as the lawful King of Sicily.

The Norman menace was now graver than ever, but for the time being nothing could be done; the new Emperor-elect of the West,[1] Conrad of Hohenstaufen, was too occupied with internal problems in Germany. The papal *curia* had somehow to readjust its policies to the idea that the boisterous new Kingdom on its southern borders was there to stay. In Constantinople John Comnenus remained steadfast in his determination to crush 'the Sicilian usurper'; but in the spring of 1143, while hunting in Cilicia, he accidentally scratched himself with a poisoned arrow and within a few days was dead of septicaemia. In Venice, too,

1. Technically, the ruler of the Empire did not become Emperor until he was crowned by the Pope in Rome. This Conrad never managed to achieve; until his death, therefore, he had to content himself with the uncrowned Emperor's title of King of the Romans.

Doge Polani was busy with affairs nearer home. In 1141 the little city of Fano appealed for help against domineering neighbours who threatened to attack her. Never one to let slip a chance to extend her authority, Venice agreed; and the terms of this first treaty ever made between the Republic and another Italian city show as clearly as anything could the position that Venice had now acquired among the populations of the Adriatic coast. Every Venetian henceforth was to enjoy in Fano the same privileges as the native citizens, with a right to Venetian judges in any lawsuit involving both cities. The Fanesi, for their part, were obliged to declare themselves subject allies of the Republic, saving only their fealty – such as it was – to the Western Empire. They were also bound to the payment of an annual tribute, in the form of 1,000 measures of oil for the illumination of St Mark's and 100 for the Doges' Palace.

Two years later there was trouble with the Paduans, who began without warning to divert the course of the Brenta. Their purpose was to shorten the river trip to the lagoon outlets; they little realized what the Venetians knew all too well – that the slightest interference with the geographical system of the lagoon risks upsetting that almost unbelievably delicate balance between land and water which is essential for Venice's survival. Faced with the prospect of vast accumulations of sand forming around Sant' Ilario and the silting up of the existing channels on which they depended, the Venetians lodged a strong protest; and when this was arrogantly rejected they immediately took up arms. The conclusion was inevitable. The Paduans could never hope to match their neighbours in a trial of strength. After a single brief and disastrous confrontation they surrendered, with the promise to pursue their project no further and to repair the damage already done. What, however, is far more important – and indeed the only reason why so trivial an incident is worth mentioning at all in this book – is the fact that in this, the first campaign in her history to be waged entirely on land, Venice engaged mercenaries to do the fighting for her, under the two leading *condottieri* of the day, Guido di Montecchio of Verona[1] commanding the cavalry and Alberto da Bragacurta the infantry. One reason was doubtless the Venetians' lack of experience on an element that always remained foreign to them; they may also, however, have felt the first stirrings of that fear that was later to become an obsession – that any native-born general, returning victorious, might enjoy a prestige and popularity unbecoming a citizen of the Republic, and possibly constituting even a danger to the state. Later centuries, when the *condottieri* were to seize power in city after city

1. The Montecchi are the Montagues of Shakespeare's *Romeo and Juliet*.

until they came to dominate most of North and Central Italy, were to show that such a fear was by no means unjustified.

The Emperor John Comnenus had been succeeded on the throne of Byzantium by his son Manuel, a young man still in his twenties, famous for his dark good looks and possessing none of his father's xenophobic tendencies. His early life had been passed in close contact with the Frankish knights of Outremer, and his admiration for Western institutions had even led him to introduce knightly tournaments to Constantinople – an innovation which, particularly when he took part in them himself, scandalized his older subjects. He was, moreover, an intellectual and a scholar who cannot have failed to be impressed by the reports he had received of the growing brilliance of the court at Palermo which, thanks to Roger's patronage of the arts and sciences, was rapidly becoming the cultural clearing-house of Europe, the one focal point where the leading thinkers of the three great civilizations of the Mediterranean – Latin, Greek and Arab – could meet together for their mutual enlightenment.

Manuel was fully aware of the danger posed by Norman Sicily. But he also knew that with two-thirds of Asia Minor – formerly the main recruiting-ground for Byzantine armies – now occupied by the Seljuk Turks and his western frontier also under constant pressure, his own Empire would have to fight for survival. Had his father been right in his determined hostility to the Sicilian Kingdom? Would it not be wiser to try and make common cause? Soon after his accession he sent an Embassy to Palermo to investigate the possibilities of an alliance, which he hoped might be cemented by the marriage of a Byzantine princess to one of the King's sons.

If these negotiations had succeeded, the consequences for Venice might have been serious indeed, with Roger of Sicily exercising effective control of both sides of the straits of Otranto. But they failed, and Manuel turned instead to the still more important question of his own marriage, to the sister-in-law of the Emperor-elect Conrad, which took place at the beginning of 1146. Just three months afterwards, on Palm Sunday, there followed an event that was to affect the whole civilized world. St Bernard of Clairvaux launched the Second Crusade.

St Bernard's excursions into the political sphere – which, unfortunately, he was throughout his life unable to resist – were almost invariably disastrous; but none ever proved so humiliating a fiasco as this immense expedition, led jointly by Conrad and King Louis VII of France with the purpose of recovering the city of Edessa from the Saracens and consolidating Frankish power in the Levant. Numberless thousands died before they ever reached the Holy Land; those that survived the journey fled after their first and only armed encounter. It is a measure of the paucity of our sources for the Venetian history of the time that we cannot be altogether sure whether Venice participated with a fleet or not. Although one chronicler – Marino Sanudo the elder, writing in the early fourteenth century – tells of the *magnum auxilium* sent by the Republic under the command of Giovanni Polani, the Doge's brother, his report is unsubstantiated by any other historian of the Crusade and can almost certainly be discounted. But the Venetians were not to be left in peace for long. In the first weeks of 1148 they received an urgent appeal from Manuel: a Sicilian fleet had sailed against his Empire.

The commander of this fleet was George of Antioch, a Levantine Greek who had risen from humble origins to be the first holder of Norman Sicily's proudest title – Emir of Emirs, at once the High Admiral[1] and chief minister of the Kingdom. He had first taken Corfu, which had surrendered without a struggle and willingly accepted a Sicilian garrison of 1,000 men. Rounding the Peloponnese and dropping further armed detachments at strategic points along the coast, he had then sailed north again as far as Euboea, raiding and pillaging as he went. A particularly rich haul had been afforded by the ancient city of Thebes, centre of the Byzantine silk manufacture, whence not only bales of damasks and brocades but also a number of highly skilled Jewish workwomen had been seized and carried off to enrich the royal silk factory (which did double duty as a harem) at Palermo. Turning back, he had finally plundered Corinth, his vessels – according to his near contemporary, Nicetas Choniates – 'by now so low in the water that they looked more like merchantmen than the pirate ships they really were'.

Nicetas was right: piracy it was. But it was also something more. King Roger was under no delusions. An attempted alliance between himself and the Byzantine Emperor having proved unworkable, he knew that it was only a question of time before Manuel, probably in conjunction with Venice and the Western Empire, launched a major offensive against him. His own pre-emptive action might precipitate the attack – no bad thing in itself if it caused Manuel to strike before he was ready – but it had at least assured him the possession of chosen strongpoints on the Balkan peninsula and, in Corfu, the principal bridgehead from which any invasion of South Italy might be expected to come.

1. The word *Admiral* is in fact derived, through Norman Sicily, from the Arabic title of *Emir*.

No Venetian ever gave anything for nothing, and Manuel had to grant further extensive trading privileges in Cyprus and Rhodes, as well as in his own capital, before he got what he wanted – the full support of the war fleet of the Republic for six months. Meanwhile he was working desperately to bring his own navy to readiness – some 500 galleys and 1,000 transports, a fitting counterpart to an army of perhaps 20,000 or 25,000 men.

From the outset, this formidable joint force was ill-starred. Though the rendezvous was fixed for April 1148, both sides were grievously delayed – the Greeks by a sudden invasion of the Kumans, a tribe from South Russia who chose this moment to sweep down across the Danube into imperial territory, the Venetians by the death of Doge Polani. It was autumn before the two navies could meet in the southern Adriatic, together to begin the siege of Corfu, and the following spring before the army could join them, accompanied by the Emperor himself in overall command.

The siege, Manuel discovered, on his arrival, was not going well. The citadel in which Roger's garrison was holding out stood on a high crag, towering above the sea and safely beyond the range of Byzantine projectiles. Nicetas reported that the Greeks seemed to be shooting at the very sky itself, while the Sicilians could release deluges of arrows and hailstorms of rocks on to the besiegers. (People wondered, he could not resist adding, how they had taken possession of it so effortlessly the previous year.) More ominous still, perhaps, was the steady worsening of relations between Greeks and Venetians – reaching a climax when the latter occupied a neighbouring islet and set fire to a number of Byzantine vessels lying offshore. They later managed to seize possession of the imperial flagship itself, on which they performed an elaborate charade, making fun of the Emperor's swarthy complexion by dressing up an Ethiopian slave in the imperial vestments and staging a mock coronation on deck in full view of their Greek allies.

Manuel was never to forgive the Venetians this insult. For the moment, however, they were his allies still, and indispensable ones at that. With patience, tact and all the charm for which he was famous, he somehow restored an uneasy harmony; then he himself assumed direct personal command of the siege operations.

Towards the end of the summer Corfu fell – probably through treachery, since Nicetas writes that the garrison commander subsequently entered the imperial service. The Emperor's joy, however, must have been mitigated by the news that George of Antioch had now taken another fleet of forty ships through the Dardanelles and across the Marmara to the very walls of Constantinople. A landing had mercifully been prevented but the Sicilians, undeterred, had sailed on some way up the Bosphorus, pillaging several rich villas along the Asiatic shore, and on their return had even for good measure shot an impudent arrow or two into the gardens of the imperial palace. Nor, once he had recaptured Corfu, was Manuel able to follow up his victory. He was summoned urgently northward to deal with a new insurrection in the Balkans – in which Roger, whose diplomatic tentacles extended far beyond his own shores, may well have been subtly implicated.

So ended the war with Sicily, from which both Venice and Byzantium had expected so much. Apart from the reconquest of a single island captured barely two years before, it had achieved nothing. Sicilian garrisons still remained strung around the Greek coast; King Roger was as secure on his throne and as powerful in Europe and the Mediter-ranean as ever he had been. Looking back on it in historical perspective, we can now see that the most noteworthy aspect of the war was also perhaps the most unedifying: for in that first sorry fracas between the two so-called allies in the water off Corfu lay the seeds of a deepening hostility between Republic and Empire which were to come to their poisonous fruition, fifty-five years later, in the Fourth Crusade.

When in the spring of 1148 Doge Polani had led his fleet out of the lagoon in response to the Byzantine appeal, the sickness that was to cause his death was already upon him. He had progressed no further than Caorle when he was forced to return, and within a few weeks he was dead. For the next seven years and seven months, Venice was ruled by Domenico Morosini. His family had already played a leading part in Venetian affairs for well over 200 years, and in the centuries to come was to provide the Republic with three other Doges besides Domenico. His reign marked, for his subjects, a happy time. By the end of 1149 peace had been made with the Sicilians; on the maps of the great Arab geo-grapher Abu Abdullah Mohammed al-Edrisi, who spent fifteen years at the court in Palermo and in whose work King Roger took an intense personal interest, the northern Adriatic was clearly labelled *Culfus Venetiarum*, and on Roger's death in 1154 his son and successor William I formally conceded all waters north of a line drawn westward from Ragusa as a Venetian preserve. Despite the Corfu incident relations continued on an ostensibly friendly basis with Byzantium, whose recent trading con-cessions were beginning to bring in most gratifying returns; while in

the Western Empire Conrad's nephew Frederick of Swabia, who succeeded his uncle in 1152, confirmed Venetian privileges without demur.
It was no wonder that Morosini's dogeship saw another building boom
in the city, marked above all by the completion, 250 years after the sinking
of its first foundations, of the campanile of St Mark.

In mainland Italy, on the other hand, the clouds were gathering fast.
The 32-year-old Frederick, whose reddish-brown hair and beard were
soon to earn him the nickname of Barbarossa, had ascended the throne
with one overriding objective. 'My wish,' he confessed frankly to the
Pope, 'is to restore to the Roman Empire its ancient greatness and
splendour.' It was a conception that left no room for compromise with
the Empire of the East, nor with Sicily; least of all with the towns and
cities of North Italy, led by Milan, whose spirit of independence, nourished
by successive Popes throughout the long years of papal–imperial struggle,
was every bit as determined as was Frederick's will to break it. The
strength of this spirit, however, seems to have genuinely surprised him
when he entered Italy in October 1154, on the way to his imperial
coronation. All the cities and major towns sent emissaries to greet him
at Roncaglia; but apart from the few who saw in the Empire a chance
to shake off Milanese domination, the overwhelming majority left him
in no doubt of their resolve to break the old feudal fetters in favour of
republican self-government. Frederick for his part was determined to
begin as he meant to go on; Milan was at present too strong for him
but her little ally Tortona, after a heroic resistance of over two months,
was destroyed until not one stone remained on another.

Having thus set what he assumed to be a salutary example, Frederick
continued, in the spring of 1155, on his journey southwards to Rome.
Predictably, in view of his general arrogance and unwillingness to
compromise, his way was not altogether smooth. His first meeting,
near Sutri, with the newly-elected Pope Adrian IV – the only Englishman
ever to occupy the Throne of St Peter – was exacerbated by his refusal
to perform the traditional courtesy of holding the papal stirrup when
Adrian dismounted. The Pope retaliated by denying him the Kiss of
Peace, and two days were lost before conversations could begin. On
this occasion Frederick was persuaded to relent; but when, a day or two
later, a delegation from the Roman Senate rode out to greet him and to
request the monetary payments and guarantees normally given by Emperors at the time of their coronation, his curt dismissal of them had more
serious results. Thanks to brilliant planning by the Pope, he was able
to slip unobserved into Rome at dawn on 17 June for a secret coronation,

but within hours the city had risen in revolt against him and by nightfall well over 1,000 Roman insurgents and imperial troops were lying dead in the streets or drowned in the Tiber.

Although Venice had sent representatives to make an *acte de présence* at Roncaglia, she had done her utmost to remain aloof from the events that followed. As an independent city-republic that had long since freed herself from imperial control, she could hardly be unsympathetic to the Lombard towns that were now striving to do the same; on the other hand her whole political and economic development had pursued so different a course from theirs that there could be no real emotional identification. Unlike them, she was a world power with a world policy – a policy which involved increasingly delicate diplomatic manoeuvring, not just with the Western Empire but with Byzantium and Norman Sicily, the Papacy and the Crusader states, to say nothing of the Saracens of both North Africa and the Middle East. At this particular moment in her history, with her relations with Manuel Comnenus growing increasingly strained and her Italian markets ever more profitable, she had no wish to antagonize Frederick Barbarossa more than was necessary. When Doge Morosini died in 1156, he left behind him a Republic still uncommitted either way.

His successor, Vitale Michiel II, did his best to steer the same middle path, but it was not long before Frederick's actions in Italy forced him to abandon it. Crossing the Alps again in 1158, at the head of an army far stronger than that which he had brought with him four years before, the Emperor called a second diet at Roncaglia, where his attitude still further enraged the Lombard cities; and though some towns still remained loyal to him, within weeks much of North Italy was in a state of open revolt. Meanwhile a great wave of revulsion against the Empire swept down through the peninsula. What was needed above all was a centre of resistance, some strong power able to focus the aspirations and ideals of those who stood for liberty against domination, republicanism against imperialism, Italian against German. Fortunately for the beleaguered cities, two such powers were near at hand: the Papacy and the Kingdom of Sicily.

Two years before, in 1156, Pope Adrian and King William of Sicily had signed a treaty at Benevento. Since then, working both separately and together, papal and Sicilian diplomatists had achieved a good deal; and in August 1159 representatives from four of the most determined of Frederick's Italian enemies – Milan, Crema, Brescia and Piacenza – met the Pope at Anagni and, in the presence of envoys from King William, swore the initial pact that was to become the nucleus of the great Lombard League. The towns promised to have no dealings with the Empire without first obtaining papal consent, while the Pope in return undertook to excommunicate the Emperor after the customary notice of forty days.

It was Adrian's last political act. He was already a sick man, and on the evening of 1 September 1159 he died of angina. His death gave Frederick Barbarossa an opportunity to sow yet more dissension. Recognizing – rightly – that the next Pope if freely elected would be sure to continue along the lines set by his predecessor, the Emperor now deliberately engineered a schism within the papal curia. Consequently, just as Cardinal Roland of Siena – who, as Adrian's Chancellor, had been the principal architect of his foreign policy – was being enthroned in St Peter's as Pope Alexander III, his colleague Cardinal Octavian of S. Cecilia suddenly seized the papal mantle and put it on himself. Alexander's supporters snatched it back; but Octavian had taken the precaution of bringing with him another, into which he somehow managed to struggle – getting it on back to front in the process. He then made a dash for the throne, sat on it, and proclaimed himself Pope Victor IV. It was hardly an edifying performance; but it worked. Frederick's ambassadors in Rome immediately recognized Victor as the rightful Pontiff. Virtually all the rest of western Europe soon gave its allegiance to Alexander, but the damage was done and the chaotic Italian political scene was further bedevilled, for the next eighteen years, by a disputed Papacy.

Faced with the need to recognize one or the other of the rival Popes, Venice could no longer stand aloof. She was moreover growing seriously alarmed at the way things were going in Lombardy; if Frederick were to continue in his present mood, he was unlikely to show any greater respect for Venetian independence than for that of any other Italian city. So she too declared for Alexander and, by implication, the Lombard rebels. The Emperor's retaliation was swift but ineffectual. Three nearby cities that had remained passively loyal to him – Padua, Verona and Ferrara – were easily persuaded to attack their proud and often domineering neighbour, but were equally easily repulsed. Perhaps their hearts were not really in it; in 1163 we find two of them, Verona and Padua, joined now by Vicenza, actually combining with Venice in an association pledged to yield no more to Barbarossa than their forefathers had yielded to Charlemagne. A subsequent attack on Grado, launched at Frederick's instigation by a German-born Patriarch of Aquileia, was even less successful. A Venetian fleet sped to the rescue and took the Patriarch prisoner with some 700 of his followers, releasing him only after he promised to send the Republic a tribute of a dozen pigs – one for each member of his cathedral chapter – every year on the Wednesday before Lent, in time to be chased by the Venetian populace on the following day (*Giovedì Grasso*) round the Piazza.

To Venice, these two incidents were little more than pinpricks. It was her good fortune that, much as Frederick Barbarossa would have liked to see her humbled at his feet, there were three other objectives on the Italian peninsula which had prior claim to his attention and against which he now marched. One was Ancona where, on territory that in Frederick's eyes formed an integral part of the Western Empire, Manuel Comnenus had some years before established a Byzantine outpost; the second, as always, was Norman Sicily; and the third was Rome, where the Emperor was determined to remove Pope Alexander from his throne and replace him with a new imperial puppet. (Frederick's former protégé, the anti-Pope Victor, had altogether failed to establish himself in the city; in 1164 he had died miserably in Lucca, where for a number of years he had eked out a living on the proceeds of not very successful brigandage and where the local authorities would not even allow him burial within the walls.)

The details of this, the most ambitious of all Frederick's Italian campaigns, need not detain us here. It is enough to say that of his first two objectives he achieved nothing; of the third, all too much. Rome, like the cities of the north, was a commune, with a civic government of its own; and the Romans, who had detested Frederick ever since his first ill-starred coronation visit, fought heroically to keep him out. St Peter's itself, hastily ringed with trenches and converted into a fortress, held out for eight days, but to no avail. The imperial troops burst through the great bronze doors leaving, in the words of a contemporary,[1] the marble pavements of the nave strewn with dead and dying, the high altar itself stained with blood. Alexander was forced into hiding, and on 30 July 1167 Victor's successor, the anti-Pope Paschal, celebrated Mass in the Basilica.

For Frederick, already crowned Emperor but now additionally invested with the golden circlet of a Patrician of Rome – a deliberate insult to the Roman Senate – this was the climax of his career. He could not know that four days later his entire army would be stricken by pestilence. So virulent was the epidemic that he had no course but to order an immediate withdrawal. By the time he regained his imperial headquarters at Pavia he had lost well over 2,000 men, including his Chancellor, Archbishop

1. Otto of St Blaise.

Rainald of Dassel, and many of his most trusted lieutenants and advisers.

It was like some dreadful visitation from the Old Testament – and indeed was considered all over Europe as divine retribution for the desecration of St Peter's and the expulsion of God's Vice-Regent on earth. But Frederick's punishment was not yet over. He was still in Pavia, nursing the remains of his shattered army, when on 1 December no less than fifteen of the leading North Italian cities formed themselves into a Greater Lombard League. It was the supreme gesture of defiance; and such was their contempt for the Emperor that they had not even thought it necessary to wait till he had left Italy before making it.

Of this League Venice was a founder member. She had no land forces to offer, but she pledged her navy to the cause anywhere in the lagoons or in the tributary rivers where navigable. She further agreed to share with her confederates any subsidies that she might receive from Constantinople or Palermo, and to obtain their consent before declaring war or concluding peace with any other state. These undertakings were not, it must be admitted, particularly rigorous. The narrow radius within which the Venetian fleet was bound to defend League interests is surely significant; there was no question of sending it beyond the range of immediate recall if a more serious crisis were to arise elsewhere. It seems clear, nevertheless, that the Republic was now looking again – if not in her commercial policy, then at least in her diplomatic alignments – more and more towards the West. By her adherence to the Lombard League in 1167 she had in fact identified herself with the affairs of mainland Italy more closely than at any former time in the five centuries of her existence.

Meanwhile, relations with Byzantium were growing worse and worse. There were a number of reasons, for which neither party was altogether free of blame. The number of Latins permanently resident in Constantinople at this time has been estimated at not less than 80,000, all enjoying the special privileges that Manuel and his predecessors, in moments of weakness, had been forced to grant. Of these, the Venetians were the most numerous, the most favoured and, in all probability, the most objectionable. Nicetas Choniates, chief of the palace secretariat in Constantinople, complains that their colony had become 'so insolent in its wealth and prosperity as to hold the imperial power in scorn'. He may have been right, up to a point: Venetians were never noted for their humbleness of demeanour and they doubtless gave their Byzantine hosts plenty of cause for complaint. But however much Manuel Comnenus may have been mocked by the Venetian sailors off Corfu no Venetian merchant, whether resident on the Rialto or the Bosphorus, would have dreamt of underestimating him. For some years now, the Republic had watched with misgiving while its chief commercial rivals – Genoa, Pisa and Amalfi – had slowly consolidated their positions in what had once been its own exclusive preserve; and its people were fully aware that this process was part of a deliberate policy by Manuel and his father to reduce Venetian influence. They were worried, too, about recent developments in Dalmatia. Since 1162 they had been at war with Stephen III of Hungary, who in the five succeeding years had managed to capture virtually every coastal city except Zara. Then, in 1167, Manuel Comnenus had entered the lists and gained a decisive victory over Stephen, taking these newly conquered territories for himself. It was an act hardly calculated to endear him to the Venetians; and when shortly afterwards he had the audacity to seek their support in establishing a permanent Byzantine colony at Ancona – with the longer-term objective of reviving the old Exarchate of Ravenna – they had left him in no doubt of their feelings.

It was in this atmosphere of mutual suspicion and resentment that, some time early in 1171, the new Genoese settlement at Galata – the district of Constantinople on the further side of the Golden Horn – was attacked and in large measure destroyed. Who was responsible we shall never know. For Manuel, however, here was precisely the chance that he had been looking for. Casting the blame squarely on the Venetians, on 12 March he gave the order for all citizens of the Republic on Byzantine territory to be placed under immediate arrest, their ships and property confiscated. A few managed to escape in a Byzantine warship, put at their disposal by a Venetian-born captain in the imperial service; but the majority were less lucky. In the capital alone, 10,000 were seized; and when all the prisons had been filled to bursting point, monasteries and convents were requisitioned to accommodate the overspill.

The reaction in Venice can be imagined when the news reached the Rialto. The impression that the attack on the Genoese had been nothing but a pretext was confirmed when the Genoese themselves declared that the Venetians had had nothing to do with the incident; the smoothness with which the operation had been carried out simultaneously across the length and breadth of the Empire showed beyond all doubt that it had been carefully planned in advance; and this reflection served in turn as a bitter reminder of how only two years before, to stamp out rumours that he was contemplating an action of this kind, the Emperor had given the emissaries of the Doge specific guarantees for the security of their countrymen – guarantees which had actually attracted further Venetian capital to the East and so increased the spoils he was now enjoying.

The last of the old ties that had bound Venice to Byzantium were forgotten. Forgotten too were the solemn promises of consultation made less than four years previously to the Lombard League. The Venetians were bent on war. Finance was a problem; for some time the government had been overspending, and Venice had in addition been paying the League heavy annual subsidies. In settlement of debts already incurred, all the revenues of the Rialto had been pledged for the next decade. A forced loan was ordered, for which every citizen would be liable according to his means, and to facilitate its collection the city was divided into the six districts, or *sestieri*, which still exist today: Castello, Cannaregio, Dorsoduro, Santa Croce, S. Polo and S. Marco. There was also a serious shortage of manpower; Venetians living abroad – such of them as were not languishing in Manuel's prisons – were recalled home and expected, if not actually forced, to rally to the colours.

Despite these difficulties, and thanks to the draconian measures he adopted to overcome them, in just over three months Doge Michiel was able to raise and man a fleet of over 120 sail. It was an extraordinary achievement, of which no other state would have been capable; and in September 1171 the Doge led his armada out of the lagoon against the Empire of the East. He stopped at various points in Istria and Dalmatia to pick up such Venetian subjects as he might find, then continued round the Peloponnese to Euboea. There he found ambassadors from Manuel awaiting him. They were in a conciliatory mood. Their master, they assured him, had no wish for war. The Doge had only to send a peace mission to Constantinople; he would then find that all differences could be satisfactorily resolved, and on terms that he would not consider unfavourable.

Vitale Michiel accepted. It was the worst mistake of his life. While his emissaries (who included Enrico Dandolo, later to play so fateful a role in European history) continued their journey to the Bosphorus and spent much of the winter in fruitless discussions with Byzantine officials, he took his fleet on to Chios to await developments. It was there that disaster struck. Plague broke out in the overcrowded ships and spread with terrible speed. By early spring thousands were dead, the survivors so weakened and demoralized through sickness and prolonged inactivity as to be unfit for war or anything else. At this point the ambassadors arrived back from Constantinople. They had been abominably treated, and their mission had proved a total failure. The Emperor obviously had not the faintest intention of changing his attitude; his only purpose had been to gain time, while he improved his own defences.

And so, to top all the Doge's other misfortunes, there was now added a further burden – shame and humiliation for his gullibility in falling into so obvious a trap. He could go no further. His expedition had been disastrous; the flower of Venetian youth lay dead or dying, without having once set eyes on the enemy.[1] The fleet, or what remained of it, was on the brink of open mutiny. His only course now was to return with all speed to Venice and face the wrath of his subjects.

He arrived in the middle of May, 1172, and immediately called a general assembly in the palace to which he reported all that had occurred, defending his own actions and decisions as best he could. He was heard in tight-lipped silence – the more so because, to crown all the other misfortunes he had inflicted upon the Republic, he was now seen to have brought back the plague as well. This final incompetence could not be forgiven. The assembly itself rose up against him; and though outside the palace a mob had gathered and was even now calling for his blood, Vitale Michiel saw that he must flee. Slipping out through a side door, he hurried along the Riva towards the convent of S. Zaccaria.

He never reached it. The way to S. Zaccaria led over the Ponte della Paglia and then, 100 yards or so further along the quay, up a narrow alley known as the Calle delle Rasse. Just as he was about to turn the corner, he was set upon by one of the mob who sprang out from the shadows of a neighbouring house and stabbed him to death.

It is hard not to feel sorry for Vitale Michiel. With the implacable Frederick Barbarossa on one side and the unpredictable Manuel Comnenus on the other, with the north of Italy now unified by the Lombard League and the south by the alliance of Norman Sicily with the greatest of twelfth-century Popes, he had had a far more delicate and difficult course to steer through the shoals of European diplomacy than any of his predecessors. For fifteen of his sixteen years as Doge he had steered it beautifully. Only in his last year, in a moment of crisis and in conditions to which he was utterly unaccustomed, did he take a wrong

1. Among them, so the story goes, perished all the surviving male members of the Giustiniani family – except one, a young monk in the monastery of S. Nicolò di Lido. Rather than allow so distinguished a line to die out, the Pope granted him temporary release from his vows. He left the monastery, married the Doge's daughter and did what was expected of him; then, his posterity assured, he returned to his monastery. His wife waited for the children to grow up; later she too took the veil.

decision. Even so, he can hardly be blamed for the plague – nor even altogether for returning with it to Venice, since to have delayed his homecoming any longer would have provoked certain mutiny.

Not surprisingly, perhaps, there is no monument to his name in Venice today; and yet, until only some thirty years ago, his death was more clearly commemorated – for those who knew the story – than that of any other Venetian. Soon after the murder, when his assassin had been brought to justice and executed, orders were given that the latter's house in the Calle delle Rasse should be razed to the ground, and that no stone building should ever be constructed on that spot. This decree was observed until after the Second World War – which is why all pictures and photographs of the Riva dating from before that time disclose, just beyond the Ponte della Paglia, on one of the most architecturally strategic sites in all Venice, a humble group of old houses of wood and plaster. Only in 1948 were the authorities at last persuaded to set the old tradition aside; and even now, as we glance up at the façade of the Danieli Royal Excelsior Hotel, some of us may wonder whether, in a slightly different and infinitely more disagreeable form, the old curse does not still linger over the spot where Vitale Michiel met his death eight centuries ago.

· 9 ·

Reconciliation

[1172–1187]

Non combattete mai con la religione . . . perchè questo obbietto ha troppo forza nella mente degl' huomini.

Never fight against religion . . . this concept has too much empire over the minds of men.

Guicciardini

The Venetians did not immediately elect another Doge. They wanted time to think. Their situation was grave in the extreme – there could be no doubt of that. They were now in a state of war with both Empires simultaneously. Their splendid new navy had been reduced to a shadow of what it had been only six months before, many vessels having been deliberately burnt in the Aegean in an effort to contain the plague. Manpower – since none of the prisoners interned in the East had yet been freed – was more than ever a problem, and one which continued to grow as the epidemic claimed increasing numbers of victims in the city and the other communities of the lagoon. The treasury was empty; national bankruptcy could be avoided only by repeating the forced loan of the previous year.[1] Worst of all was the demoralization. Vitale Michiel had been the eighth Doge in the Republic's history to meet a violent death, but the first for over 200 years. Perhaps the Venetians realized the strength of the mass hysteria that had suddenly overcome them, and were conscious of some sort of collective responsibility for the murder. They seem, at any rate, to have felt both shock and shame, a need to examine both their government and themselves.

What, basically, had gone wrong? It was clear that most of the blame, both for the failure of the expedition and for the penury of the state, lay with Michiel; but where were the checks and balances by which his actions should have been controlled? In the general tightening-up of the

---

1. These state loans – the first of their kind in the world – were soon to become a permanent feature of the Venetian economy, with 4 per cent transferable government bonds offering opportunities for endless speculation on the Rialto.

constitution under Domenico Flabanico the Doge had been provided, as in the early days, with two counsellors; he had moreover been put under an obligation to 'invite' other leading citizens – the *pregadi* – to give additional advice when necessary. With him also lay the right to call the *arengo* of all the people. But Flabanico had been dead for nearly a century and a half; by now the two counsellors had lost much of their authority, the *pregadi* seldom received their 'invitations' and the *arengo*, with the rapid increase of the city's population, was no longer a practical measure. Not only were there too many Venetians to meet together in general assembly as the inhabitants of the early lagoon settlements had done, but there was no way of controlling such large numbers. *Arenghi* had become no more than licensed mobs; recent years had shown all too clearly how little they could be trusted with important decisions of state. As a result they were hardly ever called except when the law specifically demanded them – for the election of a Doge or the declaration of war; and the ducal power was therefore virtually unfettered. There was an urgent necessity to redefine the powers of the three governing elements of the state: Doge, counsellors and people. It was a necessity that led, in 1172 and 1173, to what are arguably the most important constitutional reforms in Venetian history.

The first innovation was an assembly of 480 prominent Venetians, to be nominated by two representatives of each of the six new *sestieri*, and to hold office for one year only. Henceforward this assembly, the *Comitia Majora* – the *Maggior Consiglio*, or, in English, the Great Council – was to be responsible for appointing all the chief officials of the state, including the twelve representatives of the *sestieri*. In practice this meant that after the first year, when these representatives were elected democratically, they and the Great Council, each nominating the other, formed a closed circle which completely excluded the general populace from any say in their composition. The *arengo* was not entirely abolished; but even where it remained mandatory it was, as far as possible, shorn of its effective power. Its most jealously guarded prerogative of all, the election of the Doge, is a case in point. Formerly, as at the accession of Domenico Selvo, the people of Venice had played a very real part in the choice of their leader; their right to do so was one of the corner-stones of the constitution. Henceforth this choice was to be entrusted to eleven special electors, nominated by the Council; the name of the new Doge would simply be announced to the assembled populace as a *fait accompli*. The first attempt to follow this new procedure caused riots, and the objectors were pacified only after a compromise had been agreed upon: the successful candidate must be formally presented to them in St Mark's with the formula 'Here is your Doge, if it please you.' Thus the voice of the people was theoretically preserved; but it was a formality only, and the people knew it.

The next step in the work of reform was to increase the number of the ducal counsellors from two to six. They were to be in constant attendance on the Doge and, since their function was primarily to limit his authority, they must presumably have enjoyed some power of veto over his decisions. They and he together formed an inner council of state, later to be known as the *Signoria* or sometimes the *consiglietto*. As an outer advisory body the *pregadi*, or Senate, remained in being, and their influence also increased – especially in the field of foreign affairs, in which they took most of the important decisions which were subsequently ratified by the Council.

The effect of these measures was, in short, to weaken both the apex and the base of the administrative pyramid while strengthening it in the centre. Venice had taken a few more steps towards the oligarchical form of government that she was to perfect in the following century and to make peculiarly her own. On the other hand it was important that the curtailing of ducal power should not be reflected in any loss of prestige; further additions were accordingly made to the dignities of the Doge and the pomp and ceremonial with which he was surrounded. In future, directly after his election, he was to be carried all round the Piazza on a special circular chair – familiarly called the *pozzetto* from its resemblance to the characteristic well-heads of the city – scattering largesse to the people; thenceforth, whenever he left his palace on state business, he was to be accompanied by a long cortège of nobles, clergy and citizens.

But neither the pomp nor the largesse – limited by subsequent legislation to not less than 100 and not more than 500 ducats – was enough to make up for what had been taken away.

However much the Venetians as a whole may have resented this whittling down of their ancient rights by the new electoral system, nobody seriously questioned the wisdom of the electors when their choice fell on Sebastiano Ziani. The new Doge was highly intelligent, energetic despite his seventy years, and possessed of wide administrative experience. He was also enormously rich. It was just as well. Seeing the Republic on the verge of bankruptcy, he made his first task the restitution of the national finances and, on the advice of the *pregadi*, suspended all payments on the new government bonds. It was a brave decision, but it aroused less resentment than might have been expected. The bondholders were all Venetian citizens; they loved money but they loved Venice more, and this direct appeal to their patriotism met with an immediate response.

There could, however, be no question of continuing the war against Byzantium. Ambassadors set out again for Constantinople to sue for peace and, it was hoped, for the release of all those still in captivity. But their mission was in vain. They found Manuel Comnenus as unyielding as ever. Since what was left of the Venetian fleet was at that moment actively engaged with Frederick Barbarossa's army in the siege of Byzantine-held Ancona, his attitude was not altogether surprising; nevertheless, his rejection of this second overture was to prove a grave mistake, and one which his successors would have bitter cause to regret. Meanwhile it drove the Venetians into the arms of King William II ('the Good') of Sicily, with whom in 1175 they concluded a twenty-year treaty, obtaining commercial terms far more favourable than any that they had previously enjoyed.

And so, under the wise guidance of Sebastiano Ziani, the Republic began to recover. Its material rehabilitation would inevitably take some time; morally, on the other hand, the process was a good deal more rapid – culminating, in the summer of 1177, with an event that focused upon Venice the attention of all Christendom: the reconciliation of Pope Alexander III and Frederick Barbarossa that brought the seventeen-year schism to an end and peace, at last, to Italy. Just over a year before, on 29 May 1176 at Legnano, the Lombard League had inflicted on Barbarossa the most crushing defeat of his career. He had lost much of his army, and had narrowly escaped with his own life; but the disaster had brought him to his senses. After four long Italian campaigns he saw that the Lombard cities were as determined as ever to resist him and, since the formation of their League, well able to do so. Pope Alexander was now recognized almost everywhere – even in much of the Empire itself – as the rightful Pontiff. For Frederick to persist any longer in the policy on which he had already wasted the best years of his life would earn him the derision of Europe.

His ambassadors met the Pope at Anagni to negotiate the terms of the reconciliation. In essence, they were simple enough: on the imperial side, recognition of Alexander, restitution of church possessions and the conclusion of peace with Byzantium, Sicily and the Lombard League; on the papal, confirmation of Frederick's wife as Empress, of his son Henry as King of the Romans and of several distinguished prelates in sees which they originally owed to schismatic anti-Popes. The next question was where the great meeting was to take place. Bologna was suggested, but rejected by Frederick for its Lombard affiliations; finally, after prolonged argument, it was agreed that Pope and Emperor should meet in Venice, on condition that Frederick should not be admitted into the city until Alexander had given his consent.

Politically, no better choice could have been made. To be sure, Venice had been a founder member of the Lombard League. On the other hand her recent troubles with Byzantium had prevented her from playing a very active part in League affairs; at one moment, beneath the walls of Ancona, she had even found herself fighting side by side with the forces of the Western Empire. She possessed a record of independence longer than that of any other North Italian city, and as a great and splendid metropolis she would have no difficulty in accommodating, in the style to which they were accustomed, all the European notables – princes, bishops, ambassadors and representatives from the Lombard towns – who were expected to be present.

On 10 May 1177 the Pope arrived with his *curia*. He was received by the Doge and the Patriarchs of both Grado and Aquileia and, after High Mass in the basilica, was carried in the state barge to the Patriarchal palace at S. Silvestro, which was put at his disposal for as long as he cared to remain. Before his meeting with the Emperor there was much work to be done; during the discussions at Anagni he had had no brief to speak for either Sicily or the League, both of which would have to reach agreement with the imperial plenipotentiaries if the promised Kiss of Peace were to have the significance he intended for it. So now a second round of negotiations began in the Patriarchal chapel. Meanwhile the Emperor, to whom by the terms of the reconciliation Venetian territory was still forbidden, held himself in readiness at Ravenna.

The League representatives in particular proved hard negotiators, and the talks dragged on for the best part of two months. By the beginning of July, however, agreement was in sight and, to speed communications, the Pope agreed to allow Frederick to approach as near as Chioggia, where he could keep in daily touch with developments. Up to this point the Emperor had displayed an exemplary and for him unusual degree of restraint in a situation that he cannot have found anything but deeply humiliating; but at last he began to show signs of losing his patience. In the six years since Venice's break with Byzantium his adherents in the city had multiplied until they constituted quite an influential faction. They now encouraged him to enter it at once, in defiance of the papal veto, and so to force Alexander and the Lombards into granting more favourable terms. Frederick was clearly tempted, but declined to move without the Doge's approval. Ziani, aware that refusal might well provoke an uprising in the Emperor's favour, hesitated; the envoys from the League, in a mixture of anger and apprehension, retired to Treviso. For a moment it looked as if all the careful diplomacy of the past year was to be brought to nothing.

The situation was saved by the Sicilians. The leader of their delegation, Archbishop Romuald of Salerno, ordered his ships to be made ready for a hasty departure hinting that, if he and his mission decided to leave, his master King William would be swift to take revenge for Venice's breach of faith. The Archbishop's meaning was only too clear. In the past two years the already considerable number of Venetian merchants in Palermo, Messina and Catania had enormously increased. There was nothing to prevent William from acting as Manuel Comnenus had acted in 1171. Uncertain no longer, Ziani issued a statement confirming that entry by Frederick Barbarossa into Venice could be permitted only after the papal sanction had been given.

In retrospect, the crisis seems to have provided all the negotiators with a salutary shock. The outstanding details were now quickly settled and on 23 July 1177 agreement was complete. At the Pope's request a Venetian flotilla left for Chioggia and brought Frederick to the Lido, whither a delegation of four cardinals sailed out to greet him. In their presence he solemnly abjured his anti-Pope and made formal acknowledgement of Alexander as rightful Pontiff; they in turn lifted his seventeen-year excommunication. Now at last he could be admitted into Venice. Early next morning the Doge himself arrived at S. Nicolò di Lido, where Frederick had spent the night, with an impressive retinue of nobles and clergy. He personally escorted the Emperor to a barge specially decorated for the occasion, and together they were rowed in state to the Molo.

In Venice itself, meanwhile, the last preparations had been completed. The Venetians' love of pomp and pageantry was already well established; this was one of the greatest days in their history, and they were determined to do justice to the occasion. For days already people had been pouring into the city. Flags were flying, windows dressed. Of the several eye-witness accounts that have survived, perhaps the most vivid and informative is the so-called *De Pace Veneta Relatio*, whose author seems to have been a German churchman. We do not know his name, but he was certainly well placed, both geographically and hieratically, to record what he saw:

At daybreak, the attendants of the Lord Pope hastened to the church of St Mark the Evangelist and closed the central doors of the great portal in front of the church, and thither they brought much timber and deal planks and ladders, and so raised up a lofty and splendid throne. And they also erected two masts of pine wood of wondrous height on each side of the quay, from which hung the standards of St Mark, magnificently embroidered and so large that they touched the ground; for that quay, which is known as the *Marmoreum*, is but a stone's throw from the church. Thither the Pope arrived before the first hour of the day [6 a.m.] and, having heard Mass, soon afterwards ascended to the higher part of his throne to await the arrival of the Emperor. There he sat, with his patriarchs, cardinals, archbishops and bishops innumerable; on his right was the Patriarch of Venice, and on his left that of Aquileia.

And now there came a quarrel between the Archbishop of Milan and the Archbishop of Ravenna as to which should be seen to take precedence; and each strove to sit himself in the third place from that of the Pope, on his right side. But the Pope determined to put an end to their contention, and leaving his own exalted seat descended the steps and placed himself below them. Thus was there no third place to sit in, and neither could sit on his right. Then about the third hour there arrived the Doge's barge, in which was the Emperor, with the Doge and the cardinals that had been sent to him on the previous day; and he was led by seven archbishops and canons of the Church in solemn procession to the papal throne. And when he reached it, he threw off the red cloak he was wearing, and prostrated himself before the Pope, and kissed first his feet and then his knees.[1] But the Pope rose, and taking the head of the Emperor in both his hands he embraced him and kissed him, and made him sit at his right hand, and at last spoke the words 'Son of the Church, be welcome.' Then he took him by the hand and led him into the Basilica. And the bells rang, and the *Te Deum Laudamus* was sung. When the ceremony was done, they both left the church together. The Pope mounted his horse, and the Emperor held his stirrup and then retired to the Doges' Palace. And all this happened on Sunday, the Eve of St James.

And on the same day the Pope sent the Emperor many gold and silver jars filled with food of various kinds. And he sent also a fatted calf, with the words 'It is meet that we should make merry and be glad, for my son was dead, and is alive again; and was lost, and is found.'

For Pope Alexander, the Treaty of Venice marked at once the climax and the culmination of his pontificate. He had had to endure eighteen years of schism and ten of exile from Rome, to say nothing of the implacable hostility of one of the most formidable men ever to wear the crown of the Western Empire; and he had had to wait until he was well into his seventies before receiving his reward. Now, however, that reward had come – nor was it limited to Frederick's recognition of his legitimacy.

1. There is a splendidly anachronistic late sixteenth-century representation of the scene by Zuccari in the north-west corner of the Sala del Maggior Consiglio.

The Emperor had also admitted all the temporal rights of the Papacy over the city of Rome; and the six-year truce that he had concluded with the Lombard League was clearly only a preliminary to his acknowledgement of the independence of the individual Lombard cities. It was the most signal victory ever to have been won by a Pope over imperial pretensions – greater far than the empty triumph at Canossa exactly a century before; and it had been due above all to the wisdom and patience with which Alexander had steered his Church through one of the most troubled periods in her history.

And now that that period was over those qualities remained with him. Neither on the day of his triumph nor at any other time during the Emperor's stay in Venice did Alexander show the slightest inclination to crow over his former enemy. One or two subsequent historians of Venice, like the incorrigibly romantic Martino da Canale writing nearly a century later, have perpetuated the legend of the Pope placing his foot on Frederick's neck, of the Emperor muttering under his breath 'Not to you, but to St Peter' and Alexander replying sharply: 'To me *and* to St Peter.' But this story is told by no contemporary writer and is inconsistent with all the first-hand evidence that has come down to us. The Emperor, too, seems to have behaved impeccably. On the day following the great reconciliation, he tried to carry courtesy even further: having again held the papal stirrup on leaving the Basilica, he would have led Alexander's horse all the way to the point of embarkation if the Pope had not gently restrained him. Did he, one cannot help wondering, remember then the two days spent at Sutri when he had refused to perform the same service for Pope Adrian, on the way to Rome for his coronation twenty-two years before?

The part played by Venice in healing the schism had also been considerable, and her rewards too were correspondingly large. Financially, that memorable summer of 1177 did much to restore her prosperity. The Emperor was the city's guest for eight full weeks, leaving only on 18 September. Pope Alexander remained until mid-October, after a total stay of well over five months. For much of that time Venice was crowded as never before, with her normal floating foreign population of travellers and merchants now swollen to many times its normal size by the greatest princes and prelates of Europe, each bent on outshining his rivals in the splendour of his retinue. One, the Archbishop of Cologne, brought with him a suite of no less than 400 secretaries, chaplains and attendants; the Patriarch of Aquileia boasted 300, as did the Archbishops of Mainz and

Magdeburg. Count Roger of Andria, the second envoy of the King of Sicily, had 330; Duke Leopold of Austria, with a train of only 160, must have cut a sorry figure indeed.

Politically, too, there were benefits. It would have been uncharacteristic of the Venetians to have kept both Emperor and Pope so long in their midst without obtaining anything tangible in return; in fact they concluded special treaties with both. From Frederick Barbarossa they obtained free passage, safe conduct and full exemption from imperial tolls in all parts of the Empire, in return for similar privileges for his own subjects 'as far as Venice but no further' – as clear an acknowledgement as anyone could wish of Venetian supremacy in the Adriatic. Pope Alexander for his part showed his appreciation by granting indulgences to most of the principal churches in the city, and above all by making a final settlement of that age-old struggle between Grado and Aquileia that had brought so much strife and bitterness over the centuries to Venetian ecclesiastical affairs. By its terms the Patriarch of Grado – now permanently resident in Venice – abandoned all claims to the treasures stolen by Poppo of Aquileia a century and a half before, and was granted in return undisputed authority over the communities around the lagoon plus Istria and Dalmatia – where the consequent strengthening of Venice's hold over her subject towns can well be imagined.

There is a Venetian tradition that during his stay Pope Alexander also gave new sacramental significance to the annual Ascension Day ceremony that had been held since A.D. 1000 out in the open sea beyond the Lido port, transforming it from a service of supplication into a symbolic marriage with the Adriatic.[1] Indeed, above one of the doors in the north wall of the Sala del Maggior Consiglio in the Doges' Palace there is a painting by Vicentino of the Pope handing Doge Ziani the ring which he is shortly to cast into the waves. It is sad to have to record that, like the quite fictitious naval battle of Salvore, depicted by Tintoretto's son Domenico immediately to the right, this theory is without foundation. The offering of the golden ring – a symbol, originally, of propitiation pure and simple – was bound to assume matrimonial overtones as the years went by, and it may well have been at about this time that it did so; but though it is reasonably safe to assume that the Pope was present at the 1177 ceremony – Ascension Day falling in that year on 2 June – there is no evidence that he actively participated in it, far less that he radically changed its character.

The greatest gain of all to Venice was in prestige. Throughout that

1. See p. 79.

memorable summer, she was the focus of attention of the whole of Europe – the capital, in a very real sense, of Christendom. Her Doge was playing host to the two leaders of the Western world; his relations with them, if not quite those of an equal, were generally seen to be at least those of a friend and fellow-prince. She had been specifically chosen by both the imperial and the papal negotiators because – to quote once more from the *Relatio* – she was 'subject to God alone . . . a place where the courage and authority of the citizens could preserve peace between the partisans of each side and ensure that no discord or sedition, deliberate or involuntary, should arise'. Admittedly, she only just succeeded; but succeed she did, and in doing so she assumed a new status as a great metropolis and a European power.

The Basilica of St Mark, with the little porphyry lozenge set into the pavement just in front of the central doorway traditionally marking the spot where Frederick Barbarossa abased himself before the Pope, is the only building on the Piazza or the Piazzetta which was already standing in its present form at the time of the events here described. If, however, the general setting for that tremendous ceremony possessed much the same general aspect that it has today, this also is largely due to Doge Sebastiano Ziani. He it was who pulled down the old church of S. Geminiano,[1] who bought from the nuns of S. Zaccaria the orchard (known as the *brolo*) which lay between it and the lagoon, who filled in the old Rio Batario – the canal which ran from behind what are now the *Procuratie Vecchie*, across the front of the basilica and past the campanile to the Rio di Zecca next to the public garden – paved the whole thing over in herring-bone brick and gave Venice what we now know as the Piazza S. Marco. He also ordered that all the houses built around it should be linked with arches and colonnades, so that from the start it must have looked very much as it did when Gentile Bellini painted it in 1496 – and, despite the building of the two long lines of the *Procuratie* along the northern and southern sides, it still does today.[2]

Doge Ziani also left his mark on the Doges' Palace and the Piazzetta. The Palace as he found it was in essence that which had been built after

1. See p. 32. It was rebuilt at the far west end of the Piazza, where it stood until Napoleon demolished it for good in 1807 to make way for a ballroom in his new wing of the *Procuratie*.

2. The Bellini picture is that of *The Procession of the Cross in the Piazza S. Marco*, one of the series relating the *Miracles of the Relic of the True Cross* now in the Accademia. (Plate 10) The *Procuratie Vecchie*, to the north, were already begun, though not very far advanced, in Bellini's time. The *Procuratie Nuove*, to the south, were started at the end of the sixteenth century after the demolition of Pietro Orseolo's hospital (see p. 68).

its predecessor had been destroyed during the revolution of 976, with possible additions and embellishments made in the course of repairs after the fire of 1106. Ziani, we are told by Sansovino, 'enlarged it in every direction'; although evidence is sketchy, we can presume that it followed traditional lines and that it looked much like the few Byzantine buildings that still exist along the Grand Canal – the Fondaco dei Turchi for example, or the Palazzi Farsetti and Loredan near the Rialto bridge.

The Piazzetta, meanwhile, was cleared and enlarged just as the Piazza had been. Perhaps as part of the preparations for the arrival of Barbarossa, Pietro Tribuno's old wall was swept away. It had blocked off the approach from the water's edge for nearly 300 years – for the past five of which there had lain alongside it two of the three antique columns that Vitale Michiel had brought back from his ill-starred expedition to the East. (Unlucky as ever, he had lost the third, which had been accidentally dropped overboard during the unloading and still lies in the mud off the Molo.) Several attempts had been made to raise them, all unsuccessful. Now, however, a young Venetian engineer presented himself before the Doge. His real name was Nicolò Staratonio, but he was usually known as Barattieri. This nickname, which suggests in Italian some predilection for card-sharping, may not have been entirely undeserved; we know at any rate that he offered to raise the two columns into position in return for the right to set up public gaming-tables between them. Ziani agreed. Up went the columns, where they stand today, later to be crowned respectively with the Lion of St Mark and St Theodore with his dragon-crocodile. Up, too, went the tables. The Great Council, shortly afterwards, is said to have tried to diminish the value of the concession by designating the same spot for the holding of public executions. From what we know of the temper of the time the attempt may well have had precisely the opposite effect; but Barattieri did not abandon engineering altogether, since we hear of him again building the first Rialto bridge, on pontoons, a few years later.

Statesman, diplomatist and builder, Sebastiano Ziani proved himself also to be a constitutional reformer of rare ability. There is no need to elaborate here on the details of his further reorganization of the administrative machine, the establishment of new offices of state, the additional codification and clarification of the Law; what is more important is the philosophy which lay beneath his whole programme of reform and which tended always to support and strengthen that oligarchic principle that was already the dominant influence in Venetian political thinking. Shortly before his retirement he called a meeting of his chief magistrates, enjoining them *inter alia* to make a point of giving the positions of highest authority to the wealthiest and most powerful citizens, 'lest, seeing themselves passed over, they grow dissatisfied and are moved to violent action'. This advice was less reactionary than it sounds. Few noble Venetians looked on high office as anything but a responsibility, and often a disagreeable one, severely restrictive of personal liberty and a good deal less profitable than commerce. Civic duties, however, whether to be fulfilled at home or abroad, could not be refused without compelling reasons; from 1185 on, any such refusal actually carried heavy legal penalties.

In a reign that had lasted little more than six years, Sebastiano Ziani had achieved much. But he was already past seventy at the time of his election, and in 1178 he decided to withdraw from public life – retiring, as more than one of his predecessors had done before him, to the monastery of S. Giorgio Maggiore. There he died soon afterwards, and was later commemorated, opposite Tribuno Memmo, on the Palladian façade.[1] In his will, he left the rents of certain houses in the Merceria between the Basilica and S. Giuliano to provide food for the prisoners of the state, and other property further along the same street to his monastery, with instructions to supply a dinner every Tuesday for twelve paupers of the city and, for his own family as a lesson in humility, a frugal meal of cheap fish, wine and lentils without oil annually on the feast of St Stephen, before whose tomb a lamp was to be kept perpetually burning.

Shortly before his death, Sebastiano Ziani had made a further change in the existing machinery for the election of a Doge. Instead of the eleven electors nominated directly by the Great Council, it was resolved that the latter should henceforth select only four of its number, and that these should in their turn nominate an electoral team of forty, of whom each should have received at least three votes out of the four and not more than one should come from any single family. The result of this somewhat ungainly procedure – though it was simple enough compared with that of later years – was the election in 1178 of Orio Mastropiero, or Malipiero, an elderly diplomatist who had served on embassies to Palermo and Constantinople and had played a leading part, both as organizer and contributor, in the first state loan of Vitale Michiel. His diplomatic experience, in particular, was to serve him in good stead; for, in the East as in the West, the storm-clouds were gathering again.

On 24 September 1180 the Emperor Manuel Comnenus died after a

1. See p. 72, n.1.

long illness. For the next five years the Byzantine Empire was to be plunged into misery and confusion. Manuel's legitimate heir was his twelve-year-old son Alexius, whose mother, Mary of Antioch, assumed the regency. The first Latin ever to rule in Constantinople – she was the sister of the Norman Prince Bohemund III – Mary openly favoured her Frankish countrymen to the detriment of the Greeks and was consequently detested by her subjects. The first revolt against her failed but the second, in 1182, developed into a full-scale massacre in which virtually all the Westerners in the capital perished, including the women and children and even the sick in the hospitals. The entire Frankish quarter of the city was looted and pillaged in a holocaust compared with which the depredations suffered by the Venetians and Genoese eleven years before must have seemed insignificant indeed. Meanwhile Manuel's cousin Andronicus Comnenus marched on the capital and seized the throne. Mary was strangled, and soon afterwards her young son, who had been compelled to sign his mother's death warrant with his own hand, met his death by the bowstring. He left a fiancée, Agnes – rechristened Anna by the Byzantines – the twelve-year-old daughter of King Louis VII of France. She had arrived in Constantinople some months before, but owing to her extreme youth the wedding had not yet taken place; without further ado Andronicus, now sixty-four, married her and, according to at least one modern authority, consummated the marriage. There followed almost three years of brutality and terror, probably unparalleled in the civilized world until the days of the French Revolution. Then at last, in September 1185, Andronicus was in his turn overthrown and torn to pieces by the mob.

Some time during the previous year, news had reached the Rialto that suggested all too plainly that the brief honeymoon period between Venice and Sicily was nearing its end. King William the Good and his Queen, Joanna of England – the sister of Richard Cœur-de-Lion – were childless and looked like remaining so; next in line to the throne was William's aunt Constance, and she it was whose betrothal was now announced to Henry of Hohenstaufen, son and heir of Frederick Barbarossa. To Venice, as to all her sister-cities of the League, the prospect opened up by such a marriage was appalling. Their success in holding their own for so long against imperial claims was due in large measure to the fact that Frederick had no permanent home in Italy and that by feudal law he could not keep his German forces indefinitely south of the Alps. Henceforth the Emperor would be not merely a titular overlord, but a sovereign ruler in the peninsula.

Little, obviously, could be done while the Byzantine crisis continued; but once Andronicus was out of the way and the docile if ineffectual Isaac II Angelus was installed on the throne of Constantinople the Venetians lost no time. Diplomatic negotiations began in 1186 and a treaty was concluded in the following year. Full compensation was promised for the events of 1171, the Emperor undertaking to defend Venice and all her territories from any attack, whatever its source. In return the Venetians were to provide, on six months' notice, from 40 to 100 galleys, to be equipped in Venetian yards at imperial expense. Three out of every four Venetian residents in Byzantine territory were liable for conscription, to man these vessels under Venetian officers who would however be under the overall command of the imperial admiral. (Since each galley demanded a crew of 140 oarsmen, such figures suggest that some 18,000 Venetian males of military age were still living within the frontiers of the Empire.)

Now Isaac Angelus was a corrupt and feckless ruler – Nicetas Choniates said that he sold government offices like vegetables at a market; but why he decided to entrust his shipbuilding programme to a foreign nation with whom his Empire had been on distinctly hostile terms for the past twenty years – particularly when Constantinople possessed excellent shipyards of its own – is not an easy question to answer. Venice had it both ways. In return for the promise of imperial protection, she was given an effective stranglehold over the entire Byzantine navy. Sixteen years later, when the Empire of the East was to find itself practically defenceless against a Venetian invasion fleet, it would have only itself to blame.

The Shameful Glory

[1187–1205]

We can know little (as we care little)
Of the Metropolis: her candled churches,
Her white-gowned pederastic senators,
The cut-throat factions of her Hippodrome,
The eunuchs of her draped saloons ...

Robert Graves,
The Cuirassiers of the Frontier

The Venetian treaty with Byzantium of 1187 coincided almost exactly with a major disaster in the East. On 4 July the Saracens under Saladin shattered the army of Guy of Lusignan, King of Jerusalem, at the battle of Hattin; and three months later, on 2 October, the Holy City fell. When the news reached Rome the old Pope, Urban III, died of shock; his successor, Gregory VIII, lost no time in summoning all Christendom once again to take the Cross. For Venice, the call came at an opportune moment. She had recently embarked on one of her periodic campaigns for the recovery of Zara, which had once more yielded to the blandishments of the King of Hungary; but this time the Hungarian reaction had been stronger and swifter than expected. The papal injunction for all Christian powers to unite against the infidel afforded a welcome chance to withdraw without loss of face.

It was anyway to be expected that the Venetians should respond enthusiastically to Pope Gregory's appeal. In the general collapse of the Latin East after Hattin they too had lost much. Tyre, owing to prompt action by the Sicilian navy and a lucky miscalculation by Saladin, had remained in Christian hands; but Acre, with its Venetian quarter and prosperous commercial colony, had surrendered almost at once – together with Sidon, Beirut and other cities of the coast and hinterland. Doge Mastropiero accordingly announced a compulsory state loan, the precise amounts required from leading families being carefully assessed according to their wealth; and at Easter 1189 the war fleet set sail, carrying an inchoate and heterogeneous army from all parts of Italy.

In the months that followed, this army was swelled by others – English and French, Danish and Flemish, German and Sicilian. Of the four European sovereigns who had taken the Cross, two died before reaching the Holy Land: young William the Good of Sicily, struck down by illness at thirty-six, and old Frederick Barbarossa, drowned as he was crossing the Calycadnus river in southern Anatolia. But two others were there to lead their subjects into battle: Richard Cœur-de-Lion, already a legend for his courage and chivalry but at heart impetuous, irresponsible and faithless; and Philip Augustus, morose and utterly lacking in charm, but possessed of a wisdom and statesmanship that earned him a place among the best of France's kings while Richard had already proved himself one of England's worst.

The kindest thing that can be said about the Third Crusade is that it was a distinct improvement on the Second. It was better organized and very much better led; it achieved one notable victory when, after a two-year siege, it recaptured Acre; and if the soldiers of the Cross did not always measure up to the superb standards of chivalry set by Saladin – Richard's massacre of nearly 3,000 Saracen prisoners in cold blood after the fall of Acre is a further indelible stain on his reputation – they fought on the whole with courage and occasionally with heroism. Ultimately, however, they failed. Jerusalem remained in Muslim hands. The little Christian Kingdom of Acre might postpone for another century the final dissolution of Outremer; it could do nothing to prevent it.

As for Venice, her part in the Third Crusade – as in the Second – remains something of a mystery. After her impressive beginning, she fades out of the picture. The contemporary chroniclers scarcely give her a mention. Perhaps her contribution was limited to the transport of soldiers and equipment, in which case we may be quietly confident that she received full payment for her services before withdrawing from the fray. The Venetian merchants, certainly, acted smartly enough; they were back in possession of their quarter in Acre within days of the city's surrender. But of that mighty war fleet no more is heard. Doge Mastropiero had answered the papal summons; after that he seems to have felt that nothing more was expected of him. In any case he was not a man for foreign adventures. He preferred to concentrate on improving the judiciary at home, instituting a body of public procurators whose function was to represent the interests of the Republic in all legal proceedings, and establishing special courts for foreigners. It is in his reign, too, that we first hear of the *Quarantia*, or Council of Forty – an executive and judicial body standing half-way between the Great Council and the Doge's inner council, the *Signoria*. Its original purpose seems to have been that of a consultative assembly, like the *pregadi* on a larger scale; subsequently, however, when the latter became a standing commission and thence developed into a permanent Senate, the *Quarantia* became purely judicial.

All these changes were important enough, and Orio Mastropiero's record in the fourteen years of his dogeship is far from negligible. If he still strikes one as being somehow colourless, he is not altogether to blame; for it was his misfortune to fill a gap between the two greatest Doges of the medieval Republic and the two most momentous chapters in its history. Of Sebastiano Ziani and the Peace of Venice the story has already been told; we must now turn to a darker and more shameful triumph: that grim adventure still ludicrously known as the Fourth Crusade, and its architect Enrico Dandolo.

No one knows for certain the age of Enrico Dandolo when, after the death of his predecessor, he was proclaimed Doge of Venice on 1 January 1193. The story goes that he was eighty-five and already stone-blind, but this seems hardly credible when we read of his energy – indeed, his heroism – ten years later, on the walls of Constantinople. More probably, he was in his middle seventies on his accession – which would still make him, at the time of the Fourth Crusade, an octogenarian of several years' standing. A dedicated, almost fanatical patriot, he had spent much of his life in the service of the Republic. We hear of him, for example, in 1171 taking part in Vitale Michiel's Eastern expedition and, in the following year, as one of the Doge's ambassadors on the abortive peace mission to Manuel Comnenus.[1]

Did his loss of sight date from this time? According to his later name-sake, the historian Andrea Dandolo, Enrico's arrogance and stubbornness antagonized Manuel to such a point that he actually had him arrested and partially blinded;[2] on the other hand a contemporary and so possibly a more reliable source – an appendix to the Altino Chronicle – reports Doge Ziani as deciding to send his own mission to Constantinople only 'after seeing his predecessor's three ambassadors returned safe and sound'. This passage, combined with what we know of Manuel's character and the absence of any other references to what must have created a major outcry in Venice had it in fact occurred, surely indicates that, although blinding was a regular and recognized punishment in Byzantium, imperial

1. See p. 129.
2. *Cui Henricus Dandulus, pro salute patriae constanter resistens, visu aliqualiter obtenebratus est.*

displeasure cannot be blamed on this occasion. Another theory[1] holds that while in Constantinople Dandolo had been involved in a brawl, in the course of which his eyes had been injured. This too seems on the face of it improbable in view of the Altino testimony; besides, he was not even then in his first youth, but a mature diplomatist of well over forty. Thirty years later, however, the facts are no longer in doubt. Geoffrey de Villehardouin, who knew him well, assures us that 'although his eyes appeared normal, he could not see a hand in front of his face, having lost his sight after a head wound'.[2]

Neither his age nor his blindness, in any case, appear to have had the slightest effect on Dandolo's energies or abilities. Within weeks of his election he had launched a new campaign to recapture Zara; Pisa and Brindisi went to her aid and for several years the Venetians had to fight hard to maintain their power in the Adriatic. The situation was further aggravated when, on Christmas Day 1194, the German Emperor Henry VI assumed the Crown of Sicily in Palermo Cathedral. The Norman–Sicilian Kingdom was effectively at an end.

It was the one eventuality that the Venetians had feared more than any other; and they were not reassured by what they knew of Henry himself. Barbarossa's son possessed all his father's driving determination and strength of will – directing his hatred, however, less against the cities of North Italy than against the Eastern Empire. His aim was, quite simply, to destroy Byzantium, to reunite the old Roman Empire under his own rule, and then to increase it still further by the addition of a great Mediterranean dominion which, after one more decisive Crusade, would include the Holy Land itself. Only a few years before, such a dream might have appeared fantastic, even absurd; but the Comneni were gone, and the family of Angelus who now occupied the throne of Constantinople had proved themselves incapable of effective government. In 1195 the Emperor Isaac II, after ten years of chaos, was dethroned, blinded and imprisoned by his brother Alexius, a weak and unstable megalomaniac, who, though utterly unfitted for responsibility of any kind, had succeeded him under the name of Alexius III.[3] The Holy Land, too, looked ripe for the plucking. Saladin was dead; without his leadership and unifying

1. Runciman, *History of the Crusades*, Vol. III, p. 114.

2. '*Si avoit les iaulç en la teste biaus et si n'en veoit gote, que perdue avoit la veüe par une plaie qu'il ot el chef.*'

3. Nicetas Choniates wrote of him: 'Whatever paper might be presented to the Emperor for his signature, he signed it at once; it was of no concern to him if it contained a meaningless jumble of words, or a request to sail the land or till the sea – or, as the story has it, that Athos should be piled on Olympus.'

influence, the armies of Islam were no longer the formidable adversaries they had been in the past.

In Henry's scheme of things there was obviously no place for an independent maritime republic; and if he had succeeded in his first ambition – as he might well have done – Venice would surely have been one of his victims. Fortunately for the world he did not. In 1197, aged only thirty-two, he died at Messina. A few months later his wife Constance followed him to the grave, leaving their five-year-old son, Frederick, in the care of Pope Innocent III.

With both Empires virtually rudderless and Norman Sicily gone never to return, with Germany embroiled in a civil war over the imperial succession and both England and France similarly – though less violently – occupied with inheritance problems following the death of Cœur-de-Lion in 1199, Pope Innocent found himself without a secular rival in Europe. About Byzantium he had no strong feelings either way; but he too was enthusiastic for a Crusade. The difficulty was to find suitable leaders. The dearth of crowned heads did not worry him; previous experience had shown that kings and princes, by stirring up national rivalries and endless questions of protocol and precedence, were more trouble on such occasions than they were worth. A few great nobles would suit his purpose admirably; and Innocent was still casting round for likely candidates when he received a letter from Count Tibald of Champagne.

One day in September 1197 the effective ruler of Outremer, Henry of Champagne, was reviewing his troops from a window of his palace at Acre when a delegation from the local Pisan colony entered the room behind him. He turned to greet them, and a few moments later thoughtlessly stepped backward. His little dwarf, Scarlet, seized his clothes in an attempt to stop him, but was too late. Together the two crashed to the ground below. Scarlet escaped with a broken leg; Henry was killed.

Two years later his younger brother, Tibald, held a tournament at his castle of Ecri on the Aisne. Because of his youth – he was still only twenty-two – Tibald had not accompanied Henry to the Holy Land; but as the grandson of Louis VII and the nephew of both Philip Augustus and Coeur-de-Lion, he had the Crusades in his blood. He was energetic and ambitious, and possessed of a genuine religious fervour; and when, during the tournament, he and his friends were addressed by the celebrated preacher Fulk of Neuilly who was travelling through France stirring up support for a new expedition to the East, they needed little persuasion. A messenger was sent immediately to Pope Innocent to announce that they had taken the Cross; others hurried off to Tibald's fellow-princes in France, Germany and Flanders to enlist their participation. The response was gratifying; Pope Innocent's prayers had been spectacularly answered.

The principal problem was one of logistics. Richard Cœur-de-Lion, before leaving Palestine, had given it as his opinion that the weakest point of the Muslim East was Egypt, and that it was here that any future expeditions should primarily be directed. This made it clearer than ever that the new army would have to travel by sea, and would need ships in a quantity that could be provided from one source only – the Venetian Republic.

It was in the year 1201, during the first week of Lent, that a party of six knights led by Geoffrey de Villehardouin, Marshal of Champagne, arrived in Venice. At a special meeting of the Great Council they made their request, and eight days later they received their answer. The Republic would provide transport for 4,500 knights with their horses, 9,000 squires and 20,000 foot-soldiers, with food for nine months. The cost would be 84,000 silver marks. In addition Venice would herself provide fifty fully-equipped galleys at her own expense, on condition that she received one half of all the territories conquered.

Fortunately for posterity, Geoffrey has left a full record not only of the Crusade itself but also of these preliminary negotiations. No one was better placed to do so, and few men of his time, one suspects, could have done it better. The Old French in which he writes – in this instance, the *Langue d'Oïl* of the Île de France – is described by a turn-of-the-century English historian as 'one of the most admirable vehicles of expression that the world has seen' and by Gibbon rather more accurately as 'the rude idiom of his age and country'; but his style has clarity and pace, and in his opening pages he gives us an eye-witness account of Venetian democracy – such as it was – in action. Doge Dandolo, it appears, at various times during the deliberations consulted the *Quarantia*, the *pregadi* and the Great Council; but on a matter of such importance an *arengo* was still necessary. 'And so,' writes Geoffrey,

he assembled at least ten thousand men in the church of St Mark, the most beautiful that there is, to hear the Mass and to pray God for His guidance. And after the Mass he summoned the envoys and besought them, that they themselves should ask of the people the services they required. Geoffrey de Villehardouin, Marshal of Champagne, spoke by consent for the others . . . Then the Doge and people raised their hands and cried aloud with a single voice, 'We grant it! We grant it!' And so great was the noise and tumult, that the very earth seemed to tremble underfoot.

On the following day the contracts were concluded. Geoffrey notes in passing that the agreement withheld all mention of Egypt as the immediate objective. He gives no explanation; he and his colleagues were probably afraid – and with good reason, as it turned out – that the news would be unpopular with the rank and file, for whom Jerusalem was the only legitimate goal for a Crusade and who would see no reason to waste time anywhere else. Moreover an Egyptian expedition would necessarily involve a dangerous landing on a hostile coast, as opposed to a quiet anchorage at Christian Acre and an opportunity to recover from the journey before going into battle. The Venetians, for their part, would have been only too happy to cooperate in the deception, for they had another secret of their own: at the very moment that the negotiations were being concluded, their own ambassadors were in Cairo discussing a highly profitable trade agreement with the Sultan's Viceroy, to whom, shortly afterwards, they almost certainly gave a categorical assurance that Venice had no intention of being party to any attack on Egyptian territory.[1]

Such considerations, however, could not be allowed to affect plans for the Crusade, by which still greater prizes might be won; and it was agreed that the Crusaders should all foregather in Venice on St John's Day, 24 June 1202, when the fleet would be ready for them.

Just how Enrico Dandolo proposed to deflect the Franks from their concerted objective we shall never know. He and his agents may have been partly responsible for leaking the true facts about the Crusaders' intentions through the countries of the West; certainly these became public knowledge within a remarkably short time. But if he hoped that the popular reaction to this news would induce the leaders to change their minds he was mistaken. It was the followers who changed theirs. Many, on hearing of their proposed destination, renounced the Crusade altogether; many more decided to make for Palestine regardless, arranging their own transport from Marseilles or the Apulian ports. On the day appointed for the Venetian rendezvous, the army that gathered on the Lido numbered less than one-third of what had been expected.

For those who had arrived as planned the situation was embarrassing in the extreme. Venice had performed her share of the bargain: there lay the fleet, war galleys as well as transports – no Christian man, writes Geoffrey,

1. This allegation cannot be conclusively proved. There is no treaty extant, and though evidence for one is strong there is also a problem of its accurate dating. But most modern historians are convinced; and there would be nothing uncharacteristic in such double-dealing by Venetians at this time. For a more detailed discussion see Hopf, *Geschichte Griechenlands*, I, p. 118, and Hodgson, *Early History of Venice*, pp. 428–34.

had ever seen richer or finer – but sufficient for an army three times the size of that assembled. In their reduced numbers, the Crusaders could not hope to pay the Venetians the money they had promised. When their leader, the Marquis Boniface of Montferrat – Tibald of Champagne having died shortly after his Marshal's return the previous year – arrived in Venice, rather late, he found the whole expedition threatened before it had even set sail. Not only were the Venetians refusing point-blank to allow a single ship to leave port until the money was forthcoming; they were even threatening to cut off provisions to the waiting army, a threat made all the more serious in that the bulk of that army was confined to the Lido, and strictly forbidden to set foot in the city itself. This measure, it should be emphasized, was not intended to be deliberately offensive; it was a normal precaution on such occasions, designed to prevent distur-bances of the peace or the spread of infection. But it scarcely improved the atmosphere. Boniface emptied his own coffers, many of the other knights and barons did likewise, and every man in the army was pressed to give all he could; but the total raised, including quantities of gold and silver plate, still fell short by 34,000 marks of what was owing.

For as long as the contributions continued to come in, Dandolo kept the Crusaders in suspense. Then, as soon as he was sure that he had extracted all he could, he came forward with an offer. The city of Zara, he pointed out, had recently fallen into the hands of the King of Hungary. If, before embarking on the Crusade proper, the Franks would agree to assist Venice in its recapture, settlement of their debt could perhaps be postponed. It was a typically cynical proposal, and as soon as he heard of it Pope Innocent sent an urgent message forbidding its acceptance. But the Crusaders, as he later came to understand, had no choice.

There followed another of these ceremonies in the basilica that Enrico Dandolo, despite his years, handled so beautifully. Before a congregation that included all the leading Franks, he addressed his subjects. Geoffrey de Villehardouin, who was there, reports his speech as follows:

'Signors, you are joined with the worthiest people in the world, for the highest enterprise ever undertaken. I myself am old and feeble; I need rest; my body is infirm. But I know that no man can lead you and govern you as I, your Lord, can do. If therefore you will allow me to direct and defend you by taking the Cross, while my son remains in my place to guard the Republic, I am ready to live and die with you and the pilgrims.'

And when they heard him, they cried with one voice, 'We pray God that you will do this thing, and come with us!' . . .

So he came down from the pulpit and moved up to the altar, and knelt there.

weeping; and he had the cross sewn on to his great cotton hat, so determined was he that all men should see it.

Thus it came about that on 8 November 1202 the army of the Fourth Crusade set sail from Venice. Its 480 ships, led by the galley of the Doge himself, 'painted vermilion, with a silken vermilion awning spread above, cymbals clashing and four trumpeters sounding from the bows',[1] were, however, bound neither for Egypt nor for Palestine. Just a week later, Zara was taken and sacked. The fighting that broke out almost immediately afterwards between the Franks and Venetians over the division of the spoils scarcely augured well for the future, but peace was eventually restored and the two groups settled themselves in different parts of the city for the winter. Meanwhile the news of what had happened had reached the Pope. Outraged, Innocent at once excommunicated the entire expedition. Though he was later to reconsider, and to restrict his ban to the Venetians only, the Crusade could not be said to have got off to a good start.

Worse, however, was to follow. Early in the new year a messenger arrived with a letter for Boniface from the German King, Philip of Swabia. Now Philip was not only Barbarossa's son, brother to the Emperor Henry VI whose death five years before had left empty the imperial throne of the West; he was also the son-in-law of the deposed Emperor of Byzantium, Isaac Angelus, so that when Isaac's young son, another Alexius, had escaped in 1201 from the prison in which he and his father were being held, Philip's court had been his obvious place of refuge. There he had met Boniface shortly before the latter's departure for Venice, and there it seems likely that the three may have sketched out the plan which Philip now formally proposed in his letter. If the Crusade would escort the young Alexius to Constantinople and enthrone him there in place of his usurper uncle, Alexius in his turn would finance its subsequent conquest of Egypt, supplying in addition 10,000 soldiers of his own and afterwards maintaining 500 knights in the Holy Land at his expense. He would also submit the Church of Constantinople to the authority of Rome.

To Boniface, the scheme had much to recommend it. Apart from what appeared to be the long-term advantages to the Crusade itself and the possibility of paying off the still outstanding debt to Venice, he also saw the possibility of considerable personal gain. And why not? There were, after all, plenty of Crusaders over the past 100 years who had seen no

1. Robert of Clary.

incompatibility in following the Cross and enriching themselves in the process. When he put the idea to Dandolo – to whom, also, it probably came as a less that total surprise – the old Doge accepted it with enthusiasm. He had been in no way chastened by the excommunication; this was not the first time that Venice had defied papal wishes, and it would not be the last. His earlier military and diplomatic experiences had left him with little love for Byzantium; besides, the present Emperor had on his accession made intolerable difficulties over renewing the trading concessions granted by his predecessor. Genoese and Pisan competition was becoming ever more fierce; if Venice were to retain her former hold on the Eastern markets, decisive action would be required. Such action, finally, would involve a welcome postponement of the Egyptian expedition.

The Crusading army proved readier to accept the change of plan than might have been expected. A few refused outright and set off for Palestine on their own; the majority, however, were only too happy to lend themselves to a scheme which promised to strengthen and to enrich the Crusade while also restoring the unity of Christendom. Ever since the great schism, and even before, the Byzantines had been unpopular in the West. They had contributed little or nothing to previous Crusades, during which they were generally believed to have betrayed the Christian cause on several occasions. Young Alexius's offer of active assistance was a welcome change, and not to be despised. Finally, there must have been many among the more materialistically inclined who shared their leader's hope of personal rewards. The average Frank knew practically nothing about Byzantium, but all had been brought up on stories of its immense wealth. And to any medieval army, whether or not it bore the Cross of Christ on its standard, a fabulously rich city meant one thing only – loot.

Young Alexius himself arrived in Zara towards the end of April and a few days later the fleet set sail, stopping at Durazzo and Corfu, in both of which he was acclaimed as the rightful Emperor of the East. On 24 June 1203, a year to the day after the rendezvous in Venice, it dropped anchor off Constantinople. The usurper, Alexius III, had had plenty of warning of its arrival, but had made no serious preparations for his capital's defence; the dockyards had lain idle ever since his idiotic brother had entrusted the whole shipbuilding programme to Venice sixteen years before; and according to Nicetas Choniates – who, as a former imperial secretary, was well placed to know what was going on – he had allowed his principal admiral (who was also his brother-in-law) to sell off the

anchors, sails and rigging of his few remaining vessels, now reduced
to useless hulks and rotting in the inner harbour. His subjects seemed
half-stunned as they gathered on the walls to watch the massive war
fleet as it passed beneath them, beating its way up to the mouth of the
Bosphorus.

But the Crusaders, too, had plenty to stare at. Geoffrey reports:

You may imagine how they gazed, all those who had never before seen
Constantinople. For when they saw those high ramparts and the strong towers
with which it was completely encircled, and the splendid palaces and soaring
churches – so many that but for the evidence of their own eyes they would
never have believed it – and the length and breadth of that city which of all
others is sovereign, they never thought that there could be so rich and powerful
a place in all the world. And mark you that there was not a man so bold that he
did not tremble at the sight; nor was this any wonder, for never since the
creation of the world was there so great an enterprise.

Being in no particular hurry to begin the siege, the invaders first
landed on the Asiatic shore of the straits, near the imperial summer palace
of Chalcedon and the modern Scutari, to replenish their stores. 'The
surrounding land was fair and fertile; sheaves of new-reaped corn stood
in the fields, so that any man might take of it as much as he needed.'
There they easily repulsed a half-hearted attack by a small detachment of
Greek cavalry – it fled at the first charge – and later, with similar lack of
ceremony, dismissed an emissary from the Emperor. If, they told him,
his master were willing to surrender his throne forthwith to his nephew,
they would pray the latter to pardon him and make him a generous
settlement. If not, let him send them no more messengers, but look to
his defence.

Soon after sunrise on the morning of 5 July, they crossed the Bosphorus
and landed below Galata, on the northern side of the Golden Horn.
Being a commercial settlement, largely occupied by foreign trading
communities, Galata was unwalled; its only major fortification was
a single large round tower. This tower, however, was of vital strategic
importance; for in it stood the huge windlass for the raising and lower-
ing of the chain that was used in emergencies to block the entrance
to the Horn.[1] To defend it, a considerable force was drawn up on the
shore, the Emperor himself at its head. Perhaps – though considering
the general demoralization of the Byzantines since the coming of the

1. This original tower no longer stands, having been demolished in 1261. The present
Galata Tower is a fourteenth-century replacement.

Angeli, it is far from certain – they might have done better under different leadership; everyone knew how Alexius had seized the throne, and his character was not one to inspire either love or loyalty. The sight of well over 100 ships, disembarking men, horses and equipment with such speed and precision – for the Venetians were nothing if not efficient – filled them with terror, and scarcely had the first wave of Crusaders lowered their lances for the attack than they turned and fled, the Emperor once again in the lead.

Within the Galata Tower itself, the garrison fought more bravely, holding out for twenty-four hours; but by the following morning it had to surrender. The Venetian sailors unshackled the windlass, and the great iron chain that had stretched over 500 yards across the mouth of the Golden Horn subsided thunderously into the water. The fleet swept in, destroying such few seaworthy Byzantine vessels as it found in the inner harbour. The naval victory was complete.

Constantinople, however, did not give in. Its northern ramparts – those that ran along the shore of the Golden Horn – could not compare in strength or splendour with the tremendous walls on the landward side, erected by the Emperor Theodosius II in the fifth century; but they could still be staunchly defended. Gradually the Greeks began to regain the courage and determination that had heretofore been so conspicuously lacking. In all the 900 years of its existence, their city had not once fallen to a foreign invader. Perhaps, until now, they had never really thought it could. Awake at last to the full extent of the danger that threatened them, they prepared to resist.

The assault, when it came, was directed against the weakest point in the Byzantine defences: the sea frontage of the imperial palace of Blachernae, which occupied the angle formed by the Theodosian land walls and those following the line of the Horn, at the extreme north-west corner of the city. It was launched on the morning of Thursday 17 July, simultaneously from land and sea, with the Venetian ships riding low in the water under the weight of their siege machinery – catapults and mangonels on the forecastles, covered gangplanks and scaling-ladders suspended by rope tackles between the yard-arms. The Frankish army, attacking from land, was initially beaten back by the axe-swinging Englishmen and Danes who for nearly three centuries had formed the Emperor's famous Varangian Guard; it was the Venetians and, to a considerable degree, Enrico Dandolo in person, who decided the day.

The story of the old Doge's courage is told not just by some biased latter-day panegyrist of the Republic, but by Geoffrey de Villehardouin himself. He reports that although the Venetian assault-craft had approached so close inshore that those manning the ladders in the bows were fighting hand-to-hand with the defenders, the Venetian sailors were reluctant to beach the vessels and effect a proper landing.

And here was an extraordinary feat of boldness. For the Duke of Venice, who was an old man and stone blind, stood fully armed on the prow of his galley, with the banner of St Mark before him, and cried out to his men to drive the ship ashore if they valued their skins. And so they did, and ran the galley ashore, and he and they leapt down and planted the banner before him in the ground. And when the other Venetians saw the standard of St Mark and the Doge's galley beached before their own, they were ashamed, and followed him ashore.

As the attack gathered momentum, it soon became clear to the defenders that they had no chance. Before many hours had passed, Dandolo was able to send word to his Frankish allies that no less than twenty-five towers along the wall were already in Venetian hands. By this time his men were pouring into the city itself through breaches in the rampart, setting fire to the wooden houses until the whole Blachernae quarter was ablaze. That evening Alexius III, Emperor of Constantinople, fled secretly from his city, leaving his wife and all his children except a favourite daughter – whom he took with him, together with a few other women, 10,000 pounds of gold and a bag of jewels – to face the future as best they might.

Byzantium, at this gravest crisis in its history, was thus left without an Emperor; and it may seem surprising that, to fill the breach, a hastily convened council of state should have fetched old Isaac Angelus out of his prison and replaced him on the imperial throne. He was even blinder than Dandolo – his brother had taken the precaution of having his eyes put out when deposing him – and he had also proved himself a hopelessly incompetent ruler. He was, however, the legitimate Emperor; and by restoring him the Byzantines doubtless believed that they had removed all grounds for further intervention by the Crusaders. So, in a way, they had; but there remained the question of the promises made by young Alexius to Boniface and Dandolo. These Isaac was now obliged to ratify, agreeing at the same time to make his son co-Emperor with him. Only then did the Franks and Venetians accord him their formal recognition, after which they withdrew to the Galata side of the Golden Horn to await their expected rewards.

On 1 August 1203, Alexius IV was crowned alongside his father and assumed effective power. Immediately he began to regret the offers he had made so rashly at Zara in the spring. The imperial treasury, after his uncle's extravagances, was empty; the new taxes he was forced to introduce were openly resented by his subjects, who knew all too well where their money was going. Meanwhile the clergy – always an important political force in Constantinople – were scandalized when he began to seize and melt down their church plate and furious when they heard of his plans to subordinate them to the Pope of Rome. As autumn gave way to winter his unpopularity steadily grew, and the continued presence of the hated Franks, whose greed appeared insatiable, still further increased the tension. One night a group of them wandering through the city came upon a little mosque which stood in the Saracen quarter, behind the church of St Irene, pillaged it and burnt it to the ground. The flames spread, and for the next forty-eight hours Constantinople was engulfed in the worst fire in its history.

Alexius had been away on a brief and unsuccessful expedition against his fugitive uncle. He returned to find much of his capital in ruins and his subjects in a state of almost open warfare against the foreigners. The situation had clearly reached breaking-point; but when, a few days later, a delegation of three Crusaders and three Venetians came to demand immediate payment of the sum owing to them, there was nothing he could do. According to Villehardouin – who was, as usual, one of the delegates – the party narrowly escaped a lynching on its way to and from the imperial palace. 'And thus,' he writes, 'the war began; and each side did to the other as much harm as it could, both by sea and by land.'

Ironically enough, neither the Crusaders nor the Greeks wanted such a war. The inhabitants of Constantinople had by now one object only in mind: to be rid, once and for all, of these uncivilized thugs who were destroying their beloved city and bleeding them white into the bargain. The Franks, for their part, had not forgotten the reason they had left their homes, and increasingly resented their enforced stay among what they considered an effete and effeminate people when they should have been getting to grips with the infidel. Even if the Greek debt were to be paid in full, they themselves would not benefit materially; it would only enable them to settle their own outstanding account with the Venetians.

The key to the whole impossible affair lay, in short, with Venice – or, more accurately, with Enrico Dandolo. It was open to him at any moment to give his fleet the order to sail. Had he done so, the Crusaders would have been relieved and the Byzantines overjoyed. Formerly, his refusal had always been on the grounds that the Franks would never be able to pay him their debt until they in their turn received the money that Alexius and his father had promised them. In fact, however, that debt was now of relatively little interest to him – scarcely more than was the Crusade itself. His mind was on greater things: the overthrow of the Byzantine Empire and the establishment of a Venetian puppet on the throne of Constantinople.

And so, as prospects of a peaceful settlement receded, Dandolo's advice to his Frankish allies took on a different tone. Nothing more, he pointed out, could be expected of Isaac and Alexius, who had not scrupled to betray the friends to whom they owed their joint crown. If the Crusaders were ever to obtain their due, they would have to take it by force. Their moral justification was complete: the faithless Angeli had no further claim on their loyalties. Once inside the city, with one of their own leaders installed as Emperor, they could pay Venice what they owed her almost without noticing it and still have more than enough to finance the Crusade. This was their opportunity; they should seize it now, for it would not recur.

Within Constantinople too, it was generally agreed that Alexius IV must go; and on 25 January 1204 a great concourse of senators, clergy and people gathered in St Sophia to declare him deposed and elect a successor. During their deliberations – which dragged on inconclusively for three days before fixing on a reluctant nonentity named Nicholas Canabus – the only really effective figure at that moment on the Byzantine stage took the law into his own hands.

Alexius Ducas – nicknamed Murzuphlus on account of his eyebrows, which were black and shaggy and met in the middle – was a nobleman whose family had already produced two Emperors of its own and who now occupied the position of *protovestarius*, which gave him unrestricted access to the imperial apartments. Late at night he burst into where Alexius was sleeping, woke him with the news that his subjects had risen against him and offered him what he claimed was the only chance of escape. Muffling the Emperor in a long cloak, he led him by a side door out of the palace to where a band of fellow-conspirators was waiting. The unhappy youth was then clapped into irons and consigned to a dungeon where, having survived two attempts to poison him, he eventually succumbed to the bowstring. At about the same time his blind father also died; Villehardouin, with that impregnable naivety that characterizes his whole chronicle, attributes his demise to a sudden sickness, brought on at the news of Alexius's fate; it does not seem to have struck him that so convenient a malady might have been artificially induced.[1]

His rivals once eliminated – and Nicholas Canabus having retired with relief into obscurity – Murzuphlus was crowned in St Sophia as Alexius V. Once in control, he immediately began to show those qualities of leadership that his Empire had lacked for so long. For the first time since the Crusaders' arrival, the walls and towers were properly manned, while workmen sweated day and night strengthening them and raising them higher. To the Franks, one thing was plain: there was to be no more negotiation, far less any question of further payments on a debt for which the new Emperor in any case bore no responsibility. An all-out attempt on the city was their only chance; and now that Murzuphlus had revealed himself in his turn as a usurper – and a murderer to boot – they were morally in an even stronger position than if they had moved against Alexius, a legitimate Emperor and their erstwhile ally.

It was exactly what Enrico Dandolo had been saying for months; and from the moment of Murzuphlus's *coup* the old Doge seems to have been recognized, by Venetians and Franks alike, as the leader of the entire expedition. Boniface of Montferrat strove to maintain his influence; with the imperial crown almost within his grasp, it was more than ever vital to him that he should. But his association with the deposed Emperor had been too close, and now that Alexius IV was gone he found himself in some degree discredited. Besides, he had links with the Genoese – and Dandolo knew it.

Early in March there began a series of council meetings in the camp at Galata. They were concerned less with the plan of attack – despite Murzuphlus's work on the defences, its success was apparently considered a foregone conclusion – than with the future administration of the Empire after its conquest. It was agreed that the Crusaders and the Venetians should each appoint six delegates to an electoral committee, and that this should choose the new Emperor. If, as was expected, they decided on a Frank, then the Patriarch should be a Venetian; otherwise vice-versa. The Emperor would receive a quarter of the city and of the Empire, including the two chief palaces – Blachernae on the Golden Horn and the old Boucoleon palace on the Marmara. The remaining three-quarters should be divided equally, half to Venice and half in fief to the Crusading knights. For the Venetian portion, the Doge was specifically

---

1. A fellow Crusader, Robert of Clary, probably came closer to the truth when he wrote '*Si li fist lachier une corde u col, si le fist estranler et sen pere Kyrsaac ausi.*'

absolved from the need to do the Emperor homage. All plunder taken
was to be brought to an agreed spot and distributed in similar proportions.
Finally, the parties were to undertake not to leave Constantinople for a
full year – until March 1205 at the earliest.

The attack began on Friday morning, 9 April. It was to be directed
against that same stretch of sea wall facing the Golden Horn where
Dandolo and his men had distinguished themselves nine months before.
This time, however, it failed. The new, higher walls and towers, no longer
accessible from the Venetian mastheads, provided useful platforms from
which the Greek catapults could create havoc among the besiegers below.
By mid-afternoon the attackers had begun to re-embark their men,
horses and equipment and beat their way back to Galata and safety. The
next two days were spent in repairing the damage; then, on Monday, the
assault was renewed. This time the Venetians lashed their ships together
in pairs, thus contriving to throw twice as much weight as before against
each tower; soon, too, a strong north wind blew up, driving the vessels
far further up the beach below the walls than the oarsmen could ever have
done, and allowing the besiegers to work under cover of makeshift
shelters stretched from one mast to another. Before long, two of the
towers were overwhelmed and occupied. Almost simultaneously, the
Crusaders broke open one of the gates in the wall and surged into the city.

Murzuphlus, who had been commanding the defenders with courage
and determination, galloped through the streets doing his utmost to rally
his men. 'But', writes Nicetas,

they were all swept up in the whirlpool of despair, and had no ears either for
his orders or his remonstrances . . . Seeing that his efforts were vain, and fearing
to be served up to the Franks as a choice morsel for their table, he took flight,
accompanied by Euphrosyne, wife of the Emperor Alexius [III] and her
daughter Eudoxia, whom he passionately adored; for he was a great lover of
women and had already repudiated two wives in a manner not canonical.

The three sought refuge with the ex-Emperor in Thrace. Meanwhile
Murzuphlus duly married Eudoxia and began to gather strength for a
counter-offensive.

Once the walls were breached, the carnage was dreadful – so dreadful that
even Villehardouin was appalled. Only at nightfall, 'tired of battle and
massacre', did the conquerors call a truce and withdraw to camp in one
of the great squares of the city. 'That night, a party of the Crusaders,
fearing a counter-attack, set fire to the district which lay between them-

selves and the Greeks . . . and the city began to blaze fiercely, and it burned all that night and all the next day until evening. It was the third fire at Constantinople since the Franks arrived. And there were more houses burnt than there are to be found in the three greatest cities of the Kingdom of France.' After this, such few defenders as had not yet laid down their arms lost the spirit to continue. The next morning the Crusaders awoke to find all resistance at an end.

But for the inhabitants of Constantinople the tragedy had scarcely begun. Not for nothing had the army waited so long outside the world's richest city. Now that it was theirs and that the customary three days' looting was allowed them, they fell on it like locusts. Not since the barbarian invasions some seven centuries before had Europe witnessed such an orgy of brutality and vandalism; never in history had so much beauty, so much superb craftsmanship, been wantonly destroyed in so short a space of time. Among the witnesses – helpless, horrified, almost unable to believe that human beings who called themselves Christians could be capable of such enormities – was Nicetas Choniates:

I know not how to put any order into my account, how to begin, continue, or end. They smashed the holy images, hurled sacred relics of the Martyrs into places I am ashamed to mention, scattering everywhere the body and blood of the Saviour. These heralds of Anti-Christ seized the chalices and the patens, tore out the jewels and used them as drinking cups . . . As for their profanation of the Great Church [St Sophia], it cannot be thought of without horror. They destroyed the high altar, a work of art admired by the entire world, and shared out the pieces among themselves . . . And they brought horses and mules into the Church, the better to carry off the holy vessels and the engraved silver and gold that they had torn from the throne, and the pulpit, and the doors, and the furniture wherever it was to be found; and when some of these beasts slipped and fell, they ran them through with their swords, fouling the Church with their blood and ordure.

A common harlot was enthroned in the Patriarch's chair, to hurl insults at Jesus Christ; and she sang bawdy songs, and danced immodestly in the holy place . . . nor was there mercy shown to virtuous matrons, innocent maids or even virgins consecrated to God . . . In the streets, houses and churches there could be heard only cries and lamentations.

And these men, he continues, carried the Cross on their shoulders, the Cross on which they had sworn to pass through Christian lands without bloodshed, to take arms only against the heathen, and to abstain from the pleasures of the flesh until their holy task was done.

It was Constantinople's darkest hour – perhaps even darker than that, two and a half centuries later, which saw the city's final fall to the Ottoman Sultan. But not all its treasures perished. While the Frenchmen and Flemings abandoned themselves in a frenzy of wholesale destruction, the Venetians kept their heads. They knew beauty when they saw it. They too looted and pillaged and plundered – but they did not destroy. Instead, all that they could lay their hands on they sent back to Venice – beginning with the four great bronze horses which had dominated the Hippodrome since the days of Constantine and which, after a short period in the Arsenal, now stand above the main door of the Basilica of St Mark. The north and south faces of the Basilica are also studded with sculptures and reliefs shipped back at the same time; within, in the north transept, hangs the miraculous icon of the Virgin Nicopoeia – Bringer of Victory – which the Emperors used to carry before them into battle; while the Treasury possesses one of the greatest collections of Byzantine works of art to be found anywhere – a further monument to Venetian rapacity.

After three days of terror, order was restored. As previously arranged, all the spoils – or that part that had not been successfully concealed – were gathered together in three churches, and careful distribution made, a quarter for the Emperor when checked, the remainder to be split equally between Franks and Venetians. As soon as it was done, the Crusaders paid over to Dandolo the 50,000 silver marks they owed. These formalities satisfactorily concluded, both parties applied themselves to the next task, the imperial election.

Boniface of Montferrat, in a desperate attempt to recover his lost prestige and strengthen his own candidacy, had tracked down the Empress Margaret, widow of Isaac Angelus, and married her. He need not have bothered. Enrico Dandolo refused outright to consider him and the choice ultimately fell, thanks to fearsome Venetian pressure, on the easy-going and tractable Count Baldwin of Flanders and Hainault. On 16 May Baldwin received his coronation in St Sophia – the third Emperor to be crowned there in less than a year. And although the newly-appointed Patriarch, the Venetian Tommaso Morosini,[1] had not yet arrived in Constantinople and could not consequently officiate at the ceremony, there can have been few among those present who would have denied that the new Emperor owed his elevation to the Venetian Republic.

---

1. 'Fat as a stuffed pig,' snorted Nicetas later, 'and wearing a robe so tight that it seemed to have been sewn on to his skin.' Though already a monk, Morosini had not taken orders at the time he was selected for the Patriarchate. He was ordained deacon at once, priest a fortnight later, and Bishop the following morning.

In return, Venice had appropriated the best part of the imperial territory for her own. By the terms of her treaty with the Crusaders, she was entitled to three-eighths of the city and the Empire, plus free trade throughout the imperial dominions, from which both Genoa and Pisa were to be rigorously excluded. In Constantinople itself, Dandolo demanded the whole district surrounding St Sophia and the Patriarchate, reaching right down to the shore of the Golden Horn; for the rest, he took for Venice those areas that would reinforce her mastery of the Mediterranean and give her an unbroken chain of ports along the route from the lagoon to the Black Sea – including the western coast of the Greek mainland, the Ionian Islands, all the Peloponnese, Euboea, Naxos and Andros, Gallipoli, the Thracian seaboard, the inland city of Adrianople and finally, after a brief negotiation with Boniface, the all-important island of Crete.

Thus it emerges beyond all doubt that it was the Venetians, rather than the French or Flemings – or even Baldwin himself, who remained little more than a figurehead – who were the real victors of the Fourth Crusade; and that their victory was due, almost entirely, to Enrico Dandolo. From the very first – from that day four years before when the Frankish emissaries had arrived on the Rialto to ask the Republic's help in their holy enterprise – he had turned every development to Venetian advantage. He had regained Zara; he had protected Egypt from attack and so preserved Venice's commercial interests with the Muslim world; he had subtly redirected the Frankish forces towards Constantinople, while leaving the ostensible responsibility for the decision with them. Once there, his courage had largely inspired the first attack; his capacity for intrigue had brought down the Angeli, making essential a second siege and the physical capture of the city: his diplomatic skill had shaped a treaty which gave Venice more than she had dared to hope and laid the foundations for her commercial Empire. Refusing the Byzantine crown for himself – to accept it would have created insuperable constitutional problems at home and might well have destroyed the Republic – and declining even to serve on the electoral commission, he nevertheless knew that his influence over the election (which was held under his auspices, in the old imperial palace that he had temporarily appropriated for himself) would be tantamount to giving Venice a majority and would ensure the success of his own candidate. Finally, while encouraging the Franks to feudalize the Empire – a step which could not fail to create fragmentation and disunity and would prevent its ever becoming strong enough to obstruct Venetian expansion – he had kept Venice herself outside the feudal framework, holding her new dominions not as an imperial fief but by her own right of conquest. For a blind man not far short of ninety it was a remarkable achievement.

Yet even now old Dandolo did not rest. Outside the capital, the Greek subjects of the Empire continued their resistance. Murzuphlus was to cause no further trouble; soon after his marriage he was blinded by his jealous father-in-law, and when a year or two later he was captured by the Franks they brought him back to Constantinople and flung him to his death from a tall column in the centre of the city. But another of Alexius III's sons-in-law set up an Empire in exile at Nicaea, two of the Comneni did the same at Trebizond and, in Epirus, a bastard Angelus proclaimed himself an autonomous Despot. On all sides the erstwhile Crusaders had to fight hard to establish themselves, nowhere more fiercely than in Venice's newly acquired city of Adrianople where, just after Easter, 1205, the Emperor Baldwin fell into the hands of the Bulgars and the old Doge, who had fought determinedly at his side, was left to lead a shattered army back to Constantinople. He is not known to have been wounded; but six weeks later he was dead. His body, rather surprisingly, was not returned to Venice, but was buried in St Sophia – where, in the gallery above the south aisle, his grave may still be seen.

Enrico Dandolo had deserved well of his city; it is a source of still greater surprise that the Venetians never erected a monument to the greatest of all their Doges.[1] But in the wider context of world events, he was a disaster. Though it cannot be said of him that he gave the Crusades a bad name, that is only because the record of those successive forays over the previous century had already emerged as one of the blackest chapters in the history of Christendom. Yet the Fourth Crusade – if indeed it can be so described at all – surpassed even its predecessors in faithlessness and duplicity, brutality and greed. Constantinople, in the twelfth century, had been not just the greatest and wealthiest metropolis of the world, but also the most cultivated both intellectually and artistically and the chief repository of Europe's classical heritage, both Greek and Roman. By its sack, Western civilization suffered a loss greater even than the sack of Rome by the barbarians in the fifth century or the burning of the library of Alexandria by the soldiers of the Prophet in the seventh – perhaps the most catastrophic single loss in all its history.

Politically, too, the damage done was incalculable. Although the Latin rule along the Bosphorus lasted less than sixty years, after which the

---

1. They did, however, commemorate the main episodes of the Fourth Crusade with another of those cycles of paintings in the Doges' Palace, this one running along the south wall of the Sala del Maggior Consiglio.

Greek Empire was to struggle on for nearly two more centuries, that Empire never recovered its strength or any considerable part of its lost dominion. Under firm and forceful leadership – which was not lacking in the century to come – a strong and prosperous Byzantium might have halted the Turkish advance while there was still time. Instead, it was left economically crippled, territorially truncated, powerless to defend itself against the Ottoman tide. There are few greater ironies in history than the fact that the fate of Eastern Christendom should have been sealed – and half Europe condemned to some five hundred years of Muslim rule – by men who fought under the banner of the Cross. Those men were transported, inspired, encouraged and ultimately led by Enrico Dandolo in the name of the Venetian Republic; and, just as Venice derived the major advantage from the tragedy, so she and her magnificent old Doge must accept the major responsibility for the havoc they wrought upon the world.

Part Two

The Imperial Expansion

Once did she hold the gorgeous East in fee,
And was the safeguard of the West . . .

Wordsworth,
*Ode on the Extinction of the
Venetian Republic*

· II ·

The Latin Empire

[1205–1268]

> ... her daughters had their dowers
> From spoils of nations, and the exhaustless East
> Pour'd in her lap all gems in sparkling showers:
> In purple was she robed, and of her feast
> Monarchs partook, and deem'd their dignity increased.
>
> Byron, *Childe Harold's Pilgrimage*, IV, ii

When, on 5 August 1205, Sebastiano Ziani's son Pietro was unanimously elected Doge of Venice, the first question that confronted him was one of identity. To the long list of sonorous but mostly empty titles which had gradually become attached to the ducal throne, there had now been added a new one which meant exactly what it said: *Lord of a Quarter and Half a Quarter of the Roman Empire*. Was it any longer possible for a Doge to consider himself – as, in essence, his predecessors had always considered themselves – an Italian prince? Or must he now change his role to that of oriental despot?

It was Venice's good fortune that at this crucial turning-point in her history there emerged to direct her affairs not an ambitious adventurer but a thoughtful, clear-headed man with both feet firmly on the ground. The Zianis were enormously rich – it was popularly rumoured that their wealth was based on a golden cow, discovered by a remote ancestor in his cellar at Altino – and deeply respected in the city, where Pietro was well known for his piety and generosity. In his youth he had been a sailor, and in 1177 he had commanded the flotilla that escorted Frederick Barbarossa from Ravenna to Chioggia. He had also accompanied the Fourth Crusade to Zara and Constantinople; but he does not seem to have stayed very long, since at the time of his election he was already serving as one of the six counsellors to Renier Dandolo, Vice-Doge since his father's departure. Perhaps the bloodshed had sickened him; the Altino Chronicle – a surprisingly reliable source for this particular period – approvingly quotes one of his favourite *dicta*: 'War we can always have if we want it; peace we should zealously seek, and keep when found.'

But for a republic that suddenly and half-unexpectedly acquires a widespread overseas empire at a single swoop, peace tends to prove an elusive amenity. Long before old Dandolo's death it had become clear that the conquered subjects of Byzantium had no intention of accepting the new dispensations without a struggle. Venice might be rich and powerful, but her native-born population was small – nowhere near sufficient to pacify, administer and defend the entire portion that had been allotted to her. She could not look to Constantinople for help; Henry of Flanders, who had succeeded his brother Baldwin as Emperor, was already hard pressed to keep his own dominions in order. Under Ziani's wise guidance, the Venetians therefore made no attempt to take over all their new territories at once. Most of these were entrusted to vassals, usually the younger sons of leading Venetian families who were only too happy to set themselves up as petty princelings in Thrace, Asia Minor and the Aegean archipelago. Only a few of the most strategically important bases – Crete, Durazzo, Corfu and the two ports of Modone and Corone in the Morea – remained under the direct authority of the Republic.

Even these few key outposts were hard enough to control – especially since Venice's recent successes had aroused the furious jealousy of her two principal maritime rivals, Genoa and Pisa. Though both had possessed trading communities in Constantinople, representatives of which had manned the walls of the city alongside the Greeks during the Fourth Crusade, both had been debarred from imperial commerce after the fall of the city[1] and both were determined to prevent Venice from further consolidating her hold on the eastern Mediterranean. In 1206 the self-styled Count of Malta – in reality a Genoese freebooter named Enrico Pescatore – made an armed landing in Crete and, assisted by the local Greek population, captured several strongpoints along the coast. It took two years and two expeditions by the Venetians to dislodge him. To ensure that such a misfortune should not occur again, a certain Giacomo Tiepolo was appointed to Crete with the title of Doge and powers analogous to those of his counterpart in Venice, except that he and his successors were to hold office for two years instead of for life. A sixth of the island was allotted to each of the six *sestieri* of the city; and thus there was founded, in the following year, the Republic's first properly consti-

---

1. Pisa was in fact readmitted, on sufferance, in 1206; but all Genoese shipping was forbidden until 1218, when Greek and Bulgar pressure on the city called for an end to Venetian–Genoese hostilities.

tuted overseas colony. Even now the native Greeks remained unsubdued. Their lands had been confiscated to make fiefs for their Venetian over-lords, and they bitterly resented the flood of rapacious Latin churchmen who, not content with taking over all ecclesiastical property, even sought to impose the hated Roman rite in place of the traditional Orthodox liturgy. Throughout the century they were to keep up their resistance – as well they might.

But the difficulties in Crete, Corfu and elsewhere were less worrying to Ziani in the long term than those in Constantinople itself. When the city fell to the Crusaders, one of the first tasks of Enrico Dandolo had been to provide for the effective administration of the Venetian districts by the appointment of a governor, the *podestà*; and immediately on his death his compatriots in the city elected one of their number, Marino Zeno, to this office. In Venice, however, where it had always been understood that the *podestà* would be an appointee of the central government, the news of the election was received with some concern, and this was increased by subsequent reports that Zeno had adopted as his own the Doge's new style of 'Lord of a Quarter and Half a Quarter of the Roman Empire', and had even taken to wearing the parti-coloured stockings and scarlet buskins – formerly the prerogative of the Emperor – that Dandolo had worn before him. Could it be that success had already gone to the heads of the Venetians in the Levant, and that they were planning a break-away from the mother-city? A chilly message was dispatched to Zeno: excep-tionally on this occasion, his election would be ratified; but in future every new *podestà* would be sent out from Venice.

According to a long-established Venetian tradition, Doge Ziani at one moment seriously considered the possibility of transferring the capital of the Republic to Constantinople, just as Constantine the Great had done with the Roman Empire nine centuries before. The proposal is said to have been formally discussed in council, its adherents arguing that the focus of Venetian interests had now shifted eastward, that Venice was too far distant from her overseas possessions and that the city was notoriously liable to earthquake and flood;[1] and to have been finally rejected by a single vote, the so-called *Voto della Provvidenza*. But this story is reported only by one or two less reliable chroniclers – the most trustworthy sources for the period do not mention it at all – and although it may well be that some such idea was momentarily put forward, it seems unlikely that it was

1. This last point would have received added force from the memorable earthquake of Christmas Day 1223, which destroyed part of the monastery of S. Giorgio Maggiore and caused the total disappearance of Ammiana and Costanziaca, two small islands in the lagoon.

seriously upheld for very long, still less that it came anywhere near acceptance. One thing only is certain: Venice, by moving her capital to the shores of the Bosphorus, would have sacrificed her security as well as her identity, and would have survived little longer – perhaps even less long – than the pathetic Latin Empire which she did so much to establish. If, despite the probabilities, the 'Providence Vote' were to prove a historical fact, Venetians of all succeeding generations would have had good cause to congratulate themselves on a lucky escape.

By the time Pietro Ziani – now old and sick – resigned early in 1229, to be laid to rest a few weeks later beside his father in S. Giorgio Maggiore, Venice had recovered her political bearings and was back on course. The crucial question had been decided, and the decision was the right one: she would continue as before. She would exploit her new dominions as fully as possible, both politically and commercially, but she would not risk the advantages she already enjoyed by biting off more than she could chew.

Few Venetians can have been more thoroughly convinced of the wisdom of this policy than the new Doge, Giacomo Tiepolo; none, certainly, had better reason to mistrust the promise of Empire. As first Duke of Crete he had had his full share of trouble with the rebellious Greek population – to say nothing of some Venetian adventurers whom he had been ill-advised enough to call to his aid – and had eventually been forced to escape from the island in woman's clothes. His next post had been that of Venetian *podestà* in Constantinople, where he soon saw how rapidly the Crusader Empire was crumbling; in 1219 he had gone so far as to conclude a separate commercial treaty with the Greek Emperor-in-exile at Nicaea, addressing him as 'Emperor of the Romans' – a step which, though it can hardly have endeared him to the Latins, showed a clear political realization of where Venetian interests lay.

His dogeship itself cannot be said to have begun auspiciously. Unlike his predecessor, whose election had been unanimous, he and a rival candidate each polled twenty votes from the forty-strong electoral commission, and the issue had to be decided by lot. It was perhaps to mark his disapproval of the element of chance thus introduced – a sentiment that seems to have been widely shared, since to prevent a recurrence the number of the commissioners was thenceforth increased to forty-one – that old Ziani, lying on his deathbed, refused to receive the new Doge's courtesy call;[1] perhaps, too, it was a sign of general unease that the

1. Andrea Dandolo, who reports the incident, suggests as an additional reason that he

promissione which Tiepolo was obliged to sign on taking office was considerably more detailed, and more restrictive of the ducal power, than that of any Doge before him.

This *promissione*, in effect a sort of coronation oath, had long been a traditional feature of a Doge's accession. In early days it had been a mere formality, usually drafted by the new Doge in person, in which he simply promised to do his duty with impartiality and diligence. Gradually, however, the *promissioni* had become longer and more precise; and that which was now presented to Giacomo Tiepolo – and used as a model for a whole stream of his successors – reads almost like a legal contract. In it the Doge swears to renounce all claims on the revenue of the state – the only exception being his salary (payable quarterly), his share of the tribute from certain Istrian and Dalmatian towns, and certain specified quantities of apples, cherries and crabs from Lombardy and Treviso. He undertakes to contribute to public loans, to respect state secrets, and to enter into no communication with Pope, Emperor, or any other prince without prior permission of his Council, to whom all incoming letters from such potentates must immediately be shown. Firm measures are built in against corruption: the Doge may accept no presents except stipulated quantities of food and wine – not more than one animal or ten brace of birds at a time – and even those are forbidden if the donors have favours to ask; suppliants may offer him only such token gifts as rose-water, leaves, flowers, scented herbs or balsam. Nor is he to make any appointments of associates or successors to the dogeship.

In retrospect, the *promissione* of Giacomo Tiepolo emerges as another significant step in the long process by which the Doge of Venice was slowly reduced over the centuries from autocrat to figurehead. That process had begun at least as early as the days of Domenico Flabanico in the eleventh century, and had continued with the reforms following the assassination of Vitale Michiel. And it was not yet finished. Tiepolo himself was to institute further controls, including a board of five so-called Correctors, charged with the task of drafting each new *promissione* and helped by a trio of Inquisitors who, after careful examination of the late Doge's record, would inform the Correctors of any signs of autocratic or other undesirable tendencies; the latter would then adjust the new *promissione* accordingly. Venice, as usual, was taking no chances.

---

was of doubtful origins – *propter genus suum*. This seems odd, in view of the fact that the name of Tiepolo was one of the oldest in Venice, already known in the seventh century, and furthermore that the two Doges' wives were sisters, both daughters of Tancred of Lecce, the illegitimate and ill-starred King of Sicily.

However cynical Giacomo Tiepolo may have felt about Venice's overseas Empire, he soon found himself faced with far greater problems nearer home. They were caused by the new Emperor of the West, Henry VI's son, Frederick II of Hohenstaufen. This extraordinary figure – perhaps the most remarkable European ruler between Charlemagne and Napoleon – had received his imperial coronation in Rome in 1220. It was, perhaps, the last favour he would ever receive from a Pope; the remaining thirty years of his life were to be taken up with an unremitting struggle against the Papacy and the Italian cities of the reconstituted Lombard League, over which, like his father and grandfather before him, he was determined to re-establish control. Of this new association, founded as recently as 1198, Venice was not a member. Her neutrality, so triumphantly demonstrated by Barbarossa's submission to Pope Alexander twenty-one years before, had stood her in good stead and had been consolidated by the long imperial interregnum following Henry VI's death as well as by her own recent preoccupation with affairs in the East. Now that the storm was blowing up again she was resolved to remain, as far as possible, aloof.

It was in an effort to dispel this aloofness and to win the Republic over to his own side that Frederick visited Venice early in 1233. One would love to know more of his reactions to what he saw. From his maternal grand-father, Roger II of Sicily, and his childhood in cosmopolitan Palermo he had acquired an intellectual curiosity and a familiarity with five European languages and cultures – to say nothing of the Arabic with which he had personally beguiled the Emir of Jerusalem into restoring all the principal shrines to Christian hands – that had made him one of the most civilized men of his age and had already earned him the title of *Stupor Mundi*, Wonder of the World. In Venice, which had now taken the place of Palermo as Europe's foremost bridge, artistic and cultural as well as commercial, between East and West, he must have found much of that same multi-racial, polyglot atmosphere that had done so much to shape his life; while his love of magnificence and display – the exotic menagerie with which he habitually travelled was a source of perpetual amazement to his subjects – would have responded in full measure to the most splendid and most beautiful city he had ever seen.

It is perhaps rather more open to question whether the intellectual accomplishments of Giacomo Tiepolo and those other Venetian notables with whom he came in contact during his short stay proved equally stimulating to the ruler in whose court the sonnet was invented and who could hold his own with the foremost scientists and philosophers of his day. Frederick certainly directed upon them the full power of his formidable personality, backing it up by a confirmation of all the Republic's former privileges in the Empire and several new concessions in Apulia and Sicily. In return he received a splinter from the True Cross – but very little else. He may have made a tactical mistake in commissioning a new imperial crown from a Venetian goldsmith – an incident which caused much heart-searching among the authorities, who finally allowed the work to go forward only on the understanding that it was a strictly private and unofficial transaction. At all events, though perfect cordiality was shown on both sides, Frederick left the city a disappointed man. The Venetians remained, as before, on their guard.

In the years that followed, Venice's relations with the Empire were to deteriorate fast. For all her avowed neutrality, she had no desire to see a strong and probably covetous Frederick on her mainland doorstep. The considerations that had led her to join the first League were still largely valid, and her sympathies could not but be in some degree engaged with the Lombard cities. Before long she was acting as banker for the new League; soon, too, as the fighting grew fiercer, she was offering asylum to the Emperor's enemies. Meanwhile distinguished Venetians were increasingly sought after by the cities to serve as *podestà*. To the modern mind it seems almost inconceivable that these powerful municipalities should regularly and deliberately have appointed foreigners to conduct their affairs; but most of them were too divided – by factional interests and jealousies, ambitions and family feuds – for agreement on any native-born leader to be possible. To such divisions Venice was herself by no means immune; it is a credit to her remarkable gift for self-government that never once in her history was she even tempted to seek a foreign *podestà* of her own.

Still, she must have found the institution useful. Both Padua and Treviso, for example, had Venetians as their *podestà* by 1236, the latter no less a personage than the Doge's son Pietro. In that year it was he who led the city's heroic defence against the besieging army of Frederick II's principal lieutenant in North Italy, the dreaded Ezzelino da Romano, acquiring such a reputation in the process that when the city was forced into surrender in 1237 he was at once invited to occupy the same position in Milan.

The advantage of the *podestà* system, so far as Venice was concerned, was that she could pursue her interests discreetly on the mainland without officially jeopardizing her neutrality. As time went on, however, this neutrality became ever harder to profess, let alone to preserve. Not only was she drawn more and more into the ambit of the Lombard cities; she was also growing anxious at the continued imperial successes – particularly that of Cortenuova in 1237, where Pietro Tiepolo was taken prisoner and paraded in triumph on an elephant, or the still more ominous occasion in the following year when Ezzelino's army reached the very shores of the lagoon and destroyed the convent of S. Ilario at Fusina. Finally, in September 1239, at the instigation of Pope Gregory IX, the Venetians joined perhaps the most surprising alliance in their history – with their two bitterest rivals, Genoa and Pisa. It was even agreed that Venetian and Genoese galleys should fly the standard of the other republic alongside their own.

This arrangement, as might have been expected, did not last long; indeed, apart from a short and rather half-hearted expedition against Frederick's beloved Apulia, the alliance itself resulted in only one significant campaign. This was against the city of Ferrara, which Ezzelino and his other Ghibelline colleague, Salinguerra di Torello, were trying to develop as a commercial rival to Venice. A Venetian fleet – followed, some weeks later, by the Doge in his state barge, the *Bucintoro* – sailed up the Po and blockaded the city; and after five months Salinguerra was at last forced to seek terms. Whether or not, as it was widely alleged, the Venetians seized him during negotiations or whether he gave himself up to them of his own accord is uncertain; though over eighty, he was brought back to Venice and lived there another five years in comfortable captivity, to be honoured on his death with a state funeral and a splendid monument in S. Nicolò on the Lido. His followers in Ferrara were not so lucky; the Guelf faction led by Marquis Azzo VII of Este, which was now able to return from exile, took a merciless revenge. Meanwhile the grants and privileges demanded by Venice and readily granted by Azzo went far beyond any previous demands.

In 1241, at the reputed age of 100, Frederick II's arch-enemy Gregory IX died at last. His successor after a two-year interregnum, Innocent IV,[1] continued his policies; but, at least so far as Venice was concerned, the heat had gone out of the struggle, and the peace treaty she signed with the Emperor in 1245 did little more than confirm the existing state of affairs. To some extent this may have been due to a recrudescence of trouble in Dalmatia which for several years kept the Venetians primarily occupied elsewhere; but the underlying cause was a good deal simpler. Venice had come to realize that the Empire did not after all constitute a direct threat to her sovereignty. Never once did Frederick suggest that the Republic

1. Pope Celestine IV, who in fact succeeded Gregory but who died only eighteen days after his election, can safely be ignored.

owed him any allegiance. In all his written communications with the Doge he always scrupulously avoided referring to the Venetians as *fideles* – that dangerously emotive word, with its arrogant presumption of loyalty, which aroused such wrath among the townsmen of Lombardy. The two short miles of shallow water which separated the islands of Rialto from the mainland had somehow conferred on Venice a special, separate, status; they had saved her not only from conquest, spoliation and destruction but also, and more extraordinarily still, from being looked upon as just another – albeit the richest and most powerful – of the North Italian cities. The acquisition of her overseas Empire in the Levant had still further increased the respect in which she was held. She was no longer a city. She was a nation.

But a nation founded on trade; and that trade, as the Venetians must – at least subconsciously – have realized, owed its phenomenal success not to any territorial expansion but, paradoxically, to the very smallness of the Republic. Here was another benefit conferred by the surrounding lagoon. By virtually confining the Venetians to so restricted a space, it had created in them a unique spirit of cohesion and cooperation – a spirit which showed itself not only at times of national crisis but also, and still more impressively, in the day-to-day handling of their affairs. Among Venice's rich merchant aristocracy everyone knew everyone else, and close acquaintance led to mutual trust of a kind that in other cities seldom extended far outside the family circle. In consequence, the Venetians stood alone in their capacity for quick, efficient business administration. A trading venture, even one that involved immense initial outlay, several years' duration and considerable risk, could be arranged on the Rialto in a matter of hours. It might take the form of a simple partnership between two merchants, or that of a large corporation of the kind needed to finance a full-sized fleet or trans-Asiatic caravan; it might run for an agreed period or, more usually, it might be an *ad hoc* arrangement which would automatically be dissolved when the particular venture was completed. But it would be founded on trust, and it would be inviolable.

This system of easily formed short-term partnerships meant in practice that any Venetian with a little money to invest could have a share in trade. Artisans, widows, the aged, the sick – all could enter into what was known as a *colleganza* with some active but comparatively impecunious young merchant. They would provide two-thirds of the required capital while the merchant would contribute one-third, make the voyage and do all the work. On his return to Venice he was legally bound within one month to present his partner with a complete set of accounts, after which the proceeds would be equally divided. Some small dues might be levied by the state, but in these early days Venetian taxation was low – infinitesimal in comparison with the punitive sums levied by the Byzantines on their own merchants, or by most of the princes of feudal Europe. So profits were high, incentives great, and investment capital increased year by year.

It was the presumed failure of one of these *colleganze* that provided Shakespeare with the basic plot for *The Merchant of Venice*; by the middle of the thirteenth century there was already a considerable Jewish population in the city and its immediate neighbourhood – perhaps 3,000 or more. Many lived at Mestre, on the mainland; others – particularly those who had mercantile dealings with Dalmatia – occupied the island of Spinalunga and were in fact responsible for its change of name to Giudecca. Apart from trade, their principal occupations were, as everywhere in Europe, the lending of money – usury by Venetian citizens being forbidden in the Republic – and the practice of medicine; but apart from certain requirements as to residence there does not appear at this time to have been any legal restriction on their activities – including the exercise of their religion – still less any active persecution. Although at later stages of her history Venice did not always show herself to be more enlightened in her attitude to the Jews than were her European contemporaries, her commercial sense told her from the outset that Jewish capital could be of immense value to her economic growth; and, as usual, her commercial sense was right.

Again and again in Venice's early history we read of Doges suddenly withdrawing from the world and dying only a few weeks or months later. There was certainly no tradition of retirement on grounds of age alone. The Venetians have always been famous for their longevity – to this day their expectation of life comfortably exceeds that of the inhabitants of any other major Italian city – and Enrico Dandolo provides only one example of their still noticeable ability to continue well into their eighth or ninth decades with their energies and vitality almost unimpaired. When a Doge did at last step down from his throne, the speed with which death nearly always followed abdication suggests that he took such a decision only when he knew his life to be ebbing away. For as long as he felt able to govern his people, he did so; but when the task became too much for him, he did not cling to office.

Giacomo Tiepolo was no exception. He retired, not to a monastery like so many of his predecessors but to his own house in the Campo S. Agostino, in the spring of 1249; and he was dead before the autumn. He had served Venice well, in the Levant somehow contriving to hold together the chief elements of her new, dangerously fissile Empire, and in the West serving the interests of her struggling sister-cities (which were also her own) without ever identifying too closely with them or becoming inextricably involved in the strife between Guelf and Ghibelline which was to continue to tear them apart for another century. He had fought the Emperor Frederick – losing two sons in the process – as long and as hard as he felt necessary for the good of the Republic; but no longer and no harder. Meanwhile at home he had continued the work originally begun by Enrico Dandolo fifty years before and in 1242 had produced his celebrated *Statuto*, the most detailed and comprehensive codification of Venetian civil law yet to have appeared.

The other notable appearance in Venice during his reign was that of the two great orders of mendicant friars, the Dominicans and the Franciscans. St Dominic and St Francis had died within five years of each other, in 1221 and 1226 respectively; the results of their labours had been immediate, and by 1230 representatives of both orders had arrived in the city. To each, Doge Tiepolo granted land for a church; to the Dominicans, a marshy expanse to the north of the parish of S. Maria Formosa, to the Franciscans a ruined and long-abandoned abbey close to his own house, across the Grand Canal. By the year of his death, building operations at the two sites were well under way; and although the gigantic churches which were ultimately to rise there – SS. Giovanni e Paolo and S. Maria Gloriosa dei Frari – were not to be completed till the fifteenth century, of the former at least enough had already been constructed for the old Doge to choose it as his burial place.[1]

After four uninspiring years under an elderly pietist named Marin Morosini – who, but for the now inexplicable fact of his selection for the dogeship, would surely have taken his place among the dimmer members of one of the oldest and most brilliant of Venetian families – the election of Renier Zeno early in 1253 seems to have woken the city up again. Zeno had had an eventful, even adventurous, life. He had shown much courage in putting down one of the periodic revolts of Zara in 1242; in the following year, while returning to Venice from the Council of Lyons, he had been taken prisoner by the Count of Savoy. Released by order of the

---

1. The sacristy of SS. Giovanni e Paolo contains a picture by Vicentino of Doge Tiepolo granting the land to the Dominicans. His sarcophagus can still be seen in the arcade on the outer wall of the church, just to the left of the west door.

Emperor, he had then been summoned to the imperial court and forced to justify what Frederick described as Venice's ungrateful policy towards him. Later he had served as *podestà* of Piacenza and, more recently, of Fermo, where he received the news of his election. All this and a good deal more besides we learn from one of the most entertaining, (if not always the most reliable) of contemporary chroniclers, Martino da Canale, whose enthusiasm for Zeno occasionally smacks less of the historian than of the publicity agent – which, for all we know, he may have been. Not that the new Doge lacked any talent of his own for self-advertisement; in his irresistible Old French, Martino gives a breathless description of the tournament that was staged to mark his accession. It was held on the Piazza, '*la plus bele place qui soit en tot li monde*':

> The pavilions were set up in the square, and all were covered in silken cloth, and the square itself covered in the same manner. And the fine ladies and maidens ascended to the pavilions, and in all the palaces around more ladies appeared at the windows. And Monseigneur the Doge proceeded on foot from the church of St Mark, and all the nobles of Venice with him, and the people thronged the square . . . After him came a company of horsemen all splendidly mounted and richly armed. Then the jousts began, with all the ladies watching. Ah signors, had you been there, you could have seen many a good thrust with a lance . . .

Continually in his chronicle, Martino returns to the theme of Venetian pageantry, recalling the dazzling processions made by the Doge on the great feast-days of the Church, describing with child-like enthusiasm the cloth of gold, the silken banners and the silver trumpets, recreating scene after scene that cries out for a Gentile Bellini or a Carpaccio to capture it – both, alas, still a century and a half away in the future.

But life for Renier Zeno was not just a matter of parading around the Piazza. In 1256 he lent active support to a papal crusade against Ezzelino da Romano, who since Frederick's death had been using the imperial standard as only the most transparent of cloaks for his own personal ambitions. One of the earliest of the great *signori* of North Italy – and certainly the first to maintain his authority for twenty years and more – Ezzelino by his inhuman brutality had earned himself the reputation of an ogre, detested and feared throughout Lombardy, Friuli and the Marches. Thanks to the success of Venice's isolationist policy, he plays only a marginal part in her history: we can spare ourselves the stories of blinded prisoners and mutilated children with which the Pope justified his excommunication, noting only Martino's report of how, when in 1259 Ezzelino was at last hunted down and killed, 'the church bells rang out all over Venice, as they did on the feasts of the saints; and on the night following, the priests climbed to the tops of the bell-towers, where they lit candles and torches, so that the light and the clamour were wondrous to see and to hear'.[1] It was typical of the Venetian attitude, however, that, as Martino points out, these celebrations were occasioned less by the disappearance of a monster and the restoration of peace and security to a terrorized region, than by that of a ruler who had kept back the rents that were legally due to Venetian churches from their properties on the mainland.

But the attention of the Republic was soon turned back from Lombardy to the Levant. On 25 July 1261 a Greek general, Alexius Strategopoulos, launched a surprise attack on Constantinople and captured it, virtually without opposition; on 15 August the Emperor Michael VIII Palaeologus, fifth in that imperial line that had been ruling in exile at Nicaea, re-entered the city; and a month later he and his wife Theodora were crowned anew in St Sophia, now once more consecrated in the Orthodox faith. Byzantium was reborn; the Latin Empire of the East was finished.

For most of the fifty-six years of its existence it had been little more than a bad joke. Surrounded as he was by hostile Greek and Bulgarian states and disloyal Latin ones, maintained largely on gifts from his fellow-monarch St Louis of France and on loans from Venetian bankers who demanded his own son as security, progressively abandoned as more and more of his leading barons and clergy returned to the West – the latter usually taking with them what remained of the church treasure – the last of the Latin Emperors, Baldwin II, had been reduced to stripping the copper from the roofs of his palace and ultimately pawning the city's most precious relic, the Crown of Thorns, to Venetian merchants.[2] He and his Frankish predecessors on the imperial throne had achieved nothing but chaos, spoliation and destruction; their conquest had brought them only poverty and suffering. From the whole sad shambles of the Fourth Crusade and its consequences there had been only one real beneficiary: Venice.

And Venice, likewise, was the one serious loser when the Latin Empire collapsed. The Pope expressed his horror that Constantinople, the second

1. '*Les cloches sonerent par tote Venise, ensi com il sont acostumes de soner as festes des Saints; et la nuit apres, monterent li clers de sor li clochiers, et alumerent cierges et tortis par tos li clochers, et firent si grant luminaire et si grant soner des cloches, que ce fu une grant mervoile de veoir et de oir.*'

2. It was redeemed by St Louis, who subsequently brought it from St Mark's to Paris – where he built the Sainte-Chapelle, the world's most superb reliquary, in its honour. During the French Revolution it was entrusted for safety to the Bishop of Paris and is now to be found, bathetically encased in Second-Empire finery, in the Treasury of Notre Dame.

Rome, should once more have fallen away from the True Faith; St Louis doubtless shed a pious tear for the few remaining relics that would now elude his grasp; but on the Rialto the news meant grave political and financial crisis. For Venice had possessed not only three-eighths of Constantinople itself; her colonies and trading posts were by now scattered all over the Aegean and around the shores of the eastern Mediterranean and the Black Sea. Hitherto they had been satisfactorily protected by a powerful Venetian fleet based in the Golden Horn, but now this vital anchorage was denied them. From Michael Palaeologus they could expect nothing but implacable hostility. His Empire, admittedly, was depleted and impoverished; alone, he would scarcely have constituted a serious rival. But he was not alone. Some months before his triumph he had shrewdly allied himself with the Genoese who, for nearly a century, had been bitterly contesting Venetian supremacy in the Levant. In return for military and financial aid in the reconquest, he had promised them tax and customs concessions and districts of their own in the chief ports of the Empire, including Constantinople itself – all those privileges, in short, that Alexius Comnenus had granted to Venice in 1082 and upon which the Republic's commercial greatness had been founded.

Venetian–Genoese relations, strained at the best of times, had deteriorated still further in recent years, and since 1255 the two Republics had been in a state of open war. There had been three important naval battles off the coast of Palestine, in all of which – thanks in large measure to the courage of the dashing young admiral Lorenzo Tiepolo, son of the former Doge – the Venetians had inflicted crushing defeats on their rivals, expelling them from Acre and capturing an entire fleet of twenty-five galleys sent out from Genoa to their relief. The courage of the Genoese, on this occasion, had not been conspicuous: Martino writes of how one of their supporters from Tyre, a Frenchman named Philippe de Montfort who had himself come to their aid with a troop of cavalry, saw the water full of floundering Genoese sailors and left in disgust, scratching his head and complaining that 'they were good for nothing but brothels, and were like fish-eating birds, flinging themselves into the sea and drowning'.

De Montfort's logic seems as shaky as his ornithology; but his sentiments were clear enough. Genoa's pride had indeed been brought low. From the Genoese church of St Saba at Acre Lorenzo Tiepolo bore home in triumph three short columns, one cylindrical of porphyry and two quadrangular of carved white marble. All three were set up in the Piazzetta, at the south-west corner of the basilica, where they stand to this day.[1] But now the pendulum had swung. It was the Venetians' turn to suffer humiliation, this time in the eyes of the whole civilized world – a humiliation that the simultaneous threat to their commercial Empire can hardly have made easier to bear.

As things turned out, the economic consequences of the reconquest of Constantinople proved somewhat less catastrophic than they had feared. The operation itself had been surprisingly simple. Michael Palaeologus had needed less help from the Genoese than he had expected, and had even managed to avoid direct hostilities with Venice, whose fleet had been providentially absent from the Bosphorus when Strategopoulos had struck. The new Emperor was, moreover, a cautious man; he knew that Venetian naval power was still superior to Genoese, and that still more decisive victories than those at Acre might yet be won. His wisest course lay in playing the two Republics off against each other. He therefore permitted the Venetians to maintain their colony in Constantinople and left them certain minor commercial privileges. In other respects, however, they were made to feel their new position. Their official representative to the Emperor was downgraded from the rank of *podestà* (which was now awarded to the leading Genoese) to that of *bailo*; no longer was he invited as of right to the Emperor's table on the great feasts of the Church. Part of their own quarter of the city was re-allotted to the Genoese colony – now rapidly expanding – which a few years later was to receive in addition the entire district of Galata, across the Golden Horn. Outside the capital, they were forced to stand by, powerless, while their rivals set up trading posts where they themselves had previously enjoyed the monopoly – at Smyrna, on the islands of Chios and Lesbos and, most galling of all, along the coasts of the Black Sea, from which they were henceforth excluded.

Their sense of frustration must have been still further increased by the knowledge that their navy remained supreme. Michael Palaeologus had as yet no fleet worthy of the name, and had the Venetians decided to fight for their lost privileges he would have been incapable of opposing them. But they had their colony in Constantinople to consider; by allowing it to continue in existence, Michael had adroitly provided himself

1. The porphyry column, known as the *Pietra del Bando*, later became the traditional platform from which all Venetian laws were promulgated. In 1902 it performed an even more useful purpose by protecting the corner of the Basilica from the falling *campanile* – suffering considerable damage to itself in the process. To be perfectly honest, there is some doubt about the two square columns, which are not specifically mentioned by any of the contemporary chroniclers. It has been suggested that Tiepolo may have taken them not from St Saba but from the fortified tower called Mongioia which the Genoese had recently completed at Acre. (There is a third column, similar in style, in a corner of the Papadopoli gardens.

with a pledge for their good behaviour. Clearly, there could be as yet no question of any real diplomatic *rapprochement*; feelings were still running too high. Besides, with the deposed Emperor Baldwin busy canvassing the princes of Europe there might still remain some slender chance of his restoration. For the moment they could only accept the inevitable, and try to make the best of it.

With Genoa, on the other hand, no such considerations applied. The *casus belli* was greater than ever, and the Venetians returned with increased vigour to the attack. The fighting now spread all over the eastern Mediterranean, with countless minor engagements among the Aegean islands and off the coasts of Euboea and the Peloponnese. In one of these engagements, the Genoese were foolish enough to intercept a *carovana* bound for the Rialto – one of the immense convoys that sailed regularly from Levantine ports, bringing to Europe the silks and spices of the East – and escaped destruction only when the Venetian admiral commanding the escort very properly refused to risk the precious cargoes by giving chase. In others they were not so lucky – notably in an encounter off Trapani in western Sicily, in which over 1,100 Genoese sailors jumped overboard and were drowned while another 600, in twenty-seven galleys, were brought back captive to the lagoons.

In Constantinople, meanwhile, the insolence and arrogance of the newly privileged Genoese were making them if anything even more unpopular than the Venetians had been in the past; and, as the news of one Venetian victory after another reached the imperial palace, so Michael's sympathies began to change. He too had a war on his hands, against the remaining petty princelings of the Latin East and the Greek Despots of Epirus, none of whom were willing to return their territories to the restored Empire – an attitude for which they were receiving powerful support from the Pope and from Frederick II's son Manfred of Sicily. Michael was himself in desperate need of money to rebuild both his capital and his shattered fleet; his Genoese alliance, instead of providing it, was involving him in further heavy expenditure – for which he was getting remarkably little in return.

By 1264 Greek ambassadors were in Venice, and in the following year a treaty was drawn up offering the Republic privileges which, if they did not quite equal those that had been lost, represented at least an immense improvement on the existing state of affairs. But the Venetians were in no hurry. The Byzantine East was still in turmoil, and while the future of the Empire remained uncertain there was no point in committing themselves. It was not until 1268 that they finally made up their minds to accept

Michael's offer. Even now they would agree to nothing more than a five-year truce; for that period, however, they promised non-aggression, the withholding of all help to the enemies of the Empire and the liberation of their Greek prisoners in Crete, Modone and Corone, the three principal bases remaining to them in the Aegean. The Emperor undertook in return to respect Venetian settlements both there and elsewhere in the archipelago, and once more to allow Venetian merchants freedom to reside, travel and trade without let or hindrance throughout his dominions. His terms, in fact, could hardly have been more favourable. Two things only were missing: their three-eighths share – though it had gradually become in practice more of a titular claim than a real economic benefit – and the exclusivity that they had formerly enjoyed. For, Michael now stipulated, the Genoese would retain their existing rights. The dangers of the old policy, by which one of the Republics was given full imperial preference at the expense of the other, had now been conclusively demonstrated. Henceforth there would be free competition between them. That way Michael could profit by their rivalry without driving the less favoured party into hostile alliances.

Few short-term truces have had more lasting significance. At a stroke, Venice had effectively re-established her commercial primacy in the Levant and much of that influence which, only seven years previously, she seemed to have lost for ever. Her recovery was in part due to good luck, of which she had certainly received more than her fair share; but it also owed much to the astute diplomatic sense of Doge Zeno and his advisers. When he died within weeks of the treaty's ratification, he left behind him a people that had almost forgotten its recent humiliation, regained its self-respect, and was once more ready to face the future with confidence. In gratitude, and following that tradition of high pomp and sumptuous ceremonial that had marked his reign from the beginning, he was given a funeral as magnificent as only Venice could provide before being laid to rest in the still unfinished church of SS. Giovanni e Paolo. There, in the south-west corner, a part of his tomb is still preserved – a relief of Christ enthroned, with an attendant angel on each hand.

· 12 ·

The Wages of Arrogance

[1268–1299]

. . . How woful, that the war-cry of his name should so often reanimate the rage of the soldier, on those very plains where he himself had failed in the courage of the Christian, and so often dye with fruitless blood that very Cypriot Sea, over whose waves, in repentance and shame, he was following the Son of Consolation!

Ruskin, *The Stones of Venice*
(See epigraph to Chapter 3, p. 50)

The first seven decades of the thirteenth century had witnessed the emergence of Venice as a world power. They had seen her extensive possessions in the East first acquired, then developed and consolidated, then lost and finally in large measure regained. More significant by far in the long term, they had seen the eclipse of both Empires, the East and the West. The Byzantine Empire of the Palaeologi, though still with the better part of two centuries to run, would never be more than a frail, struggling shadow of what it had been before the Fourth Crusade. In western Europe, too, the great days of Hohenstaufen imperialism had died with Frederick II in 1250; it was nations – England, France, Spain – not empires (at least in the medieval sense), that were beginning to occupy the forefront of the stage.

For most of those seventy years Venice had been at war. She had had to fight for her new dominions, and to defend them, against Greeks, Genoese, Pisans and Saracens, to say nothing of pirates from every corner of the Mediterranean. Beneath the walls of Zara and of Constantinople, off the shores of Palestine and Pontus, of Crete, Euboea and the Peloponnese, across the waters of the Tyrrhenian and the Adriatic, the Aegean and the Euxine, her galleys had been as fully employed as her merchantmen.

At home, however, life had continued peaceably enough – or nearly. The expansion of trade had brought still greater prosperity; merchandise, wrote Martino da Canale, was pouring in from everywhere like water from fountains, and Venice continued to grow in size and splendour.

The two great churches of the Mendicant Friars rose ever higher; others, springing up in parish after parish, may have yielded to them in size but far surpassed them in opulence. The Grand Canal was already lined with *palazzi* – a few of them, such as the Cà da Mosto or the Fondaco dei Turchi, still standing to this day,[1] their lovely open loggias and arcades testifying to the confidence all Venetians felt in the security of their city at a time when, elsewhere in Europe, castles rather than palaces were still the rule. In 1264 the Piazzetta was paved for the first time, and in the same year a new Rialto bridge was built on wooden piles – the prototype of that painted by Carpaccio in the series of the 'Miracles of the Relic of the True Cross', now in the Accademia. The surface decoration of the Basilica of St Mark, tentatively begun under Domenico Selvo and continued at intervals throughout the twelfth century, gathered momentum with the addition of the glorious mosaics of the atrium and the façade.[2]

Meanwhile, in the constitutional sphere, Giacomo Tiepolo had produced his codification of the laws of the Republic and, with his *promissione*, had brought about a further curtailment of ducal authority. But in the summer of 1268, when the time came to elect a successor to Doge Zeno, there seems to have been a general feeling that this authority might still run out of control and so constitute a threat to the state. Inevitably, the influx of new wealth had brought certain previously unknown and insignificant families to new prominence and power. Between these families and those of the older aristocracy – the so-called *case vecchie* – feuds began once again to develop: feuds familiar enough in earlier centuries, but which the Republic should by then have outgrown. One of them, between the Dandolo and Tiepolo clans, actually led in Zeno's reign to an open brawl in the Piazza, as a result of which a law was hastily passed banning the representation of family emblems or coats of arms on the outside of buildings. The Venetians could not forget their old, almost

1. Both, inevitably, have suffered over the years. Part of the arcading of the Cà da Mosto has been bricked in, and two upper floors added, while the Fondaco has been restored so crudely that one would almost prefer it to look as it did before 1860 (see Plate 13). Other buildings still recognizably of the thirteenth century are the two Donà *palazzi* (on either side of the Madonnetta *traghetto* point) with the Barzizza, a little further on by the S. Silvestro *vaporetto* station; and, on the other side of the Grand Canal, the adjacent Palazzi Farsetti and Loredan, now the offices of the Municipality.

2. Of the latter, all of which are clearly visible in Gentile Bellini's picture in the Accademia (Plate 16), only one alas remains – that on the far left-hand lunette. It represents the *Translation of the Body of St Mark* and provides us with the earliest extant picture of the Basilica itself, at a date soon after the setting up of the horses of Lysippus over the central arch. The four other lunettes, now filled with mediocre work of the seventeenth and eighteenth centuries, stand out in sorry contrast.

pathological fear that one family, one individual even, might somehow gain control of the Republic. They had watched, with a horror not untinged with smugness, the career of Ezzelino da Romano and others of his kind who were even now arising in many less fortunate North Italian cities; and they were fully aware, six centuries and more before Lord Acton, of the effects of absolute power. The new system of election to the dogeship which they now devised must surely rank among the most complicated ever instituted by a civilized state. It strikes the modern mind as ridiculous, and to some extent it was. But it is worth setting down in some detail, if only as an indication of the lengths to which Venice was prepared to go in order to ensure that the supreme office of the state should not fall, either directly or indirectly, into ambitious or unscrupulous hands.

On the day appointed for the election, the youngest member of the Signoria[1] was to pray in St Mark's; then, on leaving the Basilica, he was to stop the first boy he met and take him to the Doges' Palace, where the Great Council, minus those of its members who were under thirty, was to be in full session. This boy, known as the *ballotino*, would have the duty of picking the slips of paper from the urn during the drawing of lots. By the first of such lots, the Council chose thirty of their own number. The second was used to reduce the thirty to nine, and the nine would then vote for forty, each of whom was to receive at least seven nominations. The forty would then be reduced, again by lot, to twelve, whose task was to vote for twenty-five, of whom each this time required nine votes. The twenty-five were in turn reduced to another nine; the nine voted for forty-five, with a minimum of seven votes each, and from these the *ballotino* picked out the names of eleven. The eleven now voted for forty-one – nine or more votes each – and it was these forty-one who were to elect the Doge.[2] They first attended Mass, and individually swore an oath that they would act honestly and uprightly, for the good of the Republic. They were then locked in secret conclave in the Palace, cut off from all contact or communication with the outside world and guarded by a special force of sailors, day and night, until their work was done.

So much for the preliminaries; now the election itself could begin. Each elector wrote the name of his candidate on a paper and dropped it in the urn; the slips were then removed and read, and a list drawn up of

1. The inner council of state (see p. 134).
2. Sir Henry Wotton, James I's ambassador to Venice, was later to maintain that this extraordinary procedure had been invented by a Benedictine monk: 'The whole mysterious frame therein doth much savor of the cloister.'

all the names proposed, regardless of the number of nominations for each. A single slip for each name was now placed in another urn, and one drawn. If the candidate concerned was present, he retired together with any other elector who bore the same surname, and the remainder proceeded to discuss his suitability. He was then called back to answer questions or to defend himself against any accusations. A ballot followed. If he obtained the required twenty-five votes, he was declared Doge; otherwise a second name was drawn, and so on.

With a system so tortuously involved as this, it may seem remarkable that anyone was ever elected at all; but on 23 July 1268, only sixteen days after the death of his predecessor, the vote found its way to Lorenzo Tiepolo. Martino da Canale, never one to resist describing a good celebration, tells us with relish how the bells of St Mark's rang out and the people flocked to the Basilica, surrounding their new Doge and 'tearing the clothes from his back' – which they seem to have been traditionally permitted to do 'as a sign of his humility and clemency'. Barefoot before the high altar, he took the oath of office and was invested with the banner of St Mark. Then, newly robed and enthroned on the *pozzetto*,[1] he was carried ceremonially round the Piazza, scattering coins as he went, before entering the Doges' Palace and addressing his new subjects. Meanwhile a delegation had hurried off to his house at S. Agostina to inform his wife – the niece of John de Brienne, one of the Latin Emperors in Constantinople – and to escort her to her new home.

'*Deboneire, cortois*, wise, valiant and of excellent parts', enthuses Martino, Lorenzo Tiepolo was 'a name celebrated throughout the world'. Besides his heroism in the Genoese war – still not over – he had spent some time as *podestà* of Fano and could boast a long record of service to the Republic. This record, however, had not prevented him from involving himself in the affray in the Piazza a few years before, and indeed from getting wounded in the course of it; and one of his first non-ceremonial actions as Doge was to send for the leading Dandolos and to make his peace with them. Then the celebrations began in earnest. First the Venetian fleet sailed past the Palace in review, followed by specially decorated ships from Torcello, Murano, Burano and the other island communities of the lagoon. Then, on foot, came a procession of the guilds. Martino's account is too long, and ultimately too tedious, to reproduce in detail; but it is an unrivalled source of information on the commercial life of the city at the time and shows the level of prosperity that had already been reached. The parade was led by the smiths, all crowned with garlands; then came the

1. See p. 134.

skinners, in their richest cloaks of vair and ermine – dress not normally recommended for Venice in late July; the master tailors, all in white with vermilion stars, singing lustily to the accompaniment of their own band; the weavers and quilters, the sandal-makers and mercers, the glass-blowers – already an important group – the makers of gold brocade, and the comb-cutters, bearing great lanterns full of birds, which they released as they passed the Palace. But the first prize for fantasy went to the barbers, led by two mounted knights in full armour and four ladies 'very strangely attired'.[1]

Dismounting before the Doge, they announced themselves. 'Sire, we are two knights errant, who have ridden the world to seek our fortune. After much trouble and labour we have won four fair damsels. If there be any knight at your court who wishes to risk his neck to take these strange ladies from us, we are ready to fight in their defence.' But the Doge replied that they were welcome, and that with God's will they themselves should enjoy their conquests; and that they should be honoured at his court, where no man should gainsay them.

The reign of Lorenzo Tiepolo had begun auspiciously enough; but the Doge never really fulfilled his early promise. With his accession to power, his former good luck seemed to desert him; diplomatically, too, he never quite found his touch. The 1268 harvest was disastrous, and within a few months Venice was stricken by famine. Throughout her history, her lack of agricultural land with her consequent dependence on the importation of grain for her survival had been one of her most serious weaknesses; and now there was revealed another – the jealousy of her neighbours. In vain did she appeal to Padua, Treviso and other towns for supplies, reminding them of the help she had given them during Ezzelino's reign of terror; they refused outright, Padua even going so far as to suspend payment of the annual rents which were payable in corn to Venetian churches and monasteries for their property on *terra firma*. By sending ships further afield, to Sicily and even to Russia, catastrophe was averted; but the Republic's subsequent vengeance was swift and savage. Heavy dues were imposed on all goods passing through Venice to destinations on the mainland; on the pretext that the Adriatic was an integral part of the Venetian heritage, officials were appointed at various ports along the coast to make sure that such goods were not offloaded there instead and to control river traffic along the Po and its tributaries. It was a foolish measure, since it implied a claim that was bound to provoke violent reactions far beyond the cities with which Venice was quarrelling; and

1. '*Aparilles mult estrangement*'.

it led to a three-year war with Bologna which, though it ended inconclusively, did little good to Venetian popularity in North Italy – or indeed to the Republic's reputation.

Thus, by the time Tiepolo died in August 1275 – to be laid next to his father in SS. Giovanni e Paolo – his glory had worn distinctly thin. He had simply not been able to understand that, however much Venice might consider herself a place apart, exalted and privileged, having nothing in common either in her history or traditions with her sister cities, in their eyes she was still one of their own number: richer and more powerful perhaps, thanks to a mixture of good luck, unscrupulous behaviour and boundless self-confidence, but in no way essentially superior to themselves and – on land at least – certainly not invincible. In the days when Barbarossa, Henry VI and Frederick II were making their periodic descents into Lombardy and the wars between Guelf and Ghibelline were still at their height, these cities had had other preoccupations; they had been obliged to steer a course as best they could through the stormy seas of imperial–papal politics while Venice, protected by her lagoon, could afford to focus her attentions on the infinitely more attractive East. But times were changing. As the imperial shadow faded, a new spirit and a new strength arose within them. Tired of bloodshed, they now looked for a greater share in the prosperity that Venice had so long enjoyed, and began to resent the arrogance with which she accepted it as her prerogative and her due.

The eighty-year-old Jacopo Contarini, who was somehow elected to the dogeship on Tiepolo's death, was – perhaps not surprisingly – no more sensitive to these developments than his predecessor. By this time the misguidedness of Venice's policy towards the mainland should have been self-evident. During the past five years, apart from her unsatisfactory treaty with Bologna and a five-year truce with Genoa in 1270, the Republic had been obliged to enter into agreements with at least six other cities, each of which had involved a grudging modification of her financial – though not of her territorial – claims. Again in 1274, when at the Council of Lyons Pope Gregory X[1] recognized Michael Palaeologus as Emperor and – in return for Michael's acknowledgement of papal primacy and the apparent healing of the Great Schism – effectively removed any religious justification for a Latin reconquest of Constantinople, the Pope and 500

---

1. Gregory had been elected Pope in 1271, after a three-year period during which, thanks to the machinations of Charles of Anjou, the Papacy had been without an occupant. The interregnum would have lasted longer if the authorities at Viterbo, where the conclave was being held, had not taken the somewhat extreme step of removing the roof from the palace in which the cardinals were assembled.

bishops had also found time to listen to an impassioned diatribe by a delegation from Ancona, protesting against Venetian pretensions.[1] Gregory himself urged a more conciliatory attitude, but in vain. Venice argued that she had been the defender of the Adriatic since the days of antiquity; that it was thanks to her alone that Slavs, Saracens and Normans had successively been driven back; and that Pope Alexander III had in fact invested her with rights over the entire gulf during the Ascension Day ceremony of 1177, when the traditional ring was cast, in his presence, into the waves.

This last claim, in particular, was distinctly shaky; there is no evidence that Pope Alexander had done any such thing.[2] As for the first two, the Anconitans could justly point out that Venice had been acting primarily in her own interests, that they too had done their share of defending, and that anyway neither was a reason to block their free passage up and down their home rivers. The quarrel grew steadily more acrimonious, and in 1277 gave place to open war. The first wave of the Venetian fleet, some twenty-six galleys, left at once for Ancona, but scarcely had they settled down to a siege of the city than a freak summer storm dashed most of them on to the rocks and scattered the remainder for miles up and down the coast. A few days later the second contingent, which had set out all unaware of the disaster, ran straight into the arms of the Anconitans and was captured.

Venice had paid dearly for her arrogance; but she had not yet paid in full. The new German King Rudolf of Habsburg had recently attempted to ingratiate himself with Pope Nicholas III by making him a gift of the territory of Romagna, which included Ancona; so that Venice now found herself embroiled with the Pope as well. Meanwhile, seeing her difficulties, certain discontented factions in Istria and Crete rose simultaneously in revolt. For Jacopo Contarini it was all too much. In March 1280 he resigned – or, perhaps more accurately, he was pensioned off; we know that he was voted an annual 1,500 *piccoli* for the rest of his life which, since he was already eighty-five and bedridden, was not expected to be of long duration.[3]

Contarini's successor, Giovanni Dandolo, is something of a mystery.

1. See Romanin (II, 307), who presumably bases himself on Martino da Canale (p. 682), though I can find no reference to such an intervention in the records of the Council's proceedings.

2. See p. 140.

3. The precise date of his death is unknown; and his tomb, '*in claustro fratrum minorum*' – by which Andrea Dandolo presumably means the Frari – has disappeared.

Despite his distinguished name, the sources reveal nothing of his past history except that he was serving abroad at the time of his election, and his relationship to the great Enrico is equally uncertain.[1] Within a year he had made peace with Ancona. The basic question of Venice's rights in the Adriatic he seems to have left unresolved, presumably in the interests of reaching a quick agreement; but his hands were at last free to tackle the discontents in Istria, now actively supported by the Patriarch of Aquileia – who claimed jurisdiction over the area – and the Count of Gorizia. Once again the Republic got off to a bad start. The Count and Patriarch together had managed to secure the services of a body of German mercenaries, who easily routed the Venetian force that had been sent to subdue a rebellious Trieste; whereat the Triestines, taking over the pursuit, first raided Caorle, capturing the *podestà* and burning his palace, and then advanced as far as Malamocco leaving a trail of devastation behind them.

Not since the days of Pepin, nearly five centuries before, had a hostile naval force approached so close to the city. The Venetians reacted with firmness and speed. The commander of the luckless expedition, Marin Morosini, was flung into prison where he was punished 'in accordance with his misdeeds and as an example to those who should come after him'; plans were announced for mass conscription; a new fleet, considerably larger than the previous one, was dispatched to Trieste. This time all went well. After a fierce resistance the town surrendered, to be followed by most of its neighbours; but it was not until 1285 that the Patriarch could be induced to sign an agreement of understanding with the Republic, and even then the question of his rights in Istria was left unsettled. As a result, hostilities all too soon flared up again, to bedevil Venice militarily, economically and politically for the next twenty years – until, in 1304, all patriarchal claims in the region were surrendered to the Doge in return for an annual payment of 450 marks.

And there were other troubles too. The Kingdom of Sicily, which included virtually all Italy south of Rome, had since 1266 been ruled by Louis IX's brother Charles of Anjou from his capital at Naples. On Easter Monday, 1282, however, a drunken French sergeant in Palermo began importuning a Sicilian woman outside the church of S. Spirito just as vespers were about to begin. He was set upon by her husband and killed;

---

1. A learned German, basing himself on 'manuscript genealogical lists' in the Museo Correr, concludes that Giovanni was in fact Enrico's great-grandson (Simonsfeld, *Andreas Dandolo und seine Geschichtswerke*, Munich, 1876); but Andrea himself, writing of the eleventh-century seaman Domenico Dandolo, says that he was ancestor of two Doges – Enrico and himself – and mentions neither Giovanni nor indeed Francesco, who was Doge from 1329 to 1339.

the murder led to a riot, the riot to a massacre; 2,000 Frenchmen were dead by morning. The remainder withdrew to the mainland where Charles was still in control, while the Sicilians established King Peter III of Aragon on the throne in Palermo.

In the so-called war of the Sicilian Vespers which now ensued, Venice – although technically she had declared for Charles the previous year – had no desire to take part. It had always been her policy to stay clear of Italian upheavals as far as possible, and her navy was anyway fully engaged in Istria. When therefore Pope Martin IV, who was a Frenchman and consequently a strong champion of Charles, launched a Crusade against Peter in 1284, she refused to join it and expressly forbade her own leading churchmen, the Patriarch of Grado and the Bishop of Castello, to preach it from their pulpits. The result was an interdict, the first – though not the last – that Venice ever suffered, and a decree so solemn that even she dared not disobey.

It is hard, nowadays, to imagine the despondency that settled on a medieval city when it came under the ban of the Church. The bells in the *campanili* fell silent; Mass could no longer be said; services of baptism, marriage and burial were alike prohibited, as were all the religious processions that the Venetians loved. That winter, without the great celebrations of Christmas and Epiphany to enliven it, must have seemed interminable; and with the coming of spring, like some Old Testament visitation of the wrath of God, Venice suffered an earth-quake which was in turn followed by disastrous floods. The breakwaters were swept away; houses without number were destroyed, families left homeless and starving. The measures taken for their relief were probably swifter, more generous and more effective than could have been expected in any other European city; but Venice was unable to conceal, from her own people or anyone else, that her fortunes had suddenly and sadly declined.

And yet, surprisingly, it was just at this gloomy moment in her history, while the papal interdict was still in force, that there first appeared, in 1284, one of the most lasting and internationally significant of all Venetian institutions – the golden ducat. The word itself was not new; it had been first given to a silver coin minted by Roger II of Sicily in 1140, and other silver ducats had appeared in Venice in 1202, for the payment of workmen building the fleet for the Fourth Crusade. But Giovanni Dandolo's golden ducat was conceived on quite a different scale from these. His decree stipulated that 'it must be made to the greatest possible fineness, like to the florin [of Florence] *only better*'; and so indeed it must have been, for in no other way could it have maintained, for 513 years until the fall of the Republic, its quality, reputation and value in the market-places of the world.[1]

Giovanni Dandolo reigned nine years. He died on 2 November 1289, leaving his golden memorial behind him – fortunately, since there now remains no other. But however brightly his ducats might shine, they could not blind the eyes of the Venetians to the fact that for the past twenty years nothing seemed to have gone right for them. Militarily they had suffered defeats on land and sea, with serious losses, both in ships and human lives. They had been forced to watch, powerless, while the enemy penetrated to the very confines of the lagoon. Their neighbours, on many of whom they depended for trade, were all in a greater or lesser degree unfriendly. Their chief colony, Crete, was once again in revolt. They had suffered the chilly joylessness – to say nothing of the spiritual dangers – of an interdict, the terrors of earthquake, the misery of flood; and though the ban had been lifted by Pope Martin's successor in 1285 and the devastation wrought by the natural disasters had been largely repaired, there was still little sign of markedly better times ahead. Mean-while the war with Istria continued to rumble away in the distance.

All states go through such periods of depression; and when they do it is only natural that men should look for a scapegoat. The Venetian populace had already found theirs: the fault, they believed, lay with the new commercial aristocracy, those families who had suddenly acquired wealth and power with the capture of Constantinople and were now using them to push the Republic ever further in the direction of oligarchy, whittling away at the power of the Doge and depriving the man in the street of any say in political life. Pre-eminent among these *parvenus* was the family of Dandolo, of whose two Doges to date the first had been responsible for the appearance of the new order while the second had, it was felt, exemplified all that was most objectionable in it and had led Venice into ever graver tribulations.

It was a view both illogical and unfair; but it was widely enough held to provoke massive demonstrations in the city. Resentful of the loss, by now not only *de facto* but *de jure*, of the one political privilege they had traditionally enjoyed, the people united in a huge effort to make their

---

1. It later came to be known as a *zecchino* or sequin, a word which originally simply meant that it was fresh from the *zecca*, or mint. The coin has another, documentary, interest: the portraits of successive Doges kneeling before St Mark enable us to trace the changes in their vestments over the centuries, and particularly the evolution of the ducal hat, or *corno*.

voice heard and, thronging the Piazza, demanded that the ducal throne should now be given to the leading member of the one family that stood more than any other for the old, genuinely democratic Venetian order: Doge Lorenzo Tiepolo's son Giacomo.[1]

In many respects this second Giacomo Tiepolo, who could boast a fine military record extending over more than twenty years, might have made an excellent Doge. He had, however, two overwhelming disadvantages. The first, paradoxically, was that he had been the subject of popular demand. If he were now to succeed, even by due process of election, the people would conclude that their manifestations had achieved their object and would further increase their demands for political influence. To the cautious councillors of Venice, this threatened to open the way to mob rule and to the very dangers which the whole intricacy of the electoral system had been specifically designed to avoid. Fortunately, however, there was another objection to Tiepolo's candidature with which his partisans would find it harder to disagree: he was the son and grandson of former Doges. The old traditional fear of hereditary monarchy was reawakened. The fact that his family was venerable and distinguished – one of the *case vecchie* – only increased the potential risk. Three Tiepolo Doges in sixty years would be too much. Giacomo himself seemed to agree. Rather than cause any further dissension, he retired to his villa on the mainland; and shortly afterwards, according to the established process, the 38-year-old Pietro Gradenigo was elected to the vacant throne.

The family of the new Doge belonged, like the Dandolos, to the class of merchant *nouveaux riches*. As his disparaging nickname of Pierazzo suggests, the people mistrusted him; and, as was made abundantly clear by his subsequent actions, from their point of view they were right. But after the withdrawal of their own candidate they had no alternative to put forward; they doubtless noted that the official delegation which was sent to fetch Gradenigo from Capodistria – where he had been serving as *podestà* – had included a representative of the Tiepolos; and, having received the news of his election in stony silence, they grudgingly accepted him as their new ruler.

The change of Doge brought no immediate improvement in Venetian fortunes. Particularly grave was the situation in the Levant, where the Mameluke Sultan of Egypt, Al-Ashraf Khalil, was gathering his forces

1. He may possibly have been Lorenzo's nephew rather than his son: the genealogy is not altogether clear.

for the final offensive against the last survivors of the Crusader states. Tripoli had fallen in 1289, just a few months before Gradenigo's accession; now only Acre remained, with a few dependent towns along the coast. For a century it had been the capital of the Frankish East, the place of refuge for the dispossessed Kings of Jerusalem, the Princes of Galilee and Antioch and other less splendid potentates who, according to a contemporary German chronicler,[1] could be seen still wearing their golden crowns as they walked about the awning-shaded streets. Venice, Pisa, Amalfi and, till its recent eviction, Genoa, each occupied a separate quarter of its own, but the Venetian colony was considerably larger than the rest, Acre being by now the principal point of trans-shipment for its trade with Central Asia and beyond.[2]

When, on Friday 18 May 1291, the Mameluke armies stormed the city of Acre, putting to death virtually all its inhabitants, the blow to Venice was therefore greater than that sustained by any of her commercial rivals. With the obliteration of Outremer – after Acre had fallen the smaller Christian towns could not hope to hold out and quickly suffered the same fate – she had lost at a stroke not only one of her most valuable markets but also an essential entrepôt for her caravans to the further East. To be sure, this latter misfortune was not necessarily permanent; despite energetic attempts by the Pope to launch a new Crusade and his fulminations against any Christian state that dared to have dealings with the infidel, Venice almost immediately entered into discussions with the Sultan, who was later to grant her highly favourable terms. But for the immediate future her Central Asian trade was severely threatened. Everything now depended on the northern route, by way of the Black Sea ports and the Crimea – which brought her face to face once again with her old enemy, Genoa.

Until nearly half-way through the thirteenth century the prevailing political unrest around the shores of the Black Sea had made it a largely unprofitable area for commerce, and Western traders had normally tended to unload at Constantinople; but since 1242, when the Mongols succeeded in unifying the lands of the Western steppes, trading possibilities had vastly improved. After Michael Palaeologus had recovered Constantinople, he had given the Genoese exclusive rights to Black Sea trading; and

---

1. Herman Corner; see Eckhardt, *Corpus Historicum Medii Aevi*, Vol. II, Col. 942, Leipzig, 1723.

2. Agreeable reminders of the Central Asian trade at this period can be found in the Palazzo Mastelli, on the Campo dei Mori. Set into the wall are late thirteenth-century statues of the three Mastelli brothers, all Levantine merchants (Plate 11), while on the canal side, opposite the church of the Madonna dell'Orto, is a charming stone relief of a heavily-loaded camel.

although seven years later he had allowed the Venetians to return, Genoa – with her ever-growing colony at Galata on the Bosphorus – was still dominant in the area. Under her influence Trebizond supplanted Egypt and the Levant – where the last remnants of the Crusader states were fast disappearing – as the terminal for the Indian spice caravans; while Caffa (the modern Feodosiya) in the Crimea handled the local produce of grain, fish and salt, as well as the furs and slaves from the Russian North. In short, the Venetians found themselves faced with a formidable adversary. An uneasy truce between the two Republics, first signed in 1270 but twice renewed, expired once again in 1291, the year that Acre fell. This time there could be no extension. Genoa was determined to preserve her control, Venice equally resolved to wrest it from her.

Neither side was in a hurry to declare war. For three years preparations continued, Venice entering into an alliance with Pisa, drawing up a register of all able-bodied citizens between seventeen and sixty – who were warned to be ready for instant conscription – and calling upon the richest families of the city to finance the manning and equipment of one, two or even three galleys.[1] Finally, on 7 October 1294, the fleet set sail. Its first engagement, in the far north-east corner of the Mediterranean near the Gulf of Alexandretta, was a catastrophe. The Genoese, seeing that they were outnumbered, adopted the curious tactic of lashing all their ships together to make a single huge floating platform. The almost total loss of manoeuvrability that must have resulted seems to have been outweighed by the fact that they thus exposed a much reduced surface area to their assailants while their crews, able to pass freely from one vessel to the next, could concentrate their strength wherever the fighting was fiercest. The Venetian admiral, Marco Basegio, made the cardinal mistake of underestimating his enemy. Scorning the use of fire-ships, he decided on a direct attack; but the Genoese square did not break, and in the fighting that followed Venice lost twenty-five galleys out of sixty-eight and many of her best men, including Basegio himself.

Genoa was not slow to follow up her advantage. Her navy swooped down on Crete, burning and sacking Canea; then, in 1295, cleverly drawing away the escort of galleys, it utterly destroyed the annual Venetian *carovana* – which, since the fall of Acre and with the Genoese at Galata effectively blocking the Bosphorus, was now loading at the inadequate little ports on the south coast of Asia Minor – in the half-way harbour of Modone. The following year brought still graver news, this time from

1. The only families which were considered rich enough to take on three were the Querini, Contarini, Morosini and Dandolo.

Constantinople. Once again, fighting had broken out between the Venetian and Genoese colonies in the city, in the course of which many Venetians had been massacred. Those who had escaped the slaughter, including the *bailo*, had been immediately arrested by the Emperor Andronicus II – Michael's son, who had clearly inherited all his father's proclivity for casting in his lot with the winning side – and clapped into prison.

This last outrage seemed to snap Venice out of her lethargy. A fleet of forty ships was quickly prepared and dispatched under the command of Rogerio Morosini, nicknamed Malabranca, 'the Evil Claw'. Racing through the Dardanelles and burning every Greek or Genoese ship in sight, he attacked and ravaged Galata. Then, turning up the Golden Horn, he dropped anchor beneath the walls of the imperial palace of Blachernae and destroyed one of the Emperor's galleys laid up on the shore. It was only after Andronicus had paid him a huge indemnity that he returned, with a host of Genoese prisoners, in triumph to the lagoon. At about the same time another Venetian fleet under Giovanni Soranzo burst through the Genoese blockade of the Bosphorus and into the Black Sea, where it seized Caffa and held it against furious attack from the Tartars until the coming of winter at length persuaded it to withdraw.

For three more years the war dragged on, with encounters between the two navies all over the central Mediterranean from Sicily to Cyprus and, in 1298, one more resounding victory for the Genoese off the Dalmatian coast near Curzola.[1] Once again they were numerically weaker, but they had the advantage of the wind and, in Lamba Doria, one of the most brilliant admirals of the age. The Venetian ships were surrounded, and packed so tightly together that a fire breaking out on one of them quickly spread. The crews from Chioggia in particular fought heroically but, when the battle was over, out of the ninety-five Venetian ships that had been involved sixty-five had been taken or sunk. Nine thousand men were killed or wounded, and a further 5,000 borne off captive to Genoa. One at least never arrived: the Venetian admiral, Andrea Dandolo – not to be confused with the historian Doge – is said to have killed himself by beating his head against a mast. Another, more fortunate and more sensible, whiled away his year in a Genoese gaol by dictating to a fellow-prisoner a report of his journeyings in the East – a work later to become celebrated as the *Travels* or *Description of the World*, by Marco Polo.

Despite his extraordinary career, and although he was the author of

1. Korčula.

perhaps the most influential travel book ever written, Marco Polo came
of a family entirely typical of the Venetian merchant aristocracy of his day.
His father, Nicolò Polo, was one of three brothers who were also business
partners and of whom at least one, Marco the elder, was resident at
Constantinople; but all three seem to have made regular journeys to the
Crimea and beyond, for in about 1260 we hear of Nicolò and the third
brother, Maffeo, travelling as far east as Bokhara. Here it was that they
chanced to meet envoys from the Mongol ruler Kublai Khan, and were
persuaded to accompany them back to Kublai's court in what is now
Peking.

Unlike his predecessors on the Mongol throne, Kublai Khan was
possessed of a remarkably open mind, which he combined with an almost
limitless intellectual curiosity. So impressed was he by what the Polo
brothers had to tell him about Europe and, in particular, the Christian
religion that he decided to send them back to the West as special envoys
to Pope Clement IV, with a request that the Pope in his turn should send
out a group of educated men to give his people instruction in Christianity
and the liberal arts. Back went the brothers, only to find on reaching Acre
that Clement had just died, and that no successor had yet been elected.
Rather than wait indefinitely at Acre, therefore, they decided to return
to Venice.

Had they not done so; had the Pope not died when he did; had they
set out again for the East at once as originally planned, it is unlikely that
the name of Marco Polo would ever have been heard of. But when
Nicolò got home in 1270, after ten years' absence, he found that his
wife had died and his son had grown almost to manhood; and when the
following year, after the longest interregnum in papal history, the Polos
were at last able to fulfil their mission to the new Pope Gregory X – an
old personal friend – and embark once again on their long journey back
to furthest Asia, they took young Marco with them.

Of the route they followed – through Persia, Oxiana, the Pamirs, Kash-
gar and the Gobi desert – Marco was later to give the first description
ever to reach the West, and indeed virtually the last until the middle of
the nineteenth century. It was long and hard, and took four years; at
last, however, the Venetians reached Kublai's summer palace at Shangtu.
The 21-year-old Marco was an immediate success with the Emperor, who
listened enthralled to the stories of his adventures and the wonders he
had seen on the journey, and at once took him into the imperial service.
Within a short time he was one of the Khan's most trusted officials,
travelling the length and breadth of the Empire, governing remote

cities and provinces, and carrying out missions to South India and even beyond.

Whether his father and uncle accompanied him on these missions is uncertain. What does seem clear, however, is that Kublai found all three Polos so interesting, or so useful, or both, that for many years he could not be persuaded to let them go. It was only in 1292, when an escort was needed for a Mongol princess who had been promised in marriage to the Persian Khan, that they were at last permitted to leave.

The story of their return after nearly a quarter of a century to the great house in Venice, of their non-recognition by family and friends, and of the subsequent *coup de théâtre* when they suddenly threw back their shabby oriental robes, ripped open the linings and allowed torrents of emeralds, rubies and pearls to cascade over the floor, has become part of the Polo legend. But despite the incredulity with which Marco's stories were received and the exaggeration of which he was accused – earning him the not invariably affectionate nickname of *Milion* because, it was said, he always talked in millions – the book which he dictated to his fellow-prisoner in Genoa is by no means simply the collection of tall stories it was once presumed to be. Many of his descriptions are remarkably accurate; several have been confirmed, after the passage of centuries, by research in Chinese archives. He speaks with authority not only of Kublai's brilliant court at Peking but of his whole Empire, from the far North with its dog-sledges and reindeer to Ceylon, Burma, Siam, Java, Sumatra and Japan – lands unheard of before his time – and even, by hearsay, of the Christian Empire of Abyssinia, of Madagascar and Zanzibar.

Marco Polo died in 1324 and was buried in the church of S. Lorenzo. His sarcophagus was unfortunately lost when the church was rebuilt in 1592; his will, however, has survived in the Marciana Library. There also remain a few vestiges of the old Polo house – including a superb Byzantine archway beneath which Marco must have passed countless times – in a remote corner just behind the church of S. Giovanni Crisostomo, still called, after the greatest and most celebrated of medieval travellers, the *Corte Seconda del Milion*.

After the battle of Curzola the war between Venice and Genoa entered its final phase. There were no more major engagements. A Genoese raiding party managed to attack Malamocco; in retaliation the Venetian Domenico Schiavo, who had already distinguished himself in the attack on Caffa a year or two before, penetrated into the inner harbour of Genoa with three galleys and, as a final insult, actually minted some Venetian coins there before retiring; but both sides were more than ready for peace. In the final reckoning the Venetians had undeniably come off the worse; their reputation in the Mediterranean and beyond had sustained a heavy blow and their self-confidence had been rudely shaken. But despite her splendid victories, Genoa too had suffered much. Though her prestige had never been higher, her total losses had fallen not far short of those of Venice, while her resources from which to make them good were still immeasurably inferior. By contrast the Venetians, tired as they might be, were even now preparing yet another fleet of 100 ships and recruiting teams of Catalan mercenaries to fill the gaps among their cross-bowmen.

The peace treaty, which was eventually signed in May 1299, was negotiated by Matteo Visconti, who had recently come to power in Milan and had offered his services as mediator. It was honourable to both parties; there was no suggestion of victor and vanquished. Nevertheless its terms were unusual – an indication of the narrowness of the distinction still prevailing between legitimate naval warfare and simple freebootery. It was not considered sufficient for the two Republics to pledge their mutual non-aggression; every Venetian captain was individually obliged to swear that he would not attack any Genoese vessel, and vice versa. The Genoese were specifically allowed, however, to go to the defence of any part of the Greek Empire in the event of a Venetian attack. In any war between Genoa and Pisa, the Venetians were to be debarred from Corsica, Sardinia, or any part of the Ligurian coast between Civitavecchia and Nice, always excepting Genoa itself; similarly, if there were fighting in the Adriatic, the Genoese must avoid all ports there except Venice. The treaty was to be ratified not only by the two principals, but also by Padua and Verona on the part of Venice and by Asti and Tortona on the part of Genoa.

The reference to the Greek Empire makes it clear that Venice's quarrel with Andronicus Palaeologus was still unsettled. It was to take another three years, another punitive expedition to Constantinople and the exemplary flogging of Greek prisoners on the decks of the Venetian ships beneath the walls of Blachernae before the Emperor could be brought to terms. And by then Venice herself would be radically, organically, changed.

13

The Oligarchs Triumphant

[1297–1310]

. . . Une ville comme Venise, maîtresse d'un immense et lointain empire, aurait été incapable de le gouverner si elle avait été régie par des institutions démocratiques. Comme l'aristocratie anglaise, à laquelle il ressemble, le patriciat vénétien a donné à la ville de saint Marc des familles où l'art de gouvernement était en quelque sorte héréditaire, et les hommes ont pu changer sans que changeassent les principes et l'esprit politiques. Et c'est pourquoi ce régime oligarchique a conquis en somme le respect et la confiance de ceux qui y furent soumis, par la claire conscience qu'il a donné à tous de son honnêteté et de sa sagesse, par l'ambition qu'il a manifestée de travailler en toute circonstance à la sécurité et à la grandeur de la patrie. Et c'est pourquoi enfin, au XIVe et au XVe siècle, le gouvernement de Venise était probablement un des meilleurs qu'il y eût au monde, et celui qui pouvait le plus utilement servir la cité de saint Marc.

Charles Diehl, *Venise: une République Patricienne*

Matteo Visconti, the self-styled 'Captain-General of Milan' was only one – albeit the most powerful – of the many despots who from about the middle of the thirteenth century had begun to seize control of the cities of North Italy. The Scaligeri were already established in Verona, the Este in Modena and Ferrara; in Mantua, the Gonzaga were poised ready to spring. Tyrants though they might all be in the strict classical sense, their rule was not normally oppressive; more often than not they were popular with their subjects, for whom life was a good deal more peaceful and secure than it had ever been in their fathers' and grandfathers' day.

To the Venetians, however, they were anathema. Again and again we find the Republic strengthening its defences against a similar takeover. The ducal *promissioni* with their ever more stringent measures to prevent nepotism, Renier Zeno's ban on the display of crests or escutcheons, the nightmare rigmarole of the Doge's election, the refusal to consider a third Tiepolo for the vacant throne – all these were symptoms of what, by the turn of the century, had developed into a neurosis. The dangers were in fact greatly exaggerated. Those magnificent autocrats of the mainland had their roots in a tradition which was quite alien to anything Venice had known. They were the products of the highly developed feudal system of western Europe, and of the municipal reaction against it; of the long, grinding contest between Empire and Papacy, Ghibelline and Guelf; and of the quarrels and rivalries that had at once stimulated and bedevilled the rise of the Italian communes.

Venice, on the other hand, was the child of Byzantium, where feudalism – at least until the Fourth Crusade – was unheard of. Not since Charlemagne's treaty with the Emperor Nicephorus had the Western Empire made any serious claim upon her. She was neither Guelf nor Ghibelline. Virtually alone among the major communities of North Italy, she had never been conquered or even invaded. While the rest, when they were not anxiously watching each other, had had to keep their eyes trained northwards to the Emperor beyond the Alps or southwards to the Pope in Rome, Venice had simply turned her back on Italy and looked to the East, to the world that had shaped her beginnings and held the greatest promise for her future. Her political development had thus proceeded on completely different lines from those followed by her sister-cities. They had taken the path of communal government and then, when that had failed, had veered sharply round towards autocracy. She, by contrast, had pursued an unwavering course in a single direction: that of self-perpetuating oligarchy which, when finally achieved, was to govern her – on the whole wisely and well – for almost exactly 500 years until the end came.

At the apex of the political pyramid, the power exercised by the Doge had long been declining. The process had begun with Domenico Flabanico in 1032, when he had put a stop to the practice by which Doges nominated colleagues and successors and had hemmed them round instead with counsellors and *pregadi*; it had continued with the establishment of the Great Council after the assassination of Vitale Michiel in 1172; and, as successive *promissioni* proved, it had not yet ended.[1] At the base of the same pyramid the Venetian populace had as we have already seen lost virtually all its influence and, as recently as 1289, had signally failed to reassert it. Thus the effective basis of the constitution had now become the Great Council, a seat in which was the first step to political power. For those without the advantages of wealth or family

1. A particularly instructive example was provided by the *promissione* of Jacopo Contarini in 1275. The eighty-year-old Doge was obliged to swear, *inter alia*, that he would not take a foreign wife without the consent of the Council, and that neither he nor his sons would buy land outside the Republic or take shares in government loans. Fiefs – presumably in the new Venetian colonies – held by any member of his family were to be given up within a year of his accession. His sons were further explicitly debarred from accepting any state office or employment, apart from those of ambassador or ship's captain.

connections, membership was not easy to obtain. From the start the Council had been self-electing; thus, inevitably over the years, it had grown more and more into a closed society. In 1293, to give but one instance, it included ten Foscari, eleven Morosini and no less than eighteen Contarini. Theoretically, however, and to some degree in practice also, its doors had remained open.

Now, in the last few years of the thirteenth century, Pietro Gradenigo closed them for ever.

Already in 1286, during the dogeship of Giovanni Dandolo, it had been proposed that eligibility for the Council should be restricted to those whose fathers or more distant paternal ancestors had themselves been members. The motion had been rejected by a comfortable majority – including Dandolo himself – and when Gradenigo reopened the question ten years later he met with no greater success. But the young Doge – he was still only forty-five – was renowned for his energy and determination, and on the last day of February, 1297,[1] a new law was proposed and accepted, the most important clause of which required the *Quarantia*[2] to ballot, one by one, on the names of all those who during the previous four years had had a seat in the Great Council, and decreed that all who received twelve or more votes should be members of it until Michaelmas – the normal time for its elections – 1298. When that time came the system was prolonged for a further year and the decree was again renewed in 1299, after which it became the established law of Venice.

For those debarred by these conditions, one loophole remained. Provision was made for three electors, holding office for one year only, whose task would be to submit for election, on the authority and approval of the Doge and his advisers, the names of other candidates not previously eligible. In theory, this provision might be thought to have opened the doors wide again; in fact there is reason to suspect that it was a deliberate attempt by a wily, disingenuous Doge to deceive the opposition. By retaining the power of veto over all new names, he robbed it of much of its force; and in the years that followed he made it clear through the electors that it would be applied in practice only in favour of those who had sat in the Council at some earlier date, or who could prove that a paternal forbear had done so.

These measures did nothing to diminish the size of the Council. On the contrary, as more and more Venetians hastened to prove their eligibility, its numbers – which for many years had been declining from the

1. 1296 according to the contemporary calendar, in which the new year began in March.
2. See p. 147.

original 480 – rapidly increased. Whereas in 1296 it could boast only 210 members, by 1311 there were 1,017 and, by 1340, 1,212. Naturally, not all of these would be present on any one occasion. Venice was small, her foreign interests immense; a considerable proportion of her leading citizens could always be expected to be abroad on diplomatic or commercial business. Nevertheless by 1301 the existing chamber had already become too small[1] and had given place to another, probably half-way down the eastern side of the building.[2] Thus, in the eyes of those responsible for it, the new law probably appeared not so much a restriction as a purification of the body politic; certainly the oligarchy that had so suddenly crystallized could not be described as a narrow one. And yet, for all that, there can be no denying that what has gone down in Venetian history as the *Serrata* – literally, the locking – *del Maggior Consiglio* created, at a stroke, a closed caste in the society of the Republic: a caste with its own inner elite of those who had sat in the Great Council during those four critical years between 1293 and 1297, but which also embraced those whose parentage, or whose own past record, gave them a title to membership. To guard against false claims, the barriers of privilege were raised even higher. In 1315 a list was compiled of all Venetian citizens eligible for election; and from this, in view of the rigid exclusion of all those born out of wedlock or of a non-patrician mother, it was a short step to that great register of noble marriages and births that was later to become famous as the *Libro d'Oro* – the Golden Book.

But what, it might be asked, of the other Venetians, of the immense majority who – though many of them might be rich, intelligent and cultivated – were not qualified to enter this exalted company? Understandably, there was a good deal of initial indignation; but after the passing of a generation or so, when they had had time to accustom themselves to the new dispensation, their resentment was, for the most part at any rate, a good deal less than might have been supposed. There existed – it is impossible to say for how long, since the institution had

1. It probably occupied most of the ground floor of the old Palace built by Sebastiano Ziani. According to a surviving document dated 1255, loitering in the neighbouring courtyard was forbidden, and anyone guilty of rowdiness or games-playing outside the windows was liable to be thrown into the water.

2. That which faces the prisons across the narrow Rio di Palazzo, now spanned by the Bridge of Sighs. This addition – which marked the beginning of the transformation of the Doges' Palace from Byzantine to Gothic – did not last long. Much of it disappeared when the Palace was further enlarged some forty years later. The only important features still surviving are the two traceried windows at each side of the south-east corner (See p. 235.)

grown up gradually over the years – a second social order in Venice.
This was the class of *cittadini*, the citizens. More humble than their
patrician governors, they could none the less take a modest pride in
their superiority over the mob – the same sort of pride, perhaps, that
St Paul took on being a citizen of the Roman Empire. Later they were
to become something distinctly higher, a kind of baronetage roughly
akin to the equestrian order in Rome; but even before the *Serrata* they
had established their claim to respect. The proof was already there
in 1268 when the office of Grand Chancellor had been instituted in
Venice, with an explicit proviso that it should always be held by a member
of the *cittadini*. It was an office as exalted as its name implies. The Grand
Chancellor was the effective head, not only of the ducal chancery but
of the entire civil service of the Republic. He wore purple and ranked
above Senators, yielding precedence only to the Doge and Signoria
and the Procurators of St Mark. Except for the franchise, he enjoyed
every prerogative of the nobility. He held his seals for life and when
he died was entitled to a funeral of similar splendour to that of the
Doge himself.

Other posts, less influential but of considerable importance none the
less, were open to *cittadini* and nobility alike; and it was typical of Venetian political wisdom that as time went on the *cittadini* became more and
more a bulwark of the oligarchic system, rather than a subversive element outside it – particularly since the so-called *privilegio* of citizenship
was not easily accorded. For foreigners seeking it, twenty-five years'
residence in Venice or her dominions was the initial requirement; citizenship *de extra*, which allowed its holders full protection outside the boundaries of the Republic, was even harder to obtain. Certain fortunate
individuals – craftsmen of rare skills, perhaps, or those who had rendered
some signal service – might be rewarded with immediate admission.
But by the same token it was the dream of every *cittadino* that, having
himself deserved particularly well of the state, he too might similarly
slip through the mesh above him and take his place among the
nobility.

This is not to say that no voices were raised against Pietro Gradenigo's
tremendous step. Some of the new disenfranchised chose, indeed, to
rebel – like a certain Marin Bocconio who, as early as the year 1300,
conceived a plot to murder the Doge and to overthrow his government.
He seems to have been just the sort of man who would most bitterly
resent the new dispensations – rich, ambitious, able to call on considerable
popular support, but now finding himself permanently debarred from

political advancement. Alas, he proved to be a not very gifted conspirator, and the Venetian security police was already an organization to be reckoned with. Bocconio and ten of his colleagues were arrested, and hanged in the usual place – between the two columns in the Piazzetta.[1] His attempt to defend the rights of his fellow-citizens had been a fiasco. It was not, however, the last.

On 31 January 1308, the Marquis Azzo VIII of Este died at Ferrara. For 200 years the house of Este had been one of the most powerful in North Italy. Padua and Verona, Mantua and Modena had all at various times come under its influence, and at Ferrara, through the earlier part of the thirteenth century, it had stoutly defended the Guelf cause against the Ghibelline captain, Salinguerra Torelli. Thus, when the city fell to the Venetians in 1240 and Salinguerra was taken prisoner, the Este had been the obvious choice to take over the effective government; and, although they had ruled virtually as Venetian satraps ever since, they had remained loyal champions of the Guelfs and had given successive Popes cause for complaint.

Azzo's death, however, created a problem. He left no legitimate offspring, only two brothers; but there was a natural son, Fosco, who in turn had a son, Folco; and it was this grandson whom Azzo had named as his heir. No dispensation could have been better calculated to cause trouble. The brothers, furious, disputed the will; Fosco, in an attempt to safeguard his son's inheritance, appealed for help to Venice; Venice dispatched a military force; and from his new seat at Avignon[2] Pope Clement V, determined at all costs to prevent a direct Venetian take-over in Ferrara, resurrected the long-dormant papal claim to suzerainty over the city and decreed in favour of the brothers. In face of this rapid escalation, Fosco lost his nerve. His position in Ferrara had never been strong, and he was certainly not prepared to make a stand against the Pope. Pausing only long enough to install the Venetian militia in the Castel Tedaldo, he fled to Venice, simultaneously ceding to the Republic all his son's claims.

Papal troops now entered Ferrara in their turn; and the legate, Cardinal Pelagrua, sent an embassy to the Doge, demanding the immediate recall of his forces. The Venetians stood firm. They had not sought this sudden

1. See p. 142. The most reliable source (Caresini, quoted by Romanin, III, p. 6) says that they were hanged *turpissime*, which Horatio Brown takes to mean head downwards.

2. The Papacy had removed its seat to Avignon in 1307, and was to remain there for the next seventy years.

armed confrontation, nor had they expected it; but possession of the Castel Tedaldo, commanding as it did the city and the all-important bridge over the Po, afforded them a considerable strategic advantage and they did not feel disposed to give in to threats, from whatever quarter these might come. The legate offered a compromise, whereby Venice might hold the city as a papal fief, in recognition of an annual rent of 20,000 ducats. Still they refused to yield. All rights over Ferrara, they pointed out, had been freely ceded to them by the house of Este. There was no more to be said on the matter.

Cardinal Pelagrua disagreed. On 25 October 1308, he gave the Venetians ten days in which to submit. If they persisted in their attitude, excommunication and interdict would be pronounced on the Republic of Venice, its Doge, his councillors and captains and all those who in defiance of the papal command had given advice or assistance against the forces of the Holy See. All Venetian goods and possessions in Ferrara would be declared confiscate, all commercial treaties annulled, all trade and traffic suspended. Venice – and Chioggia, whose ships had caused particular havoc among the papal transports along the Po – would be subjected to a blockade; such privileges as the Republic had ever been granted by the Pope would be withdrawn.

It was the second time within a quarter of a century that Venice had faced the ban of the Church; but whereas the interdict of 1284 had been largely confined to spiritual sanctions, this new threat affected her whole political and economic life. In its earlier stages, the problem of Ferrara had been entrusted to a special committee of the Great Council, originally twenty in number and later, as the situation deteriorated, increased to forty-five. To meet the present crisis, however, even this was not considered sufficient; the whole Council assembled, several hundred strong. Opinion was sharply divided. Most members of the *case vecchie*, led by Jacopo Querini, pressed for the Republic to capitulate: governments, they pointed out, just as much as individuals, were bound to fear God and to hold in reverence the Vicar of Christ on earth. Besides, Venice had not yet fully recovered, financially or materially, from a long period of wars; this was no moment to embark on yet another, which threatened to be more disastrous than any that had gone before.

Doge Gradenigo, as might have been expected, took the opposite view. The question at issue was political, not spiritual; and politically, the first duty of every man, be he prince or private citizen, was to the state – to increase its dominions, to strengthen its authority, to burnish its glory. Great opportunities occurred seldom; the wise statesman must recognize them and seize them. Here was just such an occasion, by which Venice stood to gain supremacy and security of communications all along the Po. Her rights to Ferrara were unassailable. As for Pope Clement, far away beyond the Alps, he was simply misinformed. Once the true position had been explained to him, it was inconceivable that he would proceed in such a way against the people of Venice, who were loyal sons of the Church and only too anxious to remain so.[1]

The debate was long and angry, and was not confined to the Council Chamber. All the old enmities between the two major factions – on the one side the *case vecchie*, populist, pro-papal, Guelfish, led by the families of Querini and Tiepolo, on the other the oligarchs, champions of territorial expansion, represented by the Gradenigos and the Dandolos – flared up again. Brawls and riots once more became commonplace; citizens went armed about the streets. At last, however, the party of the Doge proved the stronger. Ferrara was Venetian property, and would remain so. A Venetian *podestà* was appointed for the city, and the Ferraresi were granted full rights of Venetian citizenship.

The threatened consequences did not follow at once. Winter had come, and communications with Avignon were tenuous. By the early spring of 1309 it was agreed that a delegation should be sent to Pope Clement to explain 'submissively, but with dignity', the Venetian position. Alas, the decision came too late. The very day after the ambassadors were due to set out, on Maundy Thursday, 27 March, the Pope pronounced his excommunication. Its terms were even more fearsome than had been expected. In addition to the penalties already foreshadowed, the subjects of the Doge were all absolved of their oaths of loyalty to him; they were debarred from giving evidence or making wills; any man might deprive them of their liberty, or even enslave them, without penalty in this world or the next. Finally, all clergy were bound to leave the territory of the Republic within ten days after the expiry of the month's grace that was still allowed in case of a last-minute change of heart.

It says much for the courage of Pietro Gradenigo and those around him that even now Venice did not flinch. Economic and commercial ruin stared her in the face; and, as expected, on the very day that the month's grace expired and the Pope's dreadful sentence came into effect, her enemies and rivals struck. In every corner of Europe and a large

1. The summaries of these speeches are taken, via Romanin, from the Chronicle of Marco Barbaro in the Marciana Library. As Barbaro was writing in the mid-sixteenth century, however, it is more than likely that he is working on the Thucydidean principle, reporting not what was actually said, but the speeches which he himself would have made given the arguments available.

part of Asia, Venetian goods were seized, Venetian assets confiscated, Venetian ships attacked and plundered. In one direction only could Venetian merchantmen still sail out from the Rialto and be assured of a welcome: how the Republic's citizens must have blessed that day in 1297 when in a similar defiance of papal orders they had signed their commercial treaty with the Mameluke Sultan of Egypt, now – since the fall of Acre – controlling the whole Palestinian littoral. It was the one lifeline that the Pope had been powerless to cut.

But already nearly a month before, as soon as the papal Bull had been received by the Doge, the Venetian *podestà* in Ferrara had been ordered to entrench himself in the Castel Tedaldo and to make ready his defences; and when in July the Cardinal Legate proclaimed a Crusade against Venice all the necessary preparations were complete. Florence, Lucca, Ancona and a number of other towns in Tuscany, Lombardy and Romagna, spurred on by jealousy, greed and – one must be fair – perhaps a modicum of filial piety and obedience, hastened to the papal colours and closed in on Ferrara. And the siege began.

From the first, things went badly for the Republic. Her garrison fought with courage but pestilence broke out almost at once, carrying off the *podestà* and increasing numbers of his men. Reinforcements were hurried out, with Marco Querini della Ca' Grande and Giovanni Soranzo smashing through the chain that the papalists had drawn across the Po and forcing their way to the beleaguered citadel. But the enemy forces were too strong, the epidemic grew steadily more virulent, and when the fortress was stormed on 28 August those of the garrison who were still alive lacked the strength to resist. One or two, like Querini, managed to escape; the remainder were blinded or butchered, or both.

Another defeat, another humiliation; yet even now the Venetians did not immediately submit. The war dragged on, half-heartedly – on the Pope's side because of difficulties with Francesco d'Este, one of the brothers whose claims he had upheld; on Venice's because, as we shall soon see, she was occupied with a new crisis at home. Her lesson was still unlearnt. It was to take several more, costlier still, before she was brought to understand the simple truth that her prosperity was founded on trade, and not on territorial aggrandizement. Her strength lay in her unique situation, sea-girt like no other city in the world, secure and inviolable. If, by seeking adventures on *terra firma*, she were to deny herself this one supreme advantage, she could only bring about her own destruction.

As, ultimately, she did.

14

The Conspiracy and the Council

[1310]

Del mille tresento e diese
A mezzo el mese delle ceriese,
Bagiamonte passò el ponte
E per esso fo fatto il consegio di diese.

In one thousand three hundred and ten,
When the cherries were ripening again,
Old Bagiamonte
Passed over the *ponte*
And they founded the Council of Ten.

Old Venetian song, from *Splendor*
Magnificentissimae Urbis Venetiarum,
in Graevius, *Thesaurus Antiquitatum Italiae*, V

By the spring of 1310, Doge Pietro Gradenigo was the most detested man in Venice. The vast majority of his subjects were still smarting over their disenfranchisement; almost all of them held him responsible for the papal interdict, which had not only had a direct impact on the life of every man, woman and child in the Republic but had also brought trade to a virtual standstill. The merchant community in particular, faced with the dual prospect of financial ruin in this world and spiritual damnation in the next, made no secret of their loathing of the man whom they rightly saw as the author of their misfortunes.

To everyone, the news that had reached the lagoon in the last days of the previous August had come as a further shattering blow. Until that moment, there had still been a chance that the Doge's gamble might succeed. Even then, Venice would have been the loser in material terms; possession of Ferrara and mastery of the Po would have availed her little in the face of a multilateral blockade. But at least she would have had something to show for her stand, and her prestige would have remained high. Now even that possibility was gone. The war still continued, and the interdict; but no longer was there any hope of victory. All her sacrifices had been for nothing. Since then, Pietro Gradenigo's enemies had become more vocal. Both inside and outside the Council Chamber, they hammered home their message again and again: how the Doge had betrayed the Republic; how Jacopo Querini and his followers had never ceased to oppose the policies that had brought disgrace and disaster in their wake; how, if Giacomo Tiepolo had been elected as the people had wished, Venice would not now be in her present plight – at war with the Pope, her commercial Empire collapsing about her ears, deprived by a stroke of unparalleled political idiocy of the wise counsel and expertise of many of her most brilliant citizens. The *case vecchie*, who had always enjoyed the support of the people, had once again proved themselves to be far-seeing, clear-thinking and triumphantly right. As for Pietro Gradenigo's reputation for statesmanship – it lay, together with his popularity, at the bottom of the lagoon.

But Gradenigo was still Doge, and still in control. Demonstrations and street fighting, though now more frequent than ever, were ruthlessly put down by his security police, by the *Capi di Contrada*[1] and by the sinisterly-named *Signori di Notte*; and Pietro himself, heedless of public feeling, continued to behave with all his old arrogance. Tempers thus continued to rise, and in the prevailing atmosphere it did not take much to bring them to flash point. The issue that finally did so was in itself relatively insignificant: the proposal to appoint Doimo, Count of Veglia,[2] as one of the six ducal councillors. This was violently opposed by Jacopo Querini, who pointed out that Dalmatian Counts were expressly debarred from all public office except membership of the Great Council and the *pregadi*. His case, relying as it did on the written law of the Republic, was unanswerable; none the less, the appointment was confirmed.

To the Tiepolos, the Querini and their followers, it was the last straw. Fighting broke out again in the Piazza and elsewhere, in the course of which a Tiepolo was gravely wounded by a Dandolo. Civil war seemed imminent, and the government published an emergency decree making it an offence to carry arms. It was a wise measure; unfortunately it had the opposite effect to what was intended. A night or two later, Piero Querini della Ca' Grande, accosted by one of the Signori di Notte and ordered to submit to a search, replied with a violent kick which sent the official sprawling. His followers hurried to his aid, and within minutes the whole quarter was up in arms. Piero was arrested, found guilty and

---

1. At this time there were thirty *contrade*, or parishes, in Venice; an average of five to each *sestiere*.

2. Now Krk, an island on the Dalmatian coast.

punished. But the matter did not end there. His brother Marco was already nursing a personal grievance against the Doge, who had publicly accused him of cowardice at the time of his escape from Ferrara; and Marco now called a secret meeting of his friends. They readily agreed with him, as he had known they would, that Pietro Gradenigo could no longer be allowed to remain in office; but their first recommendation was, on the face of it, surprising. To lead the conspiracy, they suggested that Querini should summon, from a self-imposed exile on the mainland, his son-in-law Bajamonte Tiepolo.

Though now stigmatized – perhaps not altogether fairly – as one of the blackest villains in the history of Venice, Bajamonte Tiepolo remains a strangely mysterious figure. He was a great-grandson of Bohemund of Brienne, Prince of the petty Crusader state of Rascia in Bosnia (from whom he seems to have derived his curious Christian name), grandson of Doge Lorenzo and son of that Giacomo who had refused to contest the dogeship with Pietro Gradenigo twenty years before. Of his own background, however, we know little apart from a curious report by Marco Barbaro – writing, it must be remembered, two centuries later – to the effect that in 1300 he had been accused of extortion in the twin Peloponnesian colonies of Modone and Corone. By 1302, with the sum in question still not fully repaid, he had been nominated *podestà* at Nona and a member of the Quarantia, now the supreme judicial body in the state; but the accusation had continued to rankle, and rather than accept these appointments he had retired to his villa at Marocco across the lagoon. Not, in itself, a particularly distinguished record; but there must, one feels, have been more to Bajamonte Tiepolo than this – some quality of character or now-forgotten exploit that made him a well-known, popular and perhaps romantic figure in Venetian eyes. *Il gran cavaliere*, men called him; and when Marco Querini and his fellow-conspirators assembled to plan the overthrow of the Doge, they clearly believed his support to be in some way indispensable to their plans.

Only one voice, at this first meeting, was raised in opposition to the whole idea; that of old Jacopo Querini, who had spent much of his political life fighting Gradenigo and all he stood for but who refused categorically to lend his support to an unconstitutional act of violence. Jacopo, however, was shortly to leave on a government mission to Constantinople; within a few weeks he would be safely out of the way. Meanwhile Bajamonte arrived, and gave himself whole-heartedly to the cause. Political adventurer as he undoubtedly was, he seems to have seen the plot as a means of overthrowing not just Pietro Gradenigo but the whole Venetian constitution, and of establishing himself and his family as despots on the mainland pattern.

The date fixed for the insurrection was Monday 15 June, the Feast of St Vitus. The conspirators had divided themselves into three groups. Two of these, under Bajamonte Tiepolo and Marco Querini respectively, were to assemble on the evening before at the Querini house in S. Polo; thence, at first light, they would cross the Rialto bridge and advance by separate routes to the Piazza and the Doges' Palace. Meanwhile the third group, which had gathered at the little mainland village of Peraga under the leadership of Badoero Badoer,[1] would cross the lagoon at the last moment, wait until the government troops were fully occupied and then, it was hoped, fall on them from the rear.

It was not a particularly imaginative plan, but given the all-important element of surprise it might well have succeeded. Unfortunately, like Marin Bocconio before them, Bajamonte and his friends had under-estimated their Doge. A certain Marco Donato who had formerly been a member of the conspiracy suddenly withdrew from it. Whether or not he had been suborned we shall never know; it seems likely enough. Through him, at any rate, Gradenigo was fully informed of the *coup* several days before it was due to take place. This gave him time to summon all his most trusted lieutenants, including the *podestà* of Torcello, Murano and Chioggia, with as many armed men as they could muster; and on the eve of St Vitus they, together with the Signoria, the heads of the Quarantia, the Avogadori, the Signori di Notte and the workmen of the Arsenal who traditionally formed the Doge's personal bodyguard, all secretly assembled in the Palace. Meanwhile, on the Piazza, his Dandolo allies were out in strength.

That night there arose one of those violent summer storms to which Venice has always been subject, whipping up the waters of the lagoon to the point at which Badoer and his party were unable to cross to the city. Had they been able to get a message across to Bajamonte, he might well have postponed the whole operation. But knowing no more of their difficulties than he did of the Doge's own preparations he decided, despite the pouring rain, to proceed as planned. Marco Querini and his son Benedetto consequently set off at the head of the first detachment, galloping[2] through the narrow *calli* to shouts of '*Libertà, e Morte al Doge*

1. The family of Badoer, under its former name of Participazio, was one of the oldest in Venice, with the record number of seven Doges to its credit in the ninth and tenth centuries (see p. 45 n.).

2. At this period, before most of the canal bridges were arched high enough for boats to

Gradenigo!' – which, we are told, were scarcely audible above the howling of the wind – and entering the Piazza half-way along the north side, across what is now the Ponte dei Dai. They fell straight into the arms of the waiting Dandolos. Taken by surprise and heavily outnumbered, there was little they could do. Many of them, including the two Querinis, father and son, were killed; the remainder fled to the nearby Campo S. Luca, where they made a vague attempt to regroup but were again put to flight, even more shamingly, by the confraternity of the *Scuola della Carità* and a few members of the Painters' Guild.

Meanwhile Bajamonte, riding at the head of his company along the Merceria, had paused under the great elder tree which at that time stood by the church of S. Giuliano. Why he did so is uncertain. He may have wished to gather his forces together for the final charge into the Piazza; alternatively and more probably, one of Querini's men may have come back to warn him of the dangers ahead. But warnings were unnecessary, for by now the whole *sestiere* was in an uproar. Clearly, the local populace was not rallying to the insurgents as had been expected. There were no cheers; only insults and imprecations flung from the windows of the barricaded houses. At last Tiepolo advanced to the entrance of the Piazza, where the clock-tower now stands, at which point an old woman tipped a heavy stone mortar out of an upper window. It missed him, but struck his standard-bearer squarely on the head and killed him outright. The sight of his banner, emblazoned with the single word *Libertas*, lying in the mud – for the deluge continued and most of the streets were still unpaved – finally shattered his nerve. Sodden and bedraggled, he and his followers fled back across the Rialto bridge, destroying it behind them.

The insurrection, however, was not quite over. Although Badoer and his group on the mainland were quickly rounded up, brought to Venice and beheaded, Bajamonte managed to entrench himself in his own quarter where, soon afterwards, the survivors of the Querini party joined him. The district was heavily fortified with barricades; the inhabitants of the further side of the Grand Canal, unlike those of S. Marco, were totally loyal to the *case vecchie*; and Doge Gradenigo, despite his victory, could not risk a civil war by launching a direct attack. His terms were generous; and Bajamonte Tiepolo, after an initial show of haughty

---

pass beneath them, horses were common in Venice. In the more populous *calli* they even seem to have constituted something of a traffic problem: from 1291 horsemen riding down the Merceria to the Piazza were required to dismount at S. Salvatore. Horses were normally forbidden in the Piazza itself; they would be left by their owners tied to the little grove of elders by the present clock-tower.

intransigence, capitulated and went off to a four-year exile in Dalmatia – where, however, he had not the least intention of remaining.

Thus dispassionately described, the rebellion of Bajamonte Tiepolo sounds almost laughably inept. It was true, as he might have pleaded, that all occasions had conspired against him. The weather had slowed his progress, prevented his allies from joining him, and dampened spirits all round. Marco Donato had betrayed his trust. That halt at S. Giuliano, whatever its cause, had also lost him valuable minutes, since without it he might just possibly have arrived on the Piazza in time to save the Querini. Yet no amount of special pleading could alter or even conceal the fact that he had failed miserably – and in the process had brought upon himself, as well as lasting infamy, more than a little ridicule.

In Venice, however, what now appears as an almost trifling incident was taken very seriously indeed. Had Gradenigo not received advance warning, the plot might well have succeeded even without the help of the Badoer contingent; success or failure, it remained a formidable attempt, not just on the Doge personally, but on the whole fabric of the state – an attempt, moreover, with which three of the oldest and noblest Venetian families were identified. Having successfully put out the fire in its early stages, the government now determined to stamp out such embers as might continue to smoulder. Bajamonte's sentence had been relatively light only because they knew the strength of his following and had wisely decided against making a martyr of him; now that he was safely in exile, they systematically set about the destruction of his name and reputation. His house in S. Agostino – better known in the Venetian dialect form of S. Stin – was torn down within a day or two of his departure until not one stone was left on another; on its site was raised a so-called Column of Infamy, bearing the inscription:

Di Bajamonte fo questo tereno
E mo per lo so iniquo tradimento
S'è posto in chomun per l'altrui spavento
E per mostrar a tutti sempre seno.[1]

The Querini house was to suffer almost as sad a fate. Here the problem was that Marco and Piero had owned it jointly with a third brother,

1. This land was the property of Bajamonte
   And now, through his infamous betrayal,
   Is held by the Commune as a lesson to others.
   So let these words proclaim to all, for ever.

Giovanni, who had played no part in the conspiracy. The government first proposed, therefore, to pull down two-thirds of it only; but difficulties of demarcation arose, and it was finally decided to compensate Giovanni for his share and turn the whole building into a slaughterhouse. Next came a decree calling for the removal or erasure of all existing crests and escutcheons of the two disgraced dynasties – who were, however, permitted to adopt new arms and substitute them for the old. No exceptions were permitted; even the crests beneath the portraits of the two Tiepolo Doges in the Hall of the Great Council were changed, as were those on their tombs at SS. Giovanni e Paolo.

But if these two families – the Badoer were not for some reason penalized in this way – paid a price for their treachery, others were rewarded for theirs. Marco Donato, through whose agency Doge Gradenigo had first learnt of the plot against him, was ennobled and awarded membership of the Great Council in perpetuity for himself and his descendants.[1] Perhaps it was only fitting recognition for one who could claim to have saved the state; yet one reads with greater pleasure of the other beneficiaries. The church of S. Vio – St Vitus, on whose feast-day the uprising occurred – was presented with the stone door-jambs from Bajamonte's house and certain relief decorations from its walls;[2] and it was decreed that on every succeeding St Vitus's Day the Doge should visit it in solemn procession for a thanksgiving mass, followed by an official banquet. Meanwhile the Campo S. Luca, where the remnants of the Querini had been routed, was given a magnificent flagpole from which the Scuola della Carità and the Painters' Guild might fly their standards.[3]

And so we come to the last – indeed, the only – heroine in the drama, Giustina (or was it Lucia? – no one is quite sure) Rossi, the old lady who felled Bajamonte's standard-bearer with her mortar. When asked what the Republic could do for her to show its gratitude, she asked two things only: that she and her successors in that house should be allowed to display the banner of Venice from the fateful window on all major feast-days, and that her landlords, the Procurators of St Mark, should never raise her rent. Both requests were granted; and though nowadays on 15 June one may look in vain for a banner in her window, and though the rent of one of the most desirable commercial sites in the city is no

1. Their name is more usually shortened in the Venetian dialect to Donà, in which form it serves partially to identify at least a dozen *palazzi* on the Grand Canal and elsewhere.

2. S. Vio was demolished in 1813, but the decorations (several *paterae* and a cross) were preserved and are now set into the wall of the modern votive chapel that occupies the site, next to the Anglican church of St George.

3. The arms of both institutions and the date, MCCCX, are still visible on its base.

longer pegged at fifteen ducats a year, a glance at the upper wall will show that the *vecchia* herself has not been forgotten.[1]

Yet the deepest and most lasting imprint left on Venice by the events of St Vitus's Day 1310 took the form not of a banner, nor of a banquet, nor even of a Column of Infamy, but of an institution – one that was to last as long as the Republic itself, with a name still capable of provoking an occasional shudder of awe: the Council of Ten. It was established on 10 July 1310, by a decree of the Great Council, as a temporary measure only – a sort of Committee of Public Safety, with wide emergency powers to deal with the continuing state of unrest; and the very fact of its foundation, together with the edicts which it issued in the first three weeks of its existence, show more clearly than anything else how tense was the atmosphere in the city during the period immediately following the insurrection. On 12 July, members of the Great Council were permitted to attend armed; on the 19th it was resolved that the doors of the Council Chamber should remain open during sessions; 100 armed men in boats were deputed to patrol the lagoon and canals; a special corps of 200, chosen by the heads of the *sestieri*, were to guard the Piazza, another thirty the Doges' Palace, and ten more were appointed to each of the *contrade* to see that no man passed from one to another after nightfall. Meanwhile each *sestiere* was required to keep 1,500 men permanently under arms; on the sounding of the great tocsin from the campanile of St Mark's, half were to run immediately to the Piazza, while the rest remained to deal with any local uprisings.

When the Council of Ten was first established, its intended life-span was some two and a half months – till Michaelmas, which fell on 29 September. At first its prolongation was for another two months only, but subsequent renewals of its authority were for increasingly long periods, and in 1334 it was made a permanent body. Though its corporate powers were immense, they were subject to characteristically Venetian checks and balances to prevent any individual member's using them for his personal ends. Election – by the Great Council, from lists drawn up by itself and the Signoria respectively – was for a single year, and re-

1. The building that stands on the spot – under the clock-tower where the Merceria gives on to the Piazza – now bears a curious little plaque, erected in 1841, with a representation of the incident in relief; on the pavement below, a tablet of white marble marks the place where the mortar, and presumably the luckless standard-bearer, hit the ground. One of the banners is still preserved in the Museo Correr. I have not been able to discover how long the rent of the *Casa della Grazia del Morter* remained pegged; but a descendant, Nicolò Rossi, won an appeal against its increase a century and a half later, in 1468.

election was forbidden until a further year had passed, during which time any alleged abuses would be carefully investigated. Two members of the same family could never sit simultaneously. Furthermore the Council never allowed itself a single head; there were always three – the *Capi dei Dieci* – serving for a month at a time, a month during which they were forbidden to go out into society lest they should be exposed to bribes or baseless rumours. Finally – the most important point of all and perhaps the one most frequently forgotten – the Ten were powerless by themselves. They acted only in concert with the Doge and his six councillors, bringing their effective number to seventeen. In addition there was always present one of the Avogadori di Comun or state prosecutors, who had no vote but stood ready to advise the members on points of law. The Council met every weekday and seems to have been consistently overworked; its members, however, were unpaid, and venality or corruption was punishable by death.

As this story goes on, there will be a lot more to be said about this remarkable institution and its workings; during these early years many of its most interesting characteristics had not yet fully evolved. From the outset, however, it served two important purposes, which together explain why it so rapidly proved itself indispensable. The first of these was the gathering of intelligence, through a network of spies and undercover agents that was ultimately to spread right across Europe and even beyond. Despite popular legend Venice was never, in the modern sense of the term, a police state; but her intelligence and security services were unequalled. It was just as well. Within less than a year, an agent was reporting from Padua that Bajamonte, having broken the terms of his Dalmatian exile, was back in Lombardy with two of the Querini – one of them a priest – plotting a new rebellion; although in fact he never returned to Venice, this was largely due to the Republic's ability to keep him under continual surveillance and always to remain one jump ahead. But even the Ten could not put a stop to his intriguing – unless it was they who covertly did so in 1329, after which date he is heard of no more.

The second contribution made by the new Council in these first years of its existence was still more vital. The crisis over Ferrara had shown up a serious weakness in the constitution: the lack of any means of reaching a quick decision on a major matter of state and acting upon it with equal dispatch. In their anxiety to avoid the concentration of power, the Venetians had been obliged to accept a loss of executive efficiency that they could ill afford. All important issues had to be ratified by the Great Council which, in the decade since the *Serrata*, had grown steadily until it now numbered about 1,000 members. Inevitably, so unwieldy a body was obliged to delegate, and it was already common practice for it to appoint smaller committees of so-called *savii*, or sages, to handle specific questions. Some of these *savii* were permanent officers with defined responsibilities, not unlike present-day ministers though with rather less authority; indeed, by the middle of the century the *Collegio*, which they formed together with the Doge and his six councillors, had emerged as a fully-fledged cabinet. At this time, however, major questions of policy – to hold Ferrara, for example, in defiance of papal threats – were referred back to the Council in plenary session. It followed that, the graver the situation, the more cumbersome was the apparatus for dealing with it.

With the appearance of the Ten, all this was changed. Acting – as they always did – in conjunction with the Doge and his councillors, their decrees had the same force as those of the Great Council itself. Swift and decisive action once more became a possibility. It is arguable that, so great was the need for this streamlining of the administrative machine, the Council of Ten or something very like it would have been instituted anyway before very long; the fact none the less remains that it was called into being as a direct result of the Tiepoline conspiracy. Bajamonte had failed totally in his object; yet Venice owed him more than she ever admitted, or he ever knew.

15

The Mainland Dominion

[1311–1342]

A che mandarmi il doge tanto piombo? Il tenghi a coprire il campanile di S. Marco.

Why does the Doge send me so much lead? Let him keep it to roof the campanile of St Mark's.

Mastino della Scala, on receiving letters
from the Doge bearing leaden seals (*Barbaro Chronicle*)

When Pietro Gradenigo died on 13 August 1311, the prevailing emotion in Venice was one of relief. He had been a strong Doge – too strong, in the view of most of his subjects – but not a wise one. Stubborn and self-willed, mindful of the opinions of others only when considering the best way of imposing his own, he left the Republic in a worse condition than he found it: badly shaken by the Tiepolo plot and its aftermath, its trade reduced to a trickle, the papal interdict still in force. It was no wonder that, as much for fear of hostile demonstrations as on account of the ban of the Church, his body was borne off without ceremony to the abbey of S. Cipriano on Murano and buried there in an unmarked grave.

In their understandable desire that his successor should be as unlike him as possible, the ducal electors first veered too far in the opposite direction, choosing the elderly senator Stefano Giustinian who, rather than accept the greatness thrust upon him, fled to a monastery. Their second choice fell on a certain Marino Zorzi – who was even older – for no better reason than that they chanced to see him as he passed beneath the palace windows, carrying a large sack of bread for distribution to the inmates of the nearby prison. A fifteenth-century historian, Marino Sanudo the younger, explains his election with the words 'He was known as the Saint, since he was so good and so Catholic a man – and he was rich.' After Gradenigo, this was all the Venetians wanted of their Doge: an innocuous figurehead with a respectable if not particularly distinguished diplomatic background, plenty of money and a generous hand with which to dispense it. Zorzi's reputation for piety – he had founded and copiously endowed an orphanage some years before – may, however, have been an additional point in his favour; for any new Doge, the lifting of the interdict would be the first and most important objective.

But Marino Zorzi did not live to achieve it. He died in July 1312, having reigned less than a year. The electors met again, this time with all the windows looking out on to the street pointedly shuttered, and chose Giovanni Soranzo, the conqueror of Caffa during the war with the Genoese fifteen years before.[1] With a dazzling career behind him – as we have seen, he had also distinguished himself at Ferrara, and had subsequently risen to be Chief Procurator of St Mark's – it may well be asked why Soranzo had been passed over in favour of the ineffectual Zorzi the year before; the answer probably lies in the fact that his daughter had married the son of Marco Querini and since the Tiepolo plot had been sharing her husband's exile. At seventy-two, he might also have been considered some way past his prime; but he was to reign for sixteen years, during which Venice slowly returned to her old prosperity. Recovery began in March 1313, when Pope Clement was at last, and with much difficulty, persuaded to lift his ban. The price was high – 90,000 Florentine gold florins, a huge sum for the Republic's depleted coffers, and made more unpalatable still by the Pope's insistence on the specific currency in which it was to be paid. Nevertheless, by dint of a forced loan of 3 per cent on all incomes and the threat to the Florentine bankers in Venice that they would be instantly expelled if they did not change the money at once and at a fair rate, the government met its obligations; and the Pope in return decreed that Venetians might once again circulate freely in Ferrara and carry on their lawful commerce without interference.

It was a capitulation, of course: but to humble oneself before the Pope was somehow less shameful than to do so before a temporal ruler, and for most Venetians it was a small enough price to pay for the resumption of normal economic life and all that stemmed from it. Six months later Zara, which had taken advantage of the Republic's disarray following the Tiepolo plot to stage one of its own periodic rebellions, was successfully brought to heel. Venice was at peace again; trade, once more, had begun to flow; within the next few years treaties were concluded with the Byzantine Empire, with Sicily and Milan, with Bologna, Brescia and

1. See p. 201. Soranzo's conquest of Caffa in 1296 – and the fully-laden Genoese merchantmen which he took as prizes and brought back to Venice – had become something of a legend. It was later commemorated in the ceiling painting by Giulio dal Moro in the *Sala dello Scrutinio* of the Doges' Palace.

H

Como, with Tunisia, Trebizond and Persia. All this fortunately coincided with the destruction, by the Genoese Benedetto Zaccaria in 1291, of the Moroccan fleet which for years had done its best to close the straits of Gibraltar to Mediterranean shipping. Henceforth the straits were open, and – with Genoa having conveniently entered into a period of comparative eclipse, thanks to a long and acrimonious quarrel with her colony of Pera on the Bosphorus – Venice was able to capture much of the valuable trade with England and Flanders.

Thus, under a wise, moderate and universally respected Doge, morale soared. In the Republic itself new industries arose, with a craftsman being brought to Murano from Germany to teach new techniques in the manufacture of looking-glasses, and a whole colony of silk-workers from Lucca who, fleeing from the factional strife that was tearing their own city apart, established themselves in the Calle della Bissa off S. Bartolomeo. Such was the influx of German merchants that by 1318 a special building was necessary to accommodate them all – the first *Fondaco dei Tedeschi*.[1] The paving of streets and *campi* continued apace – doubtless to the consternation of the pigs from the monastery of S. Antonio, who enjoyed free rootling range throughout the city – including that of the main thoroughfare that led from the Piazza to S. Pietro di Castello; fifty new wells were sunk, and huge cisterns constructed for additional storage; another ingenious German was imported to build windmills. Venice also received her first municipal fire service.

At about this time, too, the Arsenal was enlarged – a development made necessary by significant advances in shipbuilding. The mariners' compass had appeared in about 1275, making possible the preparation of charts far more accurate than before. A few more years brought another innovation – the rudder. Until this time the accepted method of steering any large vessel was by means of an oar to one side of the stern, a system which was not only extremely inefficient but which imposed severe limits on size since with large ships it swiftly became unmanageable. The stern rudder, on the other hand, permitted an almost infinite degree of leverage simply by increasing the length of the tiller, and could even have a system of pulleys added if required. The immediate result was bigger ships; and, as these were capable of putting to sea in winter and summer alike, sailoring became for the first time an all-year-round

1. The original *Fondaco dei Tedeschi* was burnt to the ground in 1505; the present building – next to the Rialto bridge, and now the central post office – was completed three years later. The Canal façade was decorated by Giorgione, the side by Titian; traces of their work are said to survive, but I have never found them.

profession and seamanship in its turn underwent a spectacular improvement.

It was probably the opening-up of the English and Flemish trade, more than any other single factor, that led to the introduction in about 1320 of a revolutionary new ship design. Until this time oars had never been used for commercial vessels; they had been kept for warships, where high speeds and manoeuvrability were essential. With the sudden commercial expansion in the years following 1300, however, new considerations had arisen. Now merchantmen too needed to move quickly – and, with more precious cargoes to carry, they demanded increased protection. The answer was found in the merchant galley. It was longer and wider than war galleys, giving it a capacity, even in those early days of its development, of some 150 tons' burden, and in addition to its full complement of sail, was propelled by 200 oarsmen. The expense of maintaining such a crew – who were, incidentally, all free men[1] – was considerable; but it was easily outweighed by the saving of time in every voyage and by the vessel's virtual immunity from piracy, since few pirate ships could match it for speed and, even in the event of a surprise attack, the 200 men could immediately be armed for defence. Thanks to its manoeuvrability, the risk of shipwreck on some rocky coast could also be largely discounted.

Yet the greatest blessing of Giovanni Soranzo's reign, at least as far as the residents of the city were concerned, was peace. After the turbulence of the two previous decades, the Venetians desperately needed a chance to recover – not only materially from their immense losses, but mentally and spiritually from the upheavals they had suffered in every sphere of their daily life. Tempers needed time to cool, animosities to be forgotten, minds and opinions to adjust to changing political conditions in Italy and abroad. Soranzo gave his people just such a breathing space. It is a remarkable testament to a reign of sixteen years that its apparently most exciting single event should have been the birth of three cubs to the pair of lions, a gift of the King of Sicily, that lived in the Doges' Palace. This happy occurrence, which took place at about the hour of matins on Sunday 12 September 1316, is said to have brought flocking to the cage 'almost all the inhabitants of Venice and elsewhere' – crowds even greater, it appears, than those which had been privileged to witness the equally interesting preliminaries three and a half months before

---

1. The crews of these galleys – known as *voluntarie* – were well paid, and allowed to carry goods of their own, free of duty. The practice of using slaves and prisoners in Venetian galleys began only in the mid-sixteenth century.

– and was considered by the Doge to be a matter of such state importance that he had it legally recorded in a sworn affidavit by the official notary.

Another event which in retrospect might be considered to have been of even greater moment – the arrival in 1321 of Dante Alighieri as special emissary from Ravenna – seems to have aroused little or no interest in the city. Admittedly – and infuriatingly – the volume of state archives for that year has been lost; but the extant chronicles and early histories are unenlightening. All we know is that Dante's embassy, which was concerned with the old question of navigation rights along the Po, received a dusty answer; and that when the time came for his return Venice refused to grant him a safe conduct by the most convenient route. He was consequently obliged to make his way back through malarial swampland, as a result of which he caught a fever and died.

But however chilly Doge Soranzo may have been to strangers – and Dante, by his own admission, was not overfond of them himself – he was beloved by his subjects; and it may well have been his popularity as much as anything else that caused the Great Council to make new provision for the magnificence of his successors, increasing their salary and their retinue, commissioning a huge state jewel for festive occasions and a still more magnificent state barge, the *Bucintoro*. Their effective power, on the other hand, remained as restricted as ever; and it is significant that when Soranzo's widowed daughter returned from exile in 1314 she was immediately confined to the convent of S. Maria delle Vergini in a remote corner of Castello. The Doge by tradition made a formal visit there every year; but he could never persuade the Ten to permit her release and she was still a prisoner when he died, aged nearly ninety, on the last day of 1328. His body, girt with his sword and wearing the ceremonial gold shoes of his office, lay in state in the Hall of the Signori di Notte on the south side of the old Palace, looking out over the Molo; from there it was carried into the Basilica where his widow awaited it. After the funeral mass it was placed in the baptistery, in a plain sarcophagus which can still be seen, bearing the Soranzo coat of arms but no name or inscription.

Venetians have always had long memories. It would have taken more than fifteen years of peace and prosperity to make them forget the dark days of the papal interdict; and for their fiftieth Doge they were not slow in choosing Francesco Dandolo, whose patient and skilful advocacy at Avignon had finally induced the Pope to relent. Ruskin writes of how Dandolo 'concealed himself (according to the common tradition) beneath the Pontiff's dining-table; and thence coming out as he sat down to meat, embraced his feet, and obtained, by tearful entreaties, the removal of the terrible sentence'. Unkind historians have suggested that his nickname of *Cane*, 'the Dog', came from the day when he had appeared before His Holiness wearing a collar and chain in token of his humility; in fact, the name had been applied equally to his father before him. It was also borne, with pride, by the man who shortly before Francesco's accession had revealed himself as the Republic's most dangerous enemy.

Though Can Grande della Scala, despot of Verona, was still only thirty-seven years old, he had spent more than half of them extending his dominions and now controlled not just his native city but also Vicenza, Feltre, Belluno – which had made him master of several important Alpine passes – and, since September 1328, Padua. The new Doge thus found himself immediately confronted with the one threat to which Venice was more vulnerable than any other, that of economic blockade; and when in July 1329 the Veronese army captured Treviso, the position became desperate. Three days after his entry into Treviso, Can Grande was carried off by a sudden fever and Venice breathed again; but the respite was short. He was succeeded jointly by his nephews, one of whom, Alberto, was a pleasure-loving nonentity but the other, Mastino, was as ambitious and determined as his uncle. Mastino started as he meant to go on. Transit dues on Venetian goods, heavy tolls on produce bound for the lagoon from *terra firma* irrespective of whether it came from Venetian properties, customs-houses along the Po – the Venetians knew it all, only too well; they had done the same sort of thing themselves. They retaliated sharply, with prohibitive levies of their own on all merchandise passing through Venice to the cities under Mastino's control, but it was an unequal battle and they knew it. Padua, Treviso and the rest could be deprived only of luxuries from the East; they might suffer mild inconvenience, but no real harm. Venice, on the other hand, relied upon the mainland for her staple provisions. During the crisis of 1268 she had somehow managed to find alternative supplies, but since then her population had almost doubled. She was unlikely to be so fortunate again.

If catastrophe were to be averted, it would have to be by force of arms. Even now, in the Great Council, there were plenty of voices raised against such a solution, including that of the Doge himself. It was pointed out that Mastino's military strength would make his ultimate victory almost certain, and that such a victory might well mean the end of the Republic; that Venice for her part possessed no land army and would have to resort to mercenaries, with all the expense and risk that that entailed; and that, as the Ferrara affair had shown, interference in mainland politics always led to disaster. All these arguments were reasonable enough; they were also irrelevant. The fact was that Venice had no choice. She must fight or be destroyed.

She had one point in her favour. The speed of the Scaligeri expansion had caused alarm in other quarters as well. Even while diplomatic negotiations were in progress with potential allies, Mastino was making new enemies. Brescia fell to him in 1332; from the ruling family of Rossi he seized Parma, from the Florentines Lucca. His failures, such as his efforts to wrest Mantua from the Gonzagas or to poison Azzo Visconti of Milan, had made him as hated as his successes. And so an alliance took shape. In Venice itself a hasty census revealed 40,100 able-bodied males between the ages of twenty and sixty.[1] Following the normal custom, these were divided into groups of twelve, from each of which one man – and later, if necessary, a second or a third – would be chosen by lot to join the colours, the remainder sharing his expenses among them; but this time, we are told, many volunteered without waiting for the draw or demanding a wage. Meanwhile various other contingents from Italy, France, Germany and Burgundy – by no means all of whom were mercenaries – assembled some 30,000 strong at Ravenna under the command of Pietro de' Rossi, the most accomplished general of his day, who, as the youngest scion of the family that had ruled in Parma until it was expelled by Mastino, could be trusted to dedicate all his energies and abilities to the task in hand.

In the Basilica on 10 October 1336 Pietro received the banner of St Mark from Doge Dandolo while, both inside and outside the building, the assembled populace cheered him to the echo. A day or two later he and his army had crossed the Brenta into Paduan territory, and on 22 November – St Cecilia's Day – he took the fortress protecting the great saltworks with which Mastino had hoped to break the Venetian monopoly. Then he pressed on to Treviso. These early triumphs persuaded a few more waverers to join the alliance, among them Azzo Visconti, Luigi Gonzaga of Mantua and Obizzo d'Este, whose family had since 1317 been back in power in Ferrara; and in March 1337 a new treaty was signed in Venice, formally establishing a League vowed 'to the destruction and ruin of the brothers Alberto and Mastino, Signori della Scala'. A third

1. This figure is particularly significant in that it enables us to make an informed guess at the total population of the Republic at this time, which cannot have been much less than 200,000.

of its expenses was to be paid by Venice, a third by Florence on the understanding that Lucca would be restored to her, and a third jointly by the other Lombard cities.

Surrounded by his enemies and finding himself suddenly under attack on several fronts at once, Mastino had no alternative but to sue for peace – sending to Venice as his personal emissary Marsilio di Carrara. It was an extraordinary choice. Marsilio had been despot of Padua until Mastino had seized it from him a few years before; and although he had been allowed to continue as its governor he had since been little more than a puppet of the Scaligeri. His natural resentment had since been increased by a family feud resulting from the seduction – possibly even the rape – of the wife of his cousin Ubertino by Alberto della Scala; now at last he saw the opportunity for revenge. The story is told of how one evening during his Venetian mission he was dining alone with the Doge. He dropped his napkin on the floor, and both men leant down from their chairs to pick it up.

'What would you give me were I to deliver Padua into your hands?' whispered Marsilio.

'The lordship of the city,' replied the Doge.

It was enough. The pact had been made.[1]

At this time Mastino was fiercely defending Padua against the forces of the League; soon, however, a diversionary attack on Brescia by Azzo Visconti called him away, and on 3 August the gates were opened and Pietro de' Rossi entered the city. Alberto della Scala, wenching away as usual in his palace, was captured and sent a prisoner to Venice. His brother fought on a little longer, but to no avail. His empire collapsing around him, he finally capitulated.

The peace treaty was signed on 24 January 1339 (1338, according to the Venetian reckoning).[2] Its terms were remarkably generous. Most surprising of all, the Scaligeri were allowed to retain Lucca – although its outlying lands and fortresses were restored to Florence – and, subject to a moderate payment of restitution to the Rossi, Parma. To Venice went Padua, where the house of Carrara was restored to power under a somewhat nebulous Venetian suzerainty, and the March of Treviso. The western half of the latter she also entrusted to the Carraras; but the region

1. However pleasant it would be to believe that Francesco Dandolo's two greatest diplomatic triumphs were both achieved not at, but *under* the dinner-table, it should in all fairness be admitted that the best contemporary source for these events, Lorenzo de Monacis, reports the whispered conversation as having taken place while the two were walking under the loggia of the palace.

2. See p. 207n.

directly to the north of Venice, comprising Conegliano, Castelfranco, Sacile, Oderzo and Treviso itself, remained in her direct control.

It was the first time in Venetian history that a large and important area of *terra firma* had been annexed to the territory of the Republic. The immediate advantages were obvious. Provisions of corn and meat were now assured; the danger of blockade was diminished. So important an acquisition, coming as it did on top of the Scaligeri defeat and the elimination of what had seemed a threat to Venice's very survival, had also a profound effect on the national morale. The treaty was celebrated on St Valentine's Day with a grand tournament on the Piazza, and several of the principal allies, including the Carraras, the Gonzagas and the Estes, were admitted into the ranks of the Venetian nobility.

Less immediately apparent were the corresponding disadvantages of Venice's new rôle as a mainland power. Her major problems were those of frontier security. The recent war had greatly strengthened the position of the Visconti of Milan, who were now more powerful than the Scaligeri had ever been. Admittedly they were a good deal further away, and Padua under the Carraras might in other circumstances have served as a buffer state; but since any attack on Carrara territory would have to be considered as an attack on Venice herself, she and Milan were in effect coterminous. She would also have difficulties in future over her land frontier to the north-east, where the Patriarch of Aquileia and his neighbour the Count of Gorizia could always be trusted to stir up trouble whenever they got the chance.

But these problems still seemed far away. For the moment the Venetians applied themselves with energy and enthusiasm to the more immediate challenge presented by their new administrative responsibilities. Their previous experience of ruling an overseas colonial empire had left them few useful precedents for governing in Treviso and the other towns near by. Such places could obviously not be treated as feudal dependencies in the way that the Greek islands had been; nor, equally obviously, could they be run as glorified trading-posts like Modone, Corone, Acre or Negropont. Some new machinery must be devised; and Venice's solution for Treviso – which was to be applied, with minor variations, in most of her other mainland dependencies – was essentially a miniature version of the system that had worked so well in the Republic itself. At its head stood the *podestà* – in the smaller towns he was usually called a *capitano* or a *provveditore* – whose position was closely analogous to that of the Doge and the manner of whose election equally complex. He might be a Venetian nobleman, or a citizen of the town in question.

He too led a life rich in the outward trappings of pomp and splendour, but almost destitute of effective power. Just as the Doge was in reality the servant of the Council of Ten, so the *podestà*'s real master was another, more shadowy official – the Rector, always a Venetian, directly responsible to and in constant touch with the Senate and the Ten. He controlled the police; his was the ultimate responsibility for the entire government, civil and military, of the city or town. Day-to-day legislation, however – local taxation, communications, civic amenities and the rest – was the work of a council of the municipality, corresponding to the Great Council in Venice. In Treviso, this body numbered 300 – a considerable proportion of the educated male population. Thus it was not only an efficient system: it was also, within limits, a democratic one, particularly since Venice's policy was always to allow her subject cities as much individual freedom and independence as was compatible with security. Life under Venetian domination must have been different indeed from that lived under the autocratic despotism of a Scaliger or a Visconti.

Scarcely a year before the death of Francesco Dandolo on the last day of October 1338, the Church of the Frari was finished at last. It had been a century in the building, and its completion was marked by the almost immediate decision to pull it down again and replace it with another, much larger and facing the other way. These two operations seem to have proceeded simultaneously but slowly over the next 100 years, and must have greatly complicated the fufilment of the Doge's wish to be buried in the church. He had, however, left it much of his fortune, and the difficulty was overcome by placing his sarcophagus in the chapterhouse – to which, after a long absence vociferously lamented by Ruskin[1], it has now been restored. The painting above it by Paolo Veneziano, depicting the presentation to the Virgin of the Doge and Dogaressa by St Francis and St Elizabeth, is probably the oldest ducal portrait in Venice to be drawn from the life.

On 7 November Bartolomeo Gradenigo was elected in succession. His relationship to Doge Pietro is uncertain; but the choice of any member of the Gradenigo family was a sure sign that the Venetians were beginning to forget the events of thirty and forty years before. Not that the new Doge was likely to emulate his formidable namesake; apart from other considerations, he was already seventy-six. He seems to have been elected, quite deliberately, as a stop-gap. The first candidate proposed, and the obvious one in terms both of ability and popularity,

1. *The Stones of Venice*, Vol. III, ii, paras. 58–60.

was another Dandolo, Andrea. But Andrea was still in his early thirties, and unwilling; and there was also the traditional Venetian reluctance to elect two successive Doges from the same family, even if they were no more than distant cousins. How much better, it was felt, for the venerable old Senior Procurator of St Mark's to hold the fort for a while, breaking the sequence and allowing young Dandolo a little longer to mature.

Bartolomeo Gradenigo did just that. He was to reign only three years, but they were not without incident. They saw, first of all, the most terrible flood that Venice had ever suffered in her long, waterlogged history – a disaster which struck her on 15 February 1340 and which she survived only through the fortunate intervention of St Mark, St Nicholas and St George.[1] Two months later there arrived an embassy from Edward III of England, informing the government of the Republic that since the self-styled King Philip of France had declined to settle Anglo-French differences by single combat or by braving ravenous lions – 'who would in no wise harm a true King' – war was inevitable. Edward asked for forty or more galleys for a year, in return for which he offered to pay any sum that the Doge cared to name and also to grant to all Venetians on English soil the same privileges and immunities as were enjoyed by his own subjects. He went on to suggest that the Doge might like to send his two sons to England, where they would be received with every honour due to their rank, including knighthoods. Gradenigo replied that with a Turkish armada of 230 sail already threatening the Eastern Mediterranean Venice could not spare any of her ships to attack a Christian power in the West; none the less, the privileges so generously offered to Venetians in England were gratefully accepted. As for the invitation to his sons, he returned his 'devout and immense thanks' – but they never went.

It was a characteristically Venetian reply; but the Turkish menace was real enough. The whole of Asia Minor was now lost. The Ottoman Sultan Orhan had established his capital in Bursa, only sixty miles or so from Constantinople itself, while the once-glorious Empire of Byzantium, which had never properly recovered from the Fourth Crusade, was under attack from all its neighbours, Christian and Muslim, as well as being divided within itself by violent religious controversies and

1. The fisherman on whose boat the three saints took passage across the lagoon on their mission of deliverance was given a ring by St Mark, with instructions to hand it to the Doge. He did so, and a painting by Paris Bordone of this latter event hangs in Room VI of the Accademia.

torn apart by civil war. The imperial treasury was empty; it came as a surprise to no one when in 1343 the Emperor John V Palaeologus was obliged to pawn to Venetian merchants not only all the gold and silver from the Palace but even the imperial crown jewels.[1] If, then, the Turks were to be kept at bay, it was on Venice and to a lesser extent on Genoa that the bulk of the burden would fall, a joint responsibility that made good relations between the two Republics still more important – although, given their continuing bitter rivalry, no easier to achieve.

But for the time being there was peace, with Venice continuing to ride on a wave of commercial prosperity perhaps unparalleled in her history; and, as always when the political and economic situation allowed, the Venetians began once again to enlarge and embellish their capital. Their first foundling hospital was established near the church of S. Francesco della Vigna; a huge state granary was built on the Molo, on the land which now forms the public garden behind the *Procuratie Nuove*; and on the northernmost edge of the city there rose up the great church and convent of the Servi.[2] Far more important than any of these, however, was the reconstruction of the Doges' Palace, a work which began in January 1341 and which was finally to give the building its principal façades, to the south and west, as we know them today.

The centre of Venetian government and administration had already occupied this site, or part of it, since the days of Doge Agnello Participazio over five centuries before. Since then Doges' Palaces had come and gone; before the work began in 1341 the existing building was essentially that which had been left by Sebastiano Ziani, with the addition of the new Council Chamber that had been built along the eastern side (that which faces the prisons across the narrow Rio di Palazzo, now spanned by the Bridge of Sighs) at the beginning of the century.[3] But this Chamber had already proved to be hopelessly inadequate,

1. At the coronation of John VI Cantacuzenus in 1347, acute observers noted that the jewels in the imperial diadems were all made of glass.

2. None of these buildings has survived. The foundling hospital – known as the *Pietà* from the habit of its founder, Fra Pierazzo of Assisi, of crying '*Pietà, pietà!*' as he went from house to house for contributions – was transferred in the early sixteenth century to the present area of the Pietà where 200 years later, under Antonio Vivaldi, its female inmates constituted the best orchestra in Venice; the granary remained until 1808, when it was pulled down by Napoleon to provide more light for the *Procuratie Nuove* which he had converted into the Royal Palace; and the Servi also was demolished early in the last century. Its ruins were offered for sale, 'ground and all, or stone by stone', to Ruskin in 1852.

3. See p. 208.

and a three-man commission was now appointed to consider whether it should be further enlarged or whether, alternatively, a completely new one should be built in another part of the Palace. Wisely, the commission recommended the latter course; and it was decided that the new Chamber should occupy the major part of the south side of the building at first-floor level.

Although the Doges' Palace is, by any standards, unique, there is one particularly significant respect in which it differs from the corresponding seats of power in the mainland cities of Italy. They are, nearly all of them, dark and threatening reflections of the violence of the age in which they were built. Machiavelli was right when he pointed out that, in Florence, the Palazzo della Signoria was built as a protection for the civic authorities. So, centuries later, was John Addington Symonds when he spoke of Ferrara, 'where the Este's stronghold, moated, drawbridged, and portcullised, casting dense shadow over the water that protects the dungeons, still seems to threaten the public square and overawe the homes of men'. In Venice, by contrast, those for whom the Palace was built had no need for protection and no wish to terrify. Looking at it today, one feels that their instinct must have been to celebrate – to give thanks, with that dazzling fusion of grace, lightness and colour, for the political stability and serenity that they, alone among their neighbours, enjoyed.

The work started in the first days of 1341 under an architect of genius, Pietro Baseggio, and was to continue spasmodically for the next eighty-two years. The first stage, which was confined to the construction of the new Chamber, involved most of the south side and that facing the Piazzetta as far as the seventh column; it must have been more or less complete by July 1365, when Guariento was commissioned to cover the eastern wall with his great fresco of the Crowning of the Virgin in Paradise.[1] The central balcony on the Molo was added, as its inscription proclaims, only in 1404; even then, however, the interior decoration seems to have been unfinished, since it is recorded that the Great Council did not sit for the first time in its new Chamber until 1423. In that year too it was decided to extend the Piazzetta façade to its present length. Thus it was only in 1425 or thereabouts that the building first appeared in all its splendour – just in time, for the Renaissance was already at hand. Another half-century, and that fortunate decision

---

1. This was replaced after the fire by Tintoretto's version. The remains of Guariento's fresco are preserved in another room in the Palace.

would never have been taken; it would have been resolved instead to give the Palace an exterior aspect more in keeping with the contemporary classical taste; and the world's supreme example of secular Gothic architecture would have been lost.[1]

---

1. The Palace had an even luckier escape in 1577, when Palladio advocated pulling down the whole fire-damaged fabric and replacing it with a new Renaissance building of his own design.

16

Andrea Dandolo and Marin Falier

[1342–1355]

until this hour
What Prince has plotted for his people's freedom?
Or risked a life to liberate his subjects?

Byron, *Marino Faliero*

Rich, noble and popular, Andrea Dandolo was the outstanding Venetian of his generation. In 1333, while still in his early youth, he had been appointed *podestà* of Trieste. Three years later, during the war with the Scaligeri, he had served as *provveditore in campo*, the chief commissariat and finance officer in the field. Since then he had distinguished himself as professor of law at the University of Padua, where he had been the first Venetian to obtain a doctorate. All his life he was to remain a scholar; though he was to die well before he was fifty, he was to leave behind him a collection of the old laws of Venice, an edition of all the treaties made by the Republic with the states of the East (*Liber Albus*) and those of Italy (*Liber Blancus*) and two separate histories in Latin, one of Venice up to his own day and one of the world from its creation until 1280. In short, when Bartolomeo Gradenigo died on 28 December 1342, and was entombed in a sarcophagus that still stands in a niche at the northern end of the atrium of St Mark's, Andrea Dandolo was the obvious candidate to succeed him. Not yet forty, he was, it is true, exceptionally young for a Doge; but the imagined disadvantages of his youth were obviously outweighed by his other qualifications, and his election seemed to carry all the promise of the long, happy and peaceful dogeship he deserved.

The promise, alas, was not fulfilled. His reign began auspiciously enough, when a League that had for some time been projected by the Pope for a combined Crusade against the Turks finally came into being. This comprised the Byzantine Empire, the Kingdom of Cyprus and the Knights Hospitallers in Rhodes, as well as the Papacy and Venice herself, whose fleet of fifteen galleys captured several strategic places on the Anatolian coast, including the city of Smyrna. Smyrna was to remain in Christian hands for the next half-century; but the League itself soon fell apart, ending in characteristically Venetian fashion with a business agreement whereby, in return for an undertaking to defend the Mediterranean for Christendom, the Pope granted Venice the right to all ecclesiastical tithes levied in the Republic for the next three years.

One state in particular was notable by its absence from the League. Genoa had been technically at peace with Venice for the past forty years, but the cut-throat commercial rivalry between the two Republics had grown ever more bitter and their relations had continued, to say the least, strained. As before, the critical area of disagreement was the Crimea. It was here, and above all in the ports of Caffa and Soldaia (now Sudak) that the regular caravans brought the furs and slaves from the Russian North, the bales of silk from Central Asia, the spices from India and the further East; here that the stakes were highest, the competition fiercest, the sharp practices most unscrupulous, the brawls most frequent. In 1344 the situation improved somewhat when, as a result of an attack by the neighbouring Tartar tribesmen on Venetians and Genoese together, the Doge of Genoa – who was none other than Verdi's hero Simone Boccanegra – sent an embassy to Venice proposing an alliance which would include a boycott on Tartar goods; but the Tartars, when they were not actively hostile, were among the most profitable of trading partners, and the agreement was doomed almost before it was signed. The Genoese broke it almost at once; the Venetians, whose record was probably very little better, protested – adding for good measure that the Genoese merchants in Trebizond had unlawfully prevented them from fortifying their own quarter of the city – only to receive a reply to the effect that Trebizond was a Genoese preserve and that the Venetian presence there, and indeed anywhere else around the Black Sea coast, was permitted strictly on sufferance and by courtesy of Genoa. This was not so much an insult as an open challenge to Venice's whole legal and commercial position in the region. War was clearly inevitable; it was postponed only by a disaster in comparison with which even the future of Venetian commerce must have seemed of secondary importance.

Among those valuable if contentious cargoes brought by Venetian and Genoese merchantmen from the Crimea in the first weeks of 1348 were the most fateful quadrupeds in history: the rats that carried the Black Death to Europe. By the end of March Venice was in the grip of the plague, and as spring turned to summer and the heat grew ever more fierce, so the deaths increased until they were estimated at some 600 a day.

A three-man commission, appointed by the Doge to check the spread of the disease, found itself powerless. Special barges were designated to carry the bodies to burial in outlying islands of the lagoon, where it was decreed that they should be covered with not less than five feet of earth; but these measures soon proved inadequate, and despite their daily round of the canals and the all-too-familiar cry of '*Corpi Morti!* *Corpi Morti!*' from the wretched boatmen, many of the dead continued to lie alone and unburied in the houses. There were virtually no doctors; within the first few weeks almost all of them were dead or fled.[1] Partly to assuage the wrath of heaven by demonstrations of mercy, partly because they could no longer be adequately guarded, debtors and other miscreants were liberated from the prisons; but nothing could prevent the pestilence from running its course. When at last it abated, no less than fifty noble families had been completely wiped out; and Venice had lost three-fifths of her population.

Genoa, meanwhile, had fared little better. It might have been imagined that after such appalling visitations the rivalry between her and Venice would at least temporarily have been forgotten; and the earlier proposal for an alliance against the marauding Tartars was indeed briefly revived. But in 1350 the Genoese seized, apparently without provocation, a number of Venetian vessels as they lay at anchor in the port of Caffa. An embassy sent by Dandolo to Genoa to protest and seek compensation met with the usual rebuff; and the war that had threatened for so long broke out in earnest. The first victory went to Venice, when her fleet under Marco Ruzzini captured and destroyed ten out of fourteen Genoese ships in the harbour of Negropont.[2] But Genoa's revenge was swift: the four of her vessels that escaped sailed for Chios, an island they had recently appropriated from the Byzantines, where by good fortune they found nine more galleys ready for action. Under the command of Filippo Doria all thirteen sped back to Negropont in November, seized it and sacked it, capturing twenty-three Venetian merchantmen in the process.

The loss to Venice of one of her most valuable colonies was great; the humiliation greater still. The local *bailo* was impeached, but acquitted;

1. 'A certain Francesco of Rome was a health officer in Venice for seventeen years. When he retired he received an annuity of twenty-five gold ducats as a reward for staying in Venice during the Black Death . . . When asked why he did not flee with the rest he answered proudly: "I would rather die here than live elsewhere." ' P. S. Ziegler, *The Black Death*, quoting S. d'Irsay, *Annals of Medical History*, Vol. IX, p. 171.

2. Since the entire island – the modern Euboea – was Venetian territory, we must assume that the Genoese commander was still unaware of the outbreak of hostilities and was consequently taken by surprise.

and Ruzzini, who had been away in Crete seeking reinforcements, was made the scapegoat, charged with having delayed his return unnecessarily and deprived of his command. The war, however, was not over; more widespread, fiercer fighting was to come. Mercifully, Venice had potential allies at hand. King Peter of Aragon, eager to lessen Genoa's influence in the western Mediterranean, agreed to provide eighteen fully-armed men-of-war if Venice would pay two-thirds of their upkeep. In Constantinople similarly – so far as his calamitous finances allowed – the Emperor John VI was only too pleased to participate in the humbling of the Genoese, who not only harried his capital continually from their neighbouring colony of Galata (where their annual customs revenue was almost seven times that of Constantinople itself) but seemed to think that they could help themselves to Byzantine islands like Chios and Mitylene whenever they felt like it. On the other hand, he had no wish to drive them out only to see them immediately replaced by Venetians. He readily offered a dozen galleys, armed and manned – of which, however, Venice was once again to pay two-thirds of the cost in return for an undertaking that, in the event of a Venetian victory, Galata should be razed to the ground and the stolen islands returned to him, together with the imperial crown jewels which had now been seven years in pawn.

The diplomatic negotiations that preceded these agreements and the war preparations that followed them were prolonged; the Aragonese treaty was signed only in July 1351, and by the time the allied fleets joined up with each other in the Marmara the season was already too far advanced to allow of any very decisive operations. Each side, however, had entrusted its fortunes to an admiral of outstanding ability – Venice to Nicolò Pisani, and Genoa to yet another member of that brilliant family whose name was to blaze across the city's history for five centuries and more, Paganino Doria; and on 13 February 1352 the opposing fleets faced each other at the mouth of the Bosphorus, under the walls of Galata.

Paganino, guarding his home waters, had the advantage of position and had drawn up his ships in such a way that the attackers could not approach him without dangerously constricting their own line. Pisani saw the trap at once: the sea was rough, the days were short, to attack would be folly. But the Aragonese commander refused to listen. Before Pisani could stop him he cut his cables and bore down upon the Genoese; and the Venetians had no alternative but to follow.

The ensuing battle soon resolved itself into a straight contest between Venice and Genoa. The Byzantines retired almost at once, without engaging the enemy; the Aragonese, after their initial ill-advised heroics, lasted very little longer. It was left to the two most formidable naval powers of the time to fight it out by themselves, and so they did – savagely, with no quarter given on either side. Fire broke out, which the high winds quickly spread through both fleets; still they fought on, far into the night, by the light of their own blazing ships. Finally it was the Venetians, with wind and current both against them, who had to yield. They had lost most of their galleys and some 1,500 of their best fighting men, an appallingly high figure at any time; coming as it did less than four years after the Black Death, it was more catastrophic still. But when the dawn came the Genoese found that their own losses were almost as heavy, to the point where Paganino preferred to conceal them from his fellow-citizens in Galata for fear of causing a general panic. His, certainly, was the victory in the technical sense; but it was a victory that had cost him more dearly than many a defeat. There could be no question of his pursuing the retreating Venetians; nor, when news of the battle reached Genoa, was there any celebration. As the contemporary Genoese chronicler Giorgio Stella remarks, 'I saw no annual com-memoration of this triumph, nor did the Doge visit any church to give thanks, as is the normal custom; perhaps, because so many brave Genoese fell in the fight, the victory of that day is best forgotten.'

Despite their losses during the battle of the Bosphorus, the position of the Genoese in Galata remained as strong as ever; by contrast, that of the Emperor John VI Cantacuzenus became increasingly insecure. His anxieties were now due not only to financial problems and to the enemies by which the Empire was surrounded; there was a growing threat to his throne itself – a throne to which he had no legitimate claim, having usurped it from its rightful occupant, the sixteen-year-old John V Palaeologus, five years before. The latter had not been deposed; Cantacuzenus had preferred to marry him off to his daughter and allow him to continue as titular co-Emperor, though shorn of any real power. As the boy grew older, however, his resentment of his inferior status increased. He soon became the natural focus of opposition to his father-in-law, and by 1352 the Empire was on the brink of civil war. Canta-cuzenus had always detested the Genoese but now, desperate for allies, he could no longer afford politically – let alone economically – to oppose them. In May, with what inner feelings one can well imagine, he signed an agreement granting them a further expansion of their territory at Galata and the right to exclude all comers, including his own Greek subjects, from trade in the Sea of Azov.

For Venice it was a further blow. She managed to offset it in some degree by acquiring from the rival Emperor John Palaeologus the strategically important island of Tenedos, as security for a loan of 20,000 ducats which she was quietly confident that he could never repay; at the same time she recognized that there was no longer anything to be gained by pursuing the Genoese war in Byzantine or Black Sea waters. A further subsidy was sent to the Aragonese – whose continuing support, it was hoped, might be more effectual in the western Mediterranean than it had been in the Levant – and Nicolò Pisani, having triumphantly survived an official inquiry into the Bosphorus action and emerged with his honour unstained, set sail for the new theatre of operations.

The island of Sardinia had for some years been a bone of contention between Genoa and Aragon; and Pisani arrived there to find the Spaniards blockading the port of Alghero and simultaneously preparing to face an attack from a Genoese relief fleet that was even now on the horizon. His arrival was thus perfectly, if fortuitously, timed. The Spanish admiral readily allowed him supreme command and the Genoese were dismayed to discover, instead of the modest force they had expected, a considerable fleet awaiting them. Suddenly, as they approached, the banner of St Mark broke at every Venetian masthead; and their surprise turned to something akin to panic. They defended themselves courageously, above all in the later stages of the battle when the grappling-irons had been brought into service – Pisani had lashed all but ten of his galleys together before the engagement began – and the fighting was hand-to-hand; but they were outnumbered and outmanoeuvred. Forty-one of their ships were taken; only nineteen, including the flagship (on tow) of their humiliated admiral, Antonio Grimaldi, were able to struggle home.

The date was 29 August 1353. Venice's defeat on the Bosphorus eighteen months before had been more than adequately avenged. The news of the battle of La Lojera, as it came to be called, was received in Genoa not so much with despondency as with despair. The whole city went into mourning; men wept for the end of the once-glorious Republic, now doomed to ignominy and servitude. At first, as one reads – in both the Genoese and the Venetian chronicles – of this reaction, it all sounds rather overdone. After all, battles had been lost before; Genoa, like every other state, had had her share of defeats, and Venice had just proved how swift recovery could be. On reflection, however, one begins to understand: this was not just an ordinary wartime reverse. The Genoese knew the probable consequences only too well. Their enemies now controlled the entire Mediterranean, cutting them off not only from the Levant and the Crimea, the principal sources of their wealth, but also from their essential food supplies. The expansion of their city over the past hundred years had made increasing inroads on the narrow fertile strip between the mountains and the sea that constituted the only agricultural land they possessed; thus, like Venice, they had long been dependent on imports, either from overseas or from Lombardy. But Lombardy had for some time been closed to them, all the mountain passes having been blocked by another enemy who also had designs on their territory: Giovanni Visconti, Lord and Archbishop of Milan.

And so, in those late summer days of 1353, Genoa had good reason to mourn. She was in a desperate situation, for which she needed a desperate remedy. Before September was out, she had found one. Of the three evils by which she was threatened – Venice, Milan and starvation – she chose the least. In return for his help and support in continuation of the war, she made voluntary submission to the Archbishop, stipulating only two conditions: that her own laws should remain in force and that the red cross of her patron, St George, should still appear on the standards of her ships above the viper of the Visconti.

The Venetians were, understandably, furious. But they were also frightened. They had been robbed, at the last moment, of the satisfaction of crushing their rival once and for all. Worse, they saw Milan, already too powerful for comfort, now spreading her influence still further. It was inevitable, since Venice herself had become a mainland power with only her Carrara vassals in Padua to separate her from Milanese territory, that she and the Visconti would clash before long; and though it might have been expected that the clash, when it came, would be brought about by the Lombard towns rather than by the Genoese, the situation was none the less serious for that. Hastily she formed a league of mainland states who felt themselves similarly threatened – Montferrat and Ferrara, Verona, Padua, Mantua and Faenza; she even persuaded Charles IV of Bohemia, shortly to become Emperor of the West, to serve as its titular head. All this was achieved within a very short time and, according to the chronicle of Lorenzo de Monacis, 'at almost incredible cost'; but the Visconti could bribe too, and the numbers of the League soon fell away again – Charles himself the richer by 100,000 Venetian ducats – without striking a single blow against either of its enemies.

Archbishop Giovanni, however, was in no hurry to fight. Instead, he dispatched to Venice on a mission of peace the man who, after Dante, was widely celebrated as the greatest poet-diplomat of his time, Francesco Petrarch. Petrarch had already written to Doge Dandolo – a fellow humanist and personal friend – nearly three years before, imploring him to make peace with Genoa in the name of Italian unity. Now he renewed his appeal in the city itself, with all the rhetoric of which he was capable, exhorting the Venetians to extend the hand of friendship to his master and to accept the very favourable terms he was prepared to offer; but, as he later confessed, his journey was useless:

I threw my many words to the winds; and having come full of hope, I returned in sorrow, shame and fear . . . No words of mine, or even of Cicero himself, could have reached ears that were stubbornly stopped, or opened obstinate hearts.[1]

In truth the Venetians were no more impressed by Petrarch than they had been by Dante thirty-three years before. By now they had recovered from the initial shock of the Genoa–Visconti alliance and, as the threat of immediate attack from *terra firma* apparently receded, so their confidence and courage came flooding back. If the Archbishop really wanted peace, it could only be that he did not feel ready for war. They themselves had never been stronger – at least at sea; Visconti or no Visconti, they were resolved to follow up their victory at La Lojera and strike another, possibly decisive, blow at their rival while they could. They were not interested in flowery speeches in the Doge's audience chamber; their attention was focused on the Arsenal.

And rightly, for Genoa had already resumed the war. In the first weeks of 1354 she had sent a light raiding squadron up the Adriatic, where it attacked the islands of Lesina and Curzola[2] on the Dalmatian coast and did considerable damage before making its getaway. As soon as the news reached the lagoon, the Venetians had detailed a squadron of their own to guard the straits of Otranto between the heel of Apulia and Corfu; meanwhile fourteen heavy galleys under Nicolò Pisani had set off in pursuit of the raiders. Failing to find them, Pisani had sailed on to Sardinia, where the Aragonese were still besieging Alghero. It was a fatal mistake. Paganino Doria, back in command of what was left of the Genoese war fleet, saw his chance. With his adversary safely away to the west, he raced to the mouth of the Adriatic, somehow slipping through the newly established Venetian defences. There was

1. *Epistolae de Rebus Familiaribus*, XVIII, 16 (28 May 1354).
2. Hvar and Korčula.

no nonsense now about the coastal islands; sweeping straight up the gulf, he seized and occupied Parenzo on the Istrian coast, barely sixty miles from Venice itself.

At this moment of genuine emergency, the Venetians kept their heads. A Captain-General was appointed, with special powers to take all the measures he thought necessary for the defence of the city; under him were twelve other nobles, each with a work-force of 300 men. There followed a general mobilization of the populace; a special tax was levied, while several prominent citizens armed and equipped additional galleys at their own expense. Finally, a great boom of tree-trunks and iron chains was run across the Lido port between S. Nicolò and Sant' Andrea.

Perhaps the news of these measures – and particularly of the last – was enough to discourage Paganino from advancing further; but it is more likely that he had never really intended to do more than show the world that Genoa was not beaten at sea any more than she was on land, and that she was certainly not frightened, of Venice or of anyone else. If so, he had made his point. He returned down the Adriatic and, once back in the open sea, headed across to the Aegean. Up to this moment there is no record of any attempt by the Venetians to pursue or intercept him; but by now Nicolò Pisani had returned from Sardinia and, guessing that Paganino would sooner or later be sure to put in at the Genoese colony of Chios for revictualling, had set off in the same direction. There, a few weeks later, he found him as expected – only to learn that Doria was expecting another dozen galleys to arrive from home, and had no intention of emerging from harbour until he was ready. At this late season of the year – it was already October – there was little point in waiting for him. Containing his frustration as best he could, Pisani retired disconsolately to winter quarters at Portolungo, in the extreme south-west corner of the Peloponnese, opposite the island of Sapientza.

Paganino Doria, meanwhile, had decided against wintering in Chios. His galleys had arrived, and towards the end of the month he sailed for home. But the wind was against him and he was forced to take shelter, as luck would have it only a mile or two from where the Venetian fleet was lying. While he waited for more favourable weather, his nephew Giovanni – prompted, it appears, more by simple curiosity than by anything else – took a light trireme on a reconnaissance of the Venetian position. He returned to tell his uncle that the enemy was utterly unguarded, and ready for the taking. Paganino did not hesitate. On 4 November he sailed his galleys into Portolungo, catching the Venetians unawares. Most of the crews were ashore; those who had chanced to remain on board could put up no real resistance. 'You would have thought', laments Lorenzo, 'that one side consisted of armed men, the other of defenceless women.' The Venetian fleet numbered fifty-six, including thirty-three galleys. Every one was captured. Of the sailors, the majority escaped to Modone and a number of others were taken prisoner. Some 450, however, were killed – most of them, presumably, in cold blood.

Among those who escaped was Pisani. The fault was not altogether his; he had appointed one of his captains, Nicolò Querini, to guard the harbour entrance with twenty galleys, and it was Querini's dereliction of duty – or, as some said, his treachery – that caused the disaster. But disaster it undoubtedly was: greater far than that of the Bosphorus, greater perhaps than any defeat the Republic had ever suffered in its history. On their return to Venice both Pisani and Querini were called to account, subjected to heavy fines and deprived of their authority; but whereas Querini's deprivation was for six years only, the unfortunate Pisani was sentenced never, on land or sea, to command again.

Death, wrote Petrarch to the Archdeacon of Genoa, was kind to Andrea Dandolo, 'sparing him the sight of his country's bitter anguish and the still more biting letters that I should have written him'. The Doge had in fact died two months before the defeat of Portolungo, on 7 September 1354, and had been laid to rest in a superb Gothic sarcophagus in the baptistery of St Mark's – the last of Venice's rulers to be buried in the Basilica.[1] His death at forty-seven was a double tragedy: for Europe – which lost one of the outstanding humanists and men of letters of the century – and for Venice, since the old man who was now elected to succeed him was within a year to bring disgrace to the dogeship and to end his days on the scaffold.

Marin Falier was a member of one of the oldest noble families of Venice – it had already given two Doges to the Republic – and, at seventy-six, was still leading an active public life as Venetian ambassador to the papal court at Avignon. Until the messengers arrived with the news of his election this post must have been generally looked upon as the culmination of a lifetime spent in distinguished service to the state. As early as 1312 his name appears as one of the electors of Doge Soranzo, and as a member of the Council of Ten on several occasions between

---

1. Ruskin described his tomb, and that of St Isidore in the northern transept, as 'the best existing examples of Venetian monumental sculpture'. Dandolo had been responsible for the mosaics in both the chapel of St Isidore and the baptistery itself, where his own mosaic portrait can be seen above the altar.

1315 and 1327 he had been instrumental in the harrying – and quite possibly in the eventual liquidation – of Bajamonte Tiepolo. He had in his time commanded a fleet in the Black Sea, sat as *savio* on several special commissions and governed as *podestà* in Chioggia, Padua and Treviso; and only two years before his elevation he had been spokesman for the Republic when one of the periodic Hungarian claims to Dalmatia had been referred to the Emperor-elect Charles IV for judgment. On this last occasion Charles had knighted him for his pains, and awarded him the lordship of the Val Mareno in the Alpine foothills. Throughout his career, however, he had been known for his shortness of temper and quickness to take offence; in 1339, while *podestà* of Treviso, he had publicly slapped the face of the local bishop when the latter was late for a procession. As subsequent events were to show, advancing age had done nothing to mellow him.

The chroniclers describe with relish the sinister portents that attended his arrival in Venice. Exceptionally for the first week of October, the city is said to have been shrouded in dense fog, too thick to allow the *Bucintoro*, which had brought him from Chioggia on the last lap of the journey, to approach the Molo. Falier and his suite had to resort to *piatte*, the little flat-bottomed boats that preceded the invention of the gondola; even then they missed the official jetty by the Ponte della Paglia and were eventually put ashore on the Piazzetta, so that the Doge first approached his palace between the two columns – the traditional place of execution for malefactors.

Within a month of his enthronement – and his signing of a *promissione* that introduced serious new restrictions on the ducal power – reports coming in from the Peloponnese cast yet deeper shadows over the beginnings of his reign. But not even catastrophes like Portolungo could prevent the Venetians from enjoying the feasts of the Church; and early in 1355, on the last Thursday before Lent, we find them celebrating their *Giovedì Grasso* in the customary manner – chasing pigs round the Piazza and Piazzetta in memory of the capture of the German Patriarch of Aquileia two centuries before[1] and applauding those acrobatic performances that were already a Venetian speciality – the so-called Labours of Hercules (*Forze di Ercole*) in which a group of men climbed on each other's shoulders to form a human pyramid – or the Flight of the Turk (*Volo del Turco*), a dizzy slide down a tight-rope from the summit of the campanile to the Piazzetta.

After the public festivities were over the Doge held the usual banquet

1. See p. 126.

in the Palace. Here it was, by all accounts, that the trouble started. Among the guests was a young man – later tradition has unconvincingly identified him with Michele Steno, the future Doge – who began drunkenly forcing his attentions on one of the Dogaressa's waiting-women. Falier ordered him to be thrown out, but before leaving the Palace he some-how managed to slip into the Council Chamber and to leave a doggerel inscription on the ducal throne:

> *Marin Falier de la bella mujer*
> *Lu la mantien e altri la galde.*[1]

The effect on the Doge of this insult to his dignity may well be imagined; but his fury was even greater when the Quarantia, instead of pronouncing the severe sentence for which he had hoped, took the age and previous good character of the accused into consideration and let him off with a penalty so light as to be tantamount, in Falier's eyes, to a condonation of the offence. He was a cantankerous old man, with all the intolerance that old men so often show for the brashness and irreverence of the younger generation; the terms of his *promissione* continued to rankle; and as the weeks went by he began to develop an obsessive hatred of a ruling caste which could show such scant respect for the ducal authority and which apparently even protected its own kind from the proper process of law. With this hatred came a determination that somehow its members should atone for their *lèse-mujesté*; if the law was powerless against them, he would take it into his own hands.

Meanwhile other incidents occurred to fortify his resolve. Two highly respectable citizens, one a sea-captain, the other a certain Stefano Ghiazza, nicknamed Gisello, director of the Arsenal, lodged separate complaints that they had been publicly insulted and had suffered bodily violence at the hands of young aristocrats. When the Doge – seemingly forget-ful of his own previous treatment of the Bishop of Treviso – sympathized but pointed out the difficulty that even he himself had experienced

---

1. Marin Falier
Has a wife that is fair,
He has to keep her while other men lay 'er.

The verse is quoted by Marino Sanudo in his *Vita dei Duchi di Venezia*. He is writing well over a century afterwards, and the text may well be apocryphal. It has, nevertheless, led many later chroniclers and historians to suggest that the object of the youth's attentions was the Dogaressa herself; but though she was Falier's second wife and much younger than her husband, she was none the less well over forty and there is nothing to substantiate the assumption.

in obtaining punishment for such people, Gisello murmured darkly: 'Dangerous beasts must be tied up; if they cannot be controlled they must be destroyed.'

At that moment Falier knew that he had an ally, and a powerful one; the workers at the Arsenal were a body of highly trained and trusted artisans with a para-military organization and a long tradition of personal loyalty to the Doge, whose bodyguard they always provided on ceremonial occasions. And so the conspiracy took shape. On the night of 15 April disturbances would be deliberately provoked throughout the city, and a rumour simultaneously spread of an approaching Genoese war fleet. This would bring the nobility and populace alike crowding into the Piazza where a member of the ducal family, Bertuccio Falier, would be waiting with a body of armed men – presumably the *Arsenalotti* – ready, on the pretext of protecting the person of the Doge, to massacre all the young nobles on sight. Marin Falier would then be proclaimed Prince of Venice, and his title ratified by popular acclamation.

History provides innumerable instances of aristocrats who have turned against their own class to put themselves at the head of a popular movement; few, however, have done so in their late seventies, or from a position of at least theoretical supremacy. In such circumstances, the usual motives of ambition and self-interest can be ruled out; Falier seems to have been impelled, quite simply, by hatred and rancour, by a desire for revenge magnified and distorted by advancing senility into a single overpowering obsession. It may well be that Gisello and his associates, seeing this, worked upon it further and made the old Doge a tool with which to advance their own political ends; if so, he was less an instigator of the plot than its unconscious victim. Yet it is still impossible to feel much sympathy for a man who, having attained supreme office, attempts to use that office to destroy, by force and with the maximum degree of violence and bloodshed, the government – and, incidentally, the class – that put him there. Fortunately for Venice, he succeeded only in bringing about his own downfall.

The fourteenth century had already seen two conspiracies against the Republic, both of which had collapsed because those involved had been unable to keep their mouths shut. Now once again it was the same story. One of the conspirators, a furrier from Bergamo called Beltrame, warned a rich client to keep off the streets on 15 April. The client went straight to the Doge in all innocence to pass on the warning; but Falier's reaction aroused his suspicions and induced him to confide what he knew to other, more sympathetic, ears. From the seamen's district of Castello near the Arsenal, the principal centre of disaffection, one Marco Nigro brought a similar report; and there is reason to believe that several others, including the Doge himself, were also less discreet than might have been expected. All this suggests that the Ten received their information from at least two and perhaps even three or more independent quarters. They acted with their usual formidable speed. Their first meeting, to examine the evidence and to establish whether or not the Doge was personally implicated, was held secretly in the monastery of S. Salvatore. As soon as they were certain of the facts, they called a larger council, in the Palace this time, consisting of the Signoria, the Avogadori, the Quarantia, the Signori di Notte, the Capi di Sestieri and the Cinque della Pace.[1] Significantly, two officials named Falier, one an Avogadore and one a member of the Ten, were excluded.

By the day fixed for the *coup*, strict security measures had been put into force: in every parish and *sestiere* those in authority had had orders to arm their most trusted men and to muster them on the Piazza, thus providing a militia estimated between 6,000 and 8,000 men ready to deal with any trouble. A troop of 100 horsemen stood by to deal with emergencies elsewhere in the city. Meanwhile the arrests began; and the sentences soon followed. Bertuccio Falier was lucky – he was merely imprisoned for life; but ten of the other ringleaders were condemned to be hanged in a row from the palace windows overlooking the Piazzetta.[2] Ironically enough, they included Filippo Calendario, who had succeeded Baseggio as the chief architect of the Doges' Palace and who, up to the day of his arrest, had been working on the south front.

When the time came to decide the fate of the Doge himself the Ten, considering the responsibility to be too great for them to bear alone, applied for a *zonta*[3] – an exceptional increase in their numbers specifically provided for by their constitution to deal with grave emergencies – of twenty additional noblemen. Their verdict, however, was a foregone conclusion; Falier did not attempt to deny the charges. He made a full confession, pleaded guilty and proclaimed himself both deserving

1. Rough equivalents might be the Doge's inner council of six advisers, the three public prosecutors, the judicial council of forty, the chiefs of police, the heads of the six *sestieri* or districts of the city, and the five Justices of the Peace.

2. Nicolò Trevisan, who was at that time one of the Ten and has left a valuable account of these events, notes that they were hanged between 'red marble columns', which many historians including Romanin have identified with the two such columns beneath the second window from the left on the Piazzetta side; but, as we have seen, this western façade was not built in Falier's day. If these are indeed the columns in question, they must have belonged to the old Byzantine palace of Sebastiano Ziani.

3. The Venetian dialect equivalent of the Italian *aggiunta*.

of and fully prepared for the supreme penalty. Sentence was passed on 17 April; the next morning, at the hour of tierce, the old man was brought from his private apartments to the Council Chamber and thence to the top of the marble staircase that descended from the first-floor loggia into the inner courtyard of the Palace.[1] The insignia of office were stripped from him, his ducal *corno* being replaced by a plain round cap. In a brief speech, he asked the Republic's pardon for his treachery and confirmed the justice of his sentence. Then he laid his head upon the block. It was severed with a single stroke.[2]

The doors of the Palace, which had remained shut during the execution, were now opened and the body displayed to the people. The day following, it was taken in a common boat to the family vault in the chapel of S. Maria della Pace, between SS. Giovanni e Paolo and the Scuola di S. Marco, and buried in an unmarked grave.[3] All Falier's possessions were declared confiscate, excepting only 2,000 ducats, which he had specifically bequeathed to his widow just before his execution – an indication, if such were necessary, that he still trusted her despite the slanders she had suffered. Rich rewards were voted to those who had given information leading to the plot's discovery. Marco Nigro of Castello received 100 gold ducats a year for life, with the privilege – doubtless necessary – of being allowed to carry arms at all times for his own protection. The furrier Beltrame was awarded no less than 1,000 ducats, but was foolish enough to demand in addition the Falier property at SS. Apostoli and a permanent hereditary seat in the Great Council. When these were refused he took to speaking so bitterly against the government that he was thrown into prison, whence he emerged only to be done to death by one of his former fellow-conspirators.

Meanwhile, in their minute books, the Ten could not bring themselves to record the Doge's name in the list of those condemned. Where it should have appeared there is a blank space left, followed simply by the words *non scribatur* – 'let it not be written'. A decade later, however, when the shame and shock were past, their successors were less delicate:

1. The present *Scala dei Giganti* did not yet exist. The staircase on which the execution took place was probably on the south side of the courtyard, immediately outside the wall of the Council Chamber.

2. There is a splendid portrayal of the scene by Delacroix in the Wallace Collection. Romanticized as it may be, it is probably a good deal more accurate – and certainly more dramatic – than Byron's play *Marin Falier*.

3. The grave was opened in the middle of the last century, to reveal a skeleton with the skull laid between the knees. The bones were dispersed; the sarcophagus, after some years' service as a cistern, is now rather surprisingly to be found beneath the portico of the Museum of Natural History – the former Fondaco dei Turchi.

on 16 March 1366 they decreed that the likeness of Falier should be removed from the frieze of ducal portraits that had just been painted
around the walls of the Council Chamber and replaced by a painted
black veil bearing the words, clear and uncompromising, for all to read:
'*Hic est locus Marini Faledri decapitati pro criminibus.*'[1]

1. 'Here is the place of Marin Falier, beheaded for his crimes.' What we see today, together
with all the other ducal portraits in the Chamber, is a repainting dating from after the fire
of 1574.

17

Colonies Lost and Held

[1355-1376]

It was the fourth of June – perhaps the sixth hour of the day. I was standing at my window, looking out to sea . . . when one of those long ships that they call galleys entered the harbour, all garlanded with green boughs, its oars thrusting through the water, its sails swollen by the wind. So swift was its advance that we could soon see the joyful faces of the sailors and a group of laughing young men, crowned with leaves and waving banners above their heads in greeting to their native city, victorious but still unaware of her triumph. By now the look-outs on the highest tower had signalled the arrival and, all unbidden but in universal excitement and curiosity, the citizens came flocking to the shore. As the ship came in we could see the enemy standards draped over her stern, and no shred of doubt remained in our minds that she brought news of victory . . . And when he heard it Doge Lorenzo wished with all his people to give thanks and praises to God with splendid ceremonies throughout the city, but especially at the Basilica of St Mark the Evangelist than which there is nothing, I believe, on earth more beautiful.

> Petrarch, letter to Peter of Bologna,
> 10 August 1364 (*Epist. Sen. IV*, 3)

Giovanni Gradenigo, nicknamed *Nasone*, or Big-Nose – 'no doubt,' suggests one turn-of-the-century historian in a moment of reckless speculation, 'from some peculiarity of feature' – was elected Doge on 21 April 1355, only three days after the execution of his predecessor. It was an unusually short interregnum, possibly because of a general feeling that after the events of the past week it was important to re-establish the supreme authority with the minimum of delay. Once again, however, the Republic showed that its political institutions had flexibility and stability enough to take even the gravest domestic crisis in its stride. Any other state in Europe might have needed months, perhaps years, to recover; in Venice, by the time Doge Gradenigo ascended the newly scrubbed steps of his palace, the conspiracy of Marin Falier was nothing more than a painful memory.

The new Doge was seventy years old and a man of peace. The

Genoese war had been costly to both sides, paralysing trade and, particularly since Portolungo, confronting Venice with a serious shortage of ships and manpower; and when the three Visconti brothers who shared the Lordship of Milan after the death of their uncle the Archbishop offered reasonable terms on behalf of Genoa, Venice accepted with alacrity. The treaty was signed on 1 June 1355, each Republic undertaking – among other less important provisions – not to encroach on the home waters of the other and to keep out of the contentious Sea of Azov for three years. Both parties were to deposit 100,000 gold florins in a third city as security against any violation of their commitments.

The Genoese, who understandably felt that they had had the better of the fighting, resented the strict reciprocity on which the treaty was based. As subjects of the Visconti, they had no choice but to sign; they did so, however, with unconcealed reluctance and a strengthened resolve to shake off the Milanese yoke – which, in the following year, they managed to do. The Venetians were luckier. Not only was the peace treaty considerably more favourable to them than they had had any right to expect, but they were free, at a time when their rival Republic was obliged to devote all its energies to a struggle for independence, to rebuild their fleet and re-establish their trade. While the *Arsenalotti*, their discontent forgotten, worked overtime to keep a constant succession of galleys, galleons, frigates and brigantines pouring down the slipways, Venetian diplomats travelled to Barbary and Tartary, Egypt and Flanders, reviving old agreements and cementing new ones.

If only Venice had remained the exclusively maritime power that she had been until less than twenty years before, Giovanni Gradenigo's short reign would have been happy indeed. But she now had a dominion on the mainland, and her new territorial acquisitions had brought her a new vulnerability. In former times, whenever the Hungarian Kingdom revived its perennial claim to the towns of Dalmatia, the Venetians could take the war straight across by sea to the enemy camp. Now all that was changed; and they first began to understand the full significance of that change when in 1356 King Lajos the Great of Hungary invaded the Friuli.

This time the claim was not limited to any particular towns or islands; Lajos demanded, quite simply, all Venetian territory on the eastern coast of the Adriatic. He had originally done so three years before, but had been held off by adroit diplomacy; now, on a transparently spurious pretext, he attacked – directing the main force of his arms not even against

the area under dispute, but against the Republic itself. Sacile and Conegliano were quickly taken; Treviso was besieged. To make matters
worse, the attitude of Francesco da Carrara, Lord of Padua, was distinctly
equivocal; if Padua were to betray its allegiance, the enemy would
be on the very threshold of the Rialto.

Such was the situation when, in August 1356, Giovanni Gradenigo
died and was buried in the chapter-house of the Frari. His successor,
Giovanni Dolfin, had some initial difficulty in assuming the throne –
finding himself, at the moment of his election, under siege at Treviso;
but somehow he escaped one night and thanks to a combination of
courage, cunning and good luck, managed to slip through the Hungarian
lines. Once Doge, his first action was to clarify the position of Padua;
and no one was surprised when Carrara, emboldened by recent Hungarian successes, declared himself for Lajos. Economic sanctions were
immediately imposed on the city and a punitive expedition sent to devas-
tate the surrounding country, but such measures were of little real use;
meanwhile Serravalle and Asolo capitulated, the Bishop of Ceneda rebelled
against Venetian rule, and in beleaguered Treviso itself a plot to deliver
the city to the enemy was uncovered only hours before its implementa-
tion.

A five-month truce arranged by the Pope achieved nothing, and
when the war was resumed after Easter 1357 the Hungarian advance
continued. One or two towns successfully resisted, notably Castelfranco
and Oderzo; Treviso too held out, though its fall by now looked so imminent that its Bishop abandoned his flock and fled to Venice. Before long,
however, the Hungarians virtually controlled the shores of the lagoon
and were commandeering all the craft they could find for what was clearly
intended to be an invasion fleet. Venice replied with a ban on all lagoon
shipping. Meanwhile work began on defensive stockades, in the form of
wooden piles driven into the mud around the city.

Giovanni Dolfin was a brave man, but he was also a realist. He knew
that the Hungarians could never be turned back by defensive measures
alone, and that it was only a matter of time before the whole of Venetian
terra firma would be theirs, after which the occupation of Venice itself
must inevitably follow. Moreover the Treasury was becoming dangerously
depleted. Merchandise might still arrive in the city from the Orient,
but with the mainland in enemy hands there were no outlets for distribution. It was clear that he would have to come to terms with Lajos;
clear too that those terms would be very much more unpalatable than
those obtained from Genoa two years before.

When the Venetian envoys reached the King, they found him even more intractable than they had feared. His successes in Friuli and the Veneto had enabled him to open up a new offensive in Dalmatia, where Traù, Spalato and, most recently, Zara had all fallen, after varying degrees of resistance, to Hungarian arms. His demands were simple and sweeping: the Doge must renounce, for all time, his title of Duke of Dalmatia and Venice must surrender unconditionally all her Dalmatian possessions from the eastern corner of Istria as far south as Durazzo. In return she would be allowed to retain Istria itself, and Lajos would withdraw his forces from North Italy. There was also a vague undertaking on his part to guarantee Venetian shipping against pirates, although how Hungary, a land power, proposed to do this was not made altogether clear.

The special commission appointed by the Great Council to conduct the war – its original twenty-five members now reinforced by a *zonta* of fifty in view of the gravity of the situation – heard the Hungarian demands in a mood of rising indignation. The pine-forests of Dalmatia and its hinterland represented the chief source of timber for Venice's fleet, just as its maritime population furnished the majority of her crews. And how could her Doge, who had so recently claimed lordship over 'a quarter and a half a quarter of the Roman Empire', be expected to renounce a ducal title that had been rightfully his ever since that glorious Ascension Day three and a half centuries before?

They were strong arguments; but those on the other side were stronger still. Treviso, now on the point of collapse, and those parts of the Italian mainland that remained loyal were even more vital than was Dalmatia, which was in any case largely lost. They were the final bastion, on which the safety of the Republic itself depended. And so Lajos's terms were accepted and, on 18 February 1358, the peace treaty was signed at Zara.

The Venetians may well have felt the moral humiliation even more than the material loss; none the less, they themselves were at least partly to blame. Their tenure of Dalmatia had always been marked by a curious and, for them, most uncharacteristic vagueness. It was the one place where they never quite found their touch. From the beginning of their rule they had allowed the Dalmatians to maintain their shadowy allegiance to the Byzantine Empire; and because subject peoples inevitably prefer their distant and invisible overlords to the governors on their doorstep, the Venetians' presence along the coast had always been to a greater or a lesser extent resented. Admittedly, they tended to leave the day-to-

I

day tasks of government in the hands of the traditional local rulers –
princes or counts, bishops or rectors; but as time went on more and
more of these key positions came to be occupied by Venetians or their
nominees. Worst of all was their insistence on free facilities in all Dalmatian ports for Venetian shipping, and their requirement – not always
enforced – that all Dalmatian ships bound for Adriatic ports had to
offer their goods first in Venice. Local trade could not but suffer in
consequence, increasing Venetian unpopularity and making the inhabitants of the coastal towns easy game for Hungarian subversion.

Shorn of Dalmatia, Venice had saved her dominions on the Italian
mainland. She had seen, however, just how vulnerable they were to
attack – and so had her enemies, both actual and potential. Francesco da
Carrara, for example, despite a separate peace treaty and a surprisingly
lavish civic reception by the Doge later that summer, was still out for
what he could get. Before the year was over he had hired an army of
2,000 German mercenaries; and despite his assurances that they were
to be used not against Venice but the Visconti of Milan, the Venetians
felt understandable misgivings about the future. In an effort to consolidate and confirm their position, they even sent an embassy to Charles
IV to seek imperial recognition for their conquests on *terra firma*; but
Charles was his usual unsympathetic self and the only result of the
initiative was that two of the three envoys were arrested on the return
journey by Duke Rudolf of Austria – in revenge for the Venetian destruction of one of his castles in the recent Hungarian war – and spent
the next two years in captivity.

Their colleague, a certain Lorenzo Celsi, was luckier; he had decided
to stay on a little longer at the imperial court in Ratisbon. Had he not
done so, he like them would have been languishing in an Austrian
prison when Giovanni Dolfin died on 12 July 1361 – and would never
have been elected the fifty-sixth Doge of Venice.

It might be said – though perhaps a little unkindly – that nothing became
Giovanni Dolfin's dogeship like the manner of his accepting it. After
his dashing escape from besieged Treviso everything seemed to go wrong
for him. He could only preside, powerless, while the Republic he led
slowly succumbed to a foreign power and bought her deliverance by
a costly and humiliating peace. His subsequent diplomacy was no more
successful. Whether another more inspiring leader might have achieved
greater things in such circumstances is an open question. It seems unlikely.
Dolfin was not so much incapable as ill-starred. Despite his beautifully-

carved sarcophagus in the north-eastern apse chapel of SS. Giovanni e Paolo, the Venetians of today have little cause to remember him.

Lorenzo Celsi owed his elevation not only to his escape from the clutches of the Duke of Austria but also to two other strokes of luck that followed in quick succession. On his return to Venice he had been appointed 'Captain of the Gulf' – commander, in other words, of the home fleet in the Adriatic; soon afterwards he had departed on a mission; then, just as the elections were about to be held for a new Doge, a report reached the city that he had scored a signal triumph by capturing a group of Genoese privateers. The wave of jubilation caused by this news – it was the first victory that the Venetians had had to celebrate for a considerable time – was enough to tip the scales in his favour, and even when the report subsequently proved unfounded his new subjects had no real cause to regret their choice.

For the third time in the past four elections, a Doge had been chosen *in absentia* – a significant indication of the amount of time Venetian notables might expect to spend abroad. Lorenzo Celsi entered Venice in state on 21 August. He was a proud, overweening man – perhaps to compensate for his family's comparatively obscure origins – with a love of pomp and ceremonial that, anywhere else, might have been thought somewhat excessive: we are told that he had a cross fixed to his ducal cap to ensure that his old father would appear to do him adequate reverence. He also possessed a magnificent collection of stuffed animals and birds, and a stud of the finest horses in the city.

In short, he proved just the sort of Doge that the Venetians needed. Parades and processions and sumptuous display always acted on them like a tonic; and in the brief interlude of tranquillity that roughly coincided with Celsi's reign, he gave them full measure. To visiting foreign princes, too, he proved a munificent and impressive host; when Rudolf of Austria arrived in September 1361 to make his peace with the Republic (and as an earnest of his good intentions, to return in person the pair of luckless ambassadors after their two years' captivity) the Doge went out to meet him in the *Bucintoro* and later escorted him on horseback on a tour of the city, showing him the churches and palaces, the relics and priceless treasures that had made Venice famous throughout the world – though not, we may be sure, forgetting the Arsenal either. An even more splendid reception was reserved for Peter of Lusignan, King of Cyprus, during his two stays in Venice in 1362 and 1364 at the beginning and end of a European tour. He was lodged, with all the magnificence befitting his rank, in that great twelfth-century

Byzantine palace on the Grand Canal which then belonged to the Corner family and which still bears, on the cornice running along the upper loggia, the royal arms of Cyprus and of the House of Lusignan.[1]

Venice's most distinguished guest of all, however, was Petrarch, who arrived in 1362, a fugitive from the plague in Padua. His political and diplomatic life was over; in return for an offer to leave his library to the Republic he was given a fine house on the Riva, and there he lived with his daughter and her young family for the next five years until a petty insult, which he should have been able to ignore, set him off on his wanderings again.[2] What happened to the library is a question that has long puzzled scholars. An upstairs room in St Mark's was put aside for it, but the books themselves seem never to have been transferred there. It may well be that pique over the insult – four young Venetians had described him as an illiterate idiot – caused him to dispose of them elsewhere after all. Alternatively the blame may lie with the city authorities, who have been accused of simply failing to recognize the importance of the gift and allowing the books to moulder away in some forgotten repository.

In view of the reputation that Venice already enjoyed as a centre of learning and humanism, this second possibility seems unlikely. The government could well have pleaded, however, that at that particular moment it had other more pressing problems on its hands; for Petrarch's arrival in the city coincided almost precisely with a serious colonial crisis. Of all the Aegean colonies of the Republic the largest and most important was Crete; but the very size of the island had always made it something of a problem. In 160 years of Venetian domination, the Cretans had never really become reconciled to their foreign overlords, and as time went on many of the old Venetian families there also grew dissatisfied – particularly resenting the fact that whereas, had they remained in Venice, they would have enjoyed automatic membership of the Great Council, in Crete they were totally debarred from power since all local positions of authority were occupied by officials nominated by and

1. Because of their extensive sugar plantations at Piscopia (now Episkopi) in Cyprus this branch of the family took the name of Corner-Piscopia, which, according to the usual Venetian custom, was originally given to their palace as well. It is, however, more generally known by the name of Loredan, to which family it passed in the eighteenth century. One of the oldest palaces still standing in Venice – though the top two storeys are later additions – it is now joined to its contemporary neighbour, the Palazzo Farsetti, to form the modern *Municipio*, a few hundred yards down from the Rialto bridge towards St Mark's.

2. Petrarch's house in Venice was, according to long tradition and an inscription *in situ*, the former Palazzo delle due Torri just beyond the Ponte del Sepolcro on the Riva. The base of one of the two towers is still visible in the Calle del Doge adjoining.

sent out from the Republic. Flash-point was at last reached – just as in Britain's American colonies four centuries later – over the unilateral imposition of customs duties. Repeated assurances that the profit from these duties, being intended for the repair and improvement of the local harbour installations, would thus be to the colony's long-term benefit failed to impress the Cretans, who merely pointed out that they had not been consulted in advance; indeed, they were not even represented on the Great Council. They refused absolutely to pay unless they were first allowed to send a delegation of twenty wise men (*savii*) to Venice to express their grievances. Fatally perhaps, the Council could not resist a sharp retort: they were unaware, they said, that the colony possessed twenty such persons. The consequences of such an insult at such a time might have been foreseen: the standards of St Mark were lowered and those of St Titus, patron saint of Crete, hoisted in their place; the Venetian governor, Leonardo Dandolo, was deposed, narrowly escaping with his life; and the whole island rose in revolt.

Even now the Republic persisted in underestimating the gravity of the crisis. Not once but twice it dispatched official commissions to Candia – the chief city of the island – to explain to the malcontents the error of their ways. It was only after the second of these insufferably patronizing missions had had to flee back to its galleys to escape the mob that the Great Council seemed to shake off its lethargy. Letters were hurriedly sent to Pope and Emperor, and to Hungary, Naples and Genoa, urging them to refuse all support to the rebels; meanwhile a leading *condottiere*, the Veronese Luchino dal Verme, was engaged with 1,000 cavalry and 2,000 infantry to sail at once, with a fleet of thirty-three galleys, to Crete.

It was not, even by the standards of the time, a very large force, but it sufficed. The rebels were betrayed by their own lack of discipline. Their rabble army – much of it composed of hardened criminals, released from prison in return for the promise of unpaid military service – soon reverted to type and began murdering and plundering indiscriminately; soon, too, the old Venetian colonial families became alarmed at the increasing political aspirations of the far more numerous Greeks. In the rapidly changing atmosphere it began to look as though to continue the revolt might lead to open confessional strife, in which all Latins might be dispossessed and even massacred. They preferred to capitulate. Dal Verme and his men returned to Venice in triumph, and the ensuing celebrations were reported in breathless detail by Petrarch – sitting, for the occasion, at the Doge's right hand.

The size of the multitude was hard to reckon and hard to believe ... The Doge himself, surrounded by a number of distinguished notables, occupied the loggia above the entrance to the Basilica, where stand the four horses of gilded bronze whose ancient, unknown sculptor has imbued with such a semblance of life that one can almost hear them whinnying and stamping. The loggia itself was covered with rich, multicoloured awnings to protect those present from the heat and glare of the afternoon sun ... Below, on the Piazza, there was no room for a grain of wheat: church, towers, roofs, porches, windows, all were filled to bursting with jammed, jostling spectators ...

On the right, in a great wooden pavilion, sat four hundred ladies magnificently dressed, the very flower of beauty and nobility ... Nor should I omit to mention a party of English noblemen, kinsmen of the King, all exultant over their own recent victory.[1]

As things turned out, these rejoicings were a little premature. Though the Cretans of old Venetian stock had indeed capitulated – the ringleaders were beheaded and many others banished – the Greeks were to continue guerrilla activity until 1366. By that time, however, Lorenzo Celsi was dead. A certain air of mystery hangs about his death, since we find a decree by the Council of Ten, dated 30 July 1365, ordering the destruction of all written accusations levelled against the late Doge and requiring a public statement by his successor to the effect that these accusations had been thoroughly investigated and found to be without foundation. The decree was conscientiously obeyed, so that just what misdeeds had been imputed to Celsi we shall never know; some chroniclers have hinted that he was less innocent than the Ten wished it to be thought, and that had he not died so conveniently he might well have found himself arraigned on charges similar to those that had caused the downfall of Marin Falier. It may be; but there is no real evidence to support the theory. Celsi was given an honourable burial in S. Maria Celeste – now demolished – and, as we have seen, publicly exonerated. We can hardly withhold from him the benefit of the doubt.

The ducal election that followed the death of Lorenzo Celsi did not go undisputed. The name of Marco Corner – one of the ambassadors who had been imprisoned by the Duke of Austria – was put forward, but formal objections were raised to his candidature. He was too old, being well over eighty; he was too poor, and would be unable properly to meet the expenses and maintain the dignities of his office; he was

1. Presumably the Treaty of Calais of October 1360 which gave Aquitaine and much of northern France to England and brought to an end the first phase of the Hundred Years War.

too closely associated with foreign powers for his loyalty to be beyond suspicion; finally, he was married to a plebeian wife, whose numerous family would be bound to meddle in the affairs of state. But Corner rose spiritedly to his own defence. If his hair was white, he pointed out, it had gone white in the service of the Republic in which he was ready to continue; his poverty was a matter for pride rather than shame, a proof of his honesty and integrity; his ties of friendship with foreign princes were the natural results of a diplomatic career and reputation for fair dealing which had been of considerable benefit to Venice; finally, many Venetian noblemen had married ladies of humble origins, and his own wife and her family were well known and second to none in their loyalty and the love they bore their native city. His speech had precisely the desired effect: on 21 July 1365 he was elected.

His reign was short, but peaceful and prosperous. The last rebellious Cretan rumblings died away; pressure from the Count of Savoy to join in a new Crusade against the Turks was resisted, though two galleys were eventually sent off as a gesture of good will; trade with the Muslims of Alexandria was resumed and the Pope was even persuaded to give the resumption his somewhat reluctant blessing. At home, the decoration of the Doges' Palace continued, with the carving of the capitals of the south façade and Guariento's great fresco of Paradise gradually taking shape on the eastern wall of the Council Chamber, together with a long series of portraits of former Doges running around the frieze – cunningly arranged in such a way that Corner's own portrait appeared immediately above the ducal throne.

Alas, the fourteenth century was a turbulent time and Marco Corner was an old man; neither this happy breathing-space nor the Doge's life could be expected to last very long. Nor did they. On 13 January 1368 Venice once more found herself without a titular head, and within a few months of the state funeral and burial in SS. Giovanni e Paolo[1] the city was again at war.

It was not the fault of the new Doge, Andrea Contarini. He was as peacefully inclined as his predecessor and still less ambitious: he had in fact already retired to his estates near Padua, and when twelve of his most exalted countrymen arrived to inform him of his election and to escort him back in state to the Rialto, they at first met with a categorical refusal. Only after he had been threatened with banishment

---

1. Marco Corner's sarcophagus is still visible in the chancel, but has suffered badly from the treatment it received in the nineteenth century, when it was shifted and cut down to make way for the great Vendramin tomb on its transfer from the church of the Servi.

and the confiscation of his entire property did he agree to come quietly. Had he known the full measure of the tribulations that awaited him he might have shown even more reluctance; there must have been many occasions in the next fourteen years when he thought of his thwarted retirement with envious longing.

The first outbreak of trouble did not, it must be admitted, tax the strength or the resources of the Republic too severely. It took the form of an insurrection in Trieste. This was a city to which, in former years, Venice had seldom given much thought. It was smaller and, for geographical reasons, a good deal less important strategically than Zara and the other cities further along the coast. But with the loss of Dalmatia Trieste had acquired a new significance and, with it, a new susceptibility to political pressures from such dangerous neighbours as the King of Hungary, the Duke of Austria and the Patriarch of Aquileia. Whether one or more of these neighbours had a hand in stirring up the revolt we do not know; certainly the Duke was quick to send an army when the Triestines, finding themselves besieged by a Venetian fleet, appealed to him for help. But the Venetians were quicker still. They tightened the blockade and, in the summer of 1369, with a hastily gathered force composed partly of mercenaries and partly of their own fighting men, routed the Austrians utterly. Trieste withstood the siege for a few more months, but after the Austrian retreat the city's surrender could only be a matter of time. On 28 November it capitulated.

Meanwhile the behaviour of Francesco da Carrara was confirming all Venice's earlier suspicions. He was now building fort after fort along the Brenta, where he proposed to establish his own saltworks. Venice – whose monopoly of salt production in the area dated back almost as far as the Republic itself and by now probably accounted for some 10 per cent of its gross annual income[1] – sent a strongly-worded protest. Carrara instantly appealed to his old ally the King of Hungary, and was perhaps rather disappointed when Lajos, instead of supporting him, merely offered to mediate; but the ensuing discussions, which at one moment became so heated that swords were actually drawn in the council chamber, achieved nothing. Venice was not to be appeased. The salt monopoly was a cornerstone of her economy and must be protected at all costs. She hired another successful *condottiere* of the day, Renier dei Guaschi, to command her land army and declared war.

Now it was the turn of Padua to face a siege, while Venetian detachments set about the methodical destruction of Carrara's new forts and

1. We know that in 1454 it was bringing in 165,000 ducats, a still higher proportion.

the devastation of his lands. In Venice meanwhile a new plot was discovered: somehow Carrara had managed to suborn two members of the Senate and had planned with them the assassination of all his principal enemies in the government. The would-be assassins, who had been unwise enough to confide their business to a couple of patriotic prostitutes of the Merceria, were immediately arrested, drawn at a horse's tail from the Rialto to the Piazzetta and there quartered between the columns. Of the traitorous nobles, one was beheaded, the other sentenced to ten years in prison with banishment to follow. They were savage punishments, but even they did not allay the fears of the Venetian populace. New rumours flashed through the city: Carrara had poisoned the wells; he was about to set fire to the Arsenal. As much to preserve law and order as for any other reason, the Council of Ten voted special powers for the *Collegio* – to order special patrols for the streets and canals, to search all strangers entering Venice, to put suspected and accused persons to the torture. The measures were welcomed with general enthusiasm; in the popular opinion, Francesco da Carrara had become Antichrist.

The war continued almost four years, till the autumn of 1373. First Venice had the advantage; then, after a Hungarian army had arrived to supplement Carrara's already considerable force of German mercenaries – it was led by Lajos's nephew, Stephen of Transylvania – the pendulum swung and the Republic suffered a serious defeat at Narvesa on the Piave. Taddeo Giustinian, who had assumed supreme command from dei Guaschi, was taken prisoner, and the captured banner of St Mark was hung as a trophy in the great basilica of St Anthony in Padua. A second defeat followed, at Fossanuova; but soon afterwards, while the Hungarians were besieging a relatively insignificant Venetian fortress – so insignificant, indeed, that its name has not even come down to us – the Venetian army suddenly attacked. A Hungarian countercharge was broken by the unwavering stand of the Venetian pikemen, and Stephen of Transylvania taken prisoner.

Brought to Venice, he was honourably accommodated in the Doges' Palace, while the people rejoiced at the victory. They had good reason to do so. The King of Hungary, to secure his nephew's freedom, immediately withdrew from the war, and Carrara, now left without an ally, was forced to capitulate. The terms exacted were harsh: all his forts were to be destroyed, and an indemnity of no less than a quarter of a million ducats to be paid to Venice. Feltre was to be held by the Republic as security for his good behaviour. The only concession he managed to gain was that his son, rather than he himself, should come to Venice to ask pardon of the Doge, a ceremony that took place in the autumn of 1373 before the assembled Senate while Petrarch, who had accompanied the supplicant – his presence appears to have become indispensable on such occasions – pronounced one of his usual high-flown Latin orations in praise of peace.

But peace, even now, was not absolute. Another of Carrara's erstwhile allies, the Duke of Austria, continued to make trouble and for the next three years that ill-fated region of farms and hilltop towns around Treviso that had already suffered so much in the past half-century was once again torn apart by desultory and largely inconclusive warfare – in which, incidentally, the Venetians introduced a few small cannon, the first ever seen in Italy. Not until the end of 1376 did the Duke finally withdraw his army; but by then Venice had other preoccupations. Her long and bitter struggle with another, still more intractable rival was approaching its final phase.

18

The War with Genoa

[1372–1381]

'Alla fè di Dio, Signori Veneziani, non haverete mai pace dal Signore di Padova, ne dal nostro Comune di Genova, si primieramente non mettemo le briglie a quelli vostri cavalli sfrenati, che sono su la Reza del vostro Evangelista San Marco.'

'In God's name, my Venetian signors, you shall never have peace from the Lord of Padua, nor from our own Republic of Genoa, until we have put a bridle on those wild horses of yours that stand upon the Palace of St Mark your Evangelist.'

Admiral Pietro Doria (Quoted by Chinazzo, *Belli inter Venetos et Gennenses*, 1378)

On 17 January 1369 Peter I of Lusignan, King of Cyprus and Jerusalem, was murdered in his palace at Famagusta. He was succeeded by his fourteen-year-old son Peter II. Owing to the new King's youth and the repeated procrastinations of his uncle the Regent, there was no immediate coronation. It was only in January 1372 that young Peter received the crown of Cyprus, and in October of the same year that of Jerusalem.

This latter kingdom was purely titular; Jerusalem had been in the hands of the Infidel for nearly two centuries[1] and Peter's second coronation therefore took place at Famagusta, in the church of St Nicholas. Already on the way to the church some dispute over precedence broke out between the Venetian and Genoese representatives. Somehow peace was restored, but at the banquet following the ceremony the contingents from the two Republics began throwing bread at each other; a brawl ensued during which, despite strict laws to the contrary, many of the Genoese were found to have been carrying swords under their cloaks. In the circumstances it is hard to believe that the Venetians were entirely guiltless of similar offences, but they were a good deal more popular on the island than their rivals and the Cypriot authorities seem to have had no hesitation in laying the blame on the Genoese. Several of the latter

---

1. Since Saladin captured it in 1187 after the battle of Hattin. Later, in 1229, Frederick II had talked his way into possession of the Holy Places, but had held them only ten years.

were arrested, seized and defenestrated on the spot. Meanwhile the Famagusta mob descended on the Genoese quarter, pillaging, looting and burning the warehouses to the ground.

When the news of all this reached Genoa, the reaction was much as might have been foreseen. Such an insult to the Republic could not go unpunished; moreover, unless firm measures were taken at once, there was a danger that Cyprus might fall completely under Venetian influence – a possibility, to any patriotic Genoese, almost too horrible to contemplate. Two punitive expeditions set off in quick succession; on 6 October 1373 Famagusta surrendered to a Genoese war fleet, and a few days later the whole island made its submission. The young King himself was allowed to remain on his throne, but only in recognition of a fine of over 2,000,000 gold florins and an annual payment of 40,000; his uncle, two of his cousins and sixty members of the Cypriot nobility were carried off to Genoa as hostages for his future good behaviour. Genoa kept Famagusta for herself.

It was only to be expected that Venetian property should suffer during these last upheavals, just as Genoese had done in the previous year; and though the new masters of Cyprus made no effort to evict their rivals – indeed they received the formal Venetian protests and demands for compensation with unwonted politeness and even sympathy – this abrupt reversal of fortune in one of the key areas of the eastern Mediterranean made the renewal of the war between the two republics inevitable. The fact that it was to be delayed, against all probabilities, for nearly five more years was due less to any peaceable inclinations on either side than to a sudden turn of events in Constantinople in which both were to be closely – if not altogether creditably – involved.

The Emperor John V Palaeologus had by now managed to rid himself of his father-in-law Cantacuzenus, who in 1355 had given up all hopes of founding a new dynasty and had retired to end his days writing history from a monastic cell on Mount Athos. In all other respects, however, John's problems had increased. Adrianople, and with it much of Thrace, had fallen to the Ottoman Turks, who were virtually at the walls of Constantinople. He was furthermore heavily in debt, and the imperial treasury was empty. In a desperate bid for military and financial aid he had travelled to the West in 1369 and, in return for promises of ships, cavalry and bowmen from Urban V, had actually gone so far as to acknowledge papal supremacy; but the other princes of Europe had proved less sympathetic and when John reached Venice in 1370 he had had to submit to the worst humiliation of all – confinement in a debtors' prison. His elder son Andronicus, whom he had appointed regent in his absence, seemed content that he should remain there; it was left to his second son Manuel to send his own remaining jewels to Venice and bail his father out.

Even now, however, many of the debts were still unpaid; and in the years immediately following John's return to his beleaguered capital they tended to increase. The Venetians decided once again to take a firm line with the Emperor. The five-year truce they had promised him after his release had now expired; more important still, the fall of Cyprus to Genoa had made it essential for them to find an alternative commercial base in the eastern Mediterranean. In 1375, therefore, a Venetian embassy headed for Constantinople, to be followed in March 1376 – the Emperor having shown his usual tendency to prevaricate – by a fully-armed fleet under the Captain-General of the Sea, Marco Giustinian, with an ultimatum: if John wished to continue to live on peaceful terms with Venice for the next five years, he must at once pay all his outstanding debts and mortgage to the Republic the island of Tenedos. In recognizance for this last the Venetians would pay him a substantial lump sum and return his son's jewels. If he were to refuse these terms, he must look to his throne.

To any power with trading interests in the area, the strategic importance of Tenedos could hardly be exaggerated. Lying at the gateway to the Hellespont – according to Virgil[1] the Greeks had hidden there, watching and waiting, while the Wooden Horse was sent into Troy – it controlled the entrance to the straits and the Sea of Marmara beyond them as effectively as Galata did the mouth of the Bosphorus. If Tenedos too were to fall into the hands of the Genoese, Venetian trade with Byzantium and the Black Sea would be strangled. Once before, in 1352, Venice had temporarily acquired the island to prevent just such a disaster;[2] with Genoa in her present mood and mistress of Cyprus to boot, the need to assure the freedom of the Hellespont was even more vital than it had been twenty-four years earlier.

The sight of the Venetian fleet at the very mouth of the Golden Horn was more than enough to persuade John Palaeologus to submit. He paid up, willingly surrendering Tenedos on the terms proposed, asking only that it should continue to fly the imperial standard alongside that of St Mark and that it should be allowed to maintain its ecclesiastical allegiance to the Byzantine Patriarch. He must have known that his

1. *Aeneid*, II, 21ff.
2. See p. 243.

capitulation would provoke the wrath of the Genoese; he can hardly have suspected the scale of their revenge.

The Emperor's son Andronicus had already shown himself to be untrustworthy during his father's difficulties in Venice. In 1373 he had gone further still, allying himself with the son of the Ottoman Sultan Murad in a joint conspiracy against their two fathers. The plot had been discovered; Murad had blinded and later executed his own son and had enjoined John to do the same; but John, being of gentler disposition, had left Andronicus at least partially sighted and merely imprisoned him. His throne, however, was still insecure, and he now had a new problem to contend with – unpopularity. His people, to whom their religion meant even more than imperial survival, had never forgiven him his submission to the Pope. The action taken by the Genoese after his cession of Tenedos to Venice illustrates better than anything else both the weakness of his position in Constantinople and the strength of their own: they simply deposed him. Father and son changed places; John was incarcerated in his turn while Andronicus, released, was raised to the imperial throne.

The new Emperor's first act on his accession was to make over Tenedos to the Genoese, who immediately sent a representative to the island to claim it in the name of the Republic. The attempt was a failure. Venice herself had not yet taken possession, but the local governor remained loyal to John and refused point-blank to recognize the authority of Andronicus. He had presumably received some official intimation of the agreement with Venice: for when Marco Giustinian arrived with his fleet soon afterwards he was given a ceremonial welcome, the islanders willingly – even enthusiastically – delivering themselves into his hands. By this time, however, the Genoese in Constantinople had complained to Andronicus of the rebuff they had sustained and the Emperor, terrified of losing their support, had arrested the leaders of the Venetian mercantile community, including the *bailo* himself.

Clearly the war could not be much longer postponed. Throughout 1377 the diplomatic moves between Venice, Genoa and Constantinople become ever more loaded with protests rejected, demands refused and, finally, out-and-out threats. Genoa reminds Venice that she cannot be held responsible for attacks on Venetian persons and property in the Byzantine Empire; Venice informs Genoa that their political differences in the area cannot be discussed until the rightful Emperor is restored to power; finally a second Venetian admiral, Pietro Mocenigo, is ordered to Constantinople to demand the immediate release of the *bailo* and the

other Venetians held in custody, failing which Andronicus will be forcibly deposed in his turn, if necessary with the help of the Ottoman Sultan.

But Mocenigo never reached his destination. Soon after he had left
the lagoon, word reached Venice that Genoa had sent a fleet of galleys
to sea, with the object of joining up with a Byzantine squadron and
launching a combined attack on Tenedos. Messengers overtook the
admiral with revised instructions. He and his fleet were needed in the
Mediterranean. The war had begun.

The Genoese and Byzantines did indeed try to take Tenedos by force,
and failed. But the attempt is hardly mentioned in the early histories
– understandably, because it hardly mattered. With another of those
sudden shifts of focus which make the history of the Mediterranean
so bewildering to writer and reader alike, Tenedos – and with it the
gateway to the Hellespont, the Marmara, Constantinople and the whole
Black Sea trade – fades once more into the background. The last round
of the contest between Genoa and Venice was to be fought out, more
appropriately, on Italian territory and in Italian waters: in the Tyrrhenian,
the Adriatic and, most desperately of all, in the Venetian lagoon.

Both sides had taken good care to find allies. Genoa could, as always,
count on Francesco da Carrara and that other elderly troublemaker,
the King of Hungary; Venice had the support of King Peter of Cyprus,
who had not forgiven the Genoese their recent seizure of his island
and welcomed the chance of seeing his erstwhile conquerors brought
low. Peter's support was in fact to make little difference as such; but
it had one important consequence in that it enabled Venice to secure
the alliance of the young King's prospective father-in-law, Bernabò
Visconti of Milan. The two signed a four-year treaty in November 1377,
in which it was agreed that all conquests made at sea should go to Venice,
all those on land to Milan – including, if fortune favoured their efforts,
Genoa itself. In the Doges' Palace, meanwhile, the usual steps were
taken to put the Republic on war footing: special committees of *savii*
were formed to accelerate the making of policy decisions and to raise
money; arrangements were made to hire *condottieri* and mercenaries
for fighting on the mainland, to fortify strategic points in the Treviso
region, and to form *duodene*, those twelve-man groups from which,
by that admirable and characteristically Venetian system, one or more
persons could be selected by lot for military service and paid for by
the remainder. On this occasion no less than three men from each *duodena*
were to make themselves ready for immediate departure. Finally, in

the basilica on 22 April 1378, Vettor Pisani – nephew of that Nicolò
who had been deprived of command after Portolungo – was invested
by Doge Contarini with the banner of St Mark and enjoined to lead the
Republic to victory.

Vettor Pisani may not have been one of Venice's greatest admirals.
He was, however, to prove himself one of her greatest men – a superb
leader, adored by all who served under his command; and less than
six weeks after his appointment his family name had recovered all its
former glory. On 30 May the Venetian and Genoese fleets met off Anzio.
It was a day of violent storms and a heavy sea; the battle was fought in
driving rain, with winds rising to gale force so that close manoeuvring
became impossible and four of Pisani's galleys were actually prevented
from engaging the enemy at all. Yet somehow Venetian seamanship
prevailed, and by nightfall five Genoese galleys had been captured
and a sixth driven on to the rocks. The prisoners, including the Genoese
commander, were brought back to the Rialto where, we are told, they
were admirably looked after by the noble ladies of Venice. The people
of Genoa, by contrast, were less amicably inclined: alarmed and infuriated
– not so much by the news of the defeat as by the depredations of a
neighbouring baron whom the Venetians had encouraged to ravage
the Genoese coast while they kept the navy occupied – they stormed their
own ducal palace, deposed their Doge and set up another in his stead.

Had Pisani's fleet been a little more numerous and the weather less
unseasonable, he might well have advanced to Genoa itself and brought
the war to a swift conclusion; but he preferred not to take the risk.
Instead, he sailed to the Levant – incidentally providing an unexpected
additional escort for Valentina Visconti, one of Bernabò's thirty-eight
children, who was on her way to Cyprus to marry King Peter – and,
after an energetic but ultimately abortive pursuit of more Genoese
shipping, headed back to the Adriatic where he captured the cities of
Cattaro and Sebenico.[1] Permission to return to Venice being refused,
he finally settled his fleet at Pola for the winter.

This refusal on the part of the Venetian authorities was a serious
error of judgement. Pisani, his captains and his sailors had already
been at sea for six months and were now faced with the prospect of perhaps another year without contact with their families or friends. After
their exertions and several conspicuous successes, they felt they deserved
better. The ships, too, were in need of repair, and the cold, the damp
and the sickness which was bound to result from a winter spent in such

1. Kotor and Sibenik.

conditions were the more intolerable for being obviously unnecessary. A renewed request to return home in the spring was again rejected; and it was a resentful and demoralized body of men that awoke in Pola on the morning of 7 May 1379 to find a Genoese fleet of twenty-five sail lying at the harbour mouth.

Pisani at first refused to fight. He knew better than anyone the condition of his men and his ships. They were outnumbered; besides, in the event of their defeat, how was Venice herself to be protected? Another Venetian fleet under his fellow-admiral Carlo Zeno was shortly expected in Pola from the East; if it were to turn up, then the two together should be able to deal with the Genoese. Meanwhile it would be better to remain in harbour, out of harm's way. He was unquestionably right; but he was overruled. Captains and crews alike, weary of inactivity, clamoured to be allowed to take the offensive and even taunted their admiral with accusations of cowardice. Pisani was no coward; at this crucial moment, however, he seems to have lacked the moral courage to stand firm. He agreed to attack and, sailing out of the harbour, bore directly down upon the Genoese flagship.

It was all over quite quickly, and with results even more calamitous, perhaps, than Pisani had feared. He himself fought heroically, and was credited with having been personally responsible for the death of the Genoese admiral, Luciano Doria; but several of his captains proved slow and irresolute, and of the entire Venetian fleet only six battered galleys escaped capture or destruction and made their way, slow and creaking, to safety in the port of Parenzo. Recalled to Venice to answer for the defeat, Pisani was charged not with cowardice but with having kept insufficient watch on the harbour approaches. He was deprived of his command, sentenced to six months' imprisonment, and debarred from all office under the Republic for five years.

It seems hard to believe that Venice, poised as she was on the brink of disaster, should have deliberately deprived herself of the services of one of her two leading admirals – at a time moreover when the other, Carlo Zeno, was away in the East and, though vaguely thought to be on his way home, beyond any possibility of immediate recall. Her only justification, sad and ironic as it might be, was that Pisani was now useless to her since, apart from the half-dozen battered hulks in Parenzo, she no longer had any ships available for him to command. Unless and until Zeno arrived with his fleet, she had only her own natural defences in which to put her trust. Fortunately she could count on a few weeks' grace. The Genoese had lost their admiral; they could hardly resume the offensive until a new one had been appointed and had had time to travel out and take up his command.

During those few weeks the Venetians worked day and night to strengthen the defences of their city. It was a gigantic effort, involving virtually the entire population, men and women, nobles and commoners alike. Many of the rich put their whole fortunes at the disposal of the Republic; others fitted out ships or undertook costly building operations at their own expense. Their task was not made easier by the presence of Francesco da Carrara – now supported by 5,000 Hungarians sent by King Lajos – on the shores of the lagoon, where they had only just succeeded in saving Mestre from his clutches. But even Carrara was now a lesser danger. Though he might do his worst on the mainland, terrifying the local populations with his cannon – still a rarity in Italy – he was powerless on water and so constituted little physical threat to the city itself. The Genoese navy was another matter. An advance squadron was already in sight – waiting just beyond the Lido port, nearer than any hostile fleet had anchored for centuries past, as if mocking the Venetians' inability to move against it.

But if Venice could not destroy the Genoese, she could at least ensure that their onward progress would be hard. Leonardo Dandolo, now given the unprecedented appointment of 'General of the Lido', set about fortifying the monastery of S. Nicolò with stout walls and a triple ditch, while three heavy hulks were chained together across the lagoon entrance and the long and sinuous rows of piles which were used, then as now, to mark the shoals and channels were taken up to baffle the invaders. Meanwhile command on land was entrusted to the *condottiere* Giacomo de' Cavalli, who appeared with 4,000 horsemen, 2,000 infantry and a considerable force of cross-bowmen. These were drawn up in strength along the *lidi* and such neighbouring areas on the mainland as remained in Venetian hands, while armed boats constantly patrolled the lagoon to block communications between Carrara and the Genoese. In the city itself it was decreed that a committee consisting of two councillors, one *capo della Quarantia* and four *savii* should be on constant twenty-four-hour call at the Doges' Palace, to be relieved weekly by another similarly constituted. Among its other duties it was to listen for the tocsin which was to be sounded, in an emergency, by the bells of S. Nicolò di Lido. This alarm would be taken up from the campanile of St Mark's and further relayed by all the churches of Venice, while each parish sent its own armed contingent to the Piazza.

The arrangements were made only just in time. On 6 August a fleet of forty-seven Genoese galleys under the newly-appointed admiral Pietro Doria appeared off Chioggia.

The town of Chioggia stands on an island at the extreme southern end of the Venetian lagoon – a region which, even by local standards, strikes one as peculiarly indecisive; where the geography fails utterly to make up its mind whether to be terrestrial or aquatic, where the contours separating land from sea, blurred enough at the best of times, are rendered still more uncertain by the multiple mouths of the two rivers, the Brenta and the Adige, which disgorge their muddy waters a mile or two beyond; and where, over the past 500 years, generation after generation of military sappers and marine engineers have built dams and breakwaters, causeways and canals, diverting here, deflecting there, to the point at which the face of the landscape as it existed in the late fourteenth century, when Venice and Genoa confronted each other across the malodorous marshes, has been lost beyond recall.

For all these reasons, and despite the display of much scholarly ingenuity on points of topographical precision, many of the details of the war of Chioggia remain obscure. The broad outlines, however, are clear enough. Doria had brought his fleet down from the north, burning Grado, Caorle and Pellestrina on his way. He had also made what appears to have been a somewhat desultory attack on Malamocco but, encountering stiffer opposition than he had expected, had not persevered; none of these places was vital to his purpose. His sights were fixed on Chioggia, where the line of *lidi* met the mainland. There he had secretly arranged to meet Carrara who, having led his army of 24,000 Italians and Hungarians down the valley of the Brenta, would provide an invaluable supply line and simultaneously establish a mainland blockade of Venice while the Genoese did the same by sea.

Chioggia was defended by a garrison of 3,000 under its *podestà*, Pietro Emo. Such a force would have been more than adequate in any normal eventuality, but it could not hope to deal with an amphibious attack on this scale. Emo appealed to Venice for help, and fifty shallow-draught lagoon boats were immediately dispatched under Leonardo Dandolo; but they would have been of little use, and anyway they arrived too late. On 16 August, after a heroic but futile defence which took an immense toll of human life both Venetian and Genoese, Chioggia fell. For the first time since the days of Pepin, a fortified city within the lagoon – and one which, incidentally, commanded a direct deep-water channel to Venice – lay in enemy hands.

As the banners of Genoa, Hungary and its new lord Francesco Carrara fluttered over Chioggia and all the bells of Venice rang out the alarm, Doge and Senate met in emergency session. Still there was no news of Carlo Zeno and his fleet, without which they could not hope to defeat the invaders in pitched battle. An initial decision to sue for terms came to nothing when Carrara refused to grant safe conduct to the Venetian ambassadors, so that Venice now found herself in a more impossible situation than ever, powerless alike to make peace or to continue the war. All she could do was look to her defences in the hopes that they might delay the enemy until Zeno's arrival. Malamocco was abandoned, to enable all available troops to be concentrated around S. Nicolò on the Lido, and – more ominously still – on S. Giorgio Maggiore. All magistrates voluntarily renounced their pay; as food shortages became more severe and prices rose, the rich were ordered to provide free meals for the poor. Finally, in deference to the people's insistent demand, Vettor Pisani was released from prison.

This last decision was taken with reluctance. There was by now general agreement among government and people alike that Venice needed, at this moment of desperate crisis, a military leader to assume supreme command; but the Senate had their own candidate for the post, Taddeo Giustinian, and were understandably reluctant to reinstate a man whom they had publicly disgraced only a few weeks before. Even now, despite Pisani's magnanimous declaration that far from bearing the Republic any grudge for his past treatment he was resolved to dedicate his life to its preservation, they tried to subordinate him to Giustinian; but the people – and, in particular, the sailors who had served with him in the past and worshipped him - protested. Pisani was their man: they would follow no other. This was no moment to risk a popular uprising. Once again the Senate gave in.

They were wise to do so. The atmosphere in Venice changed overnight. Despair and defeatism vanished. Morale came flooding back, and with it a new vigour and determination. A forced loan produced the gigantic sum of over 6,000,000 lire, not to mention quantities of gold, silver and jewels voluntarily contributed by men and women from all sections of the city. At the Arsenal, work continued day and night until forty galleys had come off the slipways. A new defensive wall, with towers at each end, was built along the Lido and completed within a fortnight; a boom, protected by armed ships – some mounted with cannon – was stretched across the western end of the Grand Canal, and another stockade was erected, running from S. Nicolò di Lido right across the lagoon, behind the islands of S. Servolo and the Giudecca, to the mainland shore. All this and much more was due, in large measure, to the infectious enthusiasm of an inspired leader, Vettor Pisani. No wonder his men loved him.

But he was also lucky. If, immediately after the capture of Chioggia, Pietro Doria had followed Carrara's advice and launched an immediate attack on Venice, it is doubtful whether Pisani or anyone else would have been able to save the city. Fortunately, Pietro stuck to his original plan, to blockade it and starve it into submission. In this he failed; instead, he gave it time to recover, while at the same time he allowed the morale of his own men to drain away. Many of them, anxious to get their hands on the fabled wealth of Venice, had been disappointed by their admiral's excessive caution and resented having to stand idly by, watching while the city erected new and formidable defences and made itself daily more impregnable. And there were other, still more disquieting signs. One day in the late summer a small squadron under Giovanni Barbarigo had fallen upon three Genoese ships guarding a mainland fort and burnt them. Meanwhile Giacomo de' Cavalli was slowly advancing southwards along the *lidi* and had regained Malamocco. Almost incredibly, it seemed, the Venetians were beginning to take the offensive.

The recapture of Malamocco was perhaps less significant than it appeared. Winter was approaching, and winter must inevitably mean, for Pietro Doria, the withdrawal of his forces into Chioggia. For Vettor Pisani, on the other hand, who had good reason to know the difficulties of keeping a large war fleet in good order when away from home throughout those bitter months, it meant the opening of the next phase of his campaign. The blockaders must themselves be blockaded. Chioggia was already almost landlocked and depended on only three narrow channels: the main harbour entrance towards Pellestrina, and, a little further south, the two entrances to the harbour of Brondolo, both of which also gave access to the lagoon. All that was necessary was to sink a large, stone-filled hulk in each of these channels; the two other lagoon outlets to the north, the Lido and Malamocco ports, could then be blocked by Venetian patrols.

On mid-winter night, 21 December 1379, the expedition set out, with the hulks in tow. Accompanying Pisani on the leading vessel was the Doge himself, Andrea Contarini, now well into his eighties. By dawn they had arrived at the approaches to Chioggia. The local lookouts quickly gave the alert, and the fighting was fierce, particularly around Brondolo, where the defence was concentrated; but the hulks were duly sunk in their appointed places, and within a few hours Chioggia was effectively closed, the Genoese and all their fleet prisoners within it.

The Venetians' work, however, was not yet done. The success of the operation depended on their continued vigilance. One of the Brondolo barricades was clearly vulnerable and needed constant defence against attempts by the Genoese to remove it; there were also the northern lagoon entrances to be watched. Ships and provisions were still woefully short, and the winter storms made the task of the Venetian patrols, unaccustomed to keeping to the open seas in such conditions, both difficult and dangerous. How long they could have continued without assistance is uncertain, but fortunately the question did not have to be put to the test. On the first day of 1380 the long-awaited fleet of Carlo Zeno appeared over the horizon.

After a quick council of war with Pisani and the Doge, Zeno sailed at once with his eighteen ships to Brondolo, still the weakest and most critical point in the blockade. In the sudden storm which coincided with his arrival he was twice nearly shipwrecked, but a day or two later he succeeded in recapturing a nearby stronghold, the tower of Londo, so opening the way for the reinforcements and provisions that Venice's ally, the Duke of Ferrara, had sent up by the lower Adige. On 6 January there was even greater rejoicing when a Venetian cannon destroyed the campanile of Brondolo and it was learnt that Pietro Doria had been struck and killed by the falling debris.[1] His successor, chosen perforce from among the officers on the spot, was one Napoleone Grimaldi who in desperation tried to cut a new channel through the Lido of Sottomarina, immediately to the east of the beleaguered port; but in mid-February Pisani took Brondolo, and the entire line of *lidi* was back in Venetian hands.

The siege continued all through the winter and into the spring. In April the Venetians suffered a serious reverse when a new Genoese fleet under Marco Maruffo captured Taddeo Giustinian and the twelve ships with which he had gone to collect grain from Sicily – famine conditions in Venice being by now almost as bad as those in Chioggia itself – and then began to harry Pisani and Zeno as they ceaselessly patrolled the entrances to the lagoon. They also had trouble with mutinous mercenaries (including a number of particularly tiresome English-

---

1. These early cannon were so unwieldy that their terrified crews dared not use them more than once a day; but they were rapidly proving their value as a weapon, being capable of firing, at a short range, stone balls weighing up to 200 pounds.

men) whom they managed to control only with promises of additional prizes and double pay. By some miracle, however, the two admirals avoided a pitched sea battle with Maruffo – in which they would almost certainly have been defeated – while successfully preventing him from making contact with his compatriots inside the lagoon and simultaneously blocking every attempt by the latter to join him. At last he gave up, and withdrew to Dalmatia; and on 24 June the 4,000 beleaguered Genoese, despairing of rescue and half-dead with hunger, made their unconditional surrender.

In Venice there was jubilation. This was not just a victory; it was deliverance. Virtually the whole population, in innumerable boats of every shape and size, accompanied the *Bucintoro* as it sailed out in state to meet the old Doge, who had remained with the fleet throughout the six-month siege. And so the triumphal procession returned to the Molo,[1] bringing in its train the seventeen battered galleys, all that was left of Pietro Doria's fleet, and their abject crews. The mercenaries were paid in full as promised, one of them – an Englishman called William Gold who was not, presumably, one of the mutineers – receiving an additional 500 ducats in recognition of his exceptional valour.

The war was not quite over. Matteo Maruffo was still in the Adriatic, from which Pisani was determined that he should not escape. After weeks of that inconsequential and profitless searching of which, until modern times, so much of naval warfare consisted, Pisani at last caught up with a dozen Genoese galleys off the coast of Apulia and engaged them. They escaped, but not before he had been gravely wounded. Brought back to Manfredonia, he died there on 13 August. His monument, formerly in the Arsenal, can now be seen in the south-east apse of SS. Giovanni e Paolo. Amid the profusion of funerary sculpture in the church, it is seldom noticed; most guide-books ignore it utterly. But of all those buried in that tremendous building, none was more generally loved or more willingly followed than Vettor Pisani, and none has a better claim to the lasting gratitude of his compatriots. It would perhaps be an exaggeration to say that he saved Venice single-handed; the fact remains that she would not have survived without him.

Carlo Zeno, now in supreme command, continued the campaign over a theatre that ranged from the coast of the Peloponnese to Genoese home waters, but achieved no more decisive victories. Meanwhile,

1. See the painting by Veronese – one of his last works – on the west wall of the Sala del Maggior Consiglio.

in the Veneto, Carrara and his friends were also keeping up the pressure. The Venetians had long suspected that these mainland territories were more trouble than they were worth; they were determined none the less not to surrender them to the detested Carrara. Their solution was to offer them to the Duke of Austria, on condition only that he should at once occupy them with an army in the Republic's name. The Duke asked nothing better: confronted with a vastly superior force, Carrara had no alternative but to withdraw.

By now the heat had gone out of the war, and in 1381 the two exhausted Republics gratefully accepted the offer of Count Amadeus VI of Savoy to mediate. The ensuing peace conference at Turin was attended by representatives not just of Venice and Genoa but of all those who had played any part in the hostilities: Hungary, Padua, Aquileia, even Ancona and Florence. Venice demanded the right, as the victorious party, to table the first proposals, but the terms eventually agreed were scarcely those that might have been expected by a conqueror. She regained from Carrara the strong-points around the lagoon that were essential to her safety; but she confirmed her renunciation of Dalmatia and also of Tenedos, the immediate *casus belli*, which was surrendered to Amadeus to dispose of as he saw fit.

The truth was that, at least in the short-term view, Venice had not won the war or anything like it. Nor had Genoa. The only victors in any real sense were those two shadowy figures on the side-lines, the King of Hungary and the Duke of Austria. The events at Chioggia, heroic and inspiring as they had been, had served only the negative purpose of averting disaster. After all the devastation and bloodshed, the two protagonists were politically very much where they had been before – a situation confirmed by the Treaty of Turin, which provided for the continuation of trade in the Mediterranean and the Levant by both republics side by side.

As time went on, however, it gradually became clear that Venice's victory had been greater than she knew. Not for the first time, she was to astonish her friends and enemies alike by the speed of her economic and material recovery. Genoa, on the other hand, went into a decline. Her governmental system began to crumble; torn asunder by factional strife, she was to depose ten Doges in five years and soon fell under a French domination which was to last a century and a half. Only in 1528, under Andrea Doria, was she finally to regain her independence; but by then the world had changed. Never again would she constitute a threat to Venice.

19

The Empire Takes Shape

[1381–1405]

> The Duke cannot deny the course of law;
> For the commodity that strangers have
> With us in Venice, if it be denied,
> Will much impeach the justice of this state;
> Since that the trade and profit of this city
> Consisteth of all nations.
>
> Shakespeare, *The Merchant of Venice*

It was 4 September 1381. The Treaty of Turin had been signed the month before. Thanks had been rendered to God from every church in Venice for her deliverance from mortal danger and for her heroic victory – as the Venetians were determined to see it – over a powerful and pitiless foe. Plans were already being drawn up for the rebuilding of Chioggia. Only one more thing remained to be done before the whole epoch of Venetian–Genoese rivalries and hostilities could be regarded as closed for ever. Venice must reward, as she had promised to reward, those of her citizens who, through generosity, heroism or both, had rendered outstanding service in the hour of need. She would do so by offering them the most precious gift she had, one which many an Italian princeling had sought in vain: a place among her nobility. Even now, admission to this exclusive and exalted company was not to be taken for granted: each candidate had to submit to a proper election by secret ballot and, though in the circumstances such a procedure might have been thought to be largely a formality, it is reliably reported to have continued for the whole day and much of the night. We read with sorrow of a corn chandler named Leonardo dell' Agnello who, having offered to finance 150 mercenaries for a month, was understandably confident of election; disappointed, he died of a broken heart.

How many other candidates shared his disappointment we do not know; but on the morning of 5 September thirty new nobles, each carrying a lighted candle and followed by his family and friends, walked in procession to the Basilica for a special mass, and thence to the Palace to be formally presented to the Doge and Signoria. The ceremony was followed by a regatta and the usual celebrations in the Piazza; but what must have given the greatest joy to the populace was the fact that several of those honoured were tradesmen or artisans like themselves. Perhaps the Venetian aristocracy was not quite such a closed circle after all.

Despite the rigours of the Chioggia campaign, old Andrea Contarini was still, so far as we can gather, in reasonable health when the thirty came to do him reverence. He was to last one more winter; then, on 6 June 1382, he died. He was buried, rather surprisingly, in the cloister of S. Stefano. The sarcophagus is simple, its surroundings nowadays insalubrious;[1] Contarini, one feels, that reluctant Doge who served his country so well, merited something better – something, perhaps, more akin to that of his successor Michele Morosini who, having died of the plague after only four and a half months in office, was accorded a tomb – on the right-hand wall of the choir of SS. Giovanni e Paolo – described by Ruskin as 'the richest monument of the Gothic period in Venice'.[2]

Rich and high-principled, Morosini would have made an excellent Doge had he had time to prove his capabilities. It was no fault of his that he should have fallen victim, not only to one of those repeated outbreaks of the Black Death that punctuated the second half of the fourteenth century in Venice, but also to a contemporary misunderstanding that continues, still today, to besmirch his name. During the Chioggia crisis, when the future of Venice was at its bleakest, he is said to have made immense investments in real estate. His purpose was almost certainly to keep up property values and maintain confidence generally; and when asked the reason for such apparently rash behaviour he replied '*Se questa terra starà male, io non voglio aver ben*' – 'If this land is to come to grief, I do not wish to prosper.' Unfortunately the most popular version of Sanudo's *Lives of the Doges* misquotes him as having said '*io ne voglio aver ben*' – 'I wish to do well out of it'; and the calumny has stuck. Had the second version been the true one it would have cast serious doubts on Morosini's capacity, both moral and intellectual,

1. The cloister was rebuilt in the sixteenth century, and the atmosphere has not been improved by the offices of the Ministry of Finance to which it has now been given over.

2. Ruskin adds, as only he could have added, that the tomb furnishes 'not only the exactly intermediate condition in style between the pure Gothic and its final Renaissance corruption, but, at the same time, the exactly intermediate condition of *feeling* between the pure calmness of early Christianity, and the boastful pomp of the Renaissance faithlessness'.

to govern; and it is unthinkable that he would have been elected Doge
– particularly if, as some sources maintain, he had as a rival candidate
the surviving hero of the Genoese war, Carlo Zeno.

This last suggestion has caused much puzzled speculation among
modern historians, who have tended to suppose that Zeno was passed
over as a result of an insignificant reversal he had suffered shortly before
the end of the war. A far likelier explanation is that he was still a comparatively young man – not yet fifty – and an active one. Immured
in the Doges' Palace, his time largely taken up with state ceremonial,
he would have had little scope for his energies or talents. He could
be of far more use to the Republic in other capacities – as indeed, for
the next thirty-six years, he was.

On the death of Michele Morosini, and with Carlo Zeno still out of the
running, the choice of the electors now fell on a certain Antonio Venier.
The sixtieth Doge of Venice was at the time serving as *capitano* in Crete,
where his family – one of the oldest in the Republic – had settled some
time before; for three months the government was run by a Council
of Regency until, on 13 January 1383, Venier was able to return in
state to the Rialto, accompanied by the twelve noblemen who had been
sent to fetch him.[1]

He was, by all accounts, a stern and austere man with a highly developed
sense of justice; when his son was sentenced to a two-month prison
sentence after some foolish escapade[2] and fell seriously ill almost immediately afterwards, the Doge's refusal to grant him an early release – even
though the young man died as a result – earned Venier the respectful
admiration both of his subjects and of later historians. For the rest,
however, he seems to have devoted little time to domestic affairs. There
was no real need for him to do so. Unlike Genoa, now fast relapsing
into anarchy, Venice had emerged from six years of the most desperate
war in her history with her political system unshaken. No other state
in Italy could boast such stability, or anything approaching it. Internally,
the Republic virtually ran itself; its problems all came from abroad,

---

1. A small marble statue of a kneeling Doge (Plate 25) now in the Correr Museum, is almost
certainly a likeness of Antonio Venier. It is attributed to Jacobello dalle Masegne, his exact
contemporary who was responsible, *inter alia*, for the superb statues along the iconostasis of
St Mark's. (The museum also contains a double portrait of Venier and his successor Michele
Steno; but the painter, Lazzaro Bastiani, is first heard of in 1449 and did not die till 1512, so
this portrait cannot possibly have been done from life.)

2. He had, according to Horatio Brown, fastened to the front door of some distinguished
patrician 'a bunch of coral charms of curious form and opprobrious significance'.

and it was to the consolidation of Venice's position in Europe and the world that Antonio Venier and his advisers now applied themselves.

First of all, there was her commercial Empire to be rebuilt. The surrender of Dalmatia had been a blow, but for the time being at least she appeared to have no choice but to accept it. Besides, Dalmatia had never been an important trading partner; its value had been above all as a source of certain raw materials – wood and stone in particular – and as a base for operations further afield, with a coast that offered any number of superb natural harbours of a kind conspicuously lacking along the Italian shore of the Adriatic. Further south, the Peloponnesian ports of Modone and Corone were still safely in Venetian hands; Crete, after the collapse of another rebellion in 1363, had been enjoying an unwonted period of peace and comparative prosperity; and now that Genoa was no longer a rival Venice could settle down, without fear of hindrance or obstruction, to the task of renewing all her old trading links and establishing new ones – in the Levant, the Black Sea, and beyond to the furthest east. Permanent agents were established in all the important ports regularly visited by her ships, with warehouses in which to amass cargoes in preparation for the next arrival – speed of turn-around time was a point to which the Venetians attached great importance – and to store those recently delivered, lest prices should be forced down by too rapid a disposal. There was a Venetian agent resident in Siam ten years before the close of the century.

Nor did the Republic stop short at purely commercial expansion. Disillusioned now as to the desirability of territorial possessions on the Italian mainland and fatalistically resigned to the loss of Dalmatia, she was eager still to expand her Empire in the eastern Mediterranean. In 1356 she acquired Corfu. Taking shrewd advantage of the internal difficulties of the Kingdom of Naples to which the island nominally belonged, she suggested to the inhabitants that they needed some major power to protect them against potential aggressors; and the Corfiots in their turn – who knew perfectly well that any list of such aggressors would begin with the name of Venice herself – had little choice but to agree. A subsequent token payment to Naples was little more than a formality. By similar methods – a combination of political opportunism, business acumen, astute diplomacy and an occasional touch of blackmail – Venice was to acquire before the end of the century Scutari and Durazzo in southern Dalmatia, Nauplia and Argos in the Morea and most of the islands of the Cyclades and the Dodecanese.

Her reasons for embarking on this impressive programme of expansion were not exclusively commercial. Despite other preoccupations, she had been watching with mounting concern the progress of the Turks in their steady westward advance. In the last twenty years of the century this advance became something more like a rout. Serres fell in 1383, followed in rapid succession by Sofia, Nish, and Salonika. Finally in 1389, at the epic battle of Kosovo, the Ottoman armies crushed Serbia and destroyed the last hopes of independence for the Balkan Slavs. Bulgaria survived only four more years. Now the days of Byzantium itself were seen to be numbered. Apart from a few islands in the Aegean, the Roman Empire of the East was virtually coterminous with its capital, Constantinople, where the Emperor reigned on Turkish sufferance, aware that his only chance of maintaining his throne lay in total submission to the will of the Sultan. The feeble old John V Palaeologus died in senile debauchery in 1391;[1] his son Manuel II was a good and gifted man who in happier circumstances might have restored the Empire to something of its former greatness, but he was powerless to stem the Ottoman tide. Before his father's death he had been forced to live at the Sultan's court as a vassal – and a hostage to ensure his father's submissive behaviour – even on occasion fighting on the Turkish side against his fellow-Greeks. As reigning Emperor in Constantinople his position was scarcely less humiliating.

In such a situation it was only to be expected that when in 1396 King Sigismund of Hungary appealed to Christian Europe to join him in a combined onslaught against the Turkish threat Venice, despite past differences with his kingdom, should have responded – at least to the extent of putting her Black Sea fleet at his disposal. Unfortunately, few other European states followed her lead. The whole continent raised only some 60,000 men, and though this figure included the flower of the French knighthood, it was the latter's over-confidence and lack of discipline which was responsible more than any other single factor for the ensuing catastrophe. They had boasted before the battle that, if heaven itself were to fall, they could support it on the points of their lances; but they were no match for Sultan Bajazet. Once again living up to his nickname of *Yilderim* – lightning – he sped to meet their advance and when they reached Nicopolis on the Danube he was ready to receive them. The battle, which took place on 28 September 1396,

1. Gibbon writes that 'love, or rather lust, was his only vigorous passion; and in the embraces of the wives and virgins of the city the Turkish slave forgot the dishonour of the Emperor of the *Romans*'.

was short and bloody; bloodier still was its aftermath, when 10,000 French prisoners were beheaded in the Sultan's presence. Those who escaped, including Sigismund himself, did so on Venetian ships; a German eye-witness, who had been taken captive but whose extreme youth had saved him from execution, tells how as these vessels passed through the Dardanelles he and 300 other surviving prisoners were drawn up on the banks and made to jeer at the conquered King.[1]

The part played by Venice in this unedifying story was scarcely heroic; yet the battle of Nicopolis is important in her history since it marks the point at which most of western Europe simply ceased to concern itself with the Turkish menace until it felt directly threatened more than a century later. Incredibly enough, the dying Empire was still to endure another fifty-seven years, but by now it had become less of a shield than a liability. Manuel was obliged to establish a mosque in his capital, and a court to administer the law of Islam; still the princes of Christendom remained unmoved. Venice, and Venice alone, seemed aware of the danger. Equipped neither physically nor by temperament to lead Crusades, even she could do no more than defend her interests if they were attacked. But when she did so she defended Europe too.

The same sound, if occasionally unscrupulous, statesmanship that enabled Venice to extend her domains in the eastern Mediterranean dictated her policy on the Italian mainland, and with similar success. Her old enemy Francesco da Carrara, though balked of his expected triumph in 1380 by the Genoese collapse and the surrender of Treviso to Duke Leopold of Austria rather than to himself, had lost none of his former truculence. He had not seen Venice defeated as he had hoped; but he had seen her shaken, frightened and humbled. He himself, meanwhile, had discovered just how easily he could subdue the Venetian territories on *terra firma* and had emerged from the Genoese war stronger than when he had entered it. Clearly, the sooner he returned to the offensive the better. In 1382 he laid siege to Treviso.

The result was even more successful than he had expected. Duke Leopold had been ready enough to accept Treviso when the Venetians had offered it to him, but he was not prepared to put himself to much trouble or expense defending it. He now simply sold the city to Carrara, together with Belluno, Ceneda and Feltre and, with them, the control of one of the most important trade routes through the Dolomites and into the Tyrol. The price was 100,000 ducats; the value to Carrara,

1. Johann Schiltberger, *Hakluyt Society*, Vol. 58, 1879.

now once more in possession of virtually all the Venetian mainland, was incalculable.

Without resorting again to mercenaries, which she could at that moment ill afford, Venice had no land army worthy of the name. On the other hand she knew that Carrara had no fleet – nor, with Genoa in her present state, any hope of obtaining one. She rightly guessed, therefore, that rather than risk an advance across the lagoon he would turn his attention westward, where the last of the once-great dynasty of the Scaligeri, Antonio della Scala, still kept a rather tenuous hold on Verona and Vicenza – two ripe plums ready for the plucking. And so, serious as the situation was, she made no immediate attempt to retaliate. She would wait and see.

It was not that Doge Venier and his advisers viewed with equanimity the prospect of a Paduan empire extending over the entire Veneto up to her very doorstep. But they had also foreseen something else: that easy as Carrara might find such new conquests in themselves, they would bring him in direct confrontation with Gian Galeazzo Visconti, old Bernabò's nephew, who had recently overthrown his uncle, almost certainly poisoned him, and made himself master of Milan – a *coup* for whose success he was shortly to render thanks by laying the foundations of Milan cathedral. Scheming, dissembling, driven onward by wild ambition and an insatiable lust for power, of all his remarkable family Gian Galeazzo was the most dangerous. Confrontation with such a man would inevitably, sooner or later, mean opposition; and opposition, by Gian Galeazzo Visconti, would mean defeat. Venice, then, need only bide her time. There was no cause for her to take up arms against Carrara. He could be trusted to destroy himself.

To be sure, he was not such a fool as to march against Antonio della Scala without prior consultation with Milan; and on 19 April 1387 he and Gian Galeazzo concluded an agreement to expel the Scaligeri once and for all and to share the conquered territories between them, Verona falling to Milan and Vicenza to Padua. At first everything went as planned. After putting up a token resistance, Verona surrendered; Antonio fled to Venice and thence to Florence and Rome, only to die of poison himself shortly afterwards. But it was not for nothing that the Visconti had chosen a viper as their crest; ignoring the terms of his agreement, Gian Galeazzo seized Vicenza too.

Only now did Francesco Carrara see what Venice had seen all along – that he had been made the dupe of the Milanese who intended, now that he had outlived his usefulness, to devour him in his turn. Swallowing his pride, he appealed to Doge Venier, pointing out that Visconti would prove an infinitely greater danger to the Republic than he himself had ever been, and that the only hope of Venetian salvation lay in supporting an independent Padua as a buffer state between them. Once again, however, Visconti had forestalled him – by sending ambassadors to the Rialto offering, in return for recognition of his rights to Padua, the restitution of Ceneda and Treviso and of certain strategic strongholds around the shores of the lagoon.

It cannot have been an easy decision for the Doge to take. Carrara's argument may have been dictated by self-interest, but its strength was undeniable. Twice in less than a year, Gian Galeazzo had proved how dangerous he was as a neighbour. There was no reason to believe, when the moment came, that he would show Venice any more consideration than he had shown Verona or Padua. But the recent war, if it had done nothing else, had confirmed the Venetians in their belief that their city was impregnable; they needed control of Treviso and the mountain passes, without which their trade with central Europe was crippled; finally they knew that, useful as a buffer state might be, it could never function as such under Francesco Carrara, whom they detested and were determined to destroy. On 29 May 1388, they formally accepted the Milanese proposals.

Even now Carrara did not altogether give up hope. In the understandable belief that Venice's decision might have been prompted solely by animosity to him personally, he abdicated in favour of his son Francesco, called – to distinguish him from his father – Novello. But it was no use. A Visconti army marched on Padua, a Venetian squadron sailed up the Brenta and Francesco Novello surrendered. The Carraras, father and son, were interned at Monza and Asti respectively; and Venice settled down to watch her new and deadly neighbour.

Her policy towards Gian Galeazzo Visconti was a simple one: to get rid of him as soon as possible. Obviously she could not achieve this alone; but in the endlessly shifting kaleidoscope of North Italian politics there was one pattern that recurred time and time again: that of a single state growing too large and too powerful, thus causing its sister states to unite against it and bring about its destruction. In this pattern Venice put her trust. Gian Galeazzo was by now the most powerful prince in Europe, stronger by far than Richard II of England or the mentally unstable Charles VI of France. But he was not yet satisfied. Less than a year after he had seized Padua, he turned against Florence and Bologna.

He had overreached himself. Francesco Novello, having escaped with his family from Asti, had spent the interim drumming up opposition to the Visconti, and was the principal architect of the league that now took shape. With himself, Florence and Bologna it also included Francesco Gonzaga of Mantua, Antonio della Scala's dispossessed son Can Francesco of Verona, and Duke Robert of Bavaria. What it now needed above all else was the support of Venice. This time Venice did not hesitate. Only two years before, she had been the ally of Gian Galeazzo and the implacable enemy of the Carraras; but loyalty was a luxury that no Italian state could afford. Her diplomacy depended on preserving a balance of power by playing one enemy off against another. Effortlessly and without embarrassment she changed sides, joined the league and, while carefully avoiding open warfare, willingly gave Francesco Novello and the young della Scala leave to use her reacquired territory of Treviso as a springboard for their attempt to recover Padua.

The spring of 1390 was hot and dry; and on the night of 18 June Francesco Novello led a small force silently along the almost waterless bed of the Brenta into the centre of his native city. A wooden stockade – the only defence – was quickly breached and the people of Padua, for whom two years had been more than enough time to repent of their overhasty welcome of a Milanese master, received back their hereditary lord with open arms. His triumph may well have spelt salvation for Florence; it was certainly a serious check to the progress of Gian Galeazzo, who was forced to withdraw a considerable part of his army from Tuscany to prevent the revolt spreading to Verona – which had made a similar, though in this case unsuccessful, bid for independence – and beyond. To increase his worries he also found himself hard pressed by that extraordinary soldier of fortune the Englishman Sir John Hawkwood, now in Florentine service, who pursued him as far as the river Adda and would have inflicted severe damage but for the disastrous generalship of his French colleague Jean d'Armagnac. In short, Francesco Novello's reconquest of Padua transformed a potentially dangerous military crisis into a stalemate; and it seems to have been a relief for all parties when peace was concluded at Genoa in 1392. The young Carrara, who had been careful to obtain Venice's approval to this treaty before signing it, now appeared in person to do homage to the Doge, thanking him for his support and being in return received into the ranks of the Venetian nobility.

Having played no active role in the war, Venice was not herself a signatory of the treaty; it represented, none the less, everything she could possibly have hoped for. Not only had she recovered Treviso; by her shrewd diplomacy, and without the shedding of a drop of Venetian blood, she had also curbed the growing power of Milan and, in Padua, had substituted the well-disposed, even submissive Francesco Novello for his insufferable father. She did not deceive herself, however, that the peace signified anything more than a breathing space. Gian Galeazzo Visconti might have failed to gain all he expected, but he had lost nothing either. Already he was gathering forces for a new offensive – and three years later it came.

At first it seemed as though Gian Galeazzo's enemies might be able to hold him in check. When he marched on Mantua in 1395 Venice, Florence and Bologna, with active help from Carrara in Padua, sprang to their neighbour's defence; the fighting was inconclusive and a truce was soon declared, leading in 1400 to another brief and uneasy peace. This equilibrium was however shattered early in 1402 when the new western Emperor-elect Rupert of the Palatinate, on his way – as he hoped – to his imperial coronation in Rome, was persuaded to call a halt in Lombardy and crush his dangerously ambitious vassal. His attempt met with abject failure. Equally short of men and money, he seems to have had no idea of Gian Galeazzo's strength, or of conditions in Italy. By April, after no more than minor skirmishes, he was forced to return to Germany, broken and humiliated.

This defeat of the greatest prince of the West had a tonic effect on Visconti. He smashed his way into Bologna and then turned the whole weight of his forces against Florence. With Pisa, Siena and Lucca already under his control, there seemed no hope for the city. If it fell, Tuscany would join Lombardy, Umbria and Romagna as dependencies of Milan; how long, then, could Venice hold out? Gian Galeazzo had never been stronger or better equipped. He was still only fifty years old. His coffers were full, his men seasoned and in splendid heart. The North Italian Kingdom, stretching from Genoa to the Adriatic, on which he had focused his political ambitions seemed at last to be within his grasp.

Then, without warning, on 13 August 1402, he was struck down by fever; and three weeks later he died. To the Venetians his death must have seemed like a miracle – the more so since his vast dominions now fell to his three sons, the eldest of whom was only thirteen. His widow, who was appointed regent, proved utterly incapable of controlling either them or the rapacious generals and *condottieri* who, after years of fighting for the Visconti, now saw the opportunity of helping themselves to their lands; and by the end of the year the Duchy of Milan, the strongest power in Europe only six months before, had begun to crumble away.

Now, too, other erstwhile enemies of Gian Galeazzo began to move in – among the first being Francesco Novello Carrara, who marched on Vicenza. Knowing the internal difficulties of Milan, he seems to have expected little opposition; but he had reckoned without the Vicentines themselves who, having just escaped the clutches of one political adventurer, had no wish to fall victim to another. They could not, however, stand on their own; and so, without further fuss, they offered themselves to Venice. Their embassy reached the Rialto at much the same time as one from the Duchess of Milan herself, imploring Venetian aid against Carrara and offering both Vicenza and Verona in return.

With Gian Galeazzo gone, there was no longer any reason for the Venetians to maintain their alliance with Francesco Novello. Indeed, every instinct told them that they would have no lasting peace until his whole dynasty was destroyed. The promise of Verona and Vicenza – with Padua, which would obviously revert to them once he was out of the way – meant the possession of the three key cities of north-east Italy commanding the approach to Venice on her vulnerable, landward side. A herald was dispatched forthwith to Francesco Novello, beneath the walls of Vicenza, calling on him to withdraw. Now, for the first time, the young Carrara – hitherto an obedient ally of the Republic – showed his defiance. 'Let us make a lion of St Mark of this herald,' he is alleged to have said, and gave orders that the man's nose should be slit and his ears cut off.

The action was not only inhumane; it was also foolhardy. A diplomatic retreat by Francesco Novello at that moment, depriving Venice of her *casus belli*, might still have saved his dynasty. By that action he destroyed it – and, ultimately, himself. Driven back from Vicenza, he was obliged to immure himself in his own city of Padua where, to give him his due, he put up a courageous resistance to a Venetian siege, refusing the reasonable terms which, on more than one occasion, he was offered. At last, however, a combination of famine and a renewed outbreak of plague – that continuing scourge that overshadowed Europe throughout the later fourteenth and early fifteenth centuries – compelled him to submit. On 17 November 1404 Padua fell. Francesco was brought in chains, with his son Jacopo, to Venice. Such was the popular feeling against him – aggravated by a widespread rumour that he had been plotting to poison the wells of the city – that he and Jacopo were at first held, for their own safety, on S. Giorgio Maggiore; only some days later were they transferred to that special place of captivity on the top floor of the Doges' Palace which was kept for prisoners of high rank.

By then, however, new information had come to light about Carrara's recent activities. He had had no sinister designs on the wells; he had, however, organized a vast conspiracy to overthrow the Republic from within – a conspiracy which, as more and more of its ramifications were uncovered, was seen to involve several members of the Venetian nobility. The Council of Ten, assisted by six more officers specially co-opted for the task, sat day and night opening further channels of inquiry and interrogating hundreds of suspects, many of them under torture. The more they investigated, the more evidence they found – and all led back, ineluctably, to the Carraras. Father and son were condemned to death. The story that they were suspended in an iron cage from the roof of the palace is unfounded;[1] the two were strangled in prison on 17 January 1405, Francesco Novello defending himself to the end, heroically but in vain, with a wooden stool.

The fourteenth century had been hard for Venice – the hardest century, perhaps, in her history. It had begun with two attempts at revolution, by Marin Bocconio and, more seriously, Bajamonte Tiepolo; and half-way through its course it had produced a third, when old Marin Falier brought disgrace both to the Republic and to the dogeship and paid for it with what remained of his life. Soon afterwards, suspicions surrounding the conduct of Lorenzo Celsi had still further undermined the ducal prestige. Abroad, there had been rebellions in Crete, Trieste and elsewhere, the loss of Dalmatia, and, continuing intermittently for fifty years, the fateful trial of strength with Genoa. In mainland Italy the Republic's princely neighbours, whether della Scala, Visconti or Carrara, had given her no respite; and since 1348 the Black Death, returning remorselessly every few years to cut another great swathe through the population, never allowed itself to be forgotten.

For all that, Venice had achieved much. To begin with, she had established herself once and for all on *terra firma*: with the fall of the

1. Romanin (Vol. IV, p. 39) says that he has found only one instance of this punishment, when, in the sixteenth century, a priest found guilty of *enormi delitti* was thus suspended from the campanile of St Mark's – and even then managed to escape. The confusion probably arose from the fact that the Venetian dialect word for a cage, *cheba* (Italian *gabbia*), was also used for the small prison in the Doges' Palace.

house of Carrara she found herself in possession of considerable mainland territories, from the Tagliamento in the east to the shores of Lake Garda in the west, south to the Adige and north to the hills above Bassano. These territories she was later to increase; but they would never essentially be diminished – except for a brief period in the early sixteenth century – until the Republic itself came to an end.

By 1400 the Venetians can have had few delusions about their status as a European power. They had learnt, to their cost, just what it meant in practice to have long and often imprecise land frontiers to defend against predatory neighbours, and they knew all too well the expense of hiring mercenaries and maintaining them in the field. On the other hand there were obvious gains in prestige and in the influence that they would henceforth be able to wield in the affairs not only of Italy but of the whole continent, where their trading position would also be immeasurably strengthened. Moreover, their confidence was buttressed by the one great advantage that they alone possessed over all their rivals – an advantage that their recent tribulations had served only to confirm: in so far as any city could ever be, theirs was impregnable.

For, despite the new terrestrial image that she presented to the world, Venice still belonged to the sea. By it, and by the 3,300 ships and 36,000 seamen that she could boast by the close of the fourteenth century, she was both protected and enriched. No other major Italian city could claim to have remained inviolate for close on 1,000 years. No other could boast such wealth or, more important still, such powers of recuperation – powers that enabled her, when her treasury was drained by foreign wars and her economy lay apparently in ruins, to make a recovery so swift and so complete as to leave her enemies gasping. The effect was almost that of a conjuring trick, and she performed it again and again. But without her unique position it would never have been possible. Not only was she nearer than any of her competitors to the Eastern markets – the source of all those Oriental luxuries which Europe, having once developed a taste for them, was demanding more and more insistently; but the fact that the sea was, almost literally, her home had obliged her, from her earliest beginnings, to achieve a mastery over it that her rivals might occasionally challenge but could never match for long. Taken as a whole, over the years, the Venetians always remained better and faster shipbuilders, more accurate navigators and more resourceful seamen than anyone else.

And above all – particularly after the eclipse of Genoa – more successful merchants. By the end of the fourteenth century there was scarcely a single major commodity which was not largely transported in Venetian ships. Eastward and southward went timber from the Harz mountains and metals from the mines of Bohemia; northward and westward the spices from India and the Orient, to which had more recently been added cotton from Asia Minor and the Levant, and increasing quantities of sugar, the demand for which was now insatiable throughout Europe. The first supplies had come from Syria as early as the eleventh century, but by now Venetian entrepreneurs had introduced it in Crete and, with outstanding success, in Cyprus, when one Federico Corner established plantations on such a scale and ran them with such efficiency as to make his family within very few years the richest in Venice.[1] These two islands, together with parts of the Morea, were also the main producers of that sweet, heavy wine known as malmsey (from the port of Monemvasia whence most of it was shipped) which the English and their neighbours in northern Europe quaffed with such relish; and from the 1330s a regular and exceedingly profitable pattern had developed according to which Venetian merchant galleys carried it to English ports and there exchanged it for English wool. This they would take across to sell in Flanders, buying in return the bales of fine Flemish cloth or the finished woollen cloaks and gowns for which they could get high prices throughout Europe and even in the Levant. So lucrative did this triangular trade become that in 1349 it was nationalized and run thenceforth as a state monopoly.

Other patterns became less prosperous as the century progressed. Regular commerce with Russia, in particular, began to decline from about the 1360s, when civil war in the Mongol-occupied lands to the north and east of the Black Sea made the caravan routes unsafe. Thirty years later they were closed altogether when the cities along the Volga, which had served as essential staging posts, were destroyed by Tamburlaine. Precious furs immediately became rarer, and correspondingly more expensive, in the markets of the South. The slave trade, however, continued unabated. Despite repeated edicts by the Papacy and occasional somewhat tentative legislation by the Republic itself – going back to a law promulgated by Doge Orso Participazio in the ninth century – this had never ceased to flourish in Venice. A relatively small number of African negroes from East and West Africa and the Sahara were brought to the slave markets at S. Giorgio and the Rialto by Arab traders in gold and ivory, but the overwhelming majority of the slaves were Christians from the Caucasus – Georgians, Armenians and Circas-

1. See p. 260n.

sians – who had been taken prisoner by the Tartars and were sold by them at Black Sea ports. Most of these found their way, as domestic servants, bodyguards and concubines, to Egypt, North Africa and the Ottoman court. Occasionally, some might achieve positions of real power, as with the slave army of the Mamelukes, who were supreme in Egypt from the thirteenth century until the arrival of Napoleon, or as Janissaries or eunuchs at the Sultan's court. Others were purchased by wealthy Italian families in Tuscany and the North. The remainder, unluckiest of all, probably ended up working the vast agricultural estates in Crete and Cyprus – where Federico Corner's sugar plantations had been built up almost entirely on a slave economy.

Venice, it need hardly be said, received her full share of all these commodities; and there was another import in which she was not primarily a middleman but was herself the chief consumer. This was grain. Bitter experience had taught her that it was dangerous to rely on a single area for so vital a necessity. Drought or excessive rainfall could destroy a harvest; revolts or civil upheavals could prevent shipments; and even if both climatic and political conditions were favourable, there was always the possibility of pirates to be reckoned with. In consequence she had taken pains to diversify her sources of supply; and the Venetian grain ships that sailed up the Adriatic from the traditional cornfields of Sicily and Apulia were now joined by others coming from Anatolia and even the Black Sea.

Conversely, there was one product of her own – apart from manufactured goods – of which she was usually able to export a surplus. From the earliest days of the Republic she had jealously guarded her monopoly of the saltworks in the valley and delta of the Po and had never hesitated to fight for them when necessary. As time went on and the European demand for salt continued to increase, they became inadequate; further supplies had to be brought in from Dalmatia, Cyprus and elsewhere. But the domestic sources of production had by then come to be looked on with almost superstitious veneration and continued to enjoy a degree of protection well beyond their intrinsic worth.

There were other reasons too for her extraordinary economic resilience. Firstly she was trusted. By now she had built up a network of trading contacts half-way across the world, and a reputation for fair dealing – which did not exclude hard bargaining – that made it an easy matter to resume operations after an interruption. Secondly there was the Venetian character – tough, hardworking, determined, with an ingrained respect for wealth and a boundless ambition to acquire it. Thirdly came the firm discipline, born of long experience, imposed by the state.

For the state, where trade was concerned, left nothing to chance; and by 1400 it was taking over more and more of Venetian economic life. The days of private enterprise on the grand scale were almost gone. All the merchant galleys were built in the Arsenal and state-owned; the Republic kept the monopoly on many of the most profitable routes and cargoes. Even the ships that remained in private hands were obliged to conform to the strict specifications laid down by the Senate. The advantages were obvious. Given such conformity, all the vessels in a given convoy could be trusted to behave similarly in bad weather and so, with luck, to stay together; the convoy's speed, and consequently its arrival dates, could be more accurately estimated; standardized spares could be kept available in agencies and outposts overseas and quick convertibility to warships guaranteed in an emergency. By the end of the fourteenth century there were normally six of these major trading convoys a year, each consisting of up to 500 ships – occasionally more – and each bound for a different destination, but each sailing on appointed dates, and following specified routes, fixed months ahead. Most would be state-owned, their command – which was open to the nobility only – leased by auction to the highest bidder for the duration of the voyage; but every merchant and captain involved, whether owner or lessor, was bound by oath to obey the instructions issued by the Senate and to uphold 'the honour of St Mark'.

As always, increased public ownership led to increased taxation. A hundred years before, Venetian taxes had been among the lowest in Europe. No longer. Not only were there the soaring costs of the Arsenal and its 16,000 workers to be met; but the spread of state control had spawned hosts of civil servants, lawyers, notaries and accountants – to say nothing of a whole army of eagle-eyed tax collectors famous for their niggling accuracy – all of whom had to be paid for by the Republic. Small traders continued to be encouraged; if they could not afford, or spare, ships of their own for their ventures they always enjoyed the right – so long as they were Venetians – to demand cargo space on the state-owned convoys at fixed and reasonable rates. But for the grand old merchant adventurers like the Polos there was no longer a place. The Republic might be richer than it had ever been, and the city more beautiful; but much of the early romance had gone.

At this time, too, Venice felt herself obliged to take her first far-reaching measures against her Jewish population. These were in no sense intended as any form of racial or religious persecution, nor did the victims look upon them as such. The simple fact appears to have been that in the vastly more complicated economic system that had by now evolved, borrowing from the Jews (and, in the absence of public banks or even pawnshops, borrowing from any other source was impossible) had got seriously out of hand. In 1374 the Jews of Mestre had been encouraged to settle in Venice – technically for only five years, but this term was easily extended – and twenty years later few Venetian citizens were not, to a greater or a lesser degree, in hock. And so, after the failure of several attempts at controlling legislation, in 1395 all Jews were expelled from the city and allowed to return only for periods not exceeding fifteen days. Even then they were obliged to carry distinguishing marks – first a yellow circle on the breast, later a yellow cap, later still tall hats of prescribed colours. They were forbidden to hold real property and to keep schools; only those of them who were doctors were encouraged to continue.

Gradually, they returned, and the residence rules were again relaxed. For the next three centuries until the fall of the Republic, their fortunes would fluctuate; but their numbers remained considerable, their influence likewise. Culturally as well as economically, Venice would have been a poorer place without them.

In industry, too, the hand of the state was everywhere apparent. The most important branches were rigidly protected, with government bans on the export of certain raw materials; skilled artificers were forbidden to leave the city, while to reveal the secrets of key manufacturing processes was an offence punishable by death. (Foreign craftsmen, on the other hand, such as the German makers of looking-glasses and the silk workers from Lucca[1] were encouraged to settle in Venice and even, as an additional inducement, exempted from taxation for the first two years of their residence.) Most of the official controls on industrial standards and conditions of work[2] were imposed through the guilds, whose carefully-framed statutes were all subject to the approval of government supervisors; within broad limits, however, these organizations enjoyed a considerable measure of autonomy and proved of increasing value, as the years passed, both to their members and to the state. Unlike the guilds of other Italian towns – the *Arti* of Florence

1. See p. 226.
2. The latter, particularly those relating to children, were far in advance of any similar legislation passed in England before the nineteenth century.

for example – they never became, or attempted to become, a political force in the Republic: most of their members had been disenfranchised since the *Serrata del Gran Consiglio*, while the patricians whose power they might elsewhere have been led to oppose were, in the peculiar conditions pertaining to Venice, not feudal aristocrats but, in all probability, guild members themselves. On the other hand, the guilds provided a large number of honest, public-spirited and often wealthy tradesmen with a means of benefiting the community and so preserving their pride and self-respect. They also formed the basis for a remarkably effective system of social security, caring for their members in sickness and old age and assuming responsibility for their widows and children on their deaths. As they grew richer, their benevolence spread beyond the limits of their own membership; and of the forty-odd buildings of the Venetian *scuole* that survive today, many still testify to the wealth and importance of the organizations for which they were built.[1]

But the guilds did not have the monopoly of charitable foundations. By the end of the fourteenth century there were probably a dozen or more of these latter that had been privately endowed by wealthy citizens – sometimes, doubtless, for reasons of prestige but often for genuinely philanthropic motives. We know, for example, that old Doge Zorzi maintained a home for poor children; and similar institutions existed for the benefit of poor women, foundlings, reformed prostitutes and various other categories in need, together with free hospitals – at least one of them financed by its own chief surgeon.

Public health was, however, early accepted as a state responsibility, and to the Venetian Republic must go the honour of having founded the first national health service in Europe, if not in the world. Already in 1335 the state was paying a full-time salary to twelve doctor-surgeons who, together with all other licensed practitioners, were obliged by law to attend an annual course in anatomy, which included the dissection of corpses. After the establishment of the state-run School of Medicine in 1368, they were also required to attend monthly meetings to exchange notes on new cases and treatments. By that time any physician anywhere in Italy who achieved exceptional distinction could be sure, sooner or later, to receive an invitation to settle in Venice, accompanied by such financial inducements as would make it hard

1. Pre-eminent among these are the *Scuole* of the Carmini, of S. Giorgio degli Schiavoni, of S. Giovanni Evangelista and of S. Rocco; and, among those which have been converted to other uses, those of S. Marco (now the Civic Hospital) and of S. Maria della Carità (now the Accademia).

for him to refuse. In the field of law, on the other hand, the Republic had already become an exporter of talent, and Venetian legists were to be found in positions of authority the length and breadth of the peninsula; while as administrators – particularly in the capacity of rector and *podestà* in foreign cities – her citizens were in such demand that in 1306 it became necessary to pass a law forbidding the acceptance of these and similar posts without special permission from the Senate.

It was no wonder, therefore, that by 1400 Venice was respected and envied beyond all the cities of Europe – famed alike for her wealth, her beauty, her good government, and for a system of justice which gave impartial protection to rich and poor, aristocrat and artisan, Venetian and foreigner; for, in theory at any rate and for the most part in practice too, every man living beneath the banner of St Mark was equal in the sight of the law. It was no wonder that strangers came flocking – merchants, pilgrims bound for the Holy Land, and increasing numbers of simple travellers spurred less by commerce or piety than by curiosity and a thirst for adventure – to the point where, as a contemporary wrote, the rough accents of the Venetians were lost in the babel of strange tongues that was to be heard daily on the Piazza. Here, unlike any other sea-port on the Mediterranean, they knew that they would not be swindled – the Republic maintained a specially-trained corps of officials whose sole duty it was to look after strangers, to find them accommodation and to see that they received all the help they needed, that their wine was not watered and that they were never overcharged – and they also knew that, by the simple expedient of walking along the Riva, they could be virtually certain of finding a ship to take them on the next stage of their journey. Anyway – in the unlikely event of such a vessel not being immediately available – was Venice not a destination in herself?

Finally, it was no wonder that the native citizens of Venice accounted themselves privileged among other men, proud of the city that had given them birth and of the Empire it had won. They might, for the most part, have little or no say in the government of the Republic, but comparison of their lot with that of the populations on the mainland did not suggest that the latter were substantially better off in this or any other respect; besides, they were sensible enough to know that it was better to be well governed, even without political influence than subject to the whim of an ambitious and frequently tyrannical despot. They might feel irritated, from time to time, by the petty regulations and restrictions through which the state sought to interfere with so many aspects of their daily life; but if this was the price of living in the richest, safest, best ordered and most beautiful city in the civilized world they were prepared to pay it. In the century that was past they had worked hard, fought desperately, and suffered much. Now at last their enemies were crushed or scattered, and they looked forward to the century to come with confidence and hope.

List of Doges

726–1400

Orso Ipato	726–737	Vitale Michiel I	1096–1102
Interregnum	737–742	Ordelafo Falier	1102–1118
Teodato Ipato	742–755	Domenico Michiel	1118–1130
Galla Gaulo	755–756	Pietro Polani	1130–1148
Domenico Monegario	756–764	Domenico Morosini	1148–1156
Maurizio Galbaio	764–775	Vitale Michiel II	1156–1172
Giovanni Galbaio	775–804	Sebastiano Ziani	1172–1178
Obelario degli Antenori	804–811	Orio Mastropiero	1178–1192
Agnello Participazio	811–827	Enrico Dandolo	1192–1205
Giustiniano Participazio	827–829	Pietro Ziani	1205–1229
Giovanni Participazio I	829–836	Giacomo Tiepolo	1229–1249
Pietro Tradonico	836–864	Marin Morosini	1249–1253
Orso Participazio I	864–881	Renier Zeno	1253–1268
Giovanni Participazio II	881–887	Lorenzo Tiepolo	1268–1275
Pietro Candiano I	887	Jacopo Contarini	1275–1280
Pietro Tribuno	888–912	Giovanni Dandolo	1280–1289
Orso Participazio II	912–932	Pietro Gradenigo	1289–1311
Pietro Candiano II	932–939	Marino Zorzi	1311–1312
Pietro Participazio	939–942	Giovanni Soranzo	1312–1328
Pietro Candiano III	942–959	Francesco Dandolo	1329–1339
Pietro Candiano IV	959–976	Bartolomeo Gradenigo	1339–1342
Pietro Orseolo I	976–978	Andrea Dandolo	1343–1354
Vitale Candiano	978–979	Marin Falier	1354–1355
Tribuno Memmo	979–991	Giovanni Gradenigo	1355–1356
Pietro Orseolo II	991–1008	Giovanni Dolfin	1356–1361
Otto Orseolo	1008–1026	Lorenzo Celsi	1361–1365
Pietro Centranico	1026–1032	Marco Corner	1365–1368
Domenico Flabanico	1032–1043	Andrea Contarini	1368–1382
Domenico Contarini	1043–1071	Michele Morosini	1382
Domenico Selvo	1071–1084	Antonio Venier	1382–1400
Vitale Falier	1084–1096		

Bibliography

I. ORIGINAL SOURCES

1. Collections of Sources

(The abbreviations used elsewhere in this Bibliography and in the footnotes follow each entry in parentheses.)

Archivio Storico Italiano, 1st series (Florence, various dates). (A.S.I.)

Calendar of State Papers, Venetian, 38 vols., edited and translated by Rawdon Brown (London, 1864–1940). (C.S.P.V.)

CESSI, R., *Documenti Relativi alla Storia di Venezia anteriori al Mille. Cura di Roberto Cessi* (Padua, 1942). (C.D.R.S.V.)

Corpus Scriptorum Historiae Byzantinae (Bonn, 1828–97). (C.S.H.B.)

Cronache Veneziane Antichissime, ed. G. Monticolo (Rome, 1890). (C.V.A.)

Documenti del Commercio Veneziano, XI–XIII sec. (Rome, 1940). (D.C.V.)

GRAEVIUS, J. C., *Thesaurus Antiquitatum et Historiarum Italiae, etc.*, 10 vols. in 45 fol. (Leyden, 1704–25). (G.T.A.)

MIGNE, J. P., *Patrologia Latina*, 221 vols. (Paris, 1844–55). (M.P.L.)

MURATORI, L. A., *Rerum Italicarum Scriptores*, 25 vols. (Milan, 1723–51). (M.R.I.S.)

Recueil des Historiens des Croisades, Publ. Académie des Inscriptions et des Belles Lettres (Paris, 1841–1906). Historiens Occidentaux, 5 vols. (R.H.C.Occ.)

2. Individual Sources

Altino Chronicle, in A.S.I., Vol. 8.

CHINAZZO, D., *Belli inter Venetos et Genuenses, 1378*, in M.R.I.S., Vol. 15.

Cronica de singulis patriarchis Nove Aquileie, in C.V.A.

DANDOLO, Andrea, *Chronicon Venetum*, in M.R.I.S., Vol. 12 (new edn by E. Pastorello, Bologna, 1938–42).

GIUSTINIANI, Bernardo, *De Marci vita, ejus translatione et sepulturae loco*, in G.T.A., Vol. 5, i.

GIUSTINIANI, Bernardo, *Historia dell' origine di Venetia*, in G.T.A., Vol. 5, i. *Grado Chronicle*, in C.V.A.

INNOCENT III, Pope, *Letters*, in M.P.L., Vol. 215.

JOHN THE DEACON, *Cronaca veneziana*, in C.V.A., and M.P.L., Vol. 139.

LORENZO DE MONACIS, *Chron. de rebus Venetis*, ed. F. Cornelius, Venice, 1758 (also in M.R.I.S.), Vol. 8.

MARTIN DA CANALE, *Chron. des Veniciens*, ed. F. L. Polidori, in A.S.I., Vol. 8.

NICETAS CHONIATES, *Historia*, in C.S.H.B. (French trans. by L. Cousin in *Histoire de Constantinople*, Vol. 5, Paris, 1685).

PETER DAMIAN, St, *Vita Sancti Romualdi*, in M.P.L., Vol. 144.

PETER DAMIAN, St, *Opuscula*, in M.P.L., Vol. 145.

PETRARCH, Francesco, *Epistolae de rebus familiaribus et variae*, ed. G. Fracassetti, 3 vols., (Florence, 1859–63). (Italian trans. by G. Fracassetti, 5 vols., Florence, 1863–7).

POLO, Marco, *The Travels of Marco Polo*, tr. R. Latham (Harmondsworth, 1958).

ROBERT OF CLARY, *La Conquête de Constantinople*, ed. Lauer (Paris, 1924).

SANUTO (or SANUDO), Marino (the elder), *Liber secretorum fidelium crucis super Terrae Sanctae recuperatione*, in Bongars, *Gesta Dei per Francos*, Vol. II, Hanover, 1611.

STELLA, Georgius, *Annales Genuenses, 1298–1409*, in M.R.I.S., Vol. 17.

TREVISAN, Nicolò, *Chronicle*, in Biblioteca Marciana, Cl. xi, Ital. Codex xxxii.

VILLEHARDOUIN, Geoffrey of, *La Conquête de Constantinople*, ed. E. Faral, 2 vols. (Paris, 1938–9).

WILLIAM OF TYRE, *Belli sacri historia*, and *Historia rerum in partibus transmarinis gestarum*, in R.H.C.Occ., Vol. I.

WILLIAM OF TYRE, *A History of Deeds done beyond the Sea*, tr. with notes by E. A. Babcock and A. C. Krey (New York, 1943).

II. MODERN HISTORICAL WORKS

ARSLAN, Edoardo, *Gothic Architecture in Venice*, tr. Anne Engel (London, 1971).

BATTISTELLA, Antonio, *La Repubblica di Venezia nei suoi undici secoli di storia* (Venice, 1921).

BLANC, A., *Il dominio veneziano a Creta nel Trecento* (Naples, 1968).

BRAGADIN, M. A., *Repubbliche italiane sul mare* (Milan, 1951).

BRAVETTA, E., *Enrico Dandolo* (Milan, 1919).

BROWN, Horatio, *Studies in the History of Venice*, 2 vols. (London, 1907).

BROWN, Horatio, *Venice: An Historical Sketch of the Republic* (London, 1893).

BROWN, Horatio, *The Venetians and the Venetian Quarter in Constantinople to the close of the Twelfth Century* (London, 1893).

BROWN, Rawdon, *L'Archivio di Venezia con riguardo speciale alla storia inglese* (Venice and Turin, 1865).

CAMBRIDGE MEDIEVAL HISTORY, esp. Vol. V, Venetian chapters by R. Cessi. (Contains excellent and comprehensive bibliography.)

CARILE, Antonio, *La Cronachistica veneziana (secoli XIII–XVI) di fronte all' apartizione dei romani nel 1204* (Florence, 1969).

CECCHETTI, Bartolomeo, *La Vita dei veneziani fino al 1200* (Venice, 1870).

CESSI, Roberto, *Venezia Ducale,* 2 vols. (Padua, 1927).

CESSI, Roberto, *Le Colonie medioevali italiani in Oriente,* Part I, *La Conquista* (Bologna, 1942).

CESSI, Roberto, *Storia della repubblica di Venezia,* 2nd edn, 2 vols. (Still without sources, bibliography or index!) (Milan, 1968).

CHAMBERS, D. S., *The Imperial Age of Venice, 1380–1580* (London, 1970).

CRAWFORD, F. Marion, *Gleanings in Venetian History,* 2 vols. (London, 1905).

DARU, P., *Histoire de la république de Venise,* 9 vols. (Paris, 1821).

DEMUS, Otto, *The Church of S. Marco in Venice: History, Architecture, Sculpture,* Dumbarton Oaks Studies, 6 (Washington, D.C., 1960).

DIEHL, Charles, *Venise: une république patricienne* (Paris, 1915).

FILIASI, Giacomo, *Memorie storiche dei Veneti,* 11 vols. (Venice, 1796).

FONDAZIONE GIORGIO CINI, *Storia della civiltà veneziana,* Vols. 1–5 (Florence, 1955–66).

GALLICCIOLLI, G. B., *Delle Memorie Venete antiche profane ed ecclesiastiche ... libri tre,* 7 vols. (Venice, 1795).

GEANAKOPLOS, D. J., *Byzantine East and Latin West* (Oxford, 1966).

GFRÖRER, A. F., *Byzantinische Geschichten,* ed. J. B. Weiss, 3 vols. (Graz, 1872–7).

HAZLITT, W. C., *History of the Origin and Rise of the Venetian Republic,* 2 vols. (London, 1900).

HEYD, W., *Geschichte des Levantehandels im Mittelalter* (Stuttgart, 1879). (French translation by F. Raynaud, *Histoire du commerce du Levant au Moyen Âge,* 2 vols. Leipzig, 1936.)

HILL, Sir George, *History of Cyprus,* Vol. II (1192–1432). (Cambridge, 1948).

HODGKIN, Thomas, *Italy and her Invaders,* 11 vols. (Oxford, 1880).

HODGSON, F. C., *The Early History of Venice* (London, 1901).

HODGSON, F. C., *Venice in the Thirteenth and Fourteenth Centuries* (London, 1914).

HOPF, K., *Geschichte Griechenlands vom Beginne des Mittelalters bis auf die Neuere Zeit* (Leipzig, 1867–8).

KRETSCHMAYR, H., *Geschichte von Venedig* (Gotha, 1905–20; Stuttgart, 1934).

LANE, Frederick C., 'Recent Studies on the Economic History of Venice', *Journal of Economic History,* XXIII (1963).

LANE, Frederick C., *Venice, a Maritime Republic* (Baltimore, 1973).

LANE, Frederick C., *Venice and History* (Baltimore, 1966).

LONGWORTH, Philip, *The Rise and Fall of Venice* (London, 1974).

LOPEZ, Robert S., and RAYMOND, Irving W., *Medieval Trade in the Mediterranean World* (New York and London, 1955).

LUZZATTO, G., *Storia economica di Venezia dall' XI al XVI secolo* (Venice, 1961).

McNeill, William H., *Venice, the Hinge of Europe, 1081–1797* (Chicago, 1974).

Malagola, C., *Le Lido de Venise à travers l'histoire* (Venice, 1909).

Marin, C. A., *Storia civile e politica del commercio de' veneziani*, 8 vols. (Venice, 1796–1808).

Marzemin, G., *Le Origini romane di Venezia* (Venice, 1938).

Miller, W., *The Latins in the Levant* (London, 1908).

Miller, W., *Essays on the Latin Orient* (Cambridge, 1921).

Molmenti, P., *La Storia di Venezia nella vita privata*, 6th edn, 3 vols. (Bergamo 1923). (English translation by H. F. Brown, *Venice: Its Individual Growth from the Earliest Beginnings to the Fall of the Republic*, 6 vols., London, 1906–8).

Musatti, E., *Storia di Venezia*, 2 vols. (Milan, 1936).

Newett, Margaret, *The Sumptuary Laws of Venice in the Fourteenth and Fifteenth Centuries*. In *Historical Essays by Members of Owens College, Manchester*, ed. T. H. Tout and J. Tait (London, 1902).

Nystazapoulou-Pelekidis, Marie, *Venise et la mer noire du XIe au XVe siècles*, in *Thesaurismata: bolletino dell' Istituto Ellenico di Studi Bizantini e Post-Bizantini* (1970).

Okey, Thomas, *Venice and its Story* (London, 1930).

Quadri, A., *Abrégé de l'histoire de la république de Venise* (Venice, 1847).

Ragg, Laura M., *Crises in Venetian History* (London, 1928).

Romanin, S., *Storia documentata della repubblica di Venezia*, 2nd edn, 10 vols. (Venice 1912–21).

Roth, Cecil, *History of the Jews in Venice* (Philadelphia, 1930).

Runciman, Steven, *A History of the Crusades*, 3 vols. (Cambridge, 1951–4).

Sansovino, F., *Venetia, città nobilissima et singolare descritta in XIII libri* (Venice, 1658).

Simonsfeld, H., *Andreas Dandolo und seine Geschichtswerke* (Munich, 1876).

Sismondi, J. C. L., *History of the Italian Republics in the Middle Ages* (London, 1906).

Sottas, J., *Les Messageries maritimes de Venise aux XIV et XV siècles* (Paris, 1938).

Tamaro, A., *La Vénétie Julienne et la Dalmatie*, 3 vols. (Rome, 1918–19).

Tassini, G., *Curiosità Veneziane*, 8th edn (Venice, 1970).

Thayer, W. R., *A Short History of Venice* (New York, 1905).

Thiriet, F., *Histoire de Venise* (Paris, 1952).

Thiriet, F., 'La Romanie vénitienne au moyen âge. Le développement et l'exploitation du domaine colonial vénitien' (XII–XV siècles), *Écoles françaises d'Athènes et de Rome*, 193 (Paris, 1959).

Thiriet, F., *Régestes des délibérations du Sénat de Venise concernant la Roumanie, 1329–1463*, 3 vols. (Paris, 1959–61).

Wiel, Alathea, *Venice* (London, 1894).

III. GUIDE-BOOKS AND OTHERS

Grundy, Milton, *Venice, an Anthology Guide* (London, 1976). Extracts from past writers grouped under individual monuments; beautifully produced.

HONOUR, Hugh, *The Companion Guide to Venice* (London, 1965). By far the most useful general-purpose guide-book to the monuments of Venice for the informed visitor.

LINKS, J. G., *Venice for Pleasure* (London, 1966). Four long walks through the city described by one who knows and loves every stone of it. A little gem of a book which contains, incidentally, a much fuller bibliography of Venetian guide-books than there is space for here.

LORENZETTI, G., *Venice and its Lagoon* (Rome, 1961). An English translation by John Guthrie of one of the most comprehensive and encyclopedic guide-books to a single city ever written. Indispensable for real lovers of Venice; but the average visitor will find it overwhelming and hard to handle, and will be happier with Honour's *Companion Guide*.

McCARTHY, Mary, *Venice Observed* (London, 1956). A brilliantly written coffee-table book. Intelligent and informative, but not a guide.

MORRIS, James, *Venice* (London, 1960). Surely the best full-length essay on Venice ever written. Once again, in no sense a guide-book; but as a portrait of the city, incomparable.

PIGNATTI, Terisio, *Venice* (English translation by Judith Landry, London, 1971). A superbly produced and illustrated guide-book by one of Venice's leading art historians.

SHAW-KENNEDY, Ronald, *Art and Architecture in Venice. The Venice in Peril Guide* (London, 1972). Particularly useful for those as interested in the contents of the buildings of Venice as in the buildings themselves, since it contains lists of all the principal works of Venetian painters, sculptors and architects with their locations.

Index